T.E. Lawrence

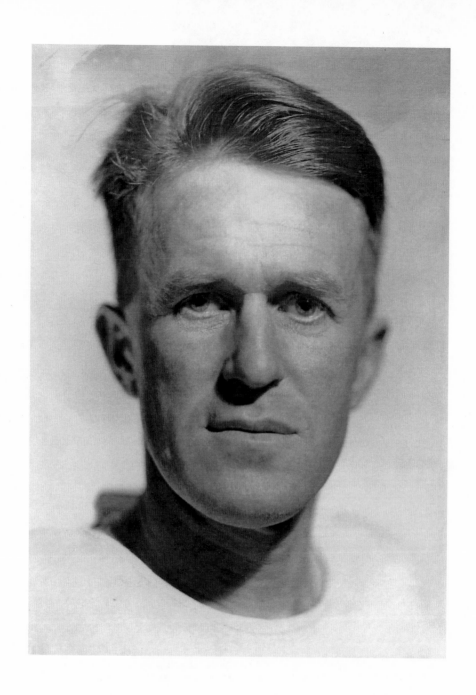

T.E. Lawrence

Biography of a Broken Hero

by Harold Orlans

McFarland & Company, Inc., Publishers
Jefferson, North Carolina, and London

Frontispiece: Howard Coster's 1931 photograph of Lawrence captures some of his inner torment. (Courtesy of the National Portrait Gallery, London.)

Library of Congress Cataloguing-in-Publication Data

Orlans, Harold, 1921–
T.E. Lawrence : Biography of a broken hero / by Harold Orlans.
p.   cm.
Includes bibliographical references and index.

ISBN-13: 978-0-7864-1307-2
(softcover : 50# alkaline paper)∞

1. Lawrence, T.E. (Thomas Edward), 1888–1935.   2. Lawrence, T.E.
(Thomas Edward), 1888–1935—Childhood and youth.   3. Lawrence, T.E.
(Thomas Edward), 1888–1935—Sexual behavior.   4. Lawrence, T.E.
(Thomas Edward), 1888–1935—Friends and associates.   5. Orientalists—Great
Britian—Biography.   6. Soldiers—Great Britian—Biography.   7. Middle
East—History—20th century.   I. Title
D568.4.L45O75   2002   940.4'15'092—dc21   2002010640

British Library cataloguing data are available

Cover art: T.E. Lawrence (*Art Today*)

Manufactured in the United States of America

*McFarland & Company, Inc., Publishers
Box 611, Jefferson, North Carolina 28640
www.mcfarlandpub.com*

To my mother, Celia (1891–1983),
who gave me *Seven Pillars of Wisdom* in 1937,

and my dear wife Kathryn,
even tempered, good natured, understanding.

Acknowledgments

I am very grateful to Jerry Caplan, Claire Keith, Claire Milne, and Kathryn Orlans for reading a draft of this book. Their detailed comments and queries have helped me to revise it and to reduce the number of errors it will inevitably retain.

Early biographers and editors who knew Lawrence—Robert Graves, Lowell Thomas, Basil Liddell Hart, Vyvyan Richards, Arnold Lawrence, Clare Smith, David Garnett—were helped and led astray by what he did and did not tell them. Later, those who did not know him, such as Flora Armitage, Richard Aldington, Suleiman Mousa, Phillip Knightley, Colin Simpson, John Mack, and Malcolm Brown, talked and corresponded with surviving friends and acquaintances. Arriving too late on the scene, I met one surviving friend, Arthur Russell, a Tank Corps comrade and pallbearer at his funeral. I could discuss Lawrence with, and learn from, only other biographers and cognoscenti. Over the years, two have been, repeatedly, most helpful, offering information, opinion, and advice and engaging in the kind of argument and reflection that advances understanding: Jeremy Wilson, Lawrence's authorized biographer, publisher of the Oxford Text and a prospective complete collection of Lawrence's letters, a careful scholar who undoubtedly knows more about Lawrence than any other living person; and Malcolm Brown, producer of BBC Lawrence documentaries, editor of Lawrence's letters and wartime dispatches, and author of two Lawrence biographies. On one memorable occasion, we talked furiously and joked about Lawrence for five and a half hours without a break. I have also had rewarding conversations and correspondence with Fred Crawford, Lawrence James, Ingrid Keith, Phillip Knightley, Paul Marriott, Maarten Schild, Colin Simpson, Valerie Thompson, and members of the Eastern States Lawrence group. Robert Archibald, Clifford Irwin, Christopher Matheson, Denis McDonnell, and Philip O'Brien have provided useful information on specific points.

I resist the temptation to name those who did not respond to requests—in one case, repeated, urgent requests. Courtesy is not compulsory and more than a few Lawrence biographers and heirs of his friends and relatives have tired of inquiries and lost whatever interest they may have had in him.

For access, starting in April 1989, to the Lawrence archive at the Bodleian Library, Oxford, which was reserved until the year 2000, I thank Michael V. Carey of the Seven Pillars of Wisdom Trust. A. J. Flavell, the Bodleian's resident Lawrence authority, and more recently Anna Dunn, who has catalogued the archive (now open to scholars), have been repeatedly helpful. Simon Masters of Random House, U.K., kindly granted permission to examine the Jonathan Cape archive at the University of Reading.

Other persons and institutions who have afforded access to materials by or about Lawrence are D. A. Rees and the Principal and Fellows of Jesus College, Oxford. In Cambridge: Odette Rogers, the Fitzwilliam Museum; Michael Harrison, Kettle's Yard; M. A. Halls, Kings College Library; A. E. B. Owen, The University Library. At the University of Reading Library, Michael Bott. In London, staff of the Department of Manuscripts, British Library, and Roderick Suddaby of the Imperial War Museum.

Three U.S. institutions with exceptional Lawrence collections are also excellent places to work, with knowledgeable and responsive staff. I thank especially Cathy Henderson and Katherine Mosley of the Harry Ransom Humanities Research Center, the University of Texas, Austin, which holds a very strong collection of Lawrence letters and documents; James Lewis and Jennie Rathbun of Harvard's Houghton Library, whose scholarly services are as admirable as its splendid holdings; and Alan Jutzi, Thomas Lange, and Leona Schonfeld of the Huntington Library, San Marino, California, whose magnificent facility houses the world's best collection of Lawrence publications, assembled by the late Edwards Metcalf. The Beinecke Library at Yale, the New York Public Library, the Firestone Library at Princeton, and the University of Virginia's Alderman Library also have significant Lawrence items.

With regard to illustrations, I thank Anna Dunn for identifying and the Bodleian Libary, University of Oxford, for copies of, and permission to reproduce, a photo (MS. Photogr. c. 122, fol. 3) of the five Lawrence brothers (1910), and one (MS. Photogr. c. 126, fol. 29r) of Lawrence on a Brough motorcycle (1925); the British Library, London, for a copy of, and permission to reproduce, Lawrence's photo (Ad MS 50584 ff116) of Dahoum (1912); Sue Donnelly and Conor Hartnett, the British Library of Political and Economic Science, London, for a copy of, and Charles Pugh of the National Trust for permission to reproduce, a photo of Charlotte Shaw (mid–1920s); Malcolm Brown, for prints of, and permission to reproduce, photographs of the garden bungalow at Polstead Road, Clouds Hill, and Lawrence's tombstone; Maggie Leighly for the map (which she prepared) of Lawrence's homes and stations in Britain; Wendy Brown, Nigel Cassidy, and John Donaldson, for a copy of, and the Museum of Classical Archaeology, University of Cambridge, for permission to reproduce, a photo of A. W. Lawrence (ca. 1945), when he was in the Faculty of Classics; Adam Grummitt, Claire Everitt, and Claire Freestone, the National Portrait Gallery (NPG), London, for a copy of, and Jeremy Wilson for permission to reproduce, a photo (RN 42677) of Lawrence's mother, Sarah (ca. 1910); NPG and Jeremy Wilson for a copy of, and the unidentified owner for permission to reproduce, a photo (RN 42684) of the Clouds Hill bookroom; NPG for copies of, and permission to reproduce, a drawing (NPG 3187) by Augustus John of Lawrence in Paris (1919) and a photo (RN 45142) of Lawrence by Howard Coster (1931).

I thank the Seven Pillars of Wisdom Trust for permission to quote writings of T. E. Lawrence, A. W. Lawrence, and contributors to *T. E. Lawrence by His Friends;* Christopher Kennington for permission to quote from unpublished writings of Celandine Kennington; St. John Armitage, Malcolm Brown, Clifford Irwin, Lawrence James, Claire Keith, Colin Simpson, and Jeremy Wilson for permission to quote from their letters, listserv postings, or conversation. Other limited quotations fall within the province of U.S. fair use and U.K. fair dealing. If any requisite copyright permission has been overlooked, I apologize and, when advised, will do my best to correct the oversight.

Contents

III. CONCLUSION

Introduction

I first encountered T. E. Lawrence in 1937, when, at 15, I read *Seven Pillars of Wisdom* (published in 1935). Lawrence's forcefulness and honesty made a powerful impression. He became my hero and long outlasted my other heroes.

Launched as the great British hero of World War I by Lowell Thomas, the American publicist, in 1919, in a wildly successful film-and-talk-show to large London audiences, Lawrence remained a hero for years after his death in 1935. That status was due to remarkable actions—leading Arab tribesmen in their wartime revolt against the Turks, and his later rejection of fame, honor, money, even his name—that seemed bold and honorable, and to the fact that we did not know him well enough to understand him. The explanations offered—that he would not profit from Britain's "betrayal" of the Arabs; that joining the RAF as a private was like vowing poverty and entering a monastery—were noble. This sense of nobility was enhanced by the sense of honesty and devastating self-criticism that *Seven Pillars* conveys. How could one doubt the honesty of a man who dealt so ruthlessly with his own motives, who was "a standing court martial" on himself?

I read the books by and about Law-rence as they appeared. *T. E. Lawrence by His Friends* (eighty of them), published in 1937, showed the range of his friendships (generals and aristocrats, soldiers and common folk, scholars, writers, artists, politicians) and talents (archeologist, photographer, map maker, intelligence officer, camel rider, guerrilla fighter, leader, manipulator, writer, linguist, mechanic). The 1938 collection of his letters edited by David Garnett, a book bigger than *Seven Pillars* yet only a selection of his correspondence, confirmed the sense of his honesty and documented his activities and feelings after Arabia. The letters strengthened the impression of Lawrence's nihilism and depression and revealed an added dimension of self-destructiveness. He served in the ranks, it seemed, because there was nothing else he wanted more to do. The letters made plain his great intelligence, knowledge, wit, and kindness. Why a man who could captivate imperialists and socialists, soldiers and pacifists, intellectuals and politicians should insist on living in barracks was puzzling.

I was not the only person to make Lawrence his hero. Millions did, for his desert exploits, his rejection of worldly rewards, his determination to live as he chose. Quite a few people regarded him as

a saint. Many admirers made him "a religion," his brother Arnold later remarked.
"I had great difficulty in not allowing myself to be used as the St. Paul of it."[1] To
Simone Weil, Lawrence "was one man
famous in history ... whom I can whole-
heartedly love and admire."[2] Victoria
Ocampo loved him and wished to edit a
book, comparable to that by his friends,
of essays by persons "who (like myself)
have become Lawrence's friends since his
death."[3] Sartre, de Beauvoir, Malraux were
fascinated by Lawrence; "while he lived,"
Eugene O'Neill wrote, "one could believe
that true honor and courage and integrity
were still alive among the leaders of men."[4]
Some of Lawrence's fascination for writers
lay in their regard for a fellow writer who,
unlike them, could lead men, a brave man
who could outthink and destroy his enemies.

In our time, no statue can long stand
in a public place unguarded and unmo-
lested: if not toppled, it will be chipped or
smeared with paint and graffiti. Vandalism is a vice of democracy: it says, *Who
dares to stand above us?*

Richard Aldington led the effort to
destroy Lawrence's reputation with a ven-
omous 1955 biography. Aldington saw not
a hero but a charlatan; not a man of
integrity but a liar, an impostor, a short
man who told tall tales, a bastard whose
achievements were fabricated. "There is
one achievement which nobody can deny
Lawrence and that was his capacity to convince others that he was a remarkable man
... but what was chiefly 'remarkable' was
his capacity for self-advertisement....
Lawrence was one of Mr. Eliot's hollow
men," Aldington wrote.[5] That is ridiculous. Lawrence's achievements in the
desert, at Akaba, advising Prince Feisal,
and blowing up trains were recognized at
the time by the area commanders and the
Imperial General Staff in London. Having
fought in France, where more men were

slaughtered in a day than in the entire
Arab revolt, Aldington took neither
Lawrence nor the revolt seriously.

Aldington's letters suggest that the
nasty tone of his biography was partly due
to his belief that Lawrence was a homosexual.[6] Yet his discussion of Lawrence's
sexuality was (unlike most of his biography) fair; he simply says that Lawrence regarded heterosexual sex as repellent and
homosexual sex, "clean," but "had no
known love affairs."[7] Aldington's main
contribution to our knowledge was his
disclosure of the fact, then little known,
that Lawrence was the illegitimate child
of unmarried parents. His larger effect
was to stem the effusive praise that had
flowed, with little correction, since Lowell
Thomas's 1919 farrago.

That effect was strengthened by the
revelation, in 1968, that, from 1923 until
his death, Lawrence had arranged to be
savagely whipped by a burly young Scotsman.[8] When I first heard this, I felt, "Poor
Lawrence." More than any other fact, that
undid his standing as a hero for me. You
must admire a hero: how can you be sorry
for him? A hero must choose, he can't be
compelled, to act, let alone succumb to a
secret vice. Those who keep Lawrence
seated on a throne interpreted the beatings as a voluntary act of contrition; I
could not see them that way. Twenty years
after Lawrence's death, Robert Graves,
who knew him well, called him "a broken
hero who tried to appear whole."[9] That
was my feeling.

Psychiatrist John Mack's 1976 biography, *A Prince of Our Disorder*, the best
study of Lawrence's character yet published, provided documentation of the
beatings and a searching discussion of
Lawrence's sexuality. Mack was sympathetic; plainly, he had as high regard for
Lawrence as a psychiatrist can have for a
patient. He valued his wartime achievements, his postwar faithfulness to the Arab

cause, his ability as an "enabler" helping others to act, his empathy and compassion. But Mack viewed the beatings as acts of inner compulsion, not freedom, and spoke of "the sadness and pathos of this terrible problem, from which Lawrence, even up to the months before his death, seemed unable to free himself."[10] With utmost kindness, he kept Lawrence off my throne. Mack's grasp of Near East affairs is weak; his vocabulary and ideas reflect parochial professional interests. But he has contributed much to our understanding of Lawrence's character, and I agree with most of his analysis.

In 1988, the hundredth anniversary of Lawrence's birth, appeared Malcolm Brown's new collection of Lawrence's letters, including letters previously unpublished (many to Mrs. Charlotte Shaw) as well as passages omitted in earlier books. They confirmed that Lawrence, gripped by demons he could not control, despised and degraded himself.

Lawrence of Arabia, historian Jeremy Wilson's massive authorized biography published in 1989, presents an account of Lawrence's life that is, by orders of magnitude, more detailed and accurate than any other. When a fact is in question, Wilson is usually reliable. However, the focus on documented facts takes it off the man hidden behind them; to one reviewer, the book "reads like *Hamlet* without the Prince." Wilson gives little attention to Lawrence's beatings, saying that Mack had already discussed them and they were "a symptom rather than a cause of his state of mind"[11]—a debatable proposition; symptoms also have consequences. Wilson is not a panegyrist; at points, he criticizes Lawrence's conduct. So did Lawrence's friends and family members. Knowing Lawrence, they offer testimony more trustworthy and illuminating than that of biographers who, not knowing him, discount his kindness and accomplishments

and invent an implausibly meretricious man. I have gone back to the observations of contemporaries and given special weight to the criticism of friends or, conversely, the praise of critics. I will often quote them directly, since quotation is more accurate and authentic than paraphrase.

After sixty years of reading and reflection, the Lawrence I see is no longer an unadulterated hero but still an extraordinary man. I can't imagine anyone— Socrates, Alexander, Shakespeare, Gandhi, Churchill—who can remain unchanged and heroic throughout one's life. Heroes are for the young. When one is young, Socrates seems braver; he seems to confront and relinquish more. Churchill was braver in 1940 than 1962, when he was too weary to leave a yacht in New York harbor to see President Kennedy in Washington. In old age, Arnold Lawrence, Vyvyan Richards, Charlotte Shaw, who had long loved Lawrence, wearied of him and the endlessly repeated questions about him; they had their own lives to finish, their own deaths to face.

Lawrence's wartime achievements were heroic; his willpower and resourcefulness were remarkable; his mind, penetrating. His character and conduct were exemplary, kind, vain, excessively fastidious, inexplicable, devious, masochistic; his later years were fundamentally tragic. Lawrence had a good sense of humor; his grin and wit could disguise his dark moods and make him good company. Admirers relish the humorous side of his time in the ranks and stories about the colonel-cum-airman flummoxing officers and snobs.[12] But there was too little genuine happiness in that period of Lawrence's life.

No new biography is needed to establish the gross facts of Lawrence's life. What we need is a better explanation of his conduct and character. The explanation should fit not just selected facts but the full range of available information and should add to our understanding of the man.

Aldington could not credit Lawrence's heroism; catching errors and lies, he claimed that Lawrence's whole life was a lie, that he was a "self-important egotist," a poor writer, not even a good motorcyclist.[13] Regarding Lawrence as a hero, Wilson finds his duplicity merely "curious," his aversion to heterosexual intercourse merely typical of Englishmen of his class and generation. Wilson minimizes the significance of his masochism and disputes evidence of his vanity, feminine traits, and homosexual inclinations.[14]

My career has been devoted to empirical social and policy research and my excursions into psychology[15] have taken the same empirical approach. I do not subscribe to the social science doctrine that one must or should have an "hypothesis" before collecting data. Ideas and spheres of interest, yes, but I never know what I will say until I sort the facts and see how they support or conflict with one or another explanation. I try to collect the broadest range of facts and opinions on every issue, paying special attention to those that question or illuminate accepted truth. Research that yields no new knowledge or insight is pointless. No one is free of bias and error, but I have tried to present and interpret the facts accurately and fairly, whether they enhance or diminish Lawrence's stature.

It has taken the better part of ten years (not full time!) to collect the facts summarized here. I have examined Lawrence's unpublished letters in British and American archives, all English language biographies, many memoirs and articles. I have acquired a substantial library by and about Lawrence, attended conferences and meetings and participated in internet discussion groups devoted to him. Jeremy Wilson confines himself largely

to primary documentary sources. John Mack interviewed many persons who knew Lawrence. Every source—government memoranda, private papers, print, the internet, interviews, conversation—has distinctive value and limitations. All can catch fragments of truth, all contain visible and invisible error. Trained as an anthropologist, I regard all written and spoken words (also objects and behavior) as possible sources of pertinent evidence. The context must be established, the evidence sifted, and particles of truth extracted from the dross. However, panning for the truth about Lawrence's character is not like panning for gold. There are reliable tests for gold; there are none for my conclusions. I think they merit attention, but they are not offered as irrefutable truths. On many matters, I doubt such truths will ever be established about that complex, wily man.

This book is divided into three parts. Part I discusses Lawrence's life in a conventional chronological sequence. As that format does not permit fuller examination of more durable aspects of his character and conduct, Part II is devoted to enduring themes: his living and spending habits; his relations with family members and friends; the elements of genius and madness, honesty and evasiveness, vanity, humility, and masochism in his nature. Part III is a conclusion.

Lawrence's larger acts in Arabia and *Seven Pillars* have been relatively overstudied. I have examined details of conduct (such as how he handled his body, property, finances, names, parents, friends) that, too small to be disguised, show the man unposed. The choice of topics is governed by the information available, a wish to highlight neglected points, and, inevitably, my own blinders and sensitivities.

Summer 2002, Bethesda, Maryland

Chronology of Lawrence's Life

1888	August 16	born in Tremadoc, Wales
1896	summer	Polstead Road, Oxford
	Sept. (–July 1907)	Oxford High School for Boys
1907	Oct. (–June 1910)	Jesus College, Oxford
1909	summer	Palestine and Syria
1910–11	winter	Jebail, Syria
1911–14	springs	Carchemish (modern Turkey)
1912–13	falls	Carchemish
1914	Jan.–Feb.	Sinai
	October	War Office, London
	Dec. (–Oct. 1916)	Military Intelligence, Cairo
1916	Oct. (–Oct. 1918)	Arabia
1917	July	Akaba
	November	Deraa
1918	Oct. 1–4	Damascus
	Oct. 27	London
1919	Jan.–Oct.	Paris Peace Conference (intermittently)
	Jan. (–July 1922)	*Seven Pillars of Wisdom* (Oxford Text)
	Oct. (–Jan. 1921)	All Souls College, Oxford and London
1921	Feb. (–July 1922)	Colonial Office, London and Mid-East
1922	August	RAF training depot, Uxbridge
	November	RAF Photography School, Farnborough
1921	January	discharged from RAF
	March (–Aug. 1925)	Royal Tank Corps, Bovington
	summer	Clouds Hill

1925	August	RAF Cadet College, Cranwell
1926	December	*Seven Pillars* subscribers' edition; sails for India
1927	Jan. (–May 1928)	RAF depot, Karachi
	March	*Revolt in the Desert*
1928	May (–Jan. 1929)	RAF, Fort Miranshah
1929	January	sails for England
	March	RAF, Mount Batten, Plymouth
1931–34		intervals at Hythe, Southampton, Cowes
1934	November	RAF, Bridlington
1935	Feb. 26	leaves RAF
	May 13 & 19	motorcycle accident & death

Prologue: A Rocket Flared and Fell

That morning in Damascus, crowds packed the roadside, windows, balconies, housetops. On the Town Hall stairs, a mob swayed, "yelling, embracing, dancing, singing." Driving from the building with Shukri el Ayubi, Saladin's descendant, flowers and splashes of perfume were thrown into their open, desert-worn, blue Rolls; women removed their veils, men threw their tarbushes in the air chanting *Feisal, Nasir, Shukri, Urens.*

"Urens" was Lt. Col. Thomas Edward Lawrence, a slight, 30-year-old Englishman in white Arab robes and headdress; the date, October 1, 1918. Early that day, the 5' 5" Lawrence, haggard, sun-scorched, his weight down to 84 pounds, had been briefly taken prisoner by Indian troops, who knew as little about their Arab allies as most Englishmen.[1]

For Lawrence, Damascus climaxed a two-year, 900-mile campaign with camel-riding Bedouin against Turkish and, at times, German troops in the deserts, mountains, and stony flats of Arabia, Palestine, and Syria. A captain on leave from his military intelligence post in Cairo, he had landed in Jidda, the Red Sea port of Mecca, in October 1916 and cre-

ated his subsequent career. He became a friend and adviser to the Arab leader Prince Feisal; a dynamiter of bridges and trains who provided the Bedouin with British weapons, gold, and Turkish loot; liaison officer to General Allenby, commander of Allied forces in the Near East; strategist, tactician, warrior, politician; a bold, astute leader who induced ungovernable tribesmen to attack the Turks, not each other. Even his enemies did not question his bravery.

On October 29, Lawrence met with the Eastern Committee of the War Cabinet to present his ideas for the future of Asian lands formerly ruled by Turkey—the ancient fertile crescent from what is now Iraq to the Mediterranean and the great Arabian peninsula. The day after, in Buckingham Palace, King George V offered him a knighthood that he declined.[2]

From January intermittently through August 1919, Lawrence was at the Paris Peace Conference and in London, advising Feisal and British officials, talking to delegates, public figures, experts, and the press to persuade them of the justice and *realpolitik* of Feisal's cause and the folly of

7

French ambitions in Syria. His reputation, intelligence, forcefulness, and Arab dress attracted great attention—Winston Churchill observed the "gravity of his demeanour, the precision of his opinions, the range and quality of his conversation."[3] But his political efforts failed. The British and French governments settled their differences in April 1920; in August, French troops drove Feisal from Damascus.

"The Last Crusade—With Allenby in Palestine and Lawrence in Arabia" was the title of a sold-out film-music-slide-and-talk show the young American journalist Lowell Thomas (he was 27, Lawrence 31) staged in London from August 1919 through March 1920. Allenby's part shrank and Lawrence's grew as Thomas repeated the performance to more than a million persons, including the king, queen, and prime minister. The show's opening was front page news. Thomas's mellifluous mixture of fact and fantasy about "The Uncrowned King of Arabia," repeated throughout the English-speaking world, made Lawrence an international celebrity. Henceforth, he was as widely known as the Prince of Wales or George Bernard Shaw and, unlike them, a hero. Why, one wonders, did all those people swallow the American showman's glowing simplicities? Were memories wet with the blood of trench warfare soothed by the mellow talk of an almost bloodless victory? Was the triumph of one Englishman in a measure the triumph of all?

In February 1921, Lawrence joined the new Middle East Department as adviser to

its head, Winston Churchill. Two years after the war had supposedly ended, 80,000 Indian and British troops fought a rebellion of Arab tribes in Iraq. Churchill's task was to restore peace, cut costs, and maintain British control.

The solution devised by Lawrence and his friends and adopted by Churchill was implemented at a March 1921 Cairo conference. Feisal was made king of Iraq and his brother Abdulla, ruler of Transjordania, a desert nation created for the purpose. Britain would control the region with air power, not ground troops. The long straight or jagged boundaries between Syria, Jordan, Palestine, Iraq, and Saudi Arabia, drawn in 1921, persist to this day. Because Iraq was cut off from the Persian Gulf, some have blamed Lawrence for its 1991 invasion of Kuwait.[4]

During the year he had agreed to serve, Lawrence revisited the Near East, trying to negotiate treaties and settle political issues. Thereafter, he wanted to quit. He was writing *Seven Pillars of Wisdom* and had other plans. Churchill would not release him. Lawrence insisted and finally had his way.

On August 30, 1922, using a pseudonym, he enlisted in the Royal Air Force as an aircraftman, the lowest rank. Except for 29 months in the Royal Tank Corps, 1923–25, he remained in the RAF until February 1935. Not three months later, swerving to avoid two bicyclists, he was thrown from his motorbike and broke his skull. After six days in a coma, he died May 19, aged 46.

I
LIFE

LAWRENCE'S HOMES and STATIONS in BRITAIN

Homes

- Ⓐ Tremadoc 1888-9
- Ⓑ Kirkcudbright 1889-91
- Ⓒ New Forest 1894-6
- Ⓓ Oxford 1896-1914, 1919-20
- Ⓔ London 1920-22
- Ⓕ Clouds Hill on & off 1923-6, 1929-35

Stations

- ① St. Just 1905
- ② Uxbridge 1922
- ③ Farnborough 1922
- ④ Bovington 1923-5
- ⑤ Cranwell 1925-6
- ⑥ Mt. Batten 1929-32
- ⑦ Hythe 1931-32
- ⑧ Southampton 1933-4
- ⑨ Bridlington 1934-5

N. IRELAND

SCOTLAND

NORTH SEA

Edinburgh

Belfast

Newcastle

IRELAND

Delvin

Isle of Man

Dublin

IRISH SEA

⑨

Manchester

Hull

Liverpool

Ⓐ

⑤

ENGLAND

WALES

0 20 40 km
0 10 20 mi

N
△

Cambridge

Oxford
Ⓓ

Thames

②

London

③

Ⓔ

①

⑥

Ⓕ ⑦ ⑧
④ Ⓒ

Dover

English Channel   Isle of Wight

Prepared by Maggie Leighly

1

Childhood and Youth, 1888–1907

Lawrence was born in Tremadoc, Wales, August 16, 1888, the second of his unmarried parents' Thomas and Sarah's five sons.

Thomas Chapman (1846–1919), a wealthy, Anglo-Irish landowner who lived at South Hill, a country estate 40 miles northwest of Dublin, and his wife Edith had four daughters, born 1874–81. About 1879, Sarah Lawrence, an illegitimate Scots working girl, then 18, came to South Hill as the children's governess. (The Protestant Anglo-Irish gentry preferred imported Protestant nannies to local Catholic girls.) They liked her and so did Thomas. His marriage was a disaster. Edith required the household to conform to her fanatical religiosity: much prayer, little entertainment, no theater. Thomas drank heavily. Self-confident, strong-willed, competent, pretty Sarah could handle a drunkard—her mother had been one.

The two fell in love. In 1885, Sarah became pregnant and left South Hill for Dublin, where her first son, Robert, was born. Chapman, entered on his birth certificate, was the name Sarah now used, while Thomas divided his time between his two homes and families. According to

one account, the illicit union was discovered by the South Hill butler, "who overheard Sarah in a grocery store giving her name … as 'Mrs. Chapman' and followed her home."[1] After the debris from the explosion settled, the errant husband relinquished his rights to the family estates to his brother in exchange for £20,000 and a lifetime annuity, and took Sarah and Robert to Wales. He could not remarry as his wife would not divorce him. On Thomas Edward's birth certificate, his parents are "Lawrence," the name they henceforth used but never legally adopted.

Concern lest their pretense be discovered led to frequent moves. "You can imagine … how yr Mother & I have suffered all these years, not knowing what day we might be recognised by some one and our sad history published far and wide," Thomas Chapman told his sons in a letter to be opened after his death.[2] A few words and a glance might arouse suspicion: what was a soft-spoken Irish gentleman doing with a much younger, ill-educated woman who spoke and misspoke in a strong Scots accent? They spent a year in Tremadoc and another in Kirkcudbright, Scotland, small, seaside towns within easy reach of Dublin; brief spells, on the Isle of Man and Jersey; over two years in Dinard, across the Channel in Brittany; two at the edge of the New Forest, near Southampton Water. A third son, William, was born in Scotland; a fourth, Frank, in Jersey.[3] The family rented houses in isolated locations; Sarah spent much time indoors.

In 1896, Thomas "Lawrence" finally bought a home in Oxford, where the boys could get a good education without the expense and scrutiny of the normally obligatory boarding school (Thomas had gone to Eton). The large, semi-detached brick house at 2 Polstead Road was at the near end of a line of new middle-class homes off Woodstock Road, a short bicycle ride to central Oxford and the City of Oxford High School for Boys that, in sequence, the brothers all attended. In 1900, seven years after Frank, the last son, Arnold, was born, when Thomas was 53 and Sarah, 38. Much that we know about T.E.'s childhood was screened by Robert, the dutiful eldest son who edited and censored his family letters, and Arnold, who lived until 1991 and, as T.E.'s literary executor, controlled use of his copyright work and access to the Lawrence archive in the Bodleian Library.

T.E. was "a big, strong, active child" who "could pull himself up over the nursery gate ... before he could walk," his mother recalled; he climbed ladders, rocks, and tall trees without fear.[4] In France, he and Robert took gym lessons; in Oxford, the parallel bars in the garden were much used; at high school, T.E.'s best sports were bicycle and foot racing and gymnastics. The brothers got on well and played vigorous games; many were war games that T.E.—"Ned" to his family and friends—invented and led.

Family members, schoolmates, and teachers draw a consistent picture of Lawrence as a child and youth. He had a quick intelligence and an independent spirit. Of

the brothers, he "was the soonest to walk, the soonest to talk ... mastered the alphabet before three, was able to read a newspaper upside down before five, ... [was] always lost in some book."[5] He read a great deal, especially history, archeology, and medieval romances, knew the Bible well, and taught Sunday school. He was a good student but weak at math and resented the regimen of conscripted study: "they were miserable sweated years of unwilling work," he later told a young friend. "...nor do I think the miseries of grown-up feelings are as bad as those of boys ... such happiness as I've had began after schooldays...." In later years, barracks revived memories of "the school-fear..., that working against hazardously-suspended penalty which made my life from eight to eighteen miserable."[6]

Lawrence early adopted the role of detached observer that marked and marred his life. He was given to attention-catching eccentricities such as walking his bicycle downhill and riding it up, and would not join in group games. Two short pieces he wrote at 15 for the high school magazine make fun of football and cricket, which he disliked "because they were organized, because they had rules." In Arabia, he would later "approve of anything ... individualistic, unorganized, unsystematic."[7] If that outlook was anarchistic, it was a personal, not political anarchism; as a former landowner, his father was a Tory and, insofar as he had political views, so was young Lawrence.

In some respects the family resembled a Salvation Army platoon commanded by Sergeant Sarah. Despite a comfortable, assured income, servants, and holidays abroad, Sarah's puritanism and childhood penury led her to impose discipline and abstemiousness. Wearing identical white and blue jerseys, the four boys rode their bicycles to school in a file, "oldest first, youngest last."[8] In class photos, their horizontally-striped, informal jerseys contrast sharply with their classmates' dark jackets, starched white collars, and ties—a bold statement of independence for parents who did not wish to call attention to themselves. Sarah demanded obedience, reliability, punctuality, neatness, cleanliness. The word *clean* appears often in *Seven Pillars of Wisdom* and in Lawrence's letters as a synonym for virtuousness and purity. When, in later life, Sarah visited the cemetery north of Oxford where Thomas Chapman was buried, she cleaned the headstone and curb with grass and water.

T.E. and Arnold spoke of their father with affection and respect; also, perhaps, with commiseration and pity at his domination by their mother, who turned the gentleman alcoholic into a church-going, mealtime-praying, home-staying, evangelical teetotaler. His wife Edith was a religious fanatic who tyrannized the household with her puritanical exactions. As a penniless mistress, Sarah must have been more compliant but, in time, as the *mater familias,* her stern religiosity differed little from Edith's; her rigorous household and family management were uncontested.

Perceptive, independent in mind and action, as strong-willed as his mother, whose facial appearance, determination, and meticulousness he shared, T.E. rebelled against her discipline and was repeatedly, severely whipped for it on his naked bottom. We are not told exactly why. Given T.E.'s lifelong inclination to prod, provoke, and test, we can imagine such deliberate offenses as being late for a meal or doing something (riding his bicycle?) that had been barred in punishment for an earlier offense.

Lawrence's childhood has often been described as happy, though his two best biographers, Mack and Wilson, warn that the "happy family" accounts of his mother and older brother, Bob, are overstated. His

"We had a very happy childhood"[9] hardly jibes with T.E.'s misery at school and beatings at home. Perhaps Bob meant "I." Compliant, he was not whipped, never married, and, after his father died, went to China as a medical missionary, accompanied by Sarah. Very likely, the idea of saving distant souls was Sarah's. The two lived together thereafter, Bob playing the part usually allotted to an unmarried daughter.

The discovery of his illegitimacy cannot have increased T.E.'s happiness or reduced the conflict with his mother. Evidently he was the one brother to learn the secret and, with characteristic self-possession, kept it to himself for years. The visitors who came at intervals to discuss finances and the management of the Irish holdings may have been indiscreet; T.E. may have fitted some remark into the puzzle of his father's trips to Ireland or suddenly grasped why his parents said "Sarah" and "Tom" or "Ned's mother" and "father," not "my wife" and "husband." The revelation that his fundamentalist parents, espousing conventional middle-class values—especially his strict mother, who beat him for minor derelictions—were hypocrites living and breeding in sin, must have weakened their moral hold and strengthened his independent resolve.

At 65½ inches, age 16, Lawrence's growth stopped, though his father and brothers William and Arnold were tall. Some writers attribute this to a leg broken while wrestling with a fellow student. Others note that Lawrence's mother and brothers Robert and Frank were short and his height approximated the national male average, 5'6". James Cadell declares that, "Just before breaking his leg Ned—like several other boys at the High School—had caught mumps.... Just one case in a thousand is unfortunate. A gland is affected which governs physical development. That was what happened to Ned." Major-General Frank Richardson, a career physician in the Royal Army Medical Corp, suggests that mumps may not only have stunted Lawrence's growth but damaged one or both testicles. "An atrophied testicle would have been likely to affect his emotional more than his physical development."[10] As Cadell and Richardson give no source, their suggestion that Lawrence had mumps remains an undocumented speculation that, if true, might explain the lifelong boyishness many observers noted.

Self-conscious about his shortness, as about almost everything, Lawrence compensated with strenuous bicycling and exercise that made him very strong for his size. He specialized in feats of endurance (such as doing with little food and sleep and taking long, fast bicycle or walking trips) at which a small man could best a large one. And he was early attracted to that great equalizer of men and nations: weapons, warfare, fortresses, and the military arts.

The attraction to guns and uniforms, to the subjection, protection, and camaraderie of military life, was displayed at 17, when T.E. ran away and enlisted in the artillery. Exactly what led him to do so is unknown; "because of trouble at home" and "Father and mother discord,"[11] he said—a rare indication that the parents sometimes quarreled. He told Charlotte Shaw about their "discordant natures ... and the inflammation of strength and weakness which followed the uprooting of their lives and principles."[12] Lawrence was in the army for perhaps three months before his father bought him out.[13]

Seventeen, he wrote, "is the age at which I suddenly found myself," referring, presumably, to his breaking away from home and his mother's domination. Even Jeremy Wilson, who indulges in little psychological speculation, senses the rising conflict between Lawrence and his mother "as he grew towards adulthood. He increasingly resented her intrusions into his private affairs, and, as he himself had a strong character, their relationship worsened."[14] Upon Lawrence's return from the army, a peace treaty must have been negotiated that restricted his mother's authority and established buffers between her and her son.

2

College and the East, 1908–1914

When, in October 1907, Lawrence entered Jesus College, Oxford, "the new freedom felt like Heaven."[1] Yet he had less freedom than most students, as, except for an obligatory term (April–June 1908), he lived at home. The reason commonly given is that his parents could not afford to lodge their numerous sons in college. However, at the end of 1908, a two-room bungalow (which, with water, electricity, stove, and a phone and buzzer connection to the house, must have cost a goodly sum—it stands to this day) was built for T.E. at the back of the garden. He spent the rest of his college years there, usually alone, reading late into the night in rooms silenced with green sheeting.

From 1906–10, Lawrence took four long bicycle trips in France and a two-week trip around Wales to inspect medieval churches, fortresses, fortifications, and battlefields as part of his deepening interest in medieval history, architecture, and warfare. A friend, brothers Will and Frank, or his father might accompany him, but the most strenuous trip he took alone in the summer of 1908: a 2,400-mile, 8-week, elliptical journey from Le Havre to the Mediterranean and back, via Gisors,

Provins, Vézélay, Avignon, Arles, Aigues-Morte, and Carcassonne to Villefranche, Niort, Tours, Chartres, and Dinan. His diet was mainly milk, bread, and fruit. He clambered around and over each structure, measuring, drawing, photographing, mapping, and recording highly detailed notes for his projected thesis on medieval military history.[2] In the coastal marshland at Aigues-Morte he caught malaria and suffered outbreaks of chills and fever the rest of his life.

Walking Through Syria

This trip pales beside his trip to Syria the next summer. The idea behind it was suggested by C. F. Bell, Assistant Keeper of the Ashmolean Museum, who said, "Why don't you go to the Holy Land and try to settle once and for all the long contested question as to whether the pointed arch and vault were copied or developed from Eastern sources by the Crusaders, or whether it was they who taught their use to the Arabs?"[3] That issue—whether the major influence on the design of crusaders' castles flowed from the west to the

Lawrence's bungalow in the garden behind the family's home at Polstead Road, Oxford (courtesy of Malcolm Brown).

east or vice versa—became the subject of Lawrence's thesis. As a thinker—and, in many ways, an actor in military and foreign affairs—Lawrence was a *provocateur* who (after escaping his socially and intellectually constricting home) questioned, or espoused the opposite of, any accepted doctrine. The accepted view was that 12th and 13th century French and British castles echoed those the crusaders had built in the Levant; Lawrence argued that the crusaders brought their design from Europe.

Once he set upon a goal, few persons or forces could stop Lawrence from pursuing and, God permitting, attaining it. His extraordinary persistence—or obduracy—resembled his mother's; his intellectual grasp, daring, cunning, stamina, and if need be ruthlessness, were his own. Resolved to visit Syria, he consulted the new Ashmolean director, David Hogarth, and Charles Doughty, patriarch of Arabian travelers. They advised him not to make the trip, especially not in the summer, alone, and on foot. "Long daily marches on foot a prudent man ... would I think consider out of the question" Doughty wrote.[4]

Dismissing their counsel, Lawrence made the trip, with camera and gun, lodging with incredulous natives and eating their food. "They ... are amazed at my traveling on foot & alone. Riding is the only honourable way of going, & everyone is dreadfully afraid of thieves." His camera was stolen; he was attacked twice by bandits and frequently by mosquitoes and fleas, was at times ill, his feet and body were blistered, cut, and sore, his clothes tattered. Yet in ten weeks, from early July to mid–September 1909, just turned 21, he walked 1,000 miles over hilly, stony, barren, sometimes roadless country in Lebanon, Palestine, and Syria, with the temperature, day and night, like a "gigantic oven."[5] Starting in Beirut, he went south to Nazareth; then, returning north, proceeded to Latakia, Antioch, Aleppo, and as far as Urfa, 25 miles inside the present Turkish border. He photographed, mapped, drew, and described 36 castles— all but one on his itinerary. In the process, he learned Arabic, learned about the local people, diet, customs, geography, social and political conditions.

He did not learn self-reliance, perseverance, endurance, or temerity: these he had. His approach was not that of a timorous tourist. He had learned architectural photography from his father and had studied architectural drawing and the techniques and terminology of fortress construction. He had practiced walking up and down a board with nails at meter intervals to measure a fortress wall without arousing the guard's suspicion. He would beguile, evade or bribe a guard to reach barred towers and recesses. One castle he explored with candles; at another, by Mt. Hermon, "I ... at last set fire to the brushwood in the inner court which burnt all the morning. Still in the evening I profited by seeing the building as a whole, as no other person can have done for 20 years— it was simply choked with rubbish."[6]

The thesis, submitted early in 1910, earned Lawrence a First in history; his tutor gave a dinner to celebrate. "[T]hey'll have to give me a First," Lawrence had told a friend. "Nobody but myself has seen all those castles, and examiners can't admit their ignorance."[7]

The Carchemish Dig

Work on the thesis had put Lawrence in touch with Hogarth, a seasoned scholar, archeologist, Near East traveler, and head of an exploratory dig the British Museum was planning at Carchemish, high on the Euphrates in northern Syria. Lawrence had passed the site on his walking tour. His performance impressed Hogarth, and Lawrence, having found the experience glorious, wanted to return to Syria. Hogarth arranged for him to join the dig on a fellowship of £100 a year. Thus, Lawrence had good money for a fledgling archeologist, security, and excitement. The years at Carchemish and roaming the country when the dig was closed were the happiest of his life.

In an insightful passage, Hogarth said, "Your true antiquary is born, not made. Sometimes an infirmity or awkwardness of body, which has disposed a boy to shun the pursuits of his fellows, may help to detach the man for the study of forgotten far off things; but it is essential that there be inborn in him the type of mind which is more curious of the past than the present, loves detail for its own sake, and cares less for ends than means."[8] That seems applicable to Lawrence in many ways: his small body, his solitary pursuits and aversion to group activities, his intense absorption in things medieval, his perception and retention of detail.

Like other English schoolchildren, Lawrence rubbed brasses, but he was unusually, even ruthlessly, thorough about it. He would trespass on church sites and unscrew brasses to examine the underside. Once, he ripped out wood to reach some brasses. "I still hear the splintering woodwork and his short laugh, almost sinister to my timorous ears," a schoolmate recalled.[9] Lawrence induced workers at Oxford construction sites to save bits of old pottery and glass that they found, paying a few pennies for them—an early instance of his easy talent for managing men. He learned how and when the objects were made, gave choice pieces to the Ashmolean, got to know the staff, and helped them arrange their brass rubbings and medieval pottery.

Thus, he had hands-on experience with old pottery and glassware, a reader's knowledge of Old World history and archeology, and at least an introduction to the literature and languages of the area—French, German, Latin, Greek, Arabic; later, he learned some Assyrian and Turkish. But he lacked the scholar's calling to seek the truth for its own sake and the willingness to devote long years to the exhaustive examination and sifting of evidence. His reading served other purposes. It enabled him to live imaginatively in other worlds; to acquire useful knowledge and skills, including that of writing; to help and impress colleagues and outmaneuver rivals by knowing more than they about a surprising range of subjects. At school, college, and during most of his life, Lawrence read prodigiously and fast. Shy, he often preferred books to people; his brother Arnold thought him "in certain respects ... book-learned rather than life-learned."[10] A photographic memory enabled him to retain what he read, heard, and saw, and a penetrating, puzzle-solving mind instantly assembled pertinent, scattered facts into a meaningful whole.

Lawrence left for Beirut by ship in December 1910. In 1908, he had written that the "little gem of a [Greek] temple" in Nimes "makes one marvel what the Parthenon must be."[11] When the ship stopped in Athens and he finally saw it, he was ecstatic: "I walked through the doorway of the Parthenon ... without really remembering where or who I was. A heaviness in the air made my eyes swim.... The building was irregular, alive with curve and subtlety ... there is an intoxication, a power of possession in its ruins, & the memories that inhabit them." There was someone captured by the past who could understand its relics and bring them to life. But not as a scholar working for the illumination of other scholars. "I am not going to put all my energies into rubbish like writing history or becoming an archaeologist," he wrote his family.[12]

The large Carchemish mound is a Hittite site overlain by Roman, Syrian, and Arab remains. It was uncertain if the site was worth excavating completely for its historical significance or the public attention notable finds might gain. Since, during World War I, Hogarth and Lawrence worked for military intelligence, some writers imagine the excavation was a cover for their spying on German engineers' construction of the Berlin to Baghdad railway, which was to bridge the Euphrates nearby. Were that the real reason for a protracted, expensive excavation, its funding would never have been in doubt.[13]

A Baronial Life

If Lawrence felt free for the first time at college, at Carchemish he was freer: free of English proprieties and pieties and the lies of legitimacy he had had to enact. Son of an unacknowledged baronet who never assumed the title, he could live here like a nobleman in the medieval world of Arab and Kurdish peasants and villagers, Turkish governors, and English overlords. The English (and other foreigners), by treaty, had special privileges in Turkish lands: "Don't you know that no Turkish officer or policeman or government official can lay hands on an Englishman, or enter his house? Much less imprison him," Lawrence writes, seeking to calm his worried family. "There would be a warship in Beyrout if anyone ... insulted us." And, "Really this country, for the foreigner, is too glorious for words: one is the baron of the feudal system."[14]

Indeed, Lawrence and Leonard Woolley, who headed the excavation under

Hogarth's distant tutelage, lived like barons. They built and furnished magnificent living quarters with Roman mosaic floors, rolled up with enormous labor, relaid, and repaired; a Roman water jug; Hittite cooking pots, coffee cups, sugar bowls, soap dishes, glass vases, stone bowls; a Phoenician basalt mortar; Greek table crockery; Damascus wall and fireplace tiles; beaten copper fire-hood and bath; Bokhara and Kurdish rugs; Aleppo carved wooden chests; a Persian box; leather-bound classics.

In earlier and later years, Lawrence was parsimonious; now he bought luxuries for himself and his family. "[T]he best carpet authority in Aleppo … priced our sitting room at about £350 in rugs … nearly half … are mine…. You [his family] will next year have as good a floor as Mr. Hogarth … which means the best in Oxford."[15] Buying antiquities for the museums and himself, Lawrence visited markets and became well known to dealers. "Woolley has brought out a deal of money to speculate in antiquities: and he is in fair way of making about 300 percent…. I have still scruples about engaging in trade!" "I was offered a huge silver chalice…. I was really tempted to throw away my salary of this year upon it."[16]

Many of Lawrence's early letters to his family are emotionally detached, full of technical details on castles and cathedrals. The letters from Carchemish give similar details on the dig and local events, but are more light-hearted; those to E. T. Leeds at the Ashmolean are often funny and even offer jocular kisses and love—for Lawrence, they are positively effusive. The self-deprecating, unhappy man of later years is not evident; he was enjoying himself too much.

Lawrence's responsibilities included recording and photographing finds, glueing fragments together, keeping the accounts, bargaining for goods, serving as Arabic-English interpreter, helping Gregorios Antoniou, the experienced Cypriot foreman who had worked for Hogarth on other digs, to manage the work crew. Knowing Arabic and the Arabs better than Woolley, Lawrence was better at finding and bargaining for objects that, siphoned off ancient sites and cemeteries, eventually made their way to private and public collections of the West.

Since the spring and fall digging depended on the timeliness of Turkish permits and British Museum funding, the number of workmen employed to remove up to 23 feet of earth and heavy stone on the ten-acre site fluctuated from 300 to none. One might expect a small, shy, young Oxonian, who looked far younger than he was (22 to 25, in the Carchemish years; at 24, he looked 16) to be uncomfortable and ineffective at managing poor, tough, illiterate hands. Nonetheless, this was one of Lawrence's effortless talents. He quickly learned the local dialects; listened to, retained, and made astute use of gossip; and turned work into a game with a small award, the firing of a gun and much commotion and praise for finds. With "the pick-men pitted against the basket-men … until with two hundred men running and yelling, half a day's output would be accomplished in an hour."[17] Lawrence matched or beat the men at feats of endurance, like walking the 50 miles to Biriedjik and back in 16 hours, which no villager had done in one day. And he was expert with a gun.

In a wild-east country where feuds were common and men wore a heavy gun-belt at home and in the fields, Lawrence's marksmanship and top-quality guns were often displayed. At Oxford, he had joined the Officers' Training Corps, practiced at the rifle range, and could fire a revolver with either hand. On his 1909 walk through Syria, he carried, and had occasion to use, a heavy, semi-automatic

Mauser. At Carchemish, he practiced often; he could hit a petrol tin at 400 yards with a rifle and a bottle at 60 yards with a Colt.

Money, practical help, and personal understanding gave Lawrence authority over the workmen. He had the power to hire, pay, and fire. The workday was 11½ hours, 5:30 A.M. to 5:00 P.M. with a half-hour morning break and 1½ hours rest at noon. The pay was 8 piastres (about 14 British pence) a day compared to 9 at the nearby German railway site, yet the men preferred the dig and moved twice as much earth as the Germans' crews. They did so because of Gregorios's experience and Lawrence's insight into Arab society and individual character and deft use of this knowledge:

> [T]he Arab day labourer is most often drawn from the worst class, and performs his task by rote, neither thinking nor caring about it…. A way of bettering this case … is by enlisting the help of the peasant farmer or his sons…. Often they do not work well side by side with the lowest class, and sometimes are only to be attracted by … sowing the superstition that certain jobs are more honourable, and therefore to be reserved for better families. If this desirable job … sets the pace for the rest (as the pick in a digging gang) the ordinary workman will be pulled up to the level of his leaders…. The happiest master is he who knows the names and relationship of all his men, for under such conditions the feudalism latent in the sedentary tribes attaches them to him; … if he has a gift of humour to temper the necessary firmness, and enough humanity to be interested in his men off the works … there is little they will not do for him.[18]

Lawrence sounds like a field biologist who has worked out the hierarchy of a wolf pack and can manage the alpha male. He and Woolley impressed a visitor with "their remarkable knowledge of men …

they know more about handling Orientals than any man I have met during my two years in Syria."[19] As lord of the Carchemish manor, Lawrence was concerned about the welfare of his men and their families. He and Woolley used their legal privileges to protect their workmen from Turkish authorities. On one occasion, 270 men seeking to avoid conscription slept at the site and in the main house; the German engineers "lost numbers of men and are crippled: we did not lose a man."[20] Lawrence served as doctor and drug dispenser; when smallpox broke out in Jerablus, the nearby village, he had the children inoculated. He advised men shopping for wives to pay £2 for a plump country girl instead of £12 for a town girl. He settled disputes among workmen and local families or between workmen and the Germans.

Landowners got their peasants into heavy debt, lending money at exorbitant rates—"1,930 percent per ann."—that they had to repay by endless labor. Most of their pay went to the landowners. "Our donkey-boy till last week was only getting 15 of 45 piastres [a month] we pay him," the rest going to the local sheikh. Resident Robin Hoods, Lawrence and Woolley fought this system, becoming "protector of-the-poor-and-enemy-of-all-the-rich-and-in-authority."[21]

Dahoum

Contributing to Lawrence's happiness at Carchemish was Dahoum, a young Arab, about 15 in 1911, perhaps the only person he ever loved and probably "S.A." to whom *Seven Pillars of Wisdom* is dedicated. Lawrence mentions Dahoum often in letters home and brought him to Oxford in the summer of 1913. Tall, very strong, "not particularly intelligent … but beautifully built and remarkably handsome,"[22] Dahoum brought water to the men and was Lawrence's generic assistant; they traveled the countryside together. "Dahoum is very useful now," Lawrence wrote, "though a savage: however we are here in the feudal system, which gives the overlord great claims: so that I have no trouble with him."[23]

Lawrence's strange sexual-cum-asexual nature will be discussed later. As he found the bodies of men, not women, attractive and Dahoum was a handsome young man, there must have been an erotic, but not, I think, a sexual element in their friendship. The marks of adolescent immaturity outweigh any suggestion of overt sexuality.

His views and goals for Dahoum merge with those he formed for the Arabs. Dahoum counted on his fingers and toes; Lawrence wanted him educated, encouraged him to read, taught him to take and develop photographs. He should not be converted to Christianity or city life, but should remain a Moslem and live in the country. Dahoum was Lawrence's noble peasant. "The perfectly hopeless vulgarity of the half–Europeanized Arab is appalling. Better a thousand times the Arab untouched. The foreigners come out here always to teach, whereas they had much better learn, for in everything but wits and knowledge the Arab is generally the better man of the two." He hoped to free the Arabs from their bondage to landowners. "If the men were living on their own land they could sell their labour ... for what it is worth: instead of starving as at present." Lawrence tried to buy the Carchemish site (which, it appeared, might be done for £30), so "our workmen can move on to it, and live out of the clutches of their sheikhs."[24] It was not feasible.

Bold, self-assured, erudite, cultivated, looking and often acting like a boy, Law-

Dahoum at Carchemish, 1912, photographed by Lawrence holding his gun (The British Library, London).

rence astonished many who met him at Carchemish. Visiting the site in May 1911, Gertrude Bell wrote of "a young man called Lawrence (he is going to make a traveller)." After Lawrence met James Elroy Flecker, British poet-consul in Beirut, his wife said, "My husband was delighted ... to hear of the 'amazing boy's' astonishing adventures." Hubert Young told his friends "there was a little man at Carchemish of whom more would be heard some day."[25]

Some found Lawrence arrogant and unpleasant. He giggled, played practical jokes but did not like being the target. Leonard Woolley perceived "his essential immaturity." After the day's dig, he would bathe and dress sumptuously in "a white and gold embroidered Arab waistcoat and a magnificent cloak of gold and silver thread, a sixty-pound garment." Armenian doctor E. H. R. Altounyan thought the "frail, pallid, silent youth ... impressive, disturbing and disagreeable," a *poseur*, "an insufferable young prig."[26]

Lawrence liked to tell, write, retell, and embellish stories. A battle between Carchemish workers and nearby German engineers became a mini-legend, half epic, half comic; a visit to a derelict fort became a mini prose-poem seeking to capture the desert's essence. With each retelling, reality and romance merged indissolubly. Michael Asher notes two accounts Lawrence gave of a caravan passing through the Aleppo market. In the first, it is a caravan of mules; in the second, camels. In both, Lawrence triumphs. He stops the caravan, buys the bells, rings them, "and the people parted ... to give me passage." "And I marched in triumph home."[27]

When the dig closed the first summer, Lawrence remained and walked again in Syria and Turkey, as two years before. This time, as his diary shows, the walk was disastrous. His feet blistered, his right instep collapsed painfully, a tooth, his right foot, a bite on his right hand were all abscessed. Initially, he had "plenty of reserve force to draw upon"; then he had severe dysentery, a high malarial fever, and fainted. "Can hardly lift hand to write this." He grew delirious—"Worst night have ever had," dragged himself back to Jerablus, and almost died. And wrote home, "I am very well."[28]

If Lawrence ever seriously contemplated an academic career, which is improbable, he now dismissed the idea. "I don't think anyone who had tasted the East as I have would give it up half-way, for a seat at high table and a chair in the Bodleian," he told his family. "I don't think that I will ever travel in the West again ... this part out here is worth a million of the rest."[29] Like William Morris, his

favorite author, Lawrence was enchanted with the medieval world. Inland Syria was wonderfully remote from his family and the sooty cities and desecrated soil of industrial Britain. His father doubted that he would ever return to live in England.

Lawrence did not just sightsee and scour bazaars for antiquities. Something impelled him to confront those who demeaned or opposed him and make them back down. Challenged, he would not retreat. Attacked and robbed in 1909, he made determined efforts, then and upon returning to the area in 1911, to find the thief and recover his goods. He made a German engineer apologize for beating Dahoum, threatening to flog him in public. Heading a group of armed Kurds, he rescued an abducted Kurdish girl. In 1913, when Turkey was at war in the Balkans and a Kurdish uprising was feared, he smuggled rifles from a British gunboat in Beirut to the British consulate in Aleppo. To his brother Will's surprised disapproval, he befriended Busrawi Agha, chief of the Melli Kurds. "They are a brave lot of brigands," Will said, but "pitiless hawks to the poor Armenians." If Bulgaria defeated Turkey, the Kurds planned to sack Aleppo; purportedly, they allotted "two bankers' houses, great collectors of objects d'art" to Lawrence. "Don't fear for Ned: if the whole country was in rebellion he would still be all right, with hundreds of horsemen at his back," Will told the family."[30]

In fact, Lawrence did not like horses, but Will, the most balanced and attractive of the five brothers, was doubtless right. When Busrawi sent a troop of horsemen to escort him on a visit, they rode and galloped six hours across the barren, hilly steppes to Busrawi's mammoth tent, where they feasted and watched racing games, "men in dazzling robes galloping splendid horses.... Yet this [Busrawi] is a man responsible for some of the biggest massacres of modern times.[31]

Lawrence had not been two months in Syria when he told his mother, "here I am Arab in habits."[32] Somehow, things *fitted*, the land, the people suited him: the long-settled order of classes—not that different from England's, but here Lawrence was one of the legitimate gentry; the dirty daytime dig and cultured evening splendor attended by servants; unearthing relics of dead empires in the dying Turkish empire; the ports and inland cities held by Turkish guns encircled, in turn, by armed Arab and Kurdish tribesmen. Lawrence admired the savage tribesmen and belittled the townsmen. When the dig closed summers and winters, he had long months free to wander. He found himself content with the life of an archaeologist. "I fought very hard ... to avoid being labeled: but the insurance people have nailed me down, now," he declared at the end of his third year in Carchemish.[33]

Questioning Lawrence's seriousness as an archeologist, Richard Aldington noted that he published little. Arnold Lawrence, a classical archeologist, agreed: "his only learned publications were his share of reports, the compilation of which was unavoidable. Contrary to general practice, he wrote no articles in archaeological journals, although he must have had ample material."[34] However, professional archeologists, like ethnographers, geographers, paleontologists, and naturalists, prize field workers who can adapt to difficult conditions, deal effectively with natives, and return with facts and artifacts their sedentary colleagues study. Whatever his status as a sedentary scholar, Lawrence was a prize field worker. Flinders Petrie, the prominent Egyptologist with whom he spent a few weeks in 1912, asked him to lead a dig in Bahrein; in 1913, Turkish officials asked him to dig for them further down the Euphrates.

In January and February 1914, while the Carchemish dig was closed, Woolley and Lawrence (with Dahoum in tow) conducted a hasty archeological survey of the Sinai for the Palestine Exploration Fund. The project was designed to put a scholarly gloss on the open military mapping undertaken at the same time by a group of Royal Engineers led by Capt. Stewart Newcombe. "We are obviously only meant as red herrings to give an archaeological colour to a political job," Lawrence explained.[35]

At Akaba, Lawrence wished to inspect an island half a mile from shore. The governor forbade it and police removed his hired boat. Lawrence and Dahoum paddled out on two water tanks. The angry governor assigned soldiers on camels to see them out of the area. "[W]e walked them out of water," Lawrence said, "and they were hungry, and we dodged up valleys and slipped their trails; until ... the last one left us."[36]

The last prewar digging season ended in June. Departing for home, Lawrence and Woolley did some genuine spying. Newcombe and three Army officers had visited Carchemish in May and taken the train to Constantinople in order to examine the route and the status of construction in the mountains. Newcombe asked the archeologists to repeat the journey and secure additional information. In June, traveling as "Jones and Robinson," they did so. Meeting an Italian engineer the Germans had just fired, Woolley, whose Italian was excellent, extracted railway drawings and information from him.[37]

On August 3, Germany went to war with France and August 4, with Britain. On October 30, Turkey and Britain were at war.

Dahoum died during the war, apparently of typhus fever. In 1919, Lawrence thought of digging again at Carchemish— even that Feisal, then King of Syria, might give him the site. He checked on its condition and learned that statues he had carved had been removed. Returning to the dig, Woolley found French officers in the archeologists' quarters and Senegalese and Algerian troops, camped nearby, fighting both Kurdish and clandestine Turkish forces. Lawrence had contacted him, early in 1919, about resuming work, but Woolley deemed it impractical: "it will not do for him to come out. I shall be working ... on sufferance of the French and I cannot afford to have with me anyone whose presence would be sure to cause friction."[38] By then, Lawrence was *persona non grata* to the French.

3

War,
1914–1918

Lawrence's three war-age brothers served in France; two died there. In the rush of taller volunteers at the outbreak of war, short Lawrence could not enlist. He worked first in Oxford on the Sinai survey report demanded by Lord Kitchener, Secretary of State for War.[1] Then, with Hogarth's help, he joined the Geographical Section of the General Staff in London as a 2d Lieutenant, preparing maps of France and the Sinai, including territory he had not visited. "So I'm writing a [military] report ... of a country I don't know.... One of the minor terrors is, that later on I'm to ... guide myself over the country with it."[2]

By the time his *Military Report on the Sinai Peninsula* was finished, Sinai and Syria mapping had moved to Cairo, whither Lawrence and Capt. Newcombe proceeded together in December. At 26, Lawrence was the youngest in a small group of able young experts on Turkish lands and peoples who made up the Military Intelligence Department. Newcombe, the director, was 34; George Lloyd, 33, and Aubrey Herbert, 32, both Members of Parliament; and Leonard Woolley, 32. Lloyd, a banker, was later Lord Lloyd, High Commissioner for Egypt; Herbert, the wealthy,

nearly blind Carnarvon scion, friend of Turkish and Balkan nationalists, was John Buchan's model for *Greenmantle.*

"I am bottle-washer and office boy pencil-sharpener and pen wiper," Lawrence declared. He made maps—"the best staff maps of the war," he boasted—and tracked the location of Turkish regiments for the information of British authorities in Egypt, Gallipoli, India, and Mesopotamia, where Indian troops, who landed in November, were advancing toward Baghdad. He monitored 136 Turkish regiments: their size, commander, guns, nearby roads, transport, supplies, and whether local people were friendly or hostile. "Following it [the Turkish army] about is like making a map of the movements of a fly before breakfast."[3]

His self-assignment was, together with his colleagues, to persuade his superiors in Egypt and London to adopt their political and strategic ideas. "The Intelligence Department ... have done invaluable work ... initiating ideas which never could have dawned [on] ... the [commanding] General.... A well-run Intelligence Department will really run him as regards policy," an observer wrote.[4] All his life, Lawrence preferred influencing and manipulating leaders to direct leadership. Now, at the bottom of massive military and governmental bureaucracies, he could influence events only by persuading those who might listen to or read what he said.

In November, viewing the scene from London, he had thought Egypt might fall; in Cairo two months later, he thought Turkey was "crumbling fast."[5] How should Turkey be defeated? Lawrence's consistent answer to that question was that defeat would be hastened by encouraging the nationalist movements of Arabs, Kurds, and other subject peoples of the extended Turkish empire. The untutored British thought everyone in Turkish uniform was Turkish; they knew little about the cultural, religious, and linguistic divisions and conflicts within the enemy armies and peoples. The intelligence officers and, later, members of the Arab Bureau that Hogarth established in March 1916, sought to educate their superiors about the ethnic, political, and military realities of the region. "I ... write geographic reports, trying to persuade 'em that Syria is not peopled entirely by Turks," Lawrence lamented.[6]

In addition to Turkey, Lawrence and his Cairo allies recognized two other enemies: the British government in India, and France. With a large Moslem population among their subjects and an army of Indian Moslems in oil-and grain-rich Mesopotamia, the governors of India did not want to promote native uprisings anywhere in their domain, which, in their view, stretched to the Red Sea. They opposed the more liberal policies of Cairo revisionist imperialists, who hoped to replace the Turkish empire with a network of native kingdoms or "brown dominions" under British protection. Only in 1921, when British policy for Mesopotamia, Arabia, Syria, and Egypt was consolidated in the Colonial Office under Winston Churchill, was the conflict between Egypt and India temporarily resolved.

Lawrence's animus against France, Britain's rival in the Levant, was manifest in a March 1915 letter to Hogarth. Though Britain had accepted France's future primacy in Syria, he hoped Britain would seize Alexandretta, at the juncture of the Anatolian and Syrian coasts. The port, he insisted, was not part of Syria. If held by the French, they could launch "naval attacks on Egypt" and "fling 100,000 men [local conscripts] against the canal in 12 days from declaration of war." A second letter spoke of his wish "to roll up Syria by way of the Hedjaz in the name of the Sherif" and "to biff the French out of ... Syria.... Won't the French be mad if we win through?"[7]

Lawrence claimed, "the Alexandretta scheme ... was, from beginning to end, my invention, put forward necessarily through my chiefs."[8] However, in November 1914 Kitchener had proposed to attack Alexandretta and in December Lloyd George proposed a British landing in Syria; "it is clear that he [Lawrence] did not initiate the [Alexandretta] project in Cairo, since [Major-General John] Maxwell [British commander in Egypt] had advocated a landing at Alexandretta [in December] ... and the idea was already under consideration in London."[9] Kitchener evidently ordered it to accompany Britain's February 1915 naval bombardment of the Dardanelles, but dropped it upon French opposition.

Lawrence's brothers Frank and Will were killed in France in May and October 1915, respectively, aged 22 and 25. "I'm rather low because first one and now another of my brothers has been killed," he wrote a friend; "they were both younger ... and it doesn't seem right, somehow, that I should go on living peacefully in Cairo."[10]

In the spring of 1916, Lawrence was

sent to Mesopotamia to accompany Aubrey Herbert, then head of naval intelligence in Mesopotamia, on a secret mission approved by the highest authorities in Cairo and London. It had two purposes: to assess the feasibility of spurring an Arab uprising in the region; and to offer a £1 million bribe to Turkish General Khalit Pasha to free General Townshend and 17,000 troops surrounded at Kut, on the Euphrates 40 miles south of Baghdad.

Herbert knew Britain's rulers; his wife dined often at 10 Downing Street; a Turkophile, he spoke Turkish and, a year earlier, had arranged a truce to bury the dead at Gallipoli. But why was Captain Lawrence, age 27, chosen? In part, he said, because he had helped the Russians capture Erzerum by putting them in touch with Arab officers in the Turkish army. In larger part, probably, because of his familiarity with Arab nationalists in Turkish lands and Egypt; their leaders were in touch with each other and, given satisfactory assurances of postwar political arrangements, might take action. "He is one of the best of our very able intelligence staff and has a thorough knowledge of the Arab question in all its bearings," Henry McMahon, High Commissioner in Cairo, advised Sir Percy Cox, his counterpart in Mesopotamia. A former Arab member of Turkey's parliament has described how, in Basra, Lawrence urged him to lead an Arab revolt, saying, "The British Government has authorised me to initiate this revolt and to offer what it may need in money and arms."[11]

A third possibility, that some Egypt officials wanted to get rid of Lawrence, can be seen in McMahon's comment, "We are very sorry to lose so valuable a man." Cox had that impression. "From Sir Henry McMahon's letter … it would appear that Lawrence is intended to remain here, and if he did I should think he would be a very valuable addition to the Intelligence Staff;

but he did not understand this at all." Colonel Gilbert Clayton, who picked Lawrence for the mission, wanted him back and cabled London asking that Lawrence "not be retained at Basra any longer than necessary."[12]

Lawrence, Herbert, and Colonel W. H. Beach, head of British intelligence in Mesopotamia, were led blindfolded to Khalit's tent, where Herbert conducted the negotiations. The "one or two million" pound offer of "financial support for the civilians of Kut"[13] was rejected and scornfully broadcast to world newspapers. The few concessions Herbert won were largely disregarded. As the British could not provide ships, the starving troops had to march to Baghdad; three-fourths died en route or as prisoners. It was a terrible disaster.

Lawrence's mission pleased few officers or officials in Mesopotamia; his manner also displeased many. Hubert Young, who had met and liked Lawrence at Carchemish, "was disappointed in him. He seemed to me thoroughly spoilt, and posing in a way that was quite unlike what I remembered." On the ship back to Cairo, Lawrence prepared a devastating report on military, political, and intelligence operations in Mesopotamia. He "spared no one…. He criticized the quality of the stones used for lithography, the system of berthing barges alongside the quays, the inefficiency of the cranes for handling stores…. And, horror of horrors, he criticized the Higher Command and the conduct of the campaign…!" When General Sir Archibald Murray, Commander of British Mediterranean forces, asked for the report, his staff toned it down to forestall an apoplectic fit.[14]

The sanitized version (the original is lost) contained astute, astonishingly detailed, wide-ranging observations with equally detailed, practical recommendations for remedying many of the itemized defects. A few extracts convey the flavor:

[T]he Intelligence Staff ... do all their examination of agents, prisoners and refugees, through interpreters..., so that many of the finer points ... are missed. Also you get gross errors.... [W]e must send them a linguist or two, who knows the inside of Turkey.

[Map] compilation and drawing [should] be done at the aerodrome, to ensure the cooperation of observers and compiler ... maps to be used for any length of time in the field [should] be printed on linen-backed paper. I have promised thirty reams of our own....

When we regulate the rivers we also drain the lakes and swamps.... We will be able to starve a rebellion by shutting down a sluice, or drown it by opening them too wide.[15]

Interviewing captured soldiers, Lawrence deduced their background from their "dress, manner, and speech." Determining their home districts, "I ... asked about my friends in them. Then they told me everything." While negotiating at Kut, he elicited General Khalil's views of the fighting ability of Arab and Kurdish troops the British had captured. "It was ... discreet but effective intelligence gathering and striking proof that Lawrence knew his job." To others, the tumultuous, fractious, warring region was a vast, buzzing confusion; to Lawrence, "it all fits into itself like a most wonderful puzzle."[16]

Intelligence work included the tedious preparation, with others, of several editions of the *Handbook of the Turkish Army*, a 1,200 page tome on Arabia, and shorter handbooks on the tribes, leaders, and geography of the region. (During World War II, American scholars prepared similar handbooks on the countries and peoples of Europe, Asia, and the Pacific islands for the use of U.S. forces.) The secret *Arab Bulletin* that Hogarth, Lawrence, and other Arab Bureau members issued from 1916 to 1918 was far more stimulating. Lawrence's contributions, many written in desert encampments, give his typically incisive appraisals of the character, politics, and military situation of the Arabs. Their striking language and insights compelled attention and brought the *Bulletin* a larger audience than was prudent for a secret publication.

The Arab Revolt

I will not recount yet again the story of the Arab revolt against the Turks that broke out in the Hejaz in June 1916, under the leadership of Sherif Hussein, or the political understandings and misunderstandings between Arab and British, and British and French, representatives. Nor will I detail the Arab campaign in the interior and the British advance up the Palestinian coast. My theme is psychological, not historical, political, or military. I am concerned with Lawrence's character and conduct, brilliant, clear, impressive, maddening, mad, or incomprehensible. The history and politics of Arab nationalist movements and their entanglements with Britain and France during and following the war have been told many times.[17]

It need only be said here that, from Turkey's entry into the war until mid–1916, Arabs served in her armies as soldiers and officers. However, Arab nationalists secretly plotted rebellion. The wary Turks withdrew Arab troops from Syria and Mesopotamia, executed many Arab leaders, and detained others in Constantinople. British diplomats sought to induce Sherif Hussein to rebel, promising help and independence for the Hejaz and, more vaguely, for the more heavily populated Arab lands to the north. Hussein, a descendent of the Prophet, was keeper of holy Mecca and Medina and the Hejaz littoral, readily controlled by the British Red

Sea fleet. The fleet protected the Arabs' long west flank; British ships supplied the Arabs with rifles, ammunition, food, water, gold.

In June and July 1916, as Arab actions against Turkish troops unfolded, confusion reigned. The Arabs had taken Mecca but not the railhead at Medina, where entrenched Turkish forces threatened to march against the poorly organized, poorly armed Arabs. Hussein asked for money, supplies, and guns. However, the revolt was a religious and diplomatic as well as military event. The guns and supplies were held by the Egyptian Expeditionary Force under General Sir Archibald Murray; the diplomacy was managed by British High Commissioner Sir Henry McMahon. The Arab Bureau was under McMahon; military intelligence, under Murray. Lawrence, formally in intelligence, served both, as did General Gilbert Clayton, his immediate commander. As McMahon and Murray feuded, they were caught in the crossfire. "[T]he jealousies and interferences of people on your own side give you far more work and anxiety than the enemy do," Lawrence complained.[18]

Clayton was evicted from intelligence and consigned to the Arab Bureau. Lawrence aimed to join him. The requested transfer being denied, "I became … quite intolerable…. I took every opportunity to rub into them their comparative ignorance and inefficiency … (not difficult!)." Lawrence asked Clayton to arrange for his transfer via London authorities, circumventing the lines of command in Egypt, and, while that was being negotiated, took leave to accompany Ronald Storrs, Oriental Secretary in Cairo, on a trip to Jidda to assess the status of the revolt.[19]

Storrs, "the most brilliant Englishman in the Near East, … was … the great man among us. His shadow would have covered our work and British policy in the East like a cloak, had he been able to deny himself the world, and to prepare his mind and body with the sternness of an athlete for a great fight," Lawrence wrote, intimating that *he* could do what Storrs could not. In his diary, Storrs noted "little Lawrence my supercerebral companion … continue to wonder whether for all his amazing knowledge, his sum total of pleasure is … any greater than mine."[20]

Entering the port of Jidda the morning of October 16, Lawrence began his adventure in Arabia: "…when at last we anchored in the outer harbour, off the white town hung between the blazing sky and its reflection in the mirage which swept and rolled over the wide lagoon, then the heat of Arabia came out like a drawn sword and struck us speechless," he recalled in *Seven Pillars*. The next words are, "It was midday." Storrs's diary says "7 A.M. Young came aboard to take us off and we reached Consulate about 9.30." Either Lawrence's memory slipped (unlikely)[21] or a mid-day sun made a more dramatic sentence.

Storrs, Lawrence, and Col. Cyril Wilson, British Consul in Jidda, met with Abdulla, Hussein's second son and Foreign Minister of the new Hejaz state. The discussion was civil but doleful, as Storrs could not supply the money or arms that had been promised or the British troops and planes that were now sought, Turkish planes over Rabegh (on the coast 80 miles north of Jidda) having greatly discombobulated the Arabs. "Lawrence remarked that very few Turkish aeroplanes last more than four or five days." Lawrence put his knowledge of the disposition of Turkish troops to good use. "As Syrian, Circassian, Anatolian, Mesopotamian names came up, Lawrence at once stated exactly which unit was in each position." Abdulla exclaimed, "Is this man God, to know everything?"[22]

With Storrs's help, Lawrence parlayed his performance into permission to inspect the situation up country and meet

Abdulla's brother Feisal, who commanded Arab forces on the Sultani Road, which the Turks would have to take if they moved out of Medina to retake Mecca. No British officer had yet gone inland. To gain authorization and a letter of introduction to Feisal, Abdulla and Storrs had to phone Hussein in Mecca and overcome his suspicions.

"Lawrence wants kicking and kicking *hard...*," Col. Wilson cabled Clayton. "I look on him as a bumptious young ass who spoils his undoubted knowledge of Syrian Arabs &c. by making himself out to be the only authority on war, engineering, HM's [His Majesty's] ships and everything else. He put every single person's back up I've met from the Admiral [Wemyss] down to the most junior fellow on the Red Sea."[23]

Though Abdulla was Sherif Hussein's heir apparent, Lawrence doubted his value as prime leader of the Arab forces. "[T]hough only thirty-five, he was putting on flesh.... Rumour made him the brain of his father and of the Arab revolt; but he seemed too easy for that.... Abdulla was too balanced, too cool, too humorous to be a prophet: especially the armed prophet." Storrs disagreed with this assessment; as a diplomat, he valued Abdulla's diplomatic talents, whereas Lawrence was assessing his military and national leadership, and (though he does not say so), *manipulability.*[24] Subsequent encounters strengthened Law-rence's judgment. He condemned Abdulla for "constant ailments ... laziness and self-indulgence ... feeble tyranny ... caprice ... love of pleasure ... insincerity" and yet other crimes of personal and military indolence. "Abdulla's theory of war," said military analyst Liddell Hart, "seemed to be that the tongue is mightier than the sword."[25]

Days later, meeting Feisal at his Wadi Safra encampment, Lawrence "felt at first glance that this was ... the leader who would bring the Arab Revolt to full glory." Lawrence saw Feisal's noble appearance and frail reality. He was "tall, graceful and vigorous, with ... a royal dignity of head and shoulders ... a careful judge of men. If he had the strength to realize his dreams he would go very far." But Feisal was also "sensitive, even unreasonable, ... ran off soon on tangents," displayed "physical weakness ... courage ... imprudence ... frailty." After "a long spell of fighting, ... he had collapsed ... and was carried away ... unconscious, with the foam flecking his lips." Here, Lawrence decided, "was offered to our hand ... a prophet who, if veiled [!], would give cogent form to the idea behind ... the Arab revolt."[26] Lawrence has been charged with presenting Feisal, in *Seven Pillars,* as stronger than he was, a charge whose validity he acknowledged. But the foregoing passages depict a man of mixed strength and weakness, an attractive reed through which Lawrence could blow.

Returning to Egypt via Port Sudan across the Red Sea, Lawrence told the authorities in Khartoum and Cairo what they wanted to hear: guns, supplies, and Arabic-speaking technical advisers, not troops, should be sent to the Arabs. Whereupon, Clayton ordered him back to Arabia to implement his own advice. He says he protested, "hated soldiering," and wanted to resume work on the *Arab Bulletin,* map-making, and monitoring Turkish troop dispositions, "all fascinating activities."[27] Perhaps: but these desk-bound activities had not always been "fascinating." Was the protest a prudent protection against failure?

Lawrence rejoined Feisal in the field and henceforth became his friend, confidant, ally, and promoter, indeed designer of his military and political cause. In Arabia and Syria, during the Paris Peace Conference and Churchill's 1921 settlement of Middle East affairs, his intimacy with Feisal remained a key to Lawrence's influence, for, no matter what policies Britain pursued, it was useful for officials to have a candid view of Feisal's position and a private way to communicate with him.

Lawrence's familiarity with the places and peoples of Syria was another key to his influence. For sheer intellectual and literary virtuosity, nothing he wrote is more impressive than the 1,600 words with which he sections Syria into five belts running from the Mediterranean to the desert, and deposes the peoples, history, terrain, tongues, faiths, feuds, and politics of each.[28] ("Syria" then also embraced what is now Lebanon, Jordan, Israel, and western Iraq.) He had tramped about and loved the country, had gained his freedom and spent happy years there, his Arabic had a Syrian accent. On his first visit to Jidda, Hussein's wish to use the Hejaz railway to advance into Syria was discussed. Syria and Mesopotamia were the region's population and power centers, the prizes of imperial and indigenous claimants beside which the vast Arabian desert was insignificant. Freeing Syria from the Turks— and the French!—became the goal he and the Arabs shared.

Fame Comes in Summer

Returning to Arabia, Lawrence rapidly immersed himself in its affairs, its deserts and water holes, families and feuds. The great empty land sounded a deep chord in him. Long before, when he first saw the Mediterranean at Aigues Mortes, he wrote home:

> The beach was hard sand as far as the eye could reach....
> I love all waste
> And solitary places: where we taste
> The pleasure of believing all we see
> Is boundless, as we wish our souls
> to be:—

> You are all wrong, Mother dear, a mountain may be a great thing, [but] ... give me a level plain, extending as far as the eye can reach....[29]

Three months after Lawrence landed in Jidda, Hogarth reported from Cairo, "T.E.L. ... writes ... that he wishes to stay away from Europe & all things European for ever & ever, & get thoroughly Arabized."[30]

In the summer of 1917, two events made Lawrence famous to Britain's leaders in Egypt and London: his secret ride behind the Turkish lines to Damascus and, three weeks later, on July 6, the Arab capture of Akaba. Lawrence rode into Syria during a pause at the Nebk oasis in the 600-mile, elliptical, counterclockwise move from the Red Sea port of Wejh through the remote desert that he, Howeitat chief Auda abu Tayi, and Feisal's deputy and cousin Sherif Nasir ibn Hussein took to attack Akaba from its unshielded rear. Their expedition was mounted independently, without British approval. On June 5, while Auda and Nasir were enlisting Howeitat tribesmen for the march on Akaba, Lawrence set forth with two men on his long, hazardous camel ride to the north.

He had mixed motives: some, almost suicidal; some, political and strategic. A diary message to Clayton said, "I've decided to go off alone to Damascus, hoping to get killed on the way: for all sakes try and clear this show up before it goes further. We are calling them to fight for us on a lie, and I can't stand it."[31] Evidently, the recruitment of men while news circulated of Britain's ceding postwar control of Syria to France deeply disturbed Lawrence.[32] "[I]t was repugnant that the innocence and the ideals of the Arabs should enlist in my sordid service," he later wrote. "I was in reckless mood.... A bodily wound would have been a grateful vent for my internal perplexities."[33]

Lawrence's practical purposes were to meet secretly with Arab leaders in Syria, warn them against an immediate uprising some were urging, and lay the ground for their help when Feisal's men would enter their territory. (Except for a small contingent, the Arabs had no standing army; their forces, recruited at negotiated sums from local Bedouin for local actions, changed constantly as the fighting moved northward through the lands and oases of rival tribes.) He reached 80 miles northeast of Damascus; dynamited a bridge at Ras Baalbek; met with the Damascus mayor outside the city and, further south, with Sheikh Hussein of the Druse and Nuri Shaalan of the great Ruwalla tribe.

Something critical happened at the latter meeting. Lawrence relates that "old Nuri ... brought out a file of documents and asked which British pledge was to be believed. In his mood, upon my answer, lay the success or failure of Feisal. My advice, uttered with some agony of mind, was to trust the latest." Jeremy Wilson thinks that Nuri, a ruthless ruler, extracted a secret pledge: "if Britain failed the Arabs, Lawrence would submit himself to dreadful retribution, perhaps even death." Lawrence kept the secret and dismissed the ride into Syria as needless, a failure, "as barren of consequence as it was unworthy in motive."[34] However, Carl Raswan, who discussed the ride with Nuri, says it helped to keep the allegiance of sheikhs whose loyalty had been shaken by word of the Sykes–Picot treaty. "I have it from Nuri ... that ... the Arabs were deserting the British in May, 1917. It was only by ... Lawrence ... taking matters up personally [with the wavering sheikhs] ... that the end of the Arab revolt was prevented."[35]

Back in Nebk June 18, Lawrence and Howeitat raiders spent five days destroying railway stretches and Turkish posts to the north, to mislead the Turks about the direction of their attack, before turning

south and marching on Akaba, which surrendered on July 6. The same day, Lawrence set out with eight men across the Sinai, reaching Cairo July 9 with news of Akaba's fall and an urgent request that a ship with food and supplies be sent to the hungry men and their captives.[36]

These pyrotechnic feats transformed Lawrence's standing from one of a number of liaison officers to a leading figure in Arab affairs. In Cairo, he met the new British Commander-in-Chief, General Edmund Allenby, and received his assurance of gold and guns. On July 15, Storrs jotted in his diary, "L.'s performance in Syria little short of miraculous...." Colonel Wilson, who had earlier called Lawrence "a bumptious ... ass," now praised "his personality, gallantry, and grit." Informing General William Robertson, Chief of the Imperial General Staff in London, of Akaba's capture, General Wingate termed Lawrence's Syrian journey "little short of marvellous" and recommended him for a Victoria Cross.[37] General Clayton told Robertson that Lawrence's was "a very remarkable performance [1,300 miles on camelback in 30 days alone would be noteworthy], calling for a display of courage, resource, and endurance."[38] Three months later, Hogarth remarked that Lawrence's reputation was "overwhelming." Returning to Cairo from a European trip, Storrs noted, "Two names had come to dominate Cairo: Allenby ... and Lawrence, no longer a meteor in renown, but a fixed star."[39]

I cite this contemporary evidence because several writers suggest that Lawrence's achievement in Arabia was largely invented by Lowell Thomas to attract crowds to his 1919 slide show; some assert that the ride into Syria never occurred.[40] George Antonius, whose 1938 history of Near East politics drew on Arabic and western sources, did not doubt it: "Lawrence went off alone on one of the most original and daring expeditions of his career and one which, for some unknown reason, is passed over in silence in all his published writings." Jeremy Wilson's carefully documented examination of the episode demonstrates that the astonishing trip did take place.[41]

Knowing the outcome of events and unable to cleanse their minds of that knowledge, historians and biographers may select and interpret early conduct in terms of its significance for later events. Thus, Lawrence's strenuous boyhood trips, interest in medieval fortresses, and spare, irregular diet have been viewed as deliberate preparation for an unknown future mission demanding great endurance. John Mack regards Lawrence's long bicycle trips across France as the "preparation of himself, of his mental and physical equipment, for a great task." Such *ex post facto* interpretation makes for a story better knit than life. In *Seven Pillars*, Lawrence commits the same error, writing as if he knew before Akaba what his position would be afterwards. "I would never again" enjoy "the security ... [of] the obscure.... Before me lay a vista of responsibility and command."[42]

Deraa

Before him lay a devastating experience. In November 1917, reconnoitering Turkish-held Deraa in muddy wet clothes, Lawrence was detained by guards and taken to the bedroom of Hajim Bey, the town governor. Hajim recognized him from an Arab traitor's recent description, sought to sodomize him, and, when Lawrence kneed him painfully, gave him to the guards for correction. Kicked, beaten, whipped savagely on the back and groin, repeatedly raped, bleeding, slobbering, and fainting, he was left in a shed. In the morning, he limped off.

If Carchemish was Lawrence's delight and the entry into Damascus his moment of triumph and exhaustion, Deraa was his time of torture, degradation, torment, and self-discovery. The description of what happened is the most searing episode in *Seven Pillars*, rewritten many times. It comes as close as Lawrence ever came—not very close, by current standards—to disclosing his sexual nature. The critical passages are piercing, remarkably candid, yet elusive; "even in this extreme self-exposure," Irving Howe observes, "where he was so honest about that side of himself which sought for masochistic pain, he could not quite bring himself to be candid about the completeness of the violation." Some writers assert that the event did not occur or was not reported honestly. Suspicion of Lawrence's honesty, founded on his personal deviousness, leads them to discount even his most notable calamity.[43]

I think it was reported honestly, for the most part, but with significant omissions. In *Seven Pillars*, the Bey says, "You must understand that I know." Lawrence writes, "I was dumbfounded.... But it was evidently a chance shot." In a 1919 letter, he explains that the Bey identified him from a description given by traitorous Abd el Kadir, who had been with Lawrence the previous week and knew his plans.[44] He deliberately misled *Seven Pillars'* readers on this point.

Precisely what transpired sexually is not clear; few persons would be explicit about such a frightening, excruciating, humiliating ordeal. Lawrence mentions repeated assaults from which he derived sexual pleasure—"a delicious warmth, probably sexual, was swelling through me." Lawrence, who could condemn himself more than his worst enemy, would not forgive himself for this pleasure and for what he considered his voluntary compliance. "It's an unforgivable matter, an irrevocable position."[45] "She wanted it" is a common defense of rapists.

"More than one member of his Staff told me that after Deraa, they felt that something had happened to Lawrence which had changed him," Ronald Storrs records. He was often depressed and bitter. Jeremy Wilson denies that Deraa was responsible for Lawrence's depression during the latter stages of the campaign, putting the onset five months earlier, during his virtually suicidal ride to Damascus.[46] Perhaps so, but Deraa did not improve his spirit.

After Deraa, Wilson states, Lawrence acquired a personal bodyguard. "The price on his head was steadily rising ... [and] he was determined never again to fall into Turkish hands alive." However, Lawrence recruited new guards and rested old ones before Deraa. They were well paid. The guardmen were "lawless," single, "cutthroats; but they cut throats only to my order." They were "blood enemies of thirty tribes, and only for my hand over them would have murdered in the ranks each day ... events forced me to live up to my bodyguard, to become as hard, as sudden, as heedless."[47]

Inglorious Realities

It was a strange revolt that Lawrence fought in, helped to shape, and did much to define and, in some respects, to invent for Western eyes. The Arabs were not a united, homogeneous people. "A first difficulty of the Arab movement," Lawrence wrote, "was to say who the Arabs were." They were scattered, feuding, nomadic bands who robbed and raided each other, pilgrim caravans to the holy cities, and settled peasants and townspeople on the coasts and fertile crescent encircling the vast inner desert. Disunited, some sided with the British, some with the Turks; many shifted allegiance, bargained with and stole from both sides, and/or held aloof until the winning side emerged. André Malraux terms the revolt "an endless series of shady dealings." "Bedouin allegiance was easily transferred as circumstances might dictate," Hubert Young writes.[48] In Mesopotamia, it was said that the British and Turks should unite to fight the Arabs, their common enemy. In Arabia and Syria, many British soldiers felt that way. "We hated the Arabs," Lawrence's armored-car driver S. C. Rolls declared. "Turkish prisoners ... are like dear friends to us compared with our Arab allies." At Amman, near the war's end, surrendered Turks and their Australian captors united to keep angry Arabs from slaughtering the Turks.[49]

"Allegiance" meant money and stores for the tribes. "It was the fattest time the [Hejaz] hills had ever known. The Sherif [Hussein] was feeding not only the fighting men, but their families, and paying two pounds a month for a man, four for a camel.... Feisal offered ... a pound a head for prisoners ... [and] paid for captured mules or rifles.... [T]he paid men were more than those mobilized; and policy often gave to great sheikhs ... money that was a polite bribe for friendly countenance."[50] Britain provided the money. In August 1917, Feisal was receiving £75,000 a month, his father Hussein, £200,000; Lawrence estimated total British payments during the revolt at £10 million.[51]

Something in Lawrence resonated with the elemental Bedouin. Their black slaves, the slave girls they sometimes married, the homosexual proclivities of men who raid and camp together are noted in *Seven Pillars;* also their lice and fleas, and the flies, mosquitoes, ticks, scorpions, and snakes that assault them. The character of their camels, upon whom their war and their lives depended, is carefully detailed. So are the camels' stink, mange, the green slaver from their lips and rear, the campground "fouled by ... men and animals."

The Arabs' japes, games, and bawdy tales, their marching songs, feasts, and hospitality are the happy counterpart of their superstition and illiteracy, the treatment of sickness by burning holes in the body and of snake-bite by Koran reading, the punishment of driving thorns into the flesh or hitting the head with a dagger's edge until the blood runs. The Bedouin, Lawrence wrote, "hurt himself … to please himself. There followed a delight in pain, … abnegation, renunciation, self-restraint."[52] It is a pithy confession.

Attacking by surprise and disappearing into the hills and desert reaches, the Bedouin were hard, elusive guerrillas. That was how Lawrence tried to use them. They could cover long distances with little rest, live on a few pounds of flour, a gazelle, or, at worst, the 200 pounds of meat each man rode on. They could be lured and led but not conscripted or ordered. That was true even of the few regular Arab troops, let alone the irregulars.[53] "These Arabs are the most ghastly material to build into a design," Lawrence lamented. "We could not mix or combine tribes, because of their distrusts: nor could we use one in the territory of another." After he blew up a train, his raiders would kill and strip the enemy and head home laden with loot. Success disabled them so that Lawrence had to recruit a fresh band. There is something (not everything) in a characterization of the revolt as "banditry, not war."[54]

The revolt did not end tribal feuds, stop one tribe from attacking or robbing another or the British, or ensure the tribes' loyalty to a common cause. "Conduct of the war in France would have been harder if each division, almost each brigade of our army had hated each other with a deadly hatred and fought when they met suddenly" was how Lawrence summed up the situation.

Approaching Wejh, the Juheina captured Billi camels; tribal war was averted only when Feisal forced their return. Shortly after, the Ageyl mutinied "and went off to kill the Ateiba." Wejh shopkeepers "were mostly Egyptians … who preferred the Turks to us." So, occupying the town that British naval guns and seamen had subdued, the Arabs "robbed the shops, broke open doors, searched every room, smashed chests and cupboards, tore down all fixed fittings, and slit each mattress and pillow for hidden treasure." The townsfolk retaliated "by stealing everything unguarded," including rice the British had just landed.[55]

Setting forth on the long, roundabout route to Akaba, Lawrence's party was attacked by hostile Arabs; a week later one of his men was killed in a night attack. Upon defeating the Turks at Aba el Lissan, Auda insisted on moving on, fearing "lest other clans of the Howeitat take us lying … asleep. Some were his blood enemies." Looting a blasted train near Mudowwara, several Arabs attacked Lawrence. "Three times I had to defend myself when they pretended not to know me and snatched at my things."[56] Near Bair, Beni Sakhr raiders fired on Lawrence's band. Escaping from the failed attempt on the Yarmuk bridge, Lawrence's Serahin robbed a group of peasants; their cries brought out mounted men to attack them. At Rumm, the Imperial Camel Corps almost fought with the Arabs, who kept their wells secret.[57] Camel-drivers stole or sold so much of the Corps' supplies that 50 men and 100 camels had to return to base. The railway south of Deraa could not be demolished due to the hostility of local Bedouin, "who threatened both to warn the Turks and attack the demolitionists." At El Taiyibe, non-Arab villagers "tried to steal ammunition…, drinking-cups, petrol-tins" and shot at the Corps' rearguard.[58]

When the revolt started, most Mecca and Jidda residents, foreigners hostile to the Bedouin, opposed an Arab state. The pro–Turk chief at Rabegh appropriated supplies the British landed and threatened to attack Feisal's rear. When the Turks advanced toward Yenbo, the Northern Harb defected.[59] At Wejh, Bedouin sold to the Turks rifles and food the British had given them. After capturing Akaba, Auda, angry that the British had not rewarded him, began treasonable negotiations with the Turkish commander at Maan.[60] Subsequently, Feisal conducted secret negotiations with the Turks. Lawrence regarded this with some sympathy for, if the Allies lost in Europe, it was the Arabs' "only way out: and I had always the lurking fear that Great Britain might ... conclude its own separate peace."[61] In April 1918, Maan townsmen joined the Turks in fighting the advancing Arabs. The Turkish garrison in Medina held out until January 1919, two months after the armistice, supplied by Turkish ally Ibn Rashid's caravans that bribed their way through the encircling Arabs; in August 1918, a German plane brought the besieged Turks a load of gold for this purpose.[62]

These mercenary, military, political, and human realities were glossed over in romanticized accounts of the revolt. In *Seven Pillars,* they are usually dealt with *en passant* as a natural feature of life in the fierce desert landscape. To my mind, they enhance Lawrence's achievement. Enemy ports, trains, tracks, bridges, and the soldiers guarding them presented relatively clear targets; it was less clear how the fractious Arabs could be managed. That Lawrence dealt successfully with both the enemy and the uncontrollable Bedouin is a measure of his genius—and luck.

Fitful Heroism

Wounded often, Lawrence was lucky not to be killed by a Turkish or Arab bullet, a mindless looter or duplicitous sheikh.

Abd el Kader, who betrayed him at Deraa, tried to stab him in Damascus. During two years of danger, Lawrence often feared for his life; "it seemed horrible to have it all cut off as he feels it will be," a friend recorded him saying. He was "not the least fearless..., but as he told me last night, each time he starts out on these stunts he simply hates it for two or three days before, until the movement, action and the glory of scenery and nature catch hold of him and make him well again."[63] Nearing the end of the campaign, Lawrence grew cautious. At Mezerib station, "Abdulla led our charge, for my days of adventure were ended.... I wanted to enter Damascus." He declined a pilot's invitation to fight enemy planes. "No: I was not going up to airfight, no matter what caste I lost with the pilot."[64]

The tension of managing the unmanageable Arabs, of shuttling between Allenby and Feisal maintaining the confidence of both while unable to confide fully in either, could make a raid upon the railway almost a relief. Lawrence "is overworked and he must be overstrained," George Lloyd reported in September 1917. Some months later, Lawrence wrote, "some day everybody will combine and down me. It is impossible for a foreigner to run another people of their own free will, indefinitely...."[65]

In February 1918, Lawrence wanted to quit. Zeid, Feisal's younger brother, had squandered £24,000 entrusted to him. To Lawrence, it was the last straw. "For a year and a half I had been in motion, riding a thousand miles each month.... In my last five actions I had been hit.... Generally I had been hungry ... and frost and dirt had poisoned my hurts into a festering mass of sores." Worst of all was the "pretence to lead the national uprising of another race." Asking a colleague to disband his bodyguard, he rode to British headquarters in Beersheba and told Hogarth, "I ... had come to beg Allenby to find me some smaller part elsewhere." But he did not tell Allenby that and returned to the field. "It might be fraud or it might be farce: no one should say that I could not play it." Years later, he recalled, "I was a very sick man, again, ... almost at breaking point."[66]

Lawrence's was a fitful war; at times, it appeared to be sustained by his personal exertions. There was little activity in Autumn 1917; "offensive operations were conducted by Lawrence himself ... with a small number of collaborators." He had to make peace as well as war, to proselytize, recruit new tribes, and revive flagging spirits. "[I]f the Billi tribe were disgruntled Lawrence had to travel ... 300 miles to smooth them down, if the Beni Sakhr failed in their demolition work Lawrence had to ... conduct the raid personally."[67] No wonder he told his family, "It will be a great comfort when one can lie down & sleep without having to think about things.... This is a job too big for me."[68]

After Akaba, Lawrence expected to be consulted by Allenby and Feisal before major decisions about the Arab campaign were taken. And the campaign changed from one of peripheral interest to the Powers (mainly for such value as the control of Mecca had to their Moslem populations) to their more central interest in strategic lands and resources. Throughout his career, Lawrence was most comfortable as the power behind the throne, an adviser to authority (Clayton, Feisal, Allenby, Churchill, Trenchard). As adviser, he was less responsible for decisions and less exposed to scrutiny; as principal, less able to escape either. His sense of responsibility was acute, excessive, beyond reason or expectation for an officer in an outpost of empire. It was the moral side of an overweening will, which could assume megalomanic proportions.

Four Days in Damascus

Whether Arabs or Australians entered Damascus first has been much debated. The issue had symbolic and, Lawrence thought, political importance in determining who might control the future government of Syria. Australian troops (though ordered by Allenby to avoid entering Damascus, if possible) passed through the northern city around 6:00 A.M., October 1, pursuing the retreating Turks. Advance Arab contingents entered about 7:30 A.M. and Lawrence, who had been detained by Indian troops, at 9:00 A.M.[69] The previous day, a provisional Arab government loyal to Hussein had been announced. At 9:30 A.M., General Henry Chauvel, commanding the Australian forces, arrived at the Town Hall.

Lawrence had concentrated so heavily on capturing or appearing to capture Damascus, he apparently gave little thought to what came next. Years later, he said "Damascus [was to lead] to Anatolia, ... Bagdad; and ... Yemen," but there is no sign that, at the time, he was physically or emotionally prepared for further conquest. "My intention," he wrote, "had been to occupy [i.e., for Feisal to occupy] from the gap of Tripoli northward to Alexandretta," but not Beirut and Lebanon, which he conceded to France but Arabs hostile to Feisal occupied.[70] Lawrence must have thought of Carchemish, but Dahoum was dead and he did not go there. Woolley did at the end of the year.

As the war wound down, Lawrence was in poor shape. "A week, two weeks, three, and I would insist upon relief. My nerve had broken; and I would be lucky if the ruin of it could be hidden so long," he wrote of his mood in early September. Hit in the elbow by a bomb fragment, he "began to cry." Five sleepless nights "made my wits woolly"; a week later, four nights of sleepless riding followed. In between came the

Lawrence entering Damascus in Rolls-Royce tender, Oct. 1, 1918 (courtesy of Rolls-Royce Motor Cars).

Turks' slaughter of Arab families at Tafas, including twenty children and forty women, and the Arabs' vengeful slaughter of the Turks, when "we killed and killed, even blowing in the heads of the fallen and of the animals."[71] "[A]t this time," Liddell Hart said, "an over-tired body dragged on a depressed mind," and Lawrence commented, "strictly speaking my will was dragging on both body & mind!" Meeting General George Barrow, commander of the British 4th Cavalry Division, at Deraa, Lawrence was deliberately provocative; he acknowledged being "very spiny and high" and behaving "with histrionic nonchalance."[72] In the railway station, Barrow saw a

> ...long ambulance train full of sick and wounded Turks.... The Arab soldiers were going through the train, tearing off the clothing of the groaning and stricken Turks, regardless of gaping wounds and broken limbs, and cutting their victims throats.... I asked Lawrence to remove the Arabs. He said he couldn't 'as it was their idea of war'. I replied, 'It is not our idea of war, and if you can't remove them, I will.' ... [and] at once gave orders for our men to clear the station.[73]

Entering Damascus in the passenger seat of a desert-dirtied Rolls, Lawrence was "crying like a baby with ... thankfulness."[74] His "dark mood in these days of triumph made an indelible impression on his companions and, because of their affection, grieved them." Lawrence's comrade T. W. Beaumont thought him "at the end of his tether."[75] Haggard and emaciated, his weight was down to 80 pounds from about 112. McBey's portrait, painted in Damascus on October 3, shows his "complete physical and mental exhaustion"; Lawrence himself found it "shockingly strange."[76]

In *Seven Pillars,* Lawrence attributes his sense of fraudulence at his role in the revolt to Britain's "betrayal" of the Arabs and the falseness of preaching "freedom" while knowing they would be under British and French control. Undoubtedly, he often felt bitter and morally compromised (also, triumphant and elated). But should these feelings be ascribed to perfidious diplomacy or to the role he freely assumed, which his singular talents and sensitivities magnified and aggravated? "General Wingate," he says, "...did not seem sensible of how false his own standing was."[77] Nor did other British officers—Newcombe, Young, Joyce, Dawnay—share his feelings. Self-mortification was a Lawrencian specialty.

As has been noted, Auda and Feisal were not political innocents but as "perfidious" as their British allies. The Arabs, like the British, were divided into factions pursuing rival policies. One of the most glaring was the division between Syrians wishing to govern themselves and those who, like Lawrence, sought a government led by the Hejazian Feisal. Lawrence himself observed that "Arab Government in Syria ... would be as much 'imposed' as the Turkish Govrnment, or a foreign protectorate.... Any wide attempt after unity would make a patched and parcelled thing."[78]

We do not know exactly what Lawrence said about the postwar status of Syria when urging Arab leaders to join the revolt. He may have promised more than he had a right to promise, Hubert Young intimates. Lawrence knew about the May 1916 Sykes–Picot Agreement assigning the Lebanese littoral to France and the inte-

rior, from the Aleppo-Damascus line east to Mosul, to the Arabs under French "advisers." Arab historian George Antonius calls it "a shocking document."[79]

Lawrence allows that, when it became known in the summer of 1917, it was the Turks' "strongest card" in trying to get the Arabs to change sides. Nonetheless, it "stipulated the establishment of independent Arab states in Damascus, Aleppo and Mosul." The treaty was, he later insisted, "the Arab sheet-anchor," giving the French "only ... the coast" and the Arabs, the rest of Syria.[80] A vigorous Arab nationalism would, Lawrence contended, "prevent the creation—by us [Britain] or others [France]—... of unduly 'colonial' schemes of exploitation." If the Arabs captured Damascus, they could make a case for governing it. That argument was strengthened by Britain's June 1918 declaration that it would "recognise the complete and sovereign independence" of "Territories liberated from Turkish rule by the action of the Arabs themselves."[81] I agree with Archibald Wavell's conclusion that Lawrence encouraged the Arabs "to believe that the imperialistic designs of Britain and France did not exist, or would be set aside, if they showed their ability as a nation to unite and to rule. His self-consciousness exaggerated to himself his 'betrayal' of the Arabs...."[82]

"[A]nyone who pushed through to success a rebellion of the weak against their masters must come out of it so stained in estimation that afterward nothing in the world would make him feel clean," Lawrence wrote, ostensibly of the revolt and plainly of himself. Lenin, who pushed through a greater rebellion in 1917, did not feel stained and Lawrence thought him the greatest man of his time.[83]

In an October 1 report from Damascus, Lawrence said he would carry on pending further instructions, but "would like to return to Palestine as I feel that if I remain here longer, it will be very difficult for my successor." Recollecting that day, he wrote, "[M]y will … broke suddenly in my hand and fell useless. It told me that this Eastern chapter in my life was ended…. Or was it just a dream from which I would awake again in the saddle, with before me other months of effort, preaching, risk?"[84]

Allenby came to Damascus on October 3. Lawrence met him, with Clayton and others in attendance; Feisal, whose train had just arrived, then joined them, Lawrence acting as interpreter. In *Seven Pillars,* Lawrence glosses over these important conversations. He criticizes many British officers but not Allenby, who is depicted as a god to be revered and obeyed. Allenby, he says, approved the Arab governments in Damascus and Deraa and quickly resolved all other outstanding difficulties. Of the conversation with Feisal, Lawrence says only that Allenby asked him to translate a Foreign Office telegram recognizing the Arabs' "status of belligerents."[85] Wavell's account is fuller:

> Allenby explained … that France was to be the protecting Power in Syria, but that Feisal, as representative of his father, King Hussein, could set up a military administration of the occupied enemy territory east of the Jordan, from Akaba to Damascus. The Lebanon was to be under direct French administration, and Feisal would have a French officer attached to him to represent French advice and guidance. It was, in fact, the Sykes–Picot Agreement, which the French Government was demanding should be observed. Feisal protested strongly, but Allenby insisted on his orders being obeyed and that Feisal must accept the situation till the peace settlement.[86]

The last paragraph of *Seven Pillars* states that, after Feisal left, Lawrence asked Allenby for "leave to go away…. In the end he agreed; and then at once I knew how much I was sorry." Wavell adds, "After Feisal had left Lawrence said that he could not consent to work with a French officer and asked for leave, which was granted." Years later, Lawrence said, "all my thought was of going home where I meant to get transferred to the French front."[87]

Colonel P. C. Joyce, nominally Lawrence's immediate superior, ran into him outside the Victoria Hotel in Damascus, "a depressed and insignificant figure in dirty unwashed Arab clothes. He had just put in his resignation to Lord Allenby and no encouragement or reasoning could make him alter his decision. 'I am going home for my work is done', was all he said to me."[88] In Cairo the following week, Lawrence remarked, "I feel like a man who has suddenly dropped a heavy load … we have, I expect, changed history in the near East. I wonder how the Powers will let the Arabs get on."[89]

4

Undiplomatic Battles,
1918–1922

After a week in Cairo, Lawrence left October 15 by boat for Italy, continuing by train through France. As sleeping berths were reserved for higher ranks, he arranged a temporary promotion to full colonel. On the boat, he obtained a letter of introduction from Earl Winterton to Lord Robert Cecil, assistant foreign secretary. "Lawrence ... may be described as 'the Soul of the Hedjaz' ... and joins exceptional brilliance to a unique personal knowledge of the Arabs."[1] Winterton, who had served with him in Arabia, later wrote, "I have worked directly under many eminent men. Of these, in my judgment, only Churchill exceeds Lawrence in stature." His description of Lawrence's powers of analysis and persuasion is worth quoting:

> When others were exhausted ... [he] could at any time of night or day present his case for a particular action or ... decision ... with complete clarity to our Arab Allies or his brother officers. In the discussion which followed he ... would often at the beginning, by ... satirical humour, seem frivolous and irresponsible. But, before the end of it, the logic of his views and the irrefutable arguments with which he presented them would be apparent.

Like Churchill, the range and fertility of his mind was almost uncanny as was his power to convey his thoughts through the written or spoken word in unforgettable language.[2]

How serious Lawrence was about serving in France cannot be determined, as the war with Germany ended November 11, eighteen days after he reached England (and the war with Turkey, October 30). On October 28, he saw Cecil, who noted that Lawrence "denounced in unmeasured terms the folly ... of the Sykes–Picot Agreement, the boundaries of which were, he said, entirely absurd and unworkable.... He was violently anti–French." Speaking of Feisal and the Arabs as "we," Lawrence turned Feisal's negotiations with the Turks to his advantage, asserting that Feisal could have taken Damascus in November 1917 and made an advantageous peace with Turkey.[3]

The next day, he met with the Eastern Committee of the War Cabinet, chaired by Lord George Curzon, who praised his achievements. At Lawrence's abrupt response, "You people don't understand yet the hole you have put us all into," Curzon broke into tears and sobs.[4] Lawrence said that Feisal wanted British or even American Zionist advisers, not French, in Syria; his brothers Zeid and Abdulla should rule new states in north and south Mesopotamia. On October 30, Lawrence went to Buckingham Palace, where George V was to award him honors he declined, remarking at one point, "Your Cabinet are an awful set of crooks."[5] Gossip spread and distorted Lawrence's astonishing directness, which struck many as unpardonably rude.

Lawrence presented his views on an Arab settlement in a memorandum and further appearances before the Eastern Committee; a minute noted, "he represented to us what we may call the extreme Arab point of view, the kind of thing that Faisal would have said." Hogarth and Clayton expressed similar views; the French and British officials for Mesopotamia and India, opposing ones. Arthur Hirtzel of the India Office stated, "At the eleventh hour Lieutenant-Colonel Lawrence has come home with a proposal to put one of the sons of King Hussein in as King of Iraq, and another as King of Northern Mesopotamia.... Without in the least wishing to deprecate Colonel Lawrence's achievements and his undoubted genius, ... he does not at all represent ... the local views."[6]

Lawrence wired King Hussein from the Foreign Office asking him to appoint Feisal his representative at the forthcoming Paris Peace Conference, adding specific instructions: Feisal should ask Allenby "for a ship to take him to France"; Hussein should telegraph the governments of Britain, France, America, and Italy that his son is going to Paris as his representative. Jeremy Wilson observes that the cabinet endorsed Feisal's presence in Paris to show the Americans, who were for "self-determination," that British proposals for Mesopotamia and Palestine had Arab support.[7]

Three anonymous articles by Lawrence on the Arabian war, in successive November issues of *The Times,* credited Feisal and the British Navy for the early Arab gains, which showed "the value of command of the sea ... in shore operations against an enemy depending entirely on land communications." Nasir, Auda, and the Howeitat figured notably; Admiral Wemyss and General Allenby were mentioned, but not Lawrence, other British officers or the Imperial Camel Corps.[8]

Lawrence's lobbying in government circles, the press, and, shortly, at the Paris Peace Conference came to naught. The areas of British and French control over the former Turkish lands in Asia were settled on December 1, when, by chance, Prime Minister Lloyd George and Premier Georges Clemenceau were alone together at the French Embassy in London. "Clemenceau ... asked what they might talk about, and Lloyd George ... replied: 'Mesopotamia and Palestine' ... 'Tell me what you want' asked Clemenceau. 'I want Mosul' [allotted to France in the Sykes–Picot Agreement] said Lloyd George. 'You shall have it' said Clemenceau. 'Anything else?' 'Yes, I want Jerusalem [i.e., Palestine] too' continued Lloyd George. 'You shall have it' said Clemenceau." In exchange, Lloyd George agreed to unified French administration of Lebanon and Syria.[9]

Paris

At the peace conference, which began in January 1919, Lawrence served both as an adviser to the British delegation and a member of Feisal's staff. He drafted the main paper Feisal presented, setting forth in broad terms goals for new nations in old lands consistent with his proposals to the British cabinet. The treatment of Arab national unity was deliciously contradictory.

The future ideal was unity, the present reality, disunity.

> [King Hussein] is convinced of the ultimate triumph of the ideal of unity, if no attempt is made now to force ... or to hinder it, by dividing the area as spoils of war.... The various provinces of Arab Asia—Syria, Irak, Jezireh [northern Iraq], Hejaz, Nejd, Yemen—are very different economically and socially, and it is impossible to constrain them into one frame of government ... the Arabs of Asia ... [expect] the Conference not to attach undue importance to superficial differences of condition ... [but] to think of them as one potential people.[10]

As Hogarth explained, Hussein and Feisal's immediate postwar goal was the formation of independent Arab states linked in a federation under Hussein; their ultimate goal was "the creation of an Arab Empire." To advance the federation, they wanted one mandatory power, either Britain or the U.S., for all the states save independent Hejaz. However, the mandatory issue was not raised in Feisal's February 6 presentation to the Council of Ten.[11] Feisal spoke in Arabic; Lawrence (who had prepared both versions) gave the English translation. Since the Italians understood neither language, President Woodrow Wilson then asked if Lawrence could put the statement into French. After a moment's hesitation, Lawrence did so and the Ten clapped in appreciation.

Lawrence served Feisal as adviser, interpreter, and translator, drafted many of his statements and letters, and represented his cause—a free Syria with access to the Mediterranean—to British and American delegates, the press, anyone who might influence the outcome. He also began to write *Seven Pillars of Wisdom,* the story of the Arab revolt and the glorification and

Lawrence at the Paris Peace Conference, 1919, drawing by Augustus John (courtesy of the National Portrait Gallery, London).

castigation of his role in it, completing seven of the eventual eleven sections or about 160,000 words.

Wearing an Arab headdress, occasionally full Arab garb, when with Feisal, who was himself a striking figure, Lawrence attracted much attention and used it to meet delegates and journalists, especially Americans. Their principle of "self-determination" seemed to favor Arab independence or at least an Arab voice in the choice of their mandatory power. "I have seen 10 American newspaper men, and given them all interviews.... Also President Wilson, and other people who have influence," Lawrence reported.[12] For a time, it appeared that the United States might accept a mandate for Syria; from May to July 1919, an American commission conducted an inquiry in Syria and Palestine.

Among the Americans Lawrence met at this time were Wilson's confidant Colonel House, historian James Shotwell, publisher F. N. Doubleday, art connoisseur

Bernard Berenson, and journalist Lincoln Steffens. Shotwell deemed him "the most winning figure" at the conference and "the most amazing youth the British Isles ever turned out"; Doubleday remained a friend thereafter. When Berenson reproached him for not keeping a luncheon engagement, Lawrence said, "'Well, look at my engagement book!' He had accepted fifteen invitations for that day."[13] When the experienced, skeptical Steffens interviewed Lawrence, "I thought I was directing the course of the conversation. It only occurred to me afterwards, with some shock, that he also had had a purpose, ... to load me up with British propaganda for the American mandate...." Steffens found the interview "the queerest I ever had in all my interviewing life."[14]

Ernest Altounyan, who had known Lawrence in prewar Syria, watched him at a Paris dinner party. "Still the manipulator, still never giving himself away, playing one person against, or with the other, always towards some end." Harold Nicolson saw a bitter man "glide along the corridors of the Majestic, the lines of resentment hardening around his boyish lips."[15] A photograph of Lawrence at Versailles, "with numb look and limp mouth," gave one writer "a frightening picture of weariness, sickness, and despair." Years later, Lawrence declared the Paris months "the worst I have lived through."[16] If so, he successfully concealed his feelings from John Maynard Keynes. Dissenting from the view that wartime experiences had "twisted" Lawrence, Keynes said, "when I knew him in the spring of 1919, ... he was a man fully in control of his nerves and quite as normal as most of us.... A year later no one could have thought the same."[17]

In May, while Feisal was in Syria for the American commission's visit, Lawrence headed for Cairo to fetch his notes and check the *Seven Pillars* draft against Arab Bureau records. He travelled on a British bomber, one of a squadron flying from Paris to Cairo. Landing at Rome, the plane hit a tree and crashed, killing both pilots; Lawrence was lucky to escape with broken ribs and collarbone. Between the accident and other delays, it took six weeks to reach Cairo. His last pilot reported, "As cheerful as ever Col. L. insisted that he was by no means fed-up with flying. In fact he was thinking of joining the Air Force."[18]

When Lawrence returned to Paris in July, the political climate had worsened. Woodrow Wilson had gone, Feisal remained in Damascus; having yielded Syria to France, British officials attacked Lawrence harshly: "there will be no peace in the Middle East until Lawrence's malign influence is withdrawn," Arthur Hirtzel stated.[19] Formerly friendly delegates turned hostile, viewing Lawrence as a free-wheeling force behind Arab opposition to what was now joint British–French policy. Lawrence "is to a large extent responsible for our troubles with the French over Syria," an official complained; "he should be definitely under orders either of the War Office or of the Peace Delegation." "We have no other channel for influencing Feisal," Robert Vansittart of the Peace Delegation replied. "He will not however prove amenable to 'orders.' It is not the best way to use him."[20]

Lawrence went home to Oxford, where he had accepted an All Souls College fellowship of £200 a year for seven years. Following a September agreement between Lloyd George and Clemenceau, French troops replaced the British in Syria. In a memorandum to the Foreign Office, Lawrence suggested, "If the French are wise and neglect the Arabs for about twelve months, they will then be implored by them to help them. If they are impatient now they only unite the Arabs against them." He advised Foreign Secretary Curzon, "...the Arabs should be our first brown dominion, and not our last brown colony. Arabs react against you if you try to drive them, ... but you can lead them without force anywhere, if nominally arm in arm."[21]

Feisal's career in Syria was brief. In March 1920, he became King, accepting the crown offered by a Syrian Congress. In April, France assumed the mandate awarded by the San Remo Conference. In July, French troops routed the Arabs, occupied Damascus, and expelled Feisal. Lawrence had told King George he might fight with the Arabs against France, but when the time came, he did not. "It was as though the mainspring of his ... will was now broken. It was never to recover its former power."[22] His will to act weakened but his power of persuasion and manipulation remained.

Superabundant Fame

After America entered the war in April 1917, Lowell Thomas, a young journalist, traveller, and Princeton speech instructor, went to Europe to report glorious Allied victories to the American public. Despite his native optimism, he found little romance in France and Italy but much in Palestine, where Allenby soon captured Jerusalem, "the holiest city of Christians and Jews [which] ... had been in Moslem hands for a thousand years, and not nine holy crusades ... could wrest it free." He also met, photographed, and spoke with Lawrence, whom Ronald Storrs introduced, in jest, as "the Uncrowned King of Arabia."

In 1919, Thomas (then 27) showed a series of war films in New York. Many seats were empty when he spoke on the war in Europe; few, "when Jerusalem and Arabia were scheduled." Prominent financier-philanthropists Edmond de Rothschild, Jacob Schiff, Paul and Felix Warburg, and Nathan Straus bought up many performances for Jewish audiences moved by Britain's promise of a Jewish homeland in Palestine. "When General Allenby freed [Jerusalem]," Schiff told Thomas, "he made our dreams come true."[23]

British impresario Percy Burton invited Thomas to give his show in London. In August, *The Last Crusade—With Allenby in Palestine and Lawrence in Arabia* opened at the Covent Garden opera house.

> Our dancer glided on stage in a brief Oriental dance of the seven veils. Fran [Thomas's wife] had set to music the Mohammmedan call to prayer and, from the wings, a lyric tenor sent this haunting ... melody ... to the farthest reaches of the theater.... I stepped into the spotlight and began to speak: "...and now come with me to the lands of mystery, history and romance." ...Afterward, the audience stood and applauded for ten minutes. Next morning ... on the front pages of the *Times,* the *Morning Post* and the *Daily Telegraph,* were reviews full of ... ardent tribute ... soon it was almost impossible to buy tickets ... for current performances.

Premier Clemenceau, Feisal, American Ambassador John Davis, General Allenby, the King and Queen, members of parliament and of the cabinet saw the show. Prime Minister Lloyd George told a reporter, "Everything that Mr. Lowell Thomas tells us about Colonel Lawrence is true.... Lawrence is one of the most remarkable and romantic figures of modern times." Thomas has been charged with "inventing" the Lawrence legend; yet his audiences, including leading national and intellectual figures, came and applauded willingly. The glowing story of almost bloodless victory in the East soothed memories of a generation butchered in Western trenches.

After seeing the performance, Lawrence had tea with Thomas and asked him to stop the show. "I was making life impossible for him," he said; "he was stopped by strangers, then swiftly surrounded by a crowd"; he was deluged with letters; women proposed marriage or affairs. Thomas could not tell if the smiling Lawrence was serious. Lawrence's mother saw the show and thanked Thomas for making "Ned's" achievements known. Lawrence came to the show and visited Thomas several times; "well aware of the propaganda value of [the] ... lectures," he was "cordial with the Thomases" and "apologetic when he missed visits."[24] The performance moved to the Royal Albert Hall, London's largest auditorium, for two months. Over a million persons saw it in London; countless others elsewhere, when Thomas toured England, Scotland, Wales, the United States, Australia, and other English-speaking lands.

The contrast between his failure in Paris and the mellifluous triumph that Thomas portrayed and Britain's classes and masses relished did not ease Lawrence's spirit. His mood swung from depression to pranks to intense work on *Seven Pillars* and writing letters and articles on the government's Arab policy.

John Buchan, who lived near Oxford, remembered how, in this period, Lawrence "would sit for hours with his head bent, never speaking."[25] A colleague observed him sitting in the All Souls common room "absorbed in his own thoughts." Some students thought him "'off his rocker,' and depressed to the point of being suicidal." Robert Graves saw him acting "very much like an undergraduate at times." He put a Hejaz flag on an All Souls spire and engineered a successful strike of college servants for better pay and hours. He conceived but did not execute other pranks: planting mushrooms to get the quadrangle returfed, stealing the Magdalen deer, giving the college a peacock named Nathaniel, after Oxford Vice-Chancellor Lord Curzon.[26]

Lawrence had always read rapidly and widely in several languages, including French, Greek, and Latin, especially in literature, poetry, history, warfare, and the Middle Ages. He sought to make *Seven Pillars* an epic to stand beside *Don Quixote*, *War and Peace*, *The Brothers Karamazov*, and *Moby Dick*. He had an excessive veneration for poets, writers, and artists and the same analytic approach to writing as to fortress construction, map-making, and guerrilla warfare. Conceiving writing as a craft whose skills could be delineated and mastered, he used his fame to meet prominent poets, writers, and publishers with whom he discussed the technique and art of making books. He sought to understand the elements of descriptive and creative writing and the degree to which the latter directly reflected the writer's experience, character, and perceptions or transmuted them into something new. Among those he met by 1920 were Siegfried Sassoon, Robert Graves, Edmund Blunden, John Masefield, Robert Bridges, Rudyard Kipling, and George Bernard Shaw.

The handwritten *Seven Pillars* manuscript was almost finished when, waiting between trains, Lawrence left it, with notes and photographs, in a bank messenger bag in a refreshment room at Reading station. It was never recovered. "I've lost the damned thing," he told Hogarth who angrily insisted he rewrite it.[27] Leaving the distractions of All Souls, Lawrence did so in an unheated Westminster loft that the architect Herbert Baker offered him. Laboring "with heavy repugnance ... from memory and my surviving notes," he rewrote most of the text in three winter months, December 1919–February 1920. The lost version would have been 250,000 words; this one, written more carelessly, was over 400,000.

Lawrence liked to punish his body.

He turned writing into a physical ordeal, producing 1,000–1,500 words an hour for 22–24 hours without food, rest, or warmth. "He refused all service and comfort," Baker said, "food, fire or hot water; he ate and bathed when he happened to go out; he kept chocolate ... for an emergency.... He worked time-less and sometimes round the sun; and once, he said, for two days ... until he became delirious."[28] "I ... excited myself with hunger and cold and sleeplessness more than did de Quincey with his opium," Lawrence wrote. "I nearly went off my head ... heaving at that beastly book."[29]

Version II, completed in mid–1920, was succeeded by revised, shortened III, a 330,000-word manuscript Lawrence prepared from September 1920 until May 1922. Whereupon he burned II with a blowtorch and, to safeguard III, had eight copies set by linotype and printed in small-type double columns by the *Oxford Times;* hence this rare 1922 edition is known as the Oxford Text. *Seven Pillars,* on which he continued to work through 1926, was an obsession, an emotional purgation, an attempted masterpiece, a history, romance, calculated political document, and self-analysis whose author esteems and despises himself inordinately, a puzzle where truth is boldly told, untold, flouted, and disguised.

Lawrence gave few details of his guerrilla methods, because, he said, of the tensions and hostilities in Syria: he did not want to help the French in any way.[30] He magnified the Arabs' sense of common nationality, their contribution to the war, their yearning for "freedom," which at best meant Arab, not Turkish, masters. He downplayed the role of the British navy in early Arab advances and the predominant role of Allied forces in the final victory. He depicted Feisal as noble and strong, "the leader who would bring the Arab Revolt to full glory," whereas elsewhere he said,

"Feisal was less than weak—he was empty:— only a great pipe waiting for a wind."[31] *Seven Pillars* trumpeted Britain's "betrayal" of the Arabs and Lawrence's bitterness at his involvement in it, a bitterness none of his fellow officers, nor Allenby, whom he worshipped, felt. Nor, before long, Lawrence himself. The epic of "betrayal" was counterbalanced by a single footnote, printed in red ink in the 1926 edition:

> 1919: but two years later Mr. Winston Churchill ... made straight all the tangle, finding solutions fulfilling (I think) our promises in letter and spirit (where humanly possible) without sacrificing any interest of our Empire or any interest of the peoples concerned. So we were quit of the war-time Eastern adventure, with clean hands, but three years too late to earn the gratitude which peoples, if not states, can pay.[32]

In a 1922 introduction to a proposed abridgement of *Seven Pillars,* Lawrence declared, "Mr. Winston Churchill ... set honesty before expediency, & sometimes even before statesmanship, in fulfilling our promises in the spirit & in the letter." He acknowledged that "The book should have been recast, to suit the new circumstances: but I am more sick of it than I am of the East: and it must go as it is."[33] Like so many of Lawrence's confessions, that was both true and untrue for he continued revising *Seven Pillars* until the limited edition was published late in 1926. Plainly, he preferred the mood of bitterness and betrayal to that of accomplishment and triumph. *The Mint* exhibits similar bitterness and suffering. Asked why he never wrote about his experience at the Colonial Office with Churchill, Lawrence replied that he might have done so had their efforts failed.

Despite his preoccupation with *Seven Pillars,* Lawrence remained involved in Arab affairs. In mid–1920, his friends Hogarth and Gertrude Bell were drafting the mandate for Iraq that Britain assumed under the San Remo Treaty. Britain's position in Iraq was, if anything, worse than France's in Syria. The attempt to impose India-style rule led to open rebellion and troops were brought from India to maintain British control.

Lawrence attacked government policy in seething communications to the press. The government in Iraq, he informed readers of *The Times*, "has 450 British executive officers ... and not a single responsible Mesopotamian. In Turkish days 70 percent of the executive civil service was local. Our 80,000 troops ... are holding down the people. In Turkish days the two army corps ... were 60 percent Arab in officers, 95 percent in other ranks." The official government language should be changed from English to Arabic; British and Indian troops should be replaced by Arabs. "...we should then hold of Mesopotamia exactly as much (or as little) as we hold of South Africa or Canada."[34] When Feisal was expelled from Syria, Lawrence observed that the French "have only followed ... the example we set them in Mesopotamia.... It is odd that we do not use poison gas.... Bombing the houses is a patchy way of getting the women and children, and our infantry always incur losses in shooting down the Arab men. By gas attacks the whole population of offending districts could be wiped out neatly."[35]

Gertrude Bell, in the Mesopotamian government, agreed that changes were needed but objected strongly that too much in his articles was "tosh.... When he says we have forced the English language on the country it's not only a lie but he knows it is. Every jot and tittle of official work is done in Arabic.... I hold him to be guilty of the unpardonable sin of wilfully darkening counsel."[36]

Lawrence's attacks on government policy were backed by MPs from all par-

ties. In May, he had helped to organize a group of experts, including Hogarth, Arnold Toynbee, Lionel Curtis, and St. John Philby, to press for a new Middle East Department which, bypassing the India Office and Foreign Secretary Curzon, could change British policy. Public sentiment and the high cost of the Iraq war were on their side. Prime Minister Lloyd George established a Middle East Department in the Colonial Office and, in January 1921, Winston Churchill became Colonial Secretary with instructions to bring peace to the region.

Advising Churchill

"The Govt. wanted me to go back East!" Lawrence remarked in September 1920.[37] In December, he met with Edward Marsh, Churchill's private secretary; the next month, he began to serve as an informal adviser and in February accepted a position as Churchill's adviser on Arab affairs. "What! Wilt thou bridle the wild ass of the desert?" Churchill had been told when he proposed to recruit Lawrence. "However, I persisted ... and to the surprise of most people, he accepted at once." Not "at once." Churchill had to ask three times before Lawrence accepted "arguments I could not resist."[38] His first condition had been that Britain honor "the war-time pledges given to the Arabs.... Winston refused my condition: but offered me direct access to himself on every point, and a free hand, subject to his discretion. This was better than any condition, because I wanted the best settlement ... possible, apart from all promises and treaties."[39]

In January, Lawrence had planned a Near East trip with Eric Kennington who was to paint portraits of the main figures in the revolt to illustrate *Seven Pillars*. Kennington had bought two train tickets which, by Lawrence's instruction, bypassed France. In the event, he travelled alone; some weeks later, Lawrence joined him briefly to help arrange sittings. Churchill wanted a March conference of senior Near East officials in Cairo; the outcome was settled beforehand. With Churchill's approval, Lawrence and Kinahan Cornwallis (adviser to Feisal in Damascus) discussed the Iraqi throne with Feisal in London in January. Feisal wanted it offered first to his brother Abdulla, who was persuaded not to accept. On March 1, Feisal agreed to accept the throne.[40] The next day, Lawrence left Cairo, "where I'll either get my way or resign—or even do both things."[41]

Lawrence and Churchill went out to Cairo by ship. Those at the meeting, convened on March 12, included the High Commissioners for Iraq and Palestine, Air Staff Chief Hugh Trenchard, Hubert Young, and Gertrude Bell. According to Lawrence, Bell "swung all the Mesop. British officials to the Feisal solution, while Winston & I swung the English people."[42] The Sunni Hejazi Feisal was imported to a heavily Shia country by "force, diplomacy, manipulation and deception."[43] Prime Minister Lloyd George told Churchill, "We think it essential that real initiative in any demand for Feisal should come from Mesopotamia." Well aware of this nicety, Churchill replied, "We are quite as fully conscious as you are of desire for securing a spontaneous movement for Feisal in Mesopotamia as a prelude to his being countenanced by us." Sayyid Talib, Feisal's chief rival, was detained after tea with Lady Percy Cox and Gertrude Bell and sent on a protracted "holiday" to Ceylon. That "spontaneous movement" made Feisal king with 96.8 percent of the vote.[44]

When the French took over Syria, Lawrence later said, "we had to transfer the focus of Arab nationalism at once to Bagdad" for which he foresaw a great future. Syria had 5 million population, Iraq 3 mil-

lion. "But Syria will only have 7,000,000 when Irak has 40,000,000."[45] In 1995, Syria had 14.7 million; Lebanon, 3.7 million; Iraq, 20.6 million.

To police Iraq economically, Britain replaced most of its troops with airplanes. The idea of doing so went back at least to February 1920, when War Minister Churchill asked Trenchard for a plan to use "some kind of asphyxiating bombs calculated to cause disablement ... but not death ... against turbulent tribes." Hearing of the scheme, Lawrence discussed it with Trenchard and his staff, named persons who could implement it in Cairo and Iraq, and outlined the political changes in London and the East which would make it feasible. "This was the sort of fixing and arranging at which Lawrence excelled."[46]

The previous November, Abdulla, aggravated by Feisal's expulsion and the proposed Jewish "homeland" in Palestine, had begun to rally tribes around Maan (then part of the Hejaz) in a threat to invade Syria. Directly after the Cairo meeting, Churchill, Samuel, Lawrence, and Abdulla met in Jerusalem and, in half an hour, agreed to detach Trans-Jordania from Palestine as a separate nation with Abdulla as king—"exact contrary to the decision reached at Cairo."[47]

In the summer of 1921, Lawrence visited Jidda several times in a futile effort to persuade Hussein to sign a treaty recognizing the new arrangements in Palestine, Jordan, and Iraq in exchange for a British subsidy and protection from Ibn Saud's expanding kingdom. Lawrence's communications with London and with Hussein, who deemed himself king of all Arab nations, yielded nothing to the conventions of diplomacy. Hussein "raises absurd new ideas daily," he cabled London.

Old man is conceited..., greedy, and stupid, but very friendly.... His ambitions are as large as his conceit, and he showed unpleasant jealousy of his sons.

I gave him my candid opinion of his character and capacity ... not only the Foreign Secretary but the King also burst into tears.... The King ... could, I think, be bullied into nearly complete surrender. Reason is entirely wasted on him since he believes himself all-wise and all-competent, and is flattered by his entourage in every idiotic thing he does.

Lawrence thought Hussein was coming round, but he changed his mind and demanded the cession to him of all Arab countries. "My reply made him send for a dagger and swear to ... kill himself. I said we would continue negotiations with his successor."[48] Hussein evidently gave as good as he got. "I would rather this swine Ibn-Saud ruled the whole of Arabia than see it under the filthy yoke of the English," he swore to Lawrence, "Get out! You are nothing but a scoundrel and an *agent provocateur*.... You have lied to me ever since the first day I saw you." John Mack is surprised that Lawrence conducted these futile negotiations, since the British mandate for Palestine and French control of Syria were "obviously intolerable" to Hussein. Arnold Lawrence thought he deliberately "bitched ... up" the negotiations to ensure their failure.[49]

That fall, Lawrence spent two months in Jordan inspecting Abdulla's unsettled regime. The two armored cars with the British units in Amman, he informed the Colonial Office, "had no ... tubes, no mechanical spares, no lamps or batteries, no jacks or pumps, no petrol ... no gun belts, no ammunition, no gun spares." The fledgling Arab legion, "the so-called Military Force, is the only unarmed body of men in the country."[50] St. John Philby, whom Lawrence chose as his successor in Jordan, admired his performance; "he seemed to know everything and everybody, but he carried all his knowledge in

his head." No bureaucrat, Lawrence threw out countless files—and a batch of passports awaiting their owners. A paper he gave Philby accounted for £100,000 expenditures, including £10,000 "lost or mislaid"; evidently he forgot £7500 later found in a safe.[51]

Lawrence's feelings revisiting many wartime sites must at best have been mixed. He was too self-conscious, too self-critical to bask easily in the role of kingmaker. The Semiramis Hotel in Cairo, he wrote his mother, was "marble & bronze..., very expensive & luxurious: horrible place: makes me Bolshevik."[52] In Jidda, Lawrence confessed, the negotiations with Hussein "had been almost too much for him and ... the mental strain ... had been worse than anything he had known during the campaign." During spells of inactivity, he revised *Seven Pillars* and was unhappy with the result. In Aden, which he visited in August, he wrote an introduction to a catalog for the London exhibition of Kennington's portraits that expresses his sense of failure as a creative writer. "There seems a hopeless line drawn between those who have creative imagination and those whose imagination is sterile."[53]

In Jordan, F. G. Peake found Lawrence "a man of moods; on some evenings he would be the best of company ...; on others, he would be depressed, incommunicative." To Arab historian George Antonius, who spent three hours with him in September, Lawrence spoke of the revolt "with apathy." Antonius felt that "his interest in the Arab problem [had] waned to a point approaching exhaustion" and that he had accepted the Cairo decisions simply to be done with the matter. However, Lawrence subsequently took credit for and defended these decisions. "I take to myself credit for some of Mr. Churchill's pacification of the Middle East.... I felt that I had gained every point I wanted.... Winston Churchill's settlement had honourably fulfilled our War obligations and my hopes."[54]

Ibn Saud occupied Mecca in October 1924 and became King of the Hejaz in 1926. Hussein fled to Cyprus and Amman, where he died in 1931. Feisal died in 1933; his grandson was assassinated and the dynasty overthrown in 1958. Abdulla was assassinated in 1951; his great grandson, the last Hashemite king, still rules Jordan.

Philby offers two vignettes of Lawrence's last days in Jordan. They were together "in the open desert on a biting cold winter's night. I dug a shallow pit ... and filled it with bushes to sleep on, overcoat and all, while he just lay down on the flat ground. By the morning I was chilled through, but he seemed to be all right." Riding on open railway trucks in "icy wind and driving sleet," Philby huddled "as near the boiler as possible." Lawrence stood on the dashboard the whole journey of three or four hours. Perhaps that was the sort of thing Lawrence had in mind when, a few months later, he said, "I'm always in physical and mental training."[55]

In November, Lawrence's mother and surviving brothers Robert, the eldest, and Arnold, the youngest, met in Jerusalem. Early that year, the Polstead Road home had been sold. Thomas Lawrence (or Chapman), Lawrence's father, had died in 1919. Robert proceeded from Palestine to China, to serve as a medical missionary, where their mother, Sarah, joined him in 1923.

Depression

Returning to London in December, to Herbert Baker's Westminster loft, Lawrence was depressed. His strain and depression toward the close of a period of significant responsibility and accomplishment paralleled that during the last stages of the revolt. He resumed his intense work on *Seven Pillars,* "biting the lines deeper,"[56] repeating the starvation, sleeplessness, and cold of two years earlier. "Lawrence was in a very nervous condition," Robert Graves wrote,

> did not eat or sleep enough, and worked over the *Seven Pillars*.... He wrote by night; his days were largely spent ... at the Colonial Office. Late in January he ... looked so bad I told him that he must take himself in hand. I asked why he didn't try to find some appropriate woman who would help him to a settled life; because if he went on experimenting with solitariness like this there would be a collapse.... He said, jokingly, that the only settling down he could contemplate was enlistment in the Army or Air Force.[57]

Churchill asked Lawrence, "'What would you like to do when all this is smoothed out? The greatest employments are open to you.' He smiled his bland, beaming, cryptic smile, and said: 'In a very few months my work here will be finished.... All you will see of me is a small cloud of dust on the horizon.'" In January 1922, when it appeared that Allenby might resign as High Commissioner in Egypt, Churchill evidently asked Lawrence if he would accept the post (which, among its glories and perquisites, paid £20,000 a year): "but ... of course I wouldn't...," he told his mother. "I don't think ever again to govern anything."[58]

He still had his All Souls fellowship, but gave up his college rooms. Months before, he had declined positions at the University of Aberystwyth and McGill University in Montreal. Now, despite his keen interest in fine printing, he declined an invitation to dine with St. John Hornby of the Ashendene Press. "I work in the Colonial Office all day, & the nights consequently are hugely valuable. So I'm not dining anywhere. "This was not the only invitation he refused; "he caused some annoyance by constantly refusing invitations to meals and by failing to visit households at which he would always have been welcome."[59] Refusing to draw his salary yet running up a large overdraft commissioning portraits, Lawrence cadged meals from friends. "I'd haunt the Duke of York Steps at lunch-time, so as to turn back with someone to his club for the food whose necessity nearly choked me."[60]

In contrast to his bullet-fast response in action and crisis, Lawrence's inner life seemed to follow slow-moving cycles of secret, deep-harbored feelings and long-pondered plans. He said that in 1918 he had resolved to enlist in the RAF and suggested that to Air Marshall Geoffrey Salmond before the Armistice. In 1921, after a dinner conversation with Air Force Chief Hugh Trenchard in Churchill's Cairo suite, he remarked, "'I'd like to join this air force of yours some day.' 'And I'd be glad to have you.' 'Even as an ordinary ranker?' 'No certainly not,' [Trenchard] … rejoined firmly. 'As an officer or nothing.'" Lawrence now wrote Trenchard:

> I'd like to join the R.A.F.—in the ranks, of course.
>
> I can't do this without your help. I'm 33…. Probably I couldn't pass your medical…. However my health is good … and I don't personally believe that I'd be below the average of your recruits…. If you think so that will end it … since I was 16 I've been writing…. I see the sort of subject I need in the beginning of your Force … and the best place to see a thing from is the ground…. It's an odd request, this…. Apologies for making it: if you say no I'll be more amused than hurt.[61]

The letter contained blatant falsehoods. If Trenchard rejected the request, Lawrence would *not* be "amused." A rejection was most unlikely to "end it": few persons were more persistent about achieving their end. Lawrence's wish to

write about the Air Force was far from the whole truth or the main reason for his enlistment. His health was not "good." He told Kennington, "I have worked myself out [on *Seven Pillars*] and am finished. Every bone in my body has been broken. My lungs are pierced, my heart is weak."[62]

Trenchard was amenable to Lawrence's enlistment if his minister and Churchill agreed. Churchill did not for several months. In February, when Lawrence's year's commitment was up, he stopped drawing his salary and spent more time revising *Seven Pillars,* though, as he knew or learned, you can only do so much with revisions. "No help, no revision, no pains taken, will make a poor draft into a good book."[63] Repeatedly, Lawrence asked Churchill to release him; Churchill refused but agreed to his taking three months leave. "I was determined to leave only with his good-will," Lawrence explained.[64]

Lawrence paid Kennington £720 for his portraits and commissioned others from Augustus John, William Roberts, William Nicholson, Paul Nash, William Rothenstein, Wyndham Lewis. Between January and July, as each section of *Seven Pillars* was finished, the *Oxford Times* set it in two-column format at a cost of £175. Lawrence had five copies bound for reading by critics and friends. Having stopped drawing his £1,300 salary, he ran out of money by April. Nonetheless, he contributed substantially to a £400 payment to Charles Doughty, ostensibly to buy the manuscript of *The Dawn in Britain* for presentation to the British Museum, actually to assist the aged poet.

Eventually, Churchill let him go (Lawrence did not tell him what he planned to do) and he submitted a formal resignation on July 4, 1922. "There are many other things I want to do," it said. But there was really only one: to enlist in the lowest rank of the RAF. He saw Trenchard who tried to persuade him to accept a commission, but "he was so insistent [on serving as a ranker] that I eventually agreed."[65] Trenchard sent RAF personnel chief Oliver Swann the following memorandum:

> It is hereby approved that Colonel T. E. Lawrence be permitted to join the Royal Air Force as an aircraft-hand under the alias of
> John Hume Ross
> AC2 No. 352087
> He is taking this step to learn what is the life of an airman. On receipt of any communication from him through any channel, asking for his release, orders are to be issued for his discharge forthwith without formality.[66]

Lawrence was well organized. Before enlisting, he sent Edward Garnett, reader for the new publishing firm Jonathan Cape, a copy of the freshly bound Oxford Text and at least four letters. They said publication should not be considered—it "never came into my mind when writing"; he had hoped the book would be "Titanic" but "it was no good."[67] Lawrence also asked George Bernard Shaw, whom he had met briefly, to read it, telling him self-denigrating half-truths and lies: "I ... successfully passed the age of 30 without having wanted to write anything" ("since I was 16 I've been writing," he told Trenchard in January); only "one other person has seen it" (three had); "it's the only book I'll write" (he was planning to write about the RAF).[68]

5

In and Out of the RAF, 1922

Some who met Lawrence found him overbearing; some, forthright and captivating; some, shy, silent, hard to reach. Before appearing for induction, he was close to emotional and physical collapse.

> Hesitating for two hours up and down a filthy street, lips and hands and knees tremulously out of control, my heart pounding in fear…. The nearest lavatory, now…. Won by a short head. My right shoe is burst along the welt and my trousers are growing fringes. One reason that taught me I wasn't a man of action was this routine melting of the bowels before a crisis.[1]

Why did he enlist? Lawrence's admirers compare the decision, the fulcrum on which his life henceforth descended, to that of a virginal man entering a monastery, renouncing fame and power for a humble life. They mistake subsequent occasions of contentment for Lawrence's state of mind upon enlisting. His own testimony and that of his family and friends show him to be hungry, distraught, disheveled, anxious, tormented. His brother Arnold thought him "physically and mentally wrecked." His friend E. T. Leeds said,

"In all respects, it was comparable to a severe breakdown in health, wrecking career and hopes and leaving the victim limp, listless and discouraged, bereft of spirit or strength…. Lawrence's sickness was of the mind, a deep and wicked sore."[2]

In military service, Lawrence said, "There is no freedom of conduct at all." He sought that enslavement. He was in an emotional condition "which allowed only negative decisions to be taken without intolerable effort. Life in the ranks, where a decision would never be required, therefore seemed the right solution."[3] The drive for captivity, abasement, punishment is the clinical mark of a masochist. In less extreme form, Lawrence sought to make himself ordinary, to disappear from public view into an indistinguishable mass of uniformed men.

Anecdotes attest to the success of the strategy: in uniform, he could pass in public unrecognized. But not in camp. Even when reporting for induction, his identity became known. Throughout his years in the ranks, he alternately hid and disclosed himself to his comrades, prominent public figures, and strangers. He humbled himself, dutifully fulfilling the functions of clerk, cleaner, storeman, mechanic. He might also act assuredly, even brazenly, as the Lawrence of old, to redress camp wrongs or address Britain's leaders as equals, at times patronizingly.

Uxbridge

When, on August 30, 1922, Lawrence reported for induction at Henrietta St., Covent Garden, things went awry. He was supposed to be "John Hume Ross," born 1894, with no prior military service. But to Capt. W. E. Johns, the officer on duty, "There was something so off-hand about his manner, almost amounting to insolence, that I took an instinctive dislike to him."[4] The Sergeant-Major was also suspicious. Johns told Ross a birth certificate and three character references were needed and, while he was away, established that Somerset House had no record of his birth. When he came back with the papers, Johns challenged them. Lawrence admitted they were fakes, left, and returned with an RAF messenger who gave Johns an order to enlist him. Johns sent him for medical examination. Observing his debilitation and whip-scarred back, the doctors refused to pass him. Thereupon, the Air Ministry sent a doctor to sign the medical papers. While waiting for the train to Uxbridge, the RAF training depot a few miles west of London, Lawrence had a long talk with Johns and acknowledged his identity. After he left, Johns phoned an Uxbridge colleague "to warn him of who was on the way. For by this time Lawrence was making it clear that he had no time for junior officers."[5] Thus, Uxbridge officers knew who Ross was before he arrived.

Lawrence apologized to "Dear Swann"—Air Vice-Marshall Sir Oliver Swann—for "the mess I made" of his induction. "I thought I was fitter.... I can only just scrape through the days.... I enjoy usually one hour of the sixteen.... In case I'm wanted by the Colonial Office I'll send you a note as often as I change station: but not more unless I want something.... Please tell the C.A.S. [Chief of Air Staff Trenchard] that I'm delighted, and most grateful to him and to you."[6] The familiarity annoyed Swann. "One would think ... I was a close correspondent of Lawrence's.... But ... I never met him until ... I was *ordered* to get him into the R.A.F. I disliked the whole business, with its secrecy and subterfuge; I discouraged communication with or from him." Lawrence treated T. B. Marson and Edward Marsh similarly, using them to convey messages he might hesitate to send their chiefs (Trenchard and Churchill, respectively) directly.[7]

The physical work and drill, the cruelty of some officers, the brutality and vulgarity of many men, excruciatingly recorded in *The Mint,* were hard for Lawrence to bear. Yet he had sought and welcomed the punishment and humiliation. David Garnett characterized his reaction as "the emotion of the weasel in the steel trap, biting the keeper's boots."[8] If the aggravations of recruit life exceeded its satisfactions he could leave at any time. However, to assess that balance correctly, it must be recognized that what gives others physical or mental pain can give a masochist perverse pleasure.

His self-imposed purgatory writing *Seven Pillars* strengthened his resolve to enlist. The company of airmen would replace solitude; eating would replace starving; the physical routine, sleepless stretches of anguished mental labor. "I sweated myself blind trying to make it [*Seven Pillars*] as good as possible. Result that I leap into the air when spoken to unexpectedly, and can't reply a word: only stand there shivering!" Lawrence wrote on his second day at Uxbridge.[9]

The last thing a man in such a state would want, one might think, would be to resume writing: which is just what Lawrence did. "[W]hat mania is it," he asked, "that drives a man who has half-killed his brain for four years over one book, so soon as it is finished, to contemplate another?" Each night he would "sit in bed, with my knees drawn up under the blankets, and write on a pad the things of the day."[10] Rewritten in 1928, the notes became *The Mint,* far slighter than *Seven Pillars* and so radically different in style—staccato, sharp, at times coarse, not rotund, profuse, deeply wrought—unknowing readers would not imagine they had the same author. James Joyce's influence is evident; Lawrence had read him and, in 1921, subscribed to Shakespeare & Co.'s limited first edition of *Ulysses.* Were the notes the extra lap a runner takes to taper off after a marathon? Lawrence doggedly continued the *Seven Pillars* marathon until December 1926.

The first night in barracks Lawrence lay awake. His "bedfellow was perfect fear" and the image that came to mind—perhaps a recollection of his 1919 crash in Rome—was of a plane "shoot[ing] downward out of control, its crew cramp themselves fearfully into their seats ... expecting the crash."[11] The image "of how I've crashed my life" recurred.[12] Lawrence was 34; the next oldest recruit in his barracks, 26; many were 19. Lawrence worried if he was up to the drills, exercise, chores.

Several themes dominate *The Mint's* early sections. None dwells on the glories of the newly forming Air Force that had supposedly impelled Lawrence to enlist. The free world of civilians and the free sky above are contrasted with recruits' servitude and imprisonment. Their lowly speech and background are noted, what brought them to this refuge, their raucous but fraternal conduct, the growth of a communal spirit. Officers are depicted as

a worm might depict birds: a totally different species; a few are kind, some take sadistic pleasure in breaking the men, body and spirit. The camp regimen is seen as largely pointless and soul-destroying, "dirty, senseless, ... arduous fatigues."[13] The abundant obscenities—farts, pricks, pissers, bollocks, cunts, fucks, buggers, bastards, arses, turds, shits, bull-shits— not the language of monastery monks!— shocked Lawrence's friends. Lawrence's attention to this language, to the sexual undertones of camp life and the sexual explosions off the base suggest that he was undergoing a kind of late adolescence, a heightened consciousness of man's carnality evinced in his searching, deeply distressed letters to Lionel Curtis.

A prominent theme is the same morbid attraction to filth, death, and decay exhibited in *Seven Pillars'* Turkish corpses and the appalling Damascus hospital. Andrew Rutherford discerns "a trace of necrophilia" in Lawrence's "preoccupation with the beauty of naked corpses"; as a boy, he slept near a brass-rubbing of "a corpse eaten by worms."[14] In 1915, he sent his family photos of dead men that his brother Frank, fighting in the French trenches, protested: "Has Ned sent any explanation of those photos of the dead men? I cannot imagine what he did it for. I could get plenty here if I ... wanted to. The human body after death is a most vile & loathesome thing."[15] Agreeing to translate Salammbô for Cape (a project soon discarded), Lawrence said, "[I]t's the description of Hanno's leprous body, after twelve days on the cross which has finally conquered me." Lawrence "kept photographs of the Turkish wounded in his home at Clouds Hill ... and often studied their gruesome details."[16] *The Mint's* dwelling on his handling rotting, maggot-infested sacks and emptying, often soaking in, bins of garbage, refuse, and manure shows his revulsion and attraction to filth and corruption.

Deep into "shit-cart," the account of that day, Lawrence drew from his "swill-stinking ... overalls" a soaked invitation to edit a new literary monthly, *Belles-Lettres*. "I stared from the lovely clouds to my foul clothes, and wondered how it would feel to go back." Rejecting the offer, he said, "an editorship could hardly be given to a man who had never had any training or written anything himself (published, that is...!)." Edward Garnett rejoined, "'training' that's all fudge. Its merely a matter of task & insight." To which Lawrence replied more (not entirely) honestly, "I don't really know why I don't want to do it."[17] Shortly after coming to Uxbridge, he asked Stiffy Breese, the drill-adjutant, for "a room in which to write undisturbed. 'Stiffy' explained with more than a touch of sarcasm that it was not possible to provide each of 1100 recruits with such a room"; he could use the camp writing room.[18]

The first month was the hardest. Lawrence was so tired, he was often late for morning parade. By October, he was over the physical hump. At 9:00 P.M., when other recruits were exhausted, he felt tolerably well. "My purgatory was passed ... and surely my nerves and sinews will never so hurt again.... I have been ... dog-tired; but not drained right out." Even the food became tolerable, if he omitted a meal. He still could not sleep through the night; "desert experience taught me to hover ... in a transparent doze, listening for the threat of any least sound or movement."[19] At 2:00 A.M., he might dress quickly and take a walk.

Trying to arrange a government pension for Charles Doughty, Lawrence contacted Prime Minister Lloyd George and other high officials. "Of the present ministry, three or four are Fellows of All Souls, & most of the others are friends of mine," he told Doughty[20]—without mentioning where he was. Few friends knew; most

wrote to Baker's Westminster office, whence mail was forwarded. In the camp canteen hung photos of the King, Trenchard, General Haig, and one of Lawrence, which he removed. For reasons only Lawrence in full flood on an analyst's couch might explain, he had in his kit the 1921 parchment designating him His Majesty's Minister Plenipotentiary to negotiate a treaty with King Hussein.

Still engrossed in *Seven Pillars*, Lawrence asked Rudyard Kipling and George Bernard Shaw to read it. Earlier, he had asked poet Laurence Binyon, whom he did not know, to read the dedicatory poem. For literary and artistic purposes, he traded readily on his fame. Kennington, Edward Garnett, and Vyvyan Richards read *Seven Pillars* immediately. The first two praised it mightily; Richards gave a more balanced judgment. Garnett's sympathy was stirred; Lawrence declared that "almost indecent" and asked him "to excise all that seems sentimental."[21]

The concise psychological profiles of sitters that he provided the artists are penetrating, witty, inimitably Lawrencian.[22] The paintings and drawings, largely irrelevant to the text, were making *Seven Pillars* an art gallery and putting Lawrence deeper in debt. The wish to earn nothing from his involvement in the revolt, which he later stressed, did not keep him from spending lavishly on the book. Publication would produce money, but Lawrence was dissatisfied with the book's literary quality and felt it impossible to publish the confessional passages.

Garnett's offer to abridge the text (as he had abridged *Arabia Deserta*) was tempting. He cut the 330,000 words almost in half and Lawrence cut them further to 150–160,000. (This invaluable copy, marked and annotated by both men, is now in the Houghton Library at Harvard.) However, Lawrence remained undecided about publication. The truncated version, omitting many brutal truths and internal conflicts, seemed false. "I hate the notion of it … and there is no doubt that I will have to do it, some time: and the motive will be money," he wrote; and two days later, "I feel less & less inclined to publish the whole work, & almost decided not to publish anything."[23]

Farnborough

In November, Lawrence was transferred to the RAF School of Photography at Farnborough, Hants., southeast of Reading. Thanking Swann in another effusive letter, he boasted (deservedly) of his photographic ability, yet "Please leave me to go through the normal training, unless I squeal about it." He soon squealed because, missing the new class by a day, he had to wait two months for the next one. "I'm already as good as the men passing out. My father … taught me before I was four … I've … exhibited … at the Camera Club." Could Swann put him into the class at once or into an active squadron or could he be remustered? Swann phoned the station commander and insisted that "Ross" start photography training promptly. When this was done, Ross solved math problems in his head and instructed the instructor on points of optics.[24]

Farnborough was much easier than Uxbridge. Lawrence lit fires, cleaned the office, and served as messenger. He did these duties well but was reprimanded for improper dress and talking back to an officer in a foreign language. Plainly, Aircraftman Ross had not subdued Colonel Lawrence, who bought an old motorcycle and sidecar to escape camp. His Farnborough routine is described in a letter:

> Today I scrubbed the kitchen out in the morning, and loafed all the afternoon…. Yesterday I washed up the dishes in the sergeants' mess in the morning (…plates were all butter and tomato sauce, and the washing water was cold) and rode to Oxford in the afternoon…. I was an errand-boy. I've also been dustman, and clerk, and pig-stye-cleaner, and housemaid, and scullion, and camp-cinema-attendant.[25]

Jock Chambers, orderly in Lawrence's barracks who became a staunch friend, was annoyed at his shirking duties. "I had a row with him because he dodged spud-peeling. I said: 'Look here, old man, if you're going to be one of us you've got to do what we do.' He said: 'It's a foolish thing, time-wasting thing' and he wouldn't do it." Lawrence, Chambers noted, was always "a rear-rank bloke [in drill] … so he didn't have to move … he knew all the tricks."[26]

By late December, Lawrence was close to signing a contract with Cape for *The War in the Desert,* the abridged Oxford Text. Dissatisfied with its "bowdlerising … favourably false"[27] rendition of the revolt and uncertain about leaving the RAF, he wavered and equivocated. He replaced his old motorbike with an expensive Brough Superior, the "Rolls Royce" of motorcycles, enabling him to cover long distances at astonishing speeds. The massive, thundering, shiny machine did not help its short, shy rider to remain anonymous.

Also in December, the irrepressible G. B. Shaw entered the scene. He had had the Oxford Text since the end of August; his wife Charlotte had pronounced it a masterpiece, but the great man had only now begun to read it. On December 1, he called it "one of the Cheops pyramids of literature and history" but far too long. "Obviously there are things in it that you cannot publish." For safety, it should be placed under seal in the British Museum and one or two other depositories and an abridgment published. On December 17, Shaw advised that he had told the two senior partners of Constable, his publisher, "it's the greatest book in the world" and was deputized to say "we should be very pleased and honoured to be entrusted with the publication." It should, Shaw now said, be published in complete form. On December 28, he repeated, "IT MUST BE PUBLISHED IN ITS ENTIRETY, UNABRIDGED. Later on an abridgment can be considered ... you must not for a moment entertain the notion of publishing an abridgment first, as no publisher would touch the whole work afterwards." The few libellous passages must be dropped or modified.[28]

Jeremy Wilson asserts that, had Shaw not intervened, Lawrence would have signed the Cape contract for an abridgment, received his money, settled his debt, left the RAF, published a limited edition, and pursued a thoroughly different career. Without the contract, he had "to remain in the ranks or seek some other ... paid work ... Shaw ... had changed the course of Lawrence's life." This reasoning is a chain of weak links. Lawrence had been encased in indecision. The press's exposure of his enlistment, not Shaw's advice, made him drop the contract; had he really wanted the money and resolved to leave the RAF, he could have signed it or made money in other ways (including editing Cape's *Belles-Lettres*). It was his inner demons, not financial need, that kept him in uniform after expulsion.[29]

Lawrence had given different estimates of how long he expected to stay in the RAF. "Seven years now before I need think of winning a meal" is how *The Mint's* account of his enlistment ends. "Less than two years won't do what I planned," he wrote Swann on September 1. "I'm quite likely to chuck the R.A.F." he told a friend in December.[30] But the RAF chucked him first.

As noted, Uxbridge officers knew Lawrence's identity before he arrived. At Farnborough, two weeks after his transfer,

Swann's phone call (which Lawrence had prompted) aroused Station Commander Guilfoyle's suspicions. Why was the RAF personnel chief interested in a lowly recruit? Guilfoyle thought Ross resembled Lawrence, whom he had seen once in Cairo during the war; a visiting officer who knew Lawrence confirmed the suspicion. What was the famous colonel doing as "Aircraftman Ross"? Was he spying for Swann or Trenchard? (Not formally, of course, but the officers were right to suspect that Lawrence passed on his observations of their conduct.) Guilfoyle tried to keep the secret, but word got out. Several of Lawrence's friends knew where he was and, in a characteristic outburst of candor, he had twice written *Daily Express* editor R. D. Blumenfeld telling him of his enlistment, the Oxford Text and its abridgment, his "excogitating" a book on the RAF, even his illegitimacy, and boasting, "don't you think it's good for me at my great age ... to be able to enlist [no mention of Trenchard's help!] and hold my own with a lusty crowd?"[31]

Two reporters appeared at Uxbridge, interviewed two officers, and, denied further interviews, waited outside the gates and spoke with airmen. "Do you think that all the conjecture and talk is in the best interests of discipline?" Guilfoyle asked Vice-Marshall Swann who consulted Trenchard who consulted his Minister, Sir Samuel Hoare. Initially, they persevered, but when the *Daily Express* ran a front page story headlined 'UNCROWNED KING' AS PRIVATE SOLDIER, the situation grew more difficult. Newsmen descended on Farnborough. Guilfoyle protested that Lawrence's presence "was prejudicial to good order and discipline." Trenchard visited to tell Lawrence he could stay in the RAF only if he accepted a commission. Lawrence refused and was discharged; his appeals for posting to a distant station such as Leuchars (in Scotland, near St. Andrews) were rejected.

Lawrence put some blame for his dismissal on the Farnborough commander: "if [he] ... was a decent size he'd treat me as average, and I'd be average" (not very likely!). He anticipated little trouble at Leuchars, where the commander, whom he knew, "is a solid and masterful person."[32] The remarks again show Lawrence's wish to serve under a man of great confidence: to be dominated by someone he felt worthy of dominating him.

As a civilian with no need to worry about the effects of publicity or publication on the supposed anonymity of Aircraftman Ross, Lawrence was now free to publish The War in the Desert. Had money to clear his overdraft been a prime concern, one might think he would do so. But money was always a minor consideration to him. His primary concern was to reenter the RAF. In part, this represented a continued drive for subjection; in part, a determination to have his way. "Since the period at Uxbridge had been a time of great suffering when he was continually on the verge of breakdown," David Garnett notes, "one wonders whether his will had not become greater than his intelligence."[33]

Lawrence was again in a poor state. "I'm rather at a loss for interest in anything," he wrote Edward Garnett. "I can't stay anywhere, for restlessness, and so haven't an address ... everything in connection with Cape and The Seven Pillars is over.... I was an ass to have dreamed of publishing anything."[34] Rejecting the abridgment, he now contemplated an expensive, unexpurgated, illustrated private edition of 2,000. Angry, frustrated, patient, hopeful, Cape prepared another contract: which, upon receiving his discharge, Lawrence refused to sign.

He wandered about London with Baker's loft as a base. He lost a packet of letters from G. B. Shaw—put them in a slit in his overalls through which they fell; a passerby returned them. He declined an invitation to go to Nepal with Robert Graves and his family, as a guest of its government. Good jobs were offered, but he insisted on an abject job. "I'm fed up with being called Colonel ... and am determined not any more to be respectable." "No one will offer me a job poor enough for my acceptance!"[35] Among those he sought were Navy supply clerk in Bermuda and lighthouse keeper. Dining with Lawrence at his London home, Air Minister Sir Samuel Hoare

found him more definite than ever in his refusal to accept a responsible post. When he was on the point of leaving very late in the evening, and was already on the doorstep, I asked him whether I should call a taxi for him. He refused the offer; he said that he had no money, and that he intended to spend the night on a seat on the Embankment. When I offered to pay both for a taxi and a room in a hotel, he again refused and walked off into the night.[36]

6

The Tank Corps, 1923–1925

When it became clear even to obdurate Lawrence that the RAF would not take him back, he tried the Navy and, more successfully, the Army. His friend Colonel Alan Dawnay contacted General Philip Chetwode (who had served under Allenby) who approached Tank Corps Commander Colonel Hugh Elles. Thus Lawrence was enlisted in the Royal Tank Corps for seven years and assigned to Bovington camp, Dorset, on March 12, 1923, as Private Thomas Edward Shaw, No. 7875698. He may have chosen "Shaw" because of the growing regard and affection between him and elderly Bernard and Charlotte Shaw. In making this arrangement, Lawrence knew that, with permission, an Army man could transfer to the RAF; "the hope of getting back into the R.A.F.," he said a year later, "is the main reason of my staying in the Army."[1]

Perhaps, as Lawrence contended, the men at Bovington were markedly worse than those at Uxbridge, but I doubt it. More likely, wounded by his ouster from the RAF, he felt worse, saw, brought out, was more offended by, and somehow reveled in their worse side. He made lasting friends at Bovington and acquired a home

nearby. His emotional descent, begun at Uxbridge, deepened.

Lawrence contrasted the Uxbridge and Bovington men. At Uxbridge, they "joined the R.A.F. as a profession—or to continue in … their trades. They talked of futures and jobs … were excited about life," wore "cleanish clothes," took pride in their work and in flight. They were "decent." At Bovington, the "unrelieved animal" men joined as a last resort because they were broke, "had failed, or were not qualified, for anything else." They had no wish to improve themselves, want nothing but food and pay; "very dirty, body & clothes," "social bed-rock," they thought little of their comrades and of themselves.[2]

Lawrence's self-hatred and self-punishment were manifested at Bovington in an intense brooding on degradation and carnality and the start of fierce whippings, with a sexual element, repeated at intervals for the rest of his life.

"I've really struck bed-rock—or base material—this time," Lawrence wrote. "The army is unspeakable: more solidly animal than I believed Englishmen could be. I hate them, and the life here: and am sure that it's good medicine for me." And:

"It's an odd penance to have set oneself, to live amongst animals for seven years … everything here disgusts me."[3] Was the foul talk at Uxbridge merely words signifying nothing? At times, Lawrence said just that: "The R.A.F. was foul-mouthed, and the cleanest little mob of fellows. These [Bovington] men are foul-mouthed, and behind their mouths is a pervading animality of spirit."[4] It is hard to credit this fully; Lawrence saw and said contradictory things in each of his many moods. Bovington comrade Alec Dixon considered his talk about the degraded Tank Corps "a ripe piece of T.E. humbug."[5] If, indeed, the Army were so bad, the perverse economy of self-degradation might have made Lawrence prefer it to the Air Force: he could more readily be defiled there. "It will be a puzzle for my biographer," he recognized, "…to reconcile my joy in the R.A.F. with my disgust with the Army."[6] Two clues to the puzzle may be his insistence on getting his own way and his friendship with Trenchard. To be an obstinate slave on a ship captained by his large, lordly friend, demonstrating both contriteness and contrariness, was strangely gratifying.[7]

Agonized Letters

From March to June 1923, Lawrence wrote Lionel Curtis, the apostle of turning the Empire into a Commonwealth, five agonized, nihilistic letters on the condition of the human animal that offer the fullest available evidence of his emotional condition at the time. Why did he enlist? "Mind-suicide" and "self-degradation." He wants to shed responsibility, "my power of moulding men and things," having lost the conviction needed to exercise that power. Taking, not giving, orders was restful. "There has not been presented to me … a single choice: everything is ordained." Pessimism is the only rational creed; "reason proves there is no hope, and we therefore hope on … on one leg of our minds."

He relishes punishing himself. "I want to stay here till … the burnt child no longer feels the fire…. [I]n sick stomachs the desire of condiment becomes a craving, till what is hateful becomes therefore wholesome." At night, the barracks seethes with "cat-calling carnality." Humanity, culture, philosophy, art breed on that carnality. "Everything with flesh in its mixture is the achievement of a moment when the lusty thought of Hut 12 has passed to action and conceived…. Hut 12 shows me the truth behind Freud. Sex is an integer in all of us." "[I]t's taken for granted as natural that you should job a woman's body, or hire out yourself, or abuse yourself in any way."[8] And he had himself abused.

By coincidence or prior arrangement, Lawrence joined the Tank Corps three days after John Bruce, a hefty 19-year old Scotsman enlisted in Aberdeen. Both were sent to Bovington for training and assigned to the same barracks. Lawrence paid Bruce £3 a week to act as his bodyguard and aide. Periodically, Bruce also whipped him severely on his naked buttocks, in accordance with detailed instructions contained in letters purportedly from "The Old Man," a distant relative of Lawrence's father, but, in fact, written by Lawrence himself. The whippings were supposed punishment for theft, indebtedness, and other imagined, half-true offenses. A classic form of masochism, they will be discussed in Chapter 21.

Excessively self-conscious, self-analytic, aware of his conflicts and contradictions (though not always of their cause) and how they mystified and dismayed his well-wishers, Lawrence called himself a case of "multiple personality."[9] One person seemed to adjust quickly and to function well at Bovington. Within a few weeks, he took his Brough to camp, made friends, visited Thomas Hardy who lived nearby, renewed contacts with friends further afield, undertook a French translation for Cape, and resumed work on *Seven Pillars*. In the summer, he leased a derelict cottage a mile away, named it Clouds Hill, and began to restore it as a secluded bolt hole. The other person, depressed by his exclusion from the RAF, wrote devastating, confessional letters to several friends and had himself brutally beaten. The first man seemed relatively content, friendly, productive; the second, distraught, involuted, self-destructive.

Alec Dixon recalled Shaw as older than most recruits, "a straight-backed little man with a finely shaped head and a good nose," a "long face ... weatherbeaten to a brick red ... a massive jaw and two restless eyes." He did barrack chores rapidly and efficiently, ate only three or four meals a week, did not drink, smoke, whistle, sing, complain, or talk about himself. The men were puzzled trying to place him. As his speech showed him to be well educated and he told a corporal he had been a major in intelligence (though his papers declared no previous military service), he was put down as an ex-officer. After he produced a new Brough worth two years' pay, donned gloves, helmet, and black leather flying suit, and took his mates on high-speed rides, he was called Broughie Shaw.[10] Most men liked and respected him, but some cadged money or fought with him. Lawrence lent or gave small sums, lent his books freely, and advised his young friends about their reading, the military, and their future careers. Thursdays, the day before payday, when cash was scarce, he bought everyone fish and chips but ate none himself. Before long, he told his friends who he was.

Despite his ostensible poverty, Lawrence unabatedly commissioned art for *Seven Pillars*, whose publication by Cape

he had quashed a few months earlier. William Roberts, Gilbert Spencer, Augustus John, and Kennington did portraits. The few Oxford Text copies were in such demand from friends and *their* friends that Lawrence was often without one. "You want a copy! Unfortunately so do I," he informed sculptress Kathleen Scott. "Of the six copies ... only one has ever been returned by a borrower: and that copy was foolishly lent a second time, and hasn't come back." Lawrence circulated the book for several reasons. What did readers— friends, participants in the revolt, writers, literary critics—*really* think of it and of the man revealed and concealed in that highly wrought mass of words? "Is any of it worth while?"[11] How much of it should be published and in what manner?

Condemning Seven Pillars

He had striven to write an epic that would join the master works of literature. Initially, he said a few good things about it. "I like parts of it. The feast in the Howeitat tents ... is well done." "It is certainly uncommon, and there's power sensible under its peculiarly frigid surface." "[I]t's a good book: in the sense that it's better than most which have been written lately."[12] But excoriation overwhelmed the thin praise and grew harsher. He lashed his writing more mercilessly than any subsequent critic. Aldous Huxley thought it lacked "freshness or spontaneity"; Richard Aldington thought it "strained, insincere and rhetorical"; Richard Hughes, "artificial"; Herbert Read, "an artificial monstrosity"; Bernard Bergonzi, "turgid"; André Malraux, "stiff and linear"; George Woodcock saw "a hollow pretentiousness of manner and sentiment."[13] Lawrence said it was "muck," "long-winded, and pretentious, and dull," "perverse," "priggish, ... hysterical," "lewd lecherous unholy," "undigestible," "a stodgy mess of mock-heroic egotism … sludge," "irre-deemable, irremediable," "rotten," "putrid rubbish," "inferior to nearly every book which I have found patience to read." "What I don't doubt at all is the inherent falsity and inferiority of my book. The thing does not ring true."[14] Yet, "I've a despairing wish to believe well of that awful book of mine, though it's a nightmare to me, and I can never agree that it's any good."[15] That sentence runs a circle of hope and despair so impenetrable one wonders what kind of response he wanted from his readers. Less, perhaps, praise (which he rejected) or practical criticism (he accepted little) than an opportunity to observe, ponder, admire, and despise the man mirrored in their comments.

When Sydney Cockerell called *Seven Pillars*, "A tremendous masterpiece," Lawrence rejoined, "no, you are wrong there. It's not a masterpiece, for it lacks form and continuity & colour … & it is not tremendous, for it can be no bigger than my petty self." Siegfried Sassoon was exasperated. "Damn you, how long do you expect me to go on reassuring you about your bloody masterpiece? It is a GREAT BOOK, blast you."[16] Lawrence visited him but failed to change his mind. Charlotte Shaw's reaction resembled Sassoon's. "How is it *conceivable, imaginable* that a man who could write the Seven Pillars can have doubts about it? If you don't know it is a 'great book' what is the use of anyone telling you so?" (None!) Lawrence replied, "it's more a storehouse than a book—has no unity, is too discursive, dispersed, heterogeneous."[17] E. M. Forster, H. G. Wells, Thomas Hardy, Bernard Shaw extolled the work. Shaw pronounced it "a masterpiece." Once, Lawrence went so far as to say, "Shaw has turned my mind slowly to consider it good."[18] But the feeling had little conviction or staying power.

Lawrence did not trust what he was told directly. Knowing his own inclination to say different things to different people, he tried to discover what was said about him and probably learned little that was new. Sassoon and Shaw praised *Seven Pillars* to others just as they did to Lawrence. However, perceiving that unstinted praise was unwelcome, E. M. Forster diligently delivered a range of criticism and suggestions for improvement. Vyvyan Richards, Robert Graves, Frederic Manning mixed praise and criticism straightforwardly.

Kipling and Shaw rebuked Lawrence for his inordinate mastication of *Seven Pillars*. "It looks to me…," Kipling said, "as if you had been on the job of that book too long. One gets stale and doubtful in such cases…. I do not hold with showing one's friends what one is doing till it is all done." To Lawrence's pained, "is there any style in my writing at all?" Shaw retorted, "As to style, what have you to do with such dilettanti rubbish…? You have something to say; and you say it as accurately and vividly as you can; and when you have done that you do not go fooling with your statement with the notion that if you do it over again five or six times you will do it five or six times better."[19] Their advice was wasted.

The charge of reticence deserves special note. *Seven Pillars* is full of Lawrence's conscious reflections and unconscious self-disclosures. Most intense in Chapters LXXX, recounting the Deraa trauma, and CIII, "Myself," marking his 30th birthday, they permeate the work. As Churchill said, "All is intense, individual, sentient…. Through all, one mind, one soul, one will-power … a prodigy, a tale of torment, and in the heart of it—a Man." Those who are captured by *Seven Pillars* are captured by the author's penetrating mind and absorbing, forceful, candid, yet elusive character. The student of crusader fortresses guards his own fortress cunningly, appearing to disclose yet withholding its key secrets. "[P]eople who read it will know me better than I know myself," he joked.[20]

But ultimate truths about Lawrence are not told. Either he is afraid to learn what they are or cannot confess them. Christopher Isherwood perceived that *Seven Pillars* "was not absolutely frank. Lawrence had been unable to bring himself to record the full history of the 'deep cleavage' in his own nature." On "the rare occasions when you attempt to give direct information about your own character," E. M. Forster said, "I don't always see that which you are willing to reveal."[21] Calling the 1926 edition "*extraordinarily truthful*," Edward Garnett nonetheless told Lawrence, "a bigger man than you would have been much more explicit ... about giving himself away."[22]

Lawrence said contradictory things about himself because he was a contradictory person. There were things he did not know and things he knew but did not say. What Thomas Mann said of Dostoevsky applies to Lawrence. "In every man's memory there are things which he does not reveal to everyone, but only to his friends. There are also things which he does not reveal to his friends, but at best to himself and only under a pledge of secrecy. And finally there are things which man hesitates to reveal even to himself."[23]

To Publish or Not

The interest the Oxford Text aroused, friends' wish for a copy, and Lawrence's mounting overdraft renewed his thoughts of publication. In May 1923, he weighed the pros and cons:

> To publish the whole book might cause a new clamour.... To censor it would mean practical re-writing, & I'm weary of the work ... also it feels a little dishonest to hide parts of the truth. Further ... the feelings of some English, some French & some Arabs might be hurt.... Against these instincts you have to set the vanity of an amateur [who] ... would like to be in print as an author: and my need of money to live quietly upon.[24]

Another factor was the impending publication of Lowell Thomas's *With Lawrence in Arabia,* issued in the U.S. in 1924 and in Britain in 1925. The prospective revival of Thomas's hero in flowing white robes while the real Lawrence was abasing himself in khaki would be a joke in poor taste; "if his book is the fulsome thing I expect, he will force the truth out of me." The idea of an abridgment returned: whatever its faults, the story would be truer than Thomas's. "What am I to do?" Lawrence asked Hogarth. "Publish the Garnett abridgement ... and use its profits to publish a limited illustrated complete edition ... publish nothing ... or print privately?"[25]

To occupy himself and make some money while deciding what to do with *Seven Pillars,* Lawrence asked Jonathan Cape for a book to translate and spent the summer turning into English Adrien le Corbeau's *Le Gigantesque,* a fictional biography of a 7,000-year-old giant California sequoia. When the camp day was over, he headed for his cottage and put in several hours translating, corresponding, or contemplating *Seven Pillars.* After *Le Gigantesque* (published as *The Forest Giant,* translated by "J. H. Ross"), he finished a second French translation but, dissatisfied with its quality, burned it.

In early December 1923, Lawrence met with D. G. Hogarth, Lionel Curtis, and Alan Dawnay in Oxford, discussed the alternatives, and resolved to print a small subscription edition of *Seven Pillars.* So far as Lawrence was concerned, the smaller, the better; for a time, he hoped a millionaire might be found to subsidize the venture. A hundred copies with the full gallery of art were planned, at £31/10 each, plus 20 copies lacking some illustrations, which

Lawrence would give to friends and persons involved in the revolt. The number of copies and price were intended (unsuccessfully) to recover the cost of production; as it rose, the number was increased. Eventually, 211 copies were printed, of which 127 were sold.

Once the decision was taken, Lawrence and his friends began to seek subscribers; Lawrence employed two printers to compose and print the text; Eric Kennington supervised the color printing of illustrations (118 drawings, paintings, and photographs by 19 individuals) by a leading firm.[26] Subscribers were asked to pay £15/15 immediately and the same amount upon completion of the work, which "may drag till the summer of '25" (in fact, December 1926). Though he was now Private T. E. Shaw, checks were to be made out to T. E. Lawrence, whose name appeared on the message to subscribers. This asserted that the illustrations were the main reason for the edition—Lawrence did not call it a "publication" or copyright it in Britain. "I am not publishing it.... I think the book exceedingly dear, an unjustifiable purchase either as investment ... or ... for reading.... I much regret the necessity ... of multiplying the book at all: but I want my illustrations reproduced...."[27]

The message stated, "Circumstances make me unable to profit" from the book. At 30 guineas, *Seven Pillars* was expensive (though far below the final production cost of £102 a copy).[28] Jeremy Wilson interprets Lawrence's refusal to make money from the production as an act of pride. "He could not stomach the idea that subscribers might think that the high price reflected personal greed."[29] Pride was converted into the principle Lawrence henceforth adopted, that he would make no money from his involvement in the Arab revolt.

Lawrence examined each prospective subscriber, returned checks from those who displeased him, and discouraged oth-

ers from subscribing. Thus, he wrote Robin Buxton, "I don't like the lady's manner: will you please return her cheques ... with a polite note.... Cuthbert Headlam has written asking for a copy. I've replied begging him to consider seriously if his bank balance can't be better employed than acquiring luxury books. He's a nice creature, & must have one if he insists." The book "is long, detailed, discursive, technical: and ... contains no political disclosures whatever" he warned an inquirer.[30] He dissuaded Clement Shorter, editor of *The Sphere,* from subscribing by asking him to promise not to review it.[31] He refused a musician's subscription "because he is too poor" and James Barrie's "because he is an insincere artist"—but then relented.

Having backed out before, Lawrence might do so again. However, once he hired printer Manning Pike, he had to give him a flow of text to set in monotype, and the increasing number of subscribers added pressure to complete the protracted labor.

"I have no idea how much of this tanking is tolerated tomfoolery, and how much genuine service," Bernard Shaw scolded. "If you are writing, or planning some new campaign, then you are justified; but if you are only acting, and devising superfluous ornaments for that old finished job of yours, you will presently find that you have lost the power of serious work, and that the end of pretending to be a common soldier is that you *are* a common soldier." Which drew the reply, "Your picture of my ending up to find that I'm a soldier, by dint of playing at it, comforts me: for it's the end I want ... with deadly seriousness."[32]

A Unicorn in the Barnyard

The second bout of training at Bovington—sixteen weeks of drill—passed more easily than the ordeal at Uxbridge and subsequent chores were less onerous. The camp day ran from 6:00 A.M. to 5:00 or 6:00 P.M. In the morning, Lawrence cleaned boots, made beds, fetched coal, lit fires, then worked as a clerk and storeman issuing and keeping track of clothing and supplies. He scored 93 percent on the Rolls-Royce armored car course, "the highest marks ever given"; when the store's records went foul, he was assigned "to enquire, check, make new ledgers, and wangle deficiencies."[33] The workday over, he ate a quick meal, read or wrote till 9:00 P.M. at the cottage or in barracks, and went to bed; after midnight, he slept little.

"Save when he grinned," Alec Dixon wrote, "his expression was strained, and there were moments when he looked grey and haggard. He was not ... a very happy man." Dixon depicts Lawrence's distinctive bearing: "he never leaned or lounged, and I never saw him to relax.... [E]xcept when on drill parade, he did not swing his arms as he walked.... He walked ... with an air of tidiness; his arms were close to his body and his toes well turned out ... he appeared to see no one about him..., looking neither to the right nor ... left."[34]

As Clouds Hill was repaired and improved, Lawrence kept some books and records there, used it more, and invited camp friends to use it. John Bruce used it occasionally to fulfill "The Old Man's" instructions.

Lawrence was generous and helpful to the men and liked by them. But he stood visibly apart, a unicorn (Robert Graves's word) amidst barnyard animals. When E. M. Forster visited Clouds Hill in March 1924, he noted Lawrence's "clammy and limp" handshake and suspected him of "practices"—"something of the Yoga kind."[35] After Lawrence's death, Forster wrote appreciatively of the "happy casualness" at Clouds Hill, drinking tea and eating out of tins with Lawrence and his sol-

dier friends. At the time, however, Forster thought Lawrence's way of life and justification of it "preposterous. He is inside a membrane of absurdity." Visiting the cottage, Gilbert Spencer felt that Lawrence "was under strain.... He wanted to be [a man among men] ... and didn't quite feel that he was, which he certainly wasn't."[36]

In mid–1924, after Bruce was transferred to another camp and no longer served as his protector, Lawrence had a rough period. Four drunken men beat him, bruising his face and re-breaking a rib. Correcting proofs revived war memories; he cried out and screamed in nightmares. "When I'd woken up the other fellows five nights running they gave me a sort of barrack-court-martial, to keep me quiet. This was humiliating, and rather painful." "[V]ery tired, disgusted: soft headed; sappy: hating myself and the T.C. [Tank Corps].... I'm ... bruised inside and out ... feel bullied ... and when dismissed I like to slink ... into the nearest patch of fern and hide there."[37]

Refusing to accept permanent eviction from the RAF, Lawrence periodically asked Trenchard to be reinstated. Blaming Air Minister Sir Samuel Hoare and the Farnborough commander for his dismissal, he cast no word of criticism at Trenchard. Trenchard, in turn, "had developed a strong affection for his wayward friend."[38] On Armistice Day 1923, he invited him to a dinner party; Lawrence must have been the lone private in khaki amidst the dress suits and bemedalled uniforms at the Army and Navy Club in London. Trenchard offered to arrange a month's leave; Lawrence declined "since returning here would be unpleasant after so long a holiday." He pled for readmission. "Do think of the many hiding-holes there are (India, Egypt and Mespot and seaplane-ships)."[39] Trenchard was willing, but the new Labor Government's Air Minister, Christopher

Thomson, who had rowed with Lawrence at the Paris Peace Conference, was not. Trenchard offered Lawrence a commission (Thomson and Hoare objected to Lawrence being in the ranks) to write the Air Force war history; he declined. On a commission, he was immovable. "My prejudice against exercising authority would prevent my becoming even an N.C.O.!" "I won't again give an order."[40]

Despairing of the RAF, Lawrence thought of other humble jobs. He considered working in a nearby garage when his seven-year Army hitch ended. Then he thought to leave sooner, perhaps the end of 1925 when *Seven Pillars* was published. "I'll look for some safer employment…. It's about that I wanted your help," he wrote Lionel Curtis. "[T]here must be no scope for voluntary effort supplementary to, or apart from, orders. That's where I fail here: the leisure lets me carry on another life when I'm off duty." He asked Curtis "to help me think of some compulsory life which shall be 24-hour in the 24"[41]—a leisureless life of total servitude. A Georgia chain gang?

In February 1925, Lawrence again appealed to Trenchard. "Please don't turn me down just because you did so last year and the year before…. I could easily get other people to help me appeal to you: only it doesn't seem fair…."[42] Nonetheless, he asked Edward Marsh to ask Churchill, then Chancellor of the Exchequer, to persuade Hoare (back as Air Minister in Stanley Baldwin's Conservative government). Hoare refused.

Distraught, Lawrence threatened suicide. He informed his banker friend Robin Buxton that, "The R.A.F. has finally made up its mind, that I am not … to serve in it again. This, of course, affects my stay in the army, by removing the motive of it. So

I may buy myself out in the autumn, to have full time for the last 3 months, to finish the Seven Pillars business."[43] Evidently "the *last* 3 months" did not register with Buxton. Four weeks later, Lawrence made it plain to Edward Garnett. Hoare's refusal and his immersion in *Seven Pillars,* he wrote, "have together convinced me that I'm no bloody good on earth. So I'm going to quit…." He would "finish the reprint and square up with Cape before I hop it! There is nothing like deliberation, order and regularity in these things. I shall bequeath you my notes [for *The Mint*]."[44] Lawrence had threatened suicide before: once, at Trenchard's home (Trenchard said, "All right, but please go into the garden. I don't want my carpets ruined") and once at Clouds Hill.[45] Alarmed, Garnett wrote Bernard Shaw who forwarded his letter to Prime Minister Baldwin "with a card to say that some decision should be made, as there is a possibility of an appalling scandal."[46]

Ever resourceful and guileful, Lawrence had already taken another approach. He asked Lionel Curtis, "John Buchan: do you ever see him? Could I? Without seeming to wish to? Naturally, in other words." Thus, he "ran into" Buchan on the street and invoked his help with Baldwin. "I don't know by what right I made that appeal to you…. It happened on the spur of the moment," he misinformed Buchan, a close friend of Baldwin. "It must be the ranks," he emphasized, "The rails, & rules & necessary subordination are so many comforts."[47] Buchan greatly admired Lawrence. Making sure that Trenchard had no objection, he wrote Baldwin, who replied, "Come and see me about that exceedingly difficult friend of yours."[48] Baldwin overrode Hoare and, on July 16, 1925, Trenchard approved Lawrence's transfer to the RAF.

7

Back in the RAF,
1925–1926

Heaven? Fulfillment? At least satisfaction and a sense of accomplishing a long-set goal for which he had endured the animal nastiness of Bovington? Not quite. "It's like a sudden port, after a voyage all out of reckoning.... I owe you the very deepest thanks," Lawrence wrote Buchan. The day he knew, he hit 108 miles an hour on Boanerges ("son of thunder").[1] The image of a ship reaching port after a long voyage appears in other letters. Lawrence spoke of peace and rest, not happiness. Writing his mother the August day he rejoined the RAF, he was deeply depressed. "Some day, you know, I will sit down & close everything: and never after write a letter or go to see a person or speak. Each day I find the satisfying of life's claims harder and harder. Existence is the heaviest burden we bear."[2]

Lawrence did surprising things out of shrewd calculation, over-clever miscalculation, over-meticulousness, or for unfathomable reasons. Thus, he told R. D. Blumenfeld, editor of the *Daily Express*, whose story had led to his expulsion from the RAF, of his impending return. "One word from you and I'm in outer darkness again."[3] By a chain of gossip, that might have bred another outburst of publicity.

Lawrence was posted to the RAF Cadet College at Cranwell, Lincolnshire, 120 miles north of London, where he knew almost no one but the commander, Air Commodore A. E. Borton, who had headed the air arm in Palestine during the war. This time, Aircraftsman T. E. Shaw, No. 338171, told everyone he met who he was. "The back of every chair in the canteen used to sprout a face whenever I entered.... A month that was. After it [they] ... settled down."[4]

Life at Cranwell

Compared to Uxbridge, life at Cranwell was relaxed. A corporal scolded Lawrence for saluting him. "Wash out all that blarsted bull-shit you've been taught." In *The Mint*, Lawrence portrays the airmen as proud of maintaining the fighter planes and enabling them to fly. "A pilot climbs in to one of *our* buses.... Hear us curse his ham-fisted cruelty to machines. *Our* machines, please: the beloved created things whose every inmost bolt ... has felt our caring fingers." He envisages a time when officer pilots and aircraftmen mechanics will be equals, "officers will only enter their airmen's rooms ... by invitation, guest-like and bare-headed, like us in an officers' mess.... The era of a real partnership ... must come." The men would set their own work standards. "Our machines fly when they're as good as it lies in our power to make them."[5] A crackerjack mechanic and craftsman of the utmost diligence, Lawrence lived up to that standard. How many other airmen did is an open question.

In *The Mint,* Lawrence jumps from Uxbridge to Cranwell, ignoring Farnborough, trying to redress the grim picture of Uxbridge with a happier account of Cranwell: also, presumably, to justify his insistence on rejoining the RAF. He succeeds only partially. The Cranwell vignettes are too mixed, slight, and unconvincing to

counterbalance the training depot brutalities. In his writing as in his adult life, Lawrence could grasp and render cruelty, suffering, and pain better than pleasure. Cranwell may be a better station than Uxbridge—the men are not there to be beaten, *minted* into shape; their plane-tending imparts dignity. But Lawrence is the same self-conscious, self-punishing man critical of military follies, rebelling against the authority he craves to submit to. He puts it more moderately—Cranwell was his refuge, the commander was his friend, he was not beaten by tcughs. But drill is still "tomfoolery"; an airman who takes it seriously is "a bull-shitter, a bobber, a creeping cunt"; the service police are "vermin"; a bad sergeant can turn the best airmen to "rebellious misery"; the men "say beastlike things in their sleep."[6] No, Cranwell is not quite the heaven he

"At Cranwell he bought a new Brough" (October 1925)—and soon wrecked it (Bodleian Library, University of Oxford).

sought or, if it is, he brings his private hell into it.

Lawrence's hut held 16 men, who awoke without bugles. Lawrence got up at 6:40, took a hot bath (if necessary, he paid the stoker to prepare hot water), made enough noise to wake the others at 7:00, had breakfast; 8:10, parade and flag-raising; 8:30, the group (15 men, corporal, and sergeant) went to the hangar to tend six planes—clean them, fill the tanks, start the engines; Lawrence was their runner and bookkeeper. Lunch at 12:45; the hangar again from 2:00 to 4:15 or 4:30. Saturday afternoon to 11:00 P.M. Sunday was free, with a pass to leave camp every other weekend. "The fellows in my hut are all right: but none of them tuned exactly to my pitch," Lawrence wrote a Bovington comrade. "Yet, it's the R.A.F. and the fact fills me with a perverse, brittle, and nevertheless complete satisfaction. Odd that a man should be so ungrateful, for the R.T.C. [Royal Tank Corps] was very good to me."[7] The beatings by toughs and Bruce, the vile language and animality were now "very good."

Other letters showed less "complete satisfaction." "Do you know what it is when you see, suddenly, that your life is all a ruin?" he asked Charlotte Shaw after a painful encounter with his past. At Cranwell, he had bought a new Brough, enabling him to visit Ayot St. Lawrence, Oxford, London, and Clouds Hill on weekend passes. One day he lunched with Feisal at Lord Winterton's estate near London, where, almost five years earlier, the three had met to discuss Feisal's becoming King of Iraq.

> [The talk turned to] old times…, as though we were once again advancing on Damascus. And I had to talk back, as though the R.A.F. clothes were a skin that I could slough off … with a laugh. But … the Lawrence who used to go about and be … familiar with that sort of people is

dead…. From henceforward my way will lie with these fellows here, degrading myself…. I've crashed my life and self and gone hopelessly wrong…, for I'm never coming back, and I want to.[8]

The Mint ends with a small hymn to the relaxed oneness of airmen. "Everywhere a relationship: no loneliness any more." That was Lawrence's aspiration, seldom realized. He thought too constantly, hated himself too much; an important function of his barrack mates was to take his mind off himself. Manual work was medicinal. At times, Lawrence would set down office paper work and go "into the hangar, scrubbing and washing machines down, although there was never any need to do so." Almost alone in camp at Christmas, he noted that the janitor had not cleaned eight dirty offices. "So I've been going down … when the place is empty, and scrubbing or sweeping or window-cleaning." "[T]he more hours work they give us the better life goes."[9]

Lawrence would return from a motorbike outing with fresh eggs and bacon to be fried and shared by all, brought tea and cakes back from the canteen, appropriated a table and officers' coal for the hut, took the group and wives by bus to a Hendon air show. Reporting these deeds, Sergeant Pugh said Lawrence "was hero-worshipped by all the flight for his never failing cheery disposition, ability to get all he could for their benefit, never complaining, and his generosity to all." Outward cheerfulness hid an inner distress that Clare Sydney Smith, who had known Lawrence in Egypt, saw when he came to tea. "Although … he looked the same, he was far more restless than when I had met him in Cairo. Sitting on his chair he would rub its sides with his hands, up and down, … and … sometimes pass two fingers over his mouth and chin, or rumple up the crest of fair hair."[10]

Disgorging Seven Pillars

The big task Lawrence set himself at Cranwell was to shed the *Seven Pillars* incubus gripping him since 1919. A book is often written to disgorge an experience. As Lawrence nursed and coddled and chewed over his experience, this book seemed to perpetuate the worst agonies of the war: the death of Dahoum, in the dedicatory poem; his killing of Farraj; the death of Tallal, his villagers, and the Turks at Tafas; Lawrence's implication in "betraying" the Arabs; his insistence on his hypocrisy and self-contempt—"I did not like … 'myself'"; the Deraa rape. "Twice you have read the thing: once you have abridged it," he wrote Edward Garnett. "I've read it twenty times, written it five times. Will there never be an end for either of us?"[11]

Nonetheless, as the proofs came in, Lawrence could not resist changes to (he hoped) improve the prose; to utilize every intial letter in the alphabet he had had designed, including X in an invented name; to obtain a page of solid black type without rivers, hyphens, or excessive white space in the last line of a paragraph. Printer Manning Pike was permitted to remove (not add) words to achieve these effects; drawings were commissioned to fill empty page bottoms at the end of chapters. The color portraits, some printed over twenty times, were assembled in a thick mass at the back of the text violating William Morris's principle that print and illustrations should be a harmonious whole. Lawrence had no kinder words for the book's appearance than for its prose. "I've printed it too elaborately: illustrated it too richly. The final effect will be like a scrofulous peacock." (When he saw it, H. S. Ede, of the Tate Gallery, was "aghast that so ugly a book should be produced.")[12] The cost was ridiculous—ultimately, more than three times the income from subscribers. Lawrence proposed to auction his valuable book collection; his Pole Hill land and the *Seven Pillars* copyright might also serve as security for his bank loan.

In March 1925, he signed a contract with Cape for a 125,000-word abridgment to be submitted a year later and published in March 1927. A special provision allowed him to stop British sales when royalties sufficed to cover his overdraft. Lawrence had to make his own abridgment, because Jonathan Cape would not part with the copy Edward Garnett had prepared, fearing it might be lost or destroyed. (Lawrence had lost *Seven Pillars* once and burned it and his *Sturly* translation once.)

The contract solved Lawrence's money problem. A £1,500 advance was paid at once, £1,500 upon delivery of the text, serial rights netted £2,000. To keep his word not to profit from the book, Lawrence established a trust which owned the copyright of the abridgment, *Revolt in the Desert;* as subscribers were promised, the complete text would not be reprinted in his lifetime. To escape the publicity that would accompany the serialization and promotion of *Revolt* (if not the distribution of *Seven Pillars*), Lawrence arranged a five-year posting to an RAF station in India. Declining Trenchard's offer to cancel the posting, he explained that "neither good-will on the part of those above me, nor correct behaviour on my part can prevent my being a nuisance in any camp where the press can get at me. Overseas they will be harmless."[13]

By December 3, 1926, 20 copies of *Seven Pillars* had gone to subscribers. The first went to King George V with a characteristic ploy. Sir John Fortescue, the King's Librarian, sent a check via bookdealer John Wilson. Lawrence returned it, because, "I'm an old-fashioned person, to whom it seems improper that Kings should buy and sell among their subjects…. F.[ortescue] is decent, and will not tell his owner: for I should prefer Him to think He is paying for it, since that is His notion of propriety."[14]

Writing to his Clouds Hill neighbor, Lawrence allowed himself a little praise. "The final book came out not so badly: the printing is lovely, some of the tail-pieces beautiful.... It is a strangely empty feeling to have finished with it, after … nine years."[15] *Seven Pillars of Wisdom,* the product of vast labor and torment, three inches thick, weighing six and a half pounds, bound in the best goatskin or pigskin by the best London binders, had no author's name on the title page or binding. On December 8, 1926, the unnamed author boarded a troopship for India.

8

India,
1927–1928

During the month's voyage to India, Lawrence read *War and Peace* again ("very good: but not more-than-human, as I first thought"), all of Pepys's *Diary* ("What a poor earth-bound lack lustre purblind worm"), *Ecclesiastes,* and Synge's *The Aran Islands*.[1] Notes he made on board the sea-sickened *Derbyshire* manifest his undue interest in filth and decay, in

> the smell of stabled humanity: the furtive creeping ... along the alleyway of the women to their latrine ... awash with a foul drainage.... [The Orderly Officer] strides boldly to the latrine.... 'God ... flooded with shit....' He ... ripped out a grating ... ordure rippled over his boots ... [thrust his hand] deep in, groped, pulled out a moist white bundle.... 'You'd think they'd have had some other place for their sanitary towels....' He shook his sleeve down ... while the released liquid gurgled contentedly down its re-opened drain.[2]

From the Karachi port, he took a train to the RAF base on Drigh Road, seven miles off. The desert country had "all sorts of haunting likenesses" to Arabia, "pack-donkeys, the colour and cut of men's clothes, an oleander bush in

flower..., camel-saddles, tamarisk." It was "a waste of sand and sandstone, with a plentiful stubble of cactus on its flat parts.... Over it blow hot and cold winds, very heavily laden with dust.... The camel-bells sound just like a water-tap dripping, drop, drop, drop, into a deep cistern."[3]

Compared to Uxbridge, Drigh Road was a holiday resort. Lawrence rose at 6:00, breakfasted, worked 7:30 to 1:00, and was free the rest of the day plus Thursdays and Sundays. Airmen had no hot water, so he used a blowtorch to heat enough for his indispensable baths. (Later, he poached on a power line to rig up a device that heated 14 gallons in 30 minutes.) He performed his chores diligently, indeed with excessive care, swept two rooms daily, searched for "mosquitoes, flies, ants, beetles, and bugs," and attacked them with spray and creosote.[4] Insects in inaccessible crevices of his cot he disposed of by taking the metal frame outdoors and heating it with the blowtorch. "He would polish his buttons and boots religiously, and cleaning the windows at his end of the room seemed to afford him pleasure."[5]

In India, even lowly airmen were a superior caste; natives did most chores, a practice Lawrence disliked. "I do wish, hourly, that our great Imperial heritage of the East would go the way of my private property." Yet he had no urge to spur reform. "I don't see myself following my inclination to stand, hat in hand, before every educated Indian, and murmur that it isn't my fault; that I'm not ... a deliberate cog of the governmental machine."[6] (What else was he?) He kept to the spacious base, over a mile square, walking and exercising there, and did not visit Karachi once.

Lawrence worked in the engine repair shops as a messenger and clerk. "I follow the course of each engine which comes in ... and note ... all that is done to it, by each man, by name, with what new parts..., what results it gives on test, and how many hours its rebuilding and adjustment occupy ... aero-engines have to 'come down' ... after 200 hours running, for complete overhaul."[7] His reports on engine maintenance had "a definite polish, not to say ornateness."[8] He behaved correctly and with deference to officers; most came to know his identity. When possible, he avoided them. The unnatural situation could produce a confrontation. One episode he related: "'But it wasn't a grin on my face, Sir. I was half-smiling, in recognition that we are playing a game by its rules....' 'Case dismissed...'—and he warned me.... 'Do it, and don't think about yourself so much.'"[9] The adjutant allowed Lawrence to use the Orderly Room and typewriter on Thursdays, one of his few privileges.

Two years earlier, Lawrence had contemplated a life that would be compulsory 24-hours a day. Now he had so much leisure he could be bored and was prompted to renewed literary activity. He might read three books a day, and asked friends to send him books and records— and to put a low value on the customs declaration, to reduce the duty. Soon he had

150 books on hand, in a year 250, some with valuable inscriptions; they circulated freely and often disappeared. As 17 of his 22 shillings weekly pay was held up for five months, he rationed his postage. G. B. Shaw brought Lawrence's penury to Prime Minister Baldwin's attention in an unsuccessful effort to get him a government pension. With fellow airmen, Lawrence was soft-spoken, direct, helpful. He volunteered for work they shirked, like Christmas guard duty. After pay arrears were rectified, he was relatively well off, since he bought little but stamps, records, and books. Before pay day, when many were broke, he lent small sums for cigarettes and food. He got a comrade to buy the best gramophone in Karachi and often listened to music.

Three Books on "Lawrence"

Lawrence had left England just in time to escape the *Daily Telegraph's* serialization of *Revolt in the Desert,* which started December 15. Released in March, over 40,000 copies were sold in three weeks. By July, 90,000 copies had been printed and Lawrence stopped further British sales; they continued in the United States, where 120,000 copies had already been sold. The trust Lawrence established received £13,000 in royalties from Cape (15% on the first 2,000 copies, 20% thereafter) and £4,000 from other sources; thus his overdraft was paid off with money to spare.

Lawrence had become John Hume Ross in 1922 and Thomas Edward Shaw in 1923. To him, "Lawrence" signified his meretricious role in Arabia, the unreal figure Lowell Thomas had created, and, above all, the coupling of his unwed parents. In subscribers' *Seven Pillars,* he initialled "Complete copy TES" in India ink. Yet "Shaw" was known to few persons, whereas "T. E. Lawrence," "Colonel Lawrence," and "Lawrence of Arabia" were known throughout the world. "T. E. Lawrence" was the name in the December 1923 notice soliciting subscribers, the name they were told to write on their checks, the name that sold *Revolt in the Desert*. At his insistence, the title page had single quotation marks around 'T. E. LAWRENCE'. They were dropped on the jacket; the inside fold spoke of "Colonel Lawrence" and "Lawrence"; the jacket back advertised a new edition of Doughty's *Travels in Arabia Deserta* "With Introduction by T. E. Lawrence."

To keep the profitable name alive after *Revolt* sales stopped and draw some of the market from Lowell Thomas's *The Boys' Life of Lawrence of Arabia,* published September 1927 in England, Cape commissioned a biography from Robert Graves (whom Lawrence chose for the purpose). Given two months to write,[10] Graves relied heavily on information Lawrence provided, paraphrased much of *Revolt,* and, to Lawrence's displeasure, added points drawn from an Oxford Text copy he borrowed from Eric Kennington. *Lawrence and the Arabs,* issued in November, sold 60,000 copies in six weeks. Lawrence could never rid himself of the name he abhorred; his mother and brothers bore it and it was cut into his gravestone. However, in June 1927, he told his solicitor, "I want to change my name formally.... I'd better be Thomas Edward Shaw in future."[11] The change was effected by deed poll on August 30.

The change made Lawrence more open, even forward, about disclosing his illegitimacy to friends and correspondents, if not the general public. Lowell Thomas, Robert Graves, and, in 1934, Basil Liddell Hart, not to mention David Hogarth and Ronald Storrs, who wrote short biographical sketches for reference works, maintained discreet silence. Some friends had known during the war; more knew by 1924; and, in 1927, in a series of letters, Lawrence referred explicitly to his illegitimacy or, less explicitly, to that of the name "Lawrence."

Writing Ventures

When Francis Yeats-Brown, literary editor of *The Spectator,* asked Lawrence to review books on the Near East in 1926, he declined with false excuses. "I have not written anything since I enlisted.... In barracks it would be quite impossible. Indeed, it's very seldom I can bring myself to answer a letter." Now, approached by Evelyn Wrench, the editor, he agreed to review "poems..., biography, criticism, novels of the XXth. Cent." anonymously, under the initials "C. D." "I'm not ambitious, financially ... and not proud, critically: for I've never imagined that my writing was any good."[12] He reviewed D. H. Lawrence, Hakluyt, Guedalla, H. G. Wells; rewrote a review of E. M. Forster's *Aspects of the Novel* twice and decided it was "not good enough."[13] Yeats-Brown thought the reviews "extraordinarily acute"; publisher Martin Secker wanted C. D. to write a book on D. H. Lawrence; Wells called the review of his short stories "the most interesting ... he had ever seen."[14] No matter: Lawrence insisted the D. H. Lawrence review was "no good. By nature I wasn't meant to write." Of the other reviews, he said, "I can't write," "it isn't worth printing," "one doesn't write good reviews merely by being interested in books." He stopped reviewing, later telling James Hanley, "I've tried reviewing. It pays, it distracts the mind, it irritates. Finally it disgusts."[15]

In 1924, Jonathan Cape had asked Lawrence to write a memoir of Charles Doughty. He asked again in February 1926, a month after Doughty died. Lawrence declined and David Hogarth undertook the work. Then, in November 1927, Hogarth died. Hogarth had helped to arrange Lawrence's first trip to Syria, had been his superior at Carchemish and the Arab Bureau, his mentor and friend thereafter; Lawrence had enormous regard for him as a scholar and a man. "Hogarth was a very wonderful man.... I owed him everything I had since I was 17." "He was ... the only person to whom I had never to explain the 'why' of what I was doing." "A great loss: the greatest, ... probably, that I'll ever have to suffer."[16] Cape now asked Lawrence to complete the Doughty biography. Lawrence agreed reluctantly, if the work could be done at Drigh Road anonymously, without reference books or original letters and documents. "I will not sign anything, whether a revise or an explanatory note." Fortunately, Hogarth's son William relieved him of the task. Hogarth's widow Laura said, "I am utterly dependent on you to write an introduction," but Lawrence did not write one.[17]

That fall, he had dysentery and felt tired for several weeks. The flies were so bad he stopped evening walks and cut down on food. His eyes troubled him so much he gave up reading for a time; he complained about his hearing and still nursed his right wrist, which had been broken in England. Others found Karachi hot; not Lawrence: "I am always shivering and catching colds."[18] Despite these ailments, he increased his workday four hours, doing two jobs and "trying to do them very exactly: just so as to leave me less strength & time and excuse for my own maunderings." His usual bedtime was 9:30. "My bed-fellows tell me that I cry in bed ... in the early hours of the night before they go to sleep.... [He lay awake later much of the night.] Always I'm wanting to cry, out here."[19]

In mid–1927, Lawrence was receiving over thirty letters a week, though Robert Graves, at his request, screened and discarded many; he replied to twenty and could tire of the labor. "Ninety percent ... are about ... business things, of which I care nothing whatever." He answered one in three (two in three, two sentences ago!) and that was "too much. It taxes my spare time valuelessly: for my opinions and ideas are not useful to anyone else, and it is no pleasure to me to put them on paper." Lawrence made a point of unloading his despair on his mother. "Life with me is much the same, from week to week, or from year to year: in camp at Farnborough, ... Bovington, or ... Drigh Road. One room is like another, ... and one airman is like another airman.... We stay still, and are physically taken care of, like stock cattle."[20]

Charlotte Shaw

If Lionel Curtis bore the burden of Lawrence's emotions at Uxbridge, Charlotte Shaw bore them in India. The playwright's childless, celibate wife, independently wealthy and independent-minded, had been seized by the Oxford Text—"I am carried off my feet by it!"[21] Thereafter, she seized on Lawrence and engaged him in an extraordinary correspondence that persisted until his death. During his two years in India, he wrote her 111 letters.[22] Charlotte was 65, Lawrence 33, when they met; in early 1927, they were 70 and 38. Theirs was something of a mother-son relation. After Charlotte's death, Bernard, reading her diary and letters, realized "there were many parts of her character that even I did not know, for she poured out her soul to Lawrence."[23] That happened with Lawrence: he could sense unspoken feelings and thoughts and capture some people without trying; if they thrust too close, he kept a set distance; no one captured him.

Charlotte offered to proofread *Seven Pillars;* thereafter, she read, proofed, and might comment on everything Lawrence wrote. She sent him books, records, chocolates, fancy foods (China tea, foie gras, marrons glacés, cake, peach-fed hams) that his comrades enjoyed. During three months of 1925, she posted twelve parcels of books and records to Bovington. The river of presents and letters flowed on to India, augmented by a notebook on the life philosophy of James P. Mills and reviews of *Revolt* and Graves's biography. Lawrence requested particular gifts. "My conscience smites me for asking you to send me that book by Wyndham Lewis.... If I choose to be poor, it is an essential condition of my self-respect ... to ... not sponge on my better-off friends." Half-heartedly, he tried to slow the flow. "Habits are chains. Break their sequence at times. Then I shall be surprised and pleased when they come, and you won't get bored sending them."[24] Lawrence refused gifts from others, pleading that he could not afford the duty. He told his mother he had instructed the post office to deliver no parcels or registered mail. But he asked Charlotte for records and books.[25]

To counterbalance her bounty, Lawrence gave Charlotte a copy of the Oxford Text, a magnificently bound *Seven Pillars* (this gold-tooled copy, with a seven-page, handwritten essay on Lawrence by Bernard Shaw, is now in the New York Public Library rare book room), a wartime notebook and diary, a hand-copied compilation of his favorite "minor" poems (published in 1971 as *Minorities*), Augustus John's famous sketch of him in Arab headdress, a clean manuscript of *The Mint,* the *Odyssey* manuscript and book.

Charlotte's father was Anglo–Irish, like Lawrence's, and her mother, like his, was domineering. Each sought to escape their mother. "I have a terror of her know-

Charlotte Shaw (mid–1920s): she and Lawrence exchanged many confessional letters (courtesy of the National Trust and the London School of Economics).

ing anything about my feelings." Lawrence wrote. "If she knew they would be damaged, violated, no longer be mine.... Arnie ... and I ... avoid her as our first rule of existence.... In all her letters she tells me she is old and lonely, and loves only us; and begs us to love her ... she makes Arnie and me profoundly unhappy ... because we cannot turn on love to her ... like a water-tap."[26]

"I've not written any letters of this sort to anyone else, since I was born," Lawrence said. Yet, in the midst of these impassioned confessions, he burned Charlotte's letters and told her so. "Lately I have, regretfully, destroyed many letters of yours: with a feeling that you would not like them shown to strangers: yet they are first class, as pictures of today, and historically valuable."[27] Lawrence had a penchant for burning. He burned a youthful manuscript on seven Eastern cities, a *Seven Pillars* manuscript, a French translation, a *Mint* manuscript, and often wished to burn other writings. The burning warned Charlotte: *Keep your distance!* Lawrence tried to excuse it. "I do not want you to feel that in burning your letters I'm doing anything wanton. It's not that.... They could not be shown to anybody else.... Nor can I keep them safely: what place have I where to keep anything?" (In the box beneath his cot where he kept *Seven Pillars*; or he could have returned them for safekeeping.)[28]

Three months later, he touched on the crime again. "I think my books do me an injustice.... I wish I'd burned them ... and whenever I come across an old letter, I wish the owner had burned that, too."[29] Charlotte, who saved Lawrence's letters, disagreed. "I think T.E. meant his letters to be published," she wrote a friend after reading David Garnett's collection.[30]

The Mint

Lawrence examined his Uxbridge notes before starting the *Spectator* reviews. He had tried to organize them at Clouds Hill; now he resumed the task. "Photographic, not artistic," he called the style. Progress was slow, sometimes retrograde: in August he said a third was done; in September, a quarter! "There is no trace of me in it...," he told Edward Garnett quite wrongly.[31] The words and topics reflect their author's perceptions and feelings like a mirror, as Lawrence later recognized. "It ... shocks & grieves me that I should ... have so given myself away. One lives decently, and keeps the lid on—to what end, if one takes the lid off and spills the pot into a book?" He came to feel that "Both *The Seven Pillars* and *The Mint* (*The Mint* especially) stink of personality."[32]

By March, the short, 70,000-word manuscript was ready. It was written four times: as notes, then pencil, type, and ink drafts. Doubtless, parts went through additional drafts: Lawrence could not leave a sentence alone. And the manuscript was much lengthened; the original notes were only 15,000 words. The work was startlingly original—"I've never read any other book of exactly the same character," Lawrence remarked—though, when published in 1955, many critics felt its time had passed. "If *The Mint* had been published in the 1920s ... it could have won Lawrence new fame as a literary innovator."[33]

Lawrence copied the manuscript in his clear hand and posted it to Edward Garnett via Charlotte Shaw, who had already seen four-fifths—all but the last part on Cranwell. He told Garnett the manuscript was sent "by an official bypass, for safety; as there is no copy," whereas Charlotte Shaw, hardly "an official," had a copy of most of it and Lawrence had the rest. (A few days later, he told Garnett, "Mrs. Shaw has seen some of it.")[34] Lawrence gave Charlotte conspiratorial instructions on wrapping and mailing. "Do not let Garnett know where it comes from ... and post it from London, not Ayot. I am asking E.G. not to lend it anyone except his son David: and he is more likely to do as I wish, if he does not know that you have seen it. This book must be kept secret."[35] More likely, the reason for this machination was to enhance the likelihood that those who knew would not talk about it. *The Mint* was a devastating attack on RAF training and officers; no matter how much Lawrence extolled Trenchard and the RAF, that fact was obvious. If the press reported it, an uproar would ensue. So there were good grounds for secrecy.

Nonetheless, Lawrence was dishonest with Garnett, involved Charlotte in his deceit, and did not tell her Trenchard would see the manuscript. Wilson finds it "curious that he should so casually have deceived two of his friends"—two of his best friends. "The truth appears to be that he had become an extremely isolated person, and after Hogarth's death there was no one he trusted completely"[36] Lawrence was too clever by half or, as Tolstoy said of Bernard Shaw, "clever-foolish." He neglected the fact that distrust, once aroused, is hard to dispel; that friends talk; that many knew one another; that he was a choice subject of gossip. He promoted talk by his insatiable desire to learn what others thought of *The Mint*. For safety's sake, Garnett prepared a few typescripts; before long, many persons read it, most at Lawrence's request.[37]

If they did not know of the deceit while he lived, his friends learned of it a month after when twelve met in London to discuss a memorial. One suggested publication of his secret book. "Lawrence had told him about this book on the understanding that he was not to whisper a word … to anybody else. Of course, we soon discovered that Lawrence had mentioned the book to each one of us on the same promise."[38]

During his stay in India, Lawrence and Trenchard exchanged friendly letters. Lawrence had given him a copy of *Seven Pillars* inscribed, "Sir Hugh Trenchard from a contented, admiring and, whenever possible, obedient servant." Acknowledging the gift "from the most disobedient mortal I have ever met," Trenchard asked Lawrence to let him know if he was unhappy "so that if necessary I can bring you home."[39] He repeated the offer several times.

When Lawrence told him about *The Mint,* Trenchard expressed his worry, even before reading it, that "it would be seized upon immediately by the Press *if they got hold of it,* and they would say what a hopeless Air Force it was." He met with Edward Garnett, who probably did not ease his concern. If *The Mint* were published, Trenchard told Lawrence, "I should hate

it, and I should feel my particular work of trying to make this force would be irretrievably damaged." He accepted Lawrence's contention that RAF recruits "have been … relatively better than the officers," but "both officers and other ranks are improving."[40] Lawrence had no intention to publish; he told Trenchard that and, in a will-like letter, asked his brother Arnold not to publish it before 1950 without permission of the RAF chief.[41] *The Mint* was published by Cape in expurgated form in 1955 and unexpurgated, in 1973. Cape considered publishing it in 1940, but decided not to. Capt. H. H. Balfour, Under-Secretary for Air, objected because it might generate criticism of the RAF during the Battle of Britain.

The real danger of publicity was a news story that might arise from typescript readers. Garnett futilely warned Lawrence that if *The* Mint were to remain secret, G. B. Shaw should not see it, because of his propensity to talk.[42] Lawrence proposed to deal with a story about the book by denying its existence. "If notes appear in the papers saying that I've written … a book about the R.A.F. … please deny it, on my behalf," he told Raymond Savage, his literary agent; and, "If it comes out in some literary gossip column … please … slap a letter in the next issue, saying that you … are authorised … to deny categorically that I have written … anything more."[43]

Many of Lawrence's friends were appalled by *The Mint's* obscenities and brutalities. Edward Marsh "was battered and oppressed by the monotonous thuddng hailstorm of *gros mots.*"[44] G. B. Shaw acknowledged its "literary power," but deemed it an indecent, unpublishable document that should be deposited in a library, barred to general readers but accessible to specialists. He urged Lawrence to remove or revise the description of old Queen Alexandra, which struck him as cruel ("the mummied thing, the bird-like head cocked on one side ... by disease, ... the enamelled face, which the famous smile scissored across all angular and heart-rending.... The body should not be kept alive after the lamp of sense has gone out"). "Would you like to read a similar description of your mother?"[45]

Ronald Storrs was dismayed by the "almost epileptic obscenity." John Buchan called it "extraordinary" and hoped it would never be published, "for it is too cruel an exposition of the sufferings of a highly-strung man." He praised Lawrence's "visualising and observing powers" as "perfectly uncanny" but "The language ... makes much of it unpublishable, and, indeed, unprintable." That was "right and proper enough in a personal journal," not a public book. "If I want to write about a stammering man I do not make all his conversation a stammer, but reserve it for the significant moment!"[46] The "account of the prolonged torture of the individual" shocked David Garnett. *Seven Pillars* had made Lawrence a hero to him; now, Lawrence "seemed ... an enemy of life."[47]

Unlike G. B. Shaw, Charlotte was deeply impressed by *The Mint*; reading it, she wrote Lawrence, "finally confirms ... my seasoned opinion that you take your place among the greatest of writers ... this thing has stirred me to the very depths of my being." Siegfried Sassoon called Lawrence "an extraordinary writer."[48] Herbert Read thought *The Mint* better than *Seven Pillars*, which he had severely criticized, more sincere and true.[49] E. M. Forster judged it "not as great ... as The Seven Pillars" but "more new, more startling and ... heartening." Edward Garnett was smitten. "It is a most *perfect* piece of writing ... a *classic*.... There's nothing like it in the least in English." In the Cranwell section, however, "you grow a little sententious in your Airman propaganda."[50] Other literary readers had a similar, partly political reaction. Regarding the RAF as an instrument of death and destruction, they liked the account of its brutalities, not splendors. Unconvinced by Cranwell's "comforting bath water," Forster hoped the book might "hinder the recrudescence of cruelty" in the military. David Garnett did not like *The Mint's* "war-spirit ... of 1915" (when he had been a conscientious objector). Insofar as it indicted the air force, H. M. Tomlinson thought it was marvelous. "Come over & help us!"[51]

Perhaps because *The Mint* was slighter than *Seven Pillars* or its style was so different, Lawrence slighted it less, at times even praised it. "I ... found it good prose.... Oh I wish I hadn't written it!" he told Charlotte Shaw and, receiving a glowing letter from her, boasted, "There never was, I fancy, such stuff put on paper before—or is this the vanity of every author?"[52] With Edward Garnett, he was harsher. "I know it's no good: but I don't like people to say so." "[I]t's pretty second-rate."[53] A year later, he told—or pled with—A. P. Wavell (not a literary man): "Its the work of my maturity ... and surely parts of it are powerful.... At least it is better done, better written, better proportioned [than *Seven Pillars*]."[54]

"A Wing-Crippled Duck"

Lawrence planned far ahead. He hoped to extend his enlistment to 1935 but thought of alternatives if an extension was denied and he had to leave in 1930. The thoughts may be ridiculous but they were earnest: all aimed at mindless labor isolated from society. "I'll try & get some quiet job, near London.... A night-watchman, door-porter, or ... chauffeur." Like service in the ranks, the last two betray a wish for repeated public humiliation. As night-watchman he could "work at night and sleep by day ... for I am solitary by nature."[55] He asked Robin Buxton and

Herbert Baker, who had designed the new Bank of England building, to help; Baker discussed it with the pertinent bank committee, so the watchman's job was a serious possibility. Lawrence described its attractions to G. B. Shaw: "[N]obody would meet me, or hear of me, much…. You come on duty as the last clerk goes…. You come off duty when the first comer opens the door in the morning." Unable to credit Lawrence's present life or future plan, Shaw had asked "What is your game *really?*" Lawrence replied, "You see, I'm all smash, inside: and I don't want to look prosperous or be prosperous, while I know that. And on the easy level of the other fellows in the R.A.F. I feel safe…. Only please don't think it is a game, just because I laugh at myself and everybody else. That's … an attempt to keep sane."[56]

In August 1927, Lawrence was 39, Shaw, 71, yet Shaw had more exuberance or, to use a Shavianism, life force. Lawrence seemed played out, tired, old; his letters speak of his weariness and aging, a sense of defeat, a readiness to close up shop. "Here in Karachi I not merely feel old, but am old," he tells Eric Kennington. "If only it were all over." He dwells on his war wounds like a legless veteran in a retirement home. "I was wounded in nine different scraps (sometimes two or three damages at once: I have about 50 scars tallied on me) and had two attacks of dysentery, besides a touch of typhoid, blackwater, and much malaria: not to mention five broken bones…. I over-exerted myself…, for I've never felt much good since."[57] "The languor deepens…," he tells Charlotte Shaw. "…always I watch myself for signs of a sudden breaking-down: one leg falling off, and white hair or baldness, and a mouthful of shed teeth…" He tells ailing David Hogarth, who died four months later, "I've turned … the corner into middle age: hair going white … and my eyesight and hearing both giving me trou-

ble…"[58] He feels like "a wing-crippled duck" and, though "I'm not consciously dying yet," sends his brother Arnold instructions about his property, copyrights, solicitor, and trustees.[59]

Lawrence's letters from Drigh Road show little joy, much weariness, and depression. "I'm like a squeezed orange." "I'm a toad rolled out under a steam roller." "[I]nside me is too vacant a place to take much exploring."[60] An airman thought Lawrence "must have experienced great loneliness…. Although his usual demeanour was one of consistent calm, marked occasionally by flashes of quiet and subtle humour, he would seem sometimes to be oppressed and utterly cast down." The camp adjutant felt "tremendous sympathy and pity" for him.[61]

John Mack thinks the letters from Karachi "reveal an increasing nihilism and self-disparagement"; Jeremy Wilson, that they "show an increasingly high morale." "He had settled in very well and was happy in Karachi."[62] Thus, Lawrence's two best biographers reach opposite conclusions from the same evidence. I agree with Mack. I see no sign that Lawrence was happy (nor does Wilson present any) and much evidence of nihilism, self-castigation, and weariness. He expresses homesickness and a wish to return to England, but feels further exile is prudent. Wilson says he "was now weary of his purposeless existence in the ranks."[63] There I agree. He was weary of barrack life in India but would not end it.

Miranshah

Lawrence's reception at a base—the degree to which he was accepted or harried—depended substantially on the base commander. Commander Guilfoyle's hostility had led to his expulsion from Farnborough. Something similar impended at

Drigh Road. Suspicious of Lawrence's correspondence with RAF brass (he was writing to Sir Geoffrey Salmond, head of the RAF in India, as well as Trenchard), the commander asked his adjutant to inquire. Lawrence showed him letters from the Air Marshalls, "both obviously private affairs." The commander, who had clashed with Lawrence in 1916, was not satisfied; "so I was sent for, cursed, and condemned to go up-country as a Bolshevik."[64] By happenstance, Salmond visited Drigh Road the next day. He halted the transfer and removed the commander. However, four months later, when a conflict with the new commander seemed to be brewing, Lawrence thought it best to leave. Earlier, he had hoped not to be posted to the Northwest Frontier. Now, he asked Salmond to send him there and, at the end of May, went to Miranshah, a small station ten miles from Afghanistan.

Miranshah was a brick-and-mud fort, 400 yards square, with an airstrip outside on the 3,000-foot-high plain; 5 British officers, 21 airmen, and 700 Indian troops manned the fort, protected by barbed wire, towers, searchlights, machine guns, and planes. Britons and Indians had separate quarters and seldom met. "Round us ... are low bare porcelain-coloured hills, with ... a broken-bottle skyline ... the quietness is so intense that I rub my ears, wondering if I am going deaf."[65] The fort had no settled commander; three or four air squadrons flew in for two months, in rotation; the commander of each flight served as base commander.

The planes patrolled the border. When he could cadge a seat, Lawrence rode along. An airman asked why he did not become a pilot. Lawrence said he would have to become an officer, which he would never do again.[66] The previous October, he had been automatically promoted to Aircraftsman 2, but further promotion required passing

an educational exam that he would not take.

When he first went to Syria, Lawrence found 90° too warm; at Karachi, he was comfortable at 100° and felt the 90° daytime temperature positively cool. Miranshah was cooler—in winter, cold. As keeper of the stores, he distributed the limited stock of blankets, taking only one; he asked a Drigh Road friend who flew in to bring him another. He worked as a clerk-typist, rewriting and filing reports, letters, duty rolls, and daily routine orders. He also served as librarian of the small camp collection, which grew as his books arrived from Drigh Road and new books came from England. His record player and most records were left behind but, on August 16, a fine new gramophone arrived as a birthday present from Charlotte and Bernard Shaw. Lawrence, who had mentioned the loss of his machine, thanked them: "it is a lovely thing, everything the heart of any man in camp could wish."[67]

With each type of literary work he tried—historical-autobiographical, translations, reviews, introductions—Lawrence was at first enthusiastic, then progressively aggravated, disgusted, and condemnatory. That was the case with his 1923 French translations; but, constraining creative latitude, translating retained an appeal. "Translating is an ingenious game, very exciting for a man who has no originalities of his own to express."[68] Lawrence considered translating several French titles for Cape and at least one for F. N. Doubleday. In October 1928, after a correspondence that Ralph Isham initiated the previous December, he contracted to translate the *Odyssey* for Bruce Rogers, the eminent American book designer, for £800, a substantial sum at the time. Because of his endless rewriting, the translation repeated, to a degree, the painful labor of *Seven Pillars*. (The pain would have been greater had Rogers not managed the book's production and sale.) The work occupied Lawrence, intermittently, until August 1931.

Lawrence had insisted that the translation be anonymous. "There will, as you rightly say, be no interest in the book, except as typography," he wrote Rogers, who noted, "I have no recollection of ever saying this."[69] By the end of June 1928, Lawrence completed the first of the *Odyssey's* 24 books and mailed it—"the sixth copying out"—as a sample. It took him over 100 hours. Satisfied, Rogers sent a draft contract, observing that, though he and his partners would keep Lawrence's anonymity, it was almost impossible to ensure it permanently. "You are very much mistaken, I think, in assuming that no one will be interested in the ... translation."[70] Lawrence merely added a clause "in which the publishers ... agree not to publish my name (any of my names!) in conjunction with this English edition ... without my permission." Always keenly interested in book composition and printing, he was pleased to be dealing with master book makers, for Emery Walker, who had worked with the Kelmscott and Dove presses, and his partner Wilfred Merton, were associated with Rogers in this project. "If you want a synopsis you shall have one for each book.... Also ... book-headings, or page headings.... It is for you to tell me." By Christmas, when he mailed Books II and III, Lawrence had put in 500 hours on the first three books, about 28 words an hour.[71]

It is hard to read Lawrence's mood at Miranshah from his letters, he disguises it so well. It could be hard to read even when you saw him: Arnold Lawrence remarked that he could appear cheerful when depressed. An episode he told Charlotte Shaw shows his ability to hide his feelings. "Mr. Russell [a Miranshah commander] is gone. As he went he said to me, 'If ever you feel you want another change, ... there is a place for you in "C" flight.' I am proud that he never saw how fed up with him I was."[72] At times his spirit seems to lift. In December, he tells Trenchard, "I'm happy at odd times," and E. M. Forster, "We have had an idyllic two and a half months.... In August & September it was horrible."[73] At times, he seems downcast and world-weary. "Not a kick in the entire body.... I am cheerful: but that's a long way from growth ... & I am so tired."[74] Lawrence describes a little bird in a funny, scatological, confessional way:

> I have a bird: it looks like a sparrow. It nests ... over my shelf of files. A dirty bird: I have brought in a varnished fabric cover to shield the files from its droppings. A misanthropic bird; a solitary bird: a silent bird. It comes in at sunset & departs at dawn.... Plop plop.... Our bombing machines can only drop six bombs, at full war load. This my sparrow puts the R.A.F. to shame.... Since sunset it has made eleven hits.[75]

Lawrence expected to spend two years at Miranshah, but his stay was abruptly terminated by the inexpungeable inanities of tabloids and governments.

In September 1928, the London *Evening News* ran, under the headline LAWRENCE OF ARABIA'S SECRET MISSION, a preposterous story about Lawrence, "in disguise," spying on "Bolshevik agents" in Amritsar. The *Sunday Express* reported that Lawrence, "concealed beneath a mocha stain and ... turban and robes," was on a secret mission in Afghanistan laying the ground for a treaty with Britain. Events like those in Evelyn Waugh's *Scoop* escalated this nonsense. In November, a tribal revolt broke out in Afghanistan; Afghan and Soviet (not to mention British and U.S.) newspapers embroidered the *Sunday Express* story; the British ambassador to Afghanistan asked permission to deny that Lawrence was in or near the country. In London, socialists burned an effigy of Lawrence; in India, hostile officials wanted him removed; the ambassador concurred. So, reluctantly, did Trenchard. He asked Geoffrey Salmond to learn if Lawrence preferred Singapore, Aden, Somaliland, or home. Choosing home, he was flown to Lahore and on January 12, 1929, took ship for England.[76]

9

Seas and Shores,
1929–1935

Lawrence left Bombay January 12, installed in a comfortable 2nd-class cabin on the *S.S. Rajputana*. During three weeks on the nearly empty liner, he read a lot and translated three books of the *Odyssey*—as many as in seven months at Miranshah. To his annoyance, the Egyptian police did not let him off the ship at Port Said to see his friend Lord Lloyd, High Commissioner for Egypt. However, he chatted with Lloyd's 16-year-old son David, who came aboard bound for Eton. "A bit grim for the kid, to be inspected by his father's friends.... Have you been stuffing the poor child with Lowell-Thomas tales?" Lawrence asked Lloyd. "The contrast between my person & my reputation is grotesque.... I wish kids didn't have to grow up. They are so beautiful, unfinished."[1]

Arch imperialist spy Lawrence of Arabia was British newspaper fodder. Suspicious of his rumored activities in Afghanistan, Labor MP Ernest Thurtle had raised parliamentary questions about his use of a pseudonym in the RAF. Boatloads of reporters and photographers circled the *Rajputana* as passengers debarked at Plymouth. Loud headlines and a photo of Lawrence on a naval launch appeared in the press, publicity that Trenchard and Air Minister Hoare did not want. Nonetheless, starting a month's leave, Lawrence met Thurtle and two other Labor MPs in the House of Commons, hoping to dispel their suspicions. "His figure was small and his uniform unimpressive," Thurtle recalled, "but there was an almost devastating air of intelligence about him and a great poise of manner." He answered their questions "with great frankness and good humour," and explained his concern lest the questions about his name betray his illegitimacy. Thurtle felt "that his was a mind of a very unusual order indeed, and that his sense of values was more unusual still." Yet "there was something enigmatic about him."[2] To explain himself more fully, Lawrence lent Thurtle *Seven Pillars* and a *Mint* typescript.

The talk with opposition members and the press's follies taxed Hoare's patience and almost led to Lawrence's expulsion from the RAF. "Why must you be more of a damned nuisance than you need be?" Trenchard demanded. "To stop Thurtle and his friends from asking any more foolish questions about me," Lawrence replied. "I'm sorry if

I upset the Minister. But I think I succeeded." He did and Thurtle became a friend and a collaborator in seeking service reforms. "Will you please shut up the *Daily News*?" Lawrence asked, or instructed, Trenchard. "It goes on chattering, and a word from you to Sir Herbert Samuel, saying that it was my wish, would end the business. A silly rag of a paper."[3] Acts of this sort that he took in ensuing years show that, at least in his personal affairs, the old Lawrence who disdained custom and authority and could get things done was still alive.

From his familiar Westminster attic, Lawrence hunted up old friends, contacted new ones with whom he had corresponded from India, spent four days with his mother in the country near Reading, visited Clouds Hill, was given a new "apolaustic" motorbike, worried about a Lawrence of Arabia film that might be released in August, and puzzled over himself. "I wander about London with my eyes on the pavement." To a man who, like a cold-blooded animal, loved hot sun and warm baths—"heaven ... will be subtropical"— the damp English winter was dismayingly cold. "I am ... frozen to death. Ugh, Brrrrr etc. It is arctic."—"I wish England could be towed some thousand miles to the South."[4] In India, he had been homesick. In London, the excitement of being back and on leave quickly died and he yearned for his barrack prison. "I do not think I shall ever go on leave, for pleasure." "Something has gone wrong with the works: I can't wind myself up to meet people." The motorbike, worth three years' pay, was a gift from five friends, Charlotte Shaw contributing over two-thirds of the total. Lawrence insisted on repaying them.[5]

Plymouth

In March, Lawrence reported to Cattewater, the RAF station near Plymouth,

"a tiny station, on a rocky peninsula.... From my bed the sea lies 30 yards to the South ... and 60 yards to the North."[6] He had known station commander Sydney Smith in Cairo and Cranwell; they liked each other and got on well. Better than any other commander, Smith understood how to use Lawrence's talents and contacts while respecting his wish to be treated as a humble airman: it was not an easy relationship to define and maintain. Lawrence was welcomed into Smith's home, where he became the seventh member of the family, which included Smith's wife Clare, their 12-year-old daughter Maureen ("Squeak"), two golden retrievers, and a cocker spaniel.

There were 150 men at Cattewater (soon renamed Mount Batten), 50 of whom lived in town. Lawrence's duties were to clean the barracks in rotation with 19 men, daily drill, duty watch, inspecting moored seaplanes, and attaching lights to them in rough weather. He was Smith's clerk, secretary, minute-taker at meetings, and drafted station standing orders, daily routine orders, and all technical correspondence for his signature. Smith gave him an office and consulted him on matters involving airmen's comfort and effectiveness. The men liked and respected Lawrence, knew his identity and pointed him or his barracks out to visitors— "That's the hut where Colonel Lawrence lives!" As usual, he lent books, records, money, advice, and help, shared candy and delicacies, and stood duty for those who wanted a night off. "He'd get on the men's level, yet he kept that little bit of reserve," a comrade recalled.[7]

In April, when the popular magazine *John Bull* reported that Lawrence was translating *The Odyssey*, he wrote Bruce Rogers, "If I were free to do so, I'd like to return you your payment and cancel the whole business." As an alternative, he suggested finding "a ghost who will put his or her name to it, and accept the public responsibility for it." Rogers had warned Lawrence that he could guarantee only his own discretion. Lawrence had told many friends about the translation and, far worse, had shown *The Mint* to many people. "I don't suppose that one person in a thousand who reads ... *John Bull* ... had ... even heard of the *Odyssey*," Rogers replied. "These rumours ... will be forgotten before the book appears."[8]

The press exists to print, if necessary to invent stories. It was impossible to suppress every story about Lawrence of Arabia. *John O'London's Weekly* reported, "Colonel Lawrence is engaged on a new translation of Homer's 'Odyssey' for an American publisher. It will be published anonymously in the summer." A Vancouver paper announced that "Aircraftman Shaw, otherwise the famous Lawrence of Arabia, has undertaken to translate Homer's 'Odyssey'." Other publications picked up the story; "all the world has been told about it," Gwen Howard, Jonathan Cape's partner, informed Lawrence.[9]

T. E. Shaw shouldered the cross of T. E. Lawrence and soldiered on: "[A]s for choking off the Press—he will be my friend for life who finds how to do that. I do nothing—and they talk. I do something—and they talk."[10] His uniform and blank face were camouflage, but his presence in the Plymouth area was common knowledge, many photographs had appeared, many people recognized him, wherever he went he might be noticed. His massive Brough attracted as much attention as a diplomat's limousine. He was stared at and talked about. Children and adults asked for his autograph. Strangers wrote him. A letter from America addressed to "Lieutenant-Colonel T. E. Lawrence, London, England" was forwarded to "Aircraftman Shaw, Royal Air Force, Plymouth." An American dealer offered £20

for his letters. A photographer or reporter might waylay him anywhere. Someone was always threatening to produce a film about the Arab revolt: robed men riding camels across sand dunes to the rhythm of Wagner's Valkyries were bound to attract large audiences. Plymouth papers ran stories about Col. Lawrence/Pvt. Shaw: Sydney Smith put them in a scrapbook. Lawrence had all the privacy of a movie star in Piccadilly or a panda in the zoo. Some strangers who thrust themselves upon him it was impossible to escape.

One, sighting him in Plymouth, screamed "Aircraftman" from a car, phoned Commander Smith the next day, and was shown around the station. Neither Smith nor Lawrence could escape their MP: rich, rambunctious, American-born Lady Nancy Astor, the first woman to sit in the House of Commons, wife of *Observer* publisher Lord Astor, social whirlwind, mistress of the Cliveden estate, Plymouth and London homes, vast properties and wealth. She and Lawrence launched a bantering friendship and correspondence. Soon he said, "I do not know when, or with whom, I have ever maintained for so long so hot a correspondence,"[11] while his longer, more earnest correspondence with Charlotte Shaw, whom the Astors knew, continued.

Labor ousted the Conservatives in May 1929, giving Lawrence's new friend Ernest Thurtle added influence in his campaign to end the death penalty for cowardice in war. Supporting the cause, Lawrence gave Thurtle a sentence to advance it—"I have run too far too fast under fire ... to dare throw a stone at the fearfullest creature. You see, I might hit myself in the eye." He also proposed that, with several months' notice, service men be free to buy themselves out. This would "effect a revolution in the attitude of officers & N.C.O.s ... [and] modify discipline profoundly, for the good, by making it voluntary."[12]

He urged Trenchard to eliminate or reform such practices as the need to carry a bayonet and swagger stick, laying out clothes in kit inspection, assigning men to posts far from home, and compulsory Church attendance. "It is the trifles that irritate and do most harm." The most trifling reform, permitting the top two buttons of overcoats to be undone, was achieved first. Lawrence congratulated Trenchard and pressed him to continue the good work. "Don't rest on your laurels yet. Have a bayonet put in your IN tray every morning: and say to yourself 'I must get rid of that today'."[13] In time, most of the reforms were adopted.

"I hope you will come down [to Plymouth] before the end of July. I've a suggestion to make.... And one should get everything possible out of you in your last year," Lawrence wrote Trenchard, due to leave the RAF in December. As Trenchard did not visit, Lawrence wrote again. He wanted a new airship, R100 or R101, to detour southward on a trial flight to Karachi and fly over the 'Empty Quarter' of Arabia. "No European has ever crossed it, nor any Arab.... Nothing but an airship can do it, and I want it to be one of ours which gets the plum.... I do not ask to be let go, myself ... the important thing is to get it done."[14] Lawrence asked G. B. Shaw to speak to the new Air Minister, Lord Thomson, whom he knew, about the flight. Shaw sent a letter and imprudently suggested that Lawrence make the trip. Thomson, who had clashed with Lawrence in Paris, disliked the idea.

Near Expulsion

Lawrence's initiatives about this flight over Arabia, which he had foresworn any involvement in, and RAF reforms were a sign of his rising spirit due, perhaps, to Sydney Smith's care and grooming.

However, he was soon slapped down. Smith was responsible for arranging the Schneider Trophy international air race on a course around the Solent. The race was based at Calshot, on the coast south of Southampton, near Lawrence's boyhood home by the New Forest. As Smith's secretary, Lawrence joined him at meetings in London and Calshot and the September 7 race between British and Italian planes. During the event, attended by Prime Minister Ramsay MacDonald, Lord Thomson, Trenchard, and other dignitaries, Marshall Balbo, leader of the Italian crews, complained to Lawrence, whom he knew, about green scum on his slipway. Lawrence got it cleaned. Noting this, Thomson asked why he was doing it—and photographs of the two appeared in the newspapers. Thomson was annoyed.

He was annoyed again when Trenchard asked if Lawrence might join a pilot friend on a European seaplane tour. The answer was NO. "You must ... see me," Trenchard told Lawrence. When they met, he said Thomson had almost expelled him. He must "stop leading from the ranks," act like an airman, not an officer, not fly in any government plane or leave the country, and not speak to any "great" person—Churchill, Air Under Secretary Philip Sassoon, and Lady Astor were specified but not Thurtle or G. B. Shaw (who was peeved by the omission). Effectively quarantined, Lawrence stayed in camp for several months and put in more time on the *Odyssey*. The translation of Book IX, on the Cyclops, "is V.G." (very good) he tells Charlotte Shaw, while telling E. M. Forster that the translation will "crush flat to the ground and wither" his writing hopes. "It is impossible to reconcile such letters," Jeremy Wilson observes;[15] but it may be noted that Lawrence's harshest remarks about his writing were made to established writers, as if to forestall criticism by getting a stronger blow in first.

Lawrence refused George Lloyd's invitation to ride by camel across Arabia, which, during the war, they had agreed to do. The line or lines between self-effacement and advertisement that Lawrence drew on different occasions are beyond my comprehension. The mood of the moment seemed to govern. A month after rejecting Lloyd's invitation, he allowed publisher Peter Davies to issue a pamphlet promoting *Her Privates We,* a war novel by "Private 19022." The pamphlet reproduced a phone conversation with Davies in which Lawrence had identified the anonymous author as Frederic Manning from similarities with *Scenes and Portraits,* a much different, earlier work. Perhaps he regarded the pamphlet as inconsequential or, proud of his feat, let Davies use the proscribed name "Lawrence" to help a writer he admired. So he hid and advertised himself, calmed and provoked the Air Minister.

The truth is, Lawrence was obsessed with himself. He circulated *The Mint* widely because he was more interested in what readers thought of it and him than afraid of the possible publicity. In 1930, he almost had twelve copies printed, which would have broken his pledge to Trenchard and jeopardized his enlistment.[16] He conducted a large correspondence and might reply with surprising candor to strangers. "I'm very weary of being stared at and discussed and praised. What can one do to be forgotten?" he asked Jock Chambers. The answer was, *nothing.* He could not walk about London without being stopped by half a dozen people. At Mount Batten, his happiest station, his mood fluctuated between contentment, moroseness, and self-absorption. "Each morning he would stand alone—with his tea and rockcake—and stare through a window to the sea beyond. His gaze was intense, he seemed oblivious of his immediate surroundings."[17]

"Each time I leave camp now it is with regret. Inside the cage is home." "Some unformed impulse keeps me in camp," Lawrence wrote Henry Williamson, whom he had half-promised to visit. "I am always ... saying 'I will go out this week-end': and when the time comes ... I moon about ... in camp.... I feel afraid and hesitant outside.... I think I have only been outside three times this summer."[18]

What was wrong may have been too much peacefulness, an unappeased tension released a fortnight later by a fierce beating by John Bruce, swimming in the frigid North Sea, and punishing horse rides on the rocky Scottish coast at Collieston, north of Aberdeen. We do not know what replaced these ordeals during Lawrence's stay in India, but he arranged a ferocious beating before leaving England, upon returning, and in September 1929, when Bruce reported, "he came all the way from ... Plymouth, had breakfast and a flogging and caught the next train back." The worst beating was at Collieston. Two months later, Lawrence thanked David Garnett for the gift of a red-leather, seven-volume Nonesuch Shakespeare. His remarks about Shakespeare have a confessional flavor. "What a queer great man. Dimly I feel that something went so wrong with his life that he lost heart, foreswore London, and abandoned his work.... It could only be some internal vice."[19]

In February 1931, Lawrence was standing with Clare Smith drinking coffee and watching pontoon planes fire at targets at sea. As one plane began to descend, he said. "That plane looks queer." Instead of levelling off, it flew into the water, went under, and, minutes later, rose partly submerged. Sydney Smith appeared, not knowing what had happened. With his approval, Lawrence took charge, drove a motorboat to the scene, dove in to recover trapped men, and directed rescue efforts. Three men were saved, nine drowned including the officer at the controls.[20] "It was due to bad piloting on the part of a man who ... should never have flown with passengers," Lawrence said.

> It was horrible to see a huge Flying Boat so cast away by incompetence.... At the Enquiry ... I propose to say just what I saw ... to bring the responsibility home upon an Air-Marshall Webb-Bowen at the Air Ministry, who refused to listen to reports made to him on 3 separate occasions, regarding this officer's unfitness to fly ... such a case had better not happen again, and I have facts enough to prevent it happening again if I publish them.[21]

With Lady Astor's help, Lawrence steered a careful course to change Air Ministry rules on fitness to fly and air-sea rescue procedures and yet protect himself and Sydney Smith. He succeeded. His testimony was impeccably precise and factual. "The tail of the machine came up, her main planes crashed into the water and folded back together. The hull dived straight to the bottom, and the tail swung very slowly towards Batten breakwater, until it rested upside down only a few feet above the water." Lawrence described the hearing to Lady Astor: "The Coroner ... asked all the nibbly, difficult, hurtful questions, so innocently ... that everything came out.... They have set the reforms afoot.... I am watching very closely and will move another little lever or two when or if it is necessary.... I need hardly say how grateful I am to you for your help."[22]

Months before, a rich friend of Sydney Smith's had given him and Lawrence an American motorboat—they named it the *Biscuit*—that could do 46 m.p.h. That boat and the plane crash made Lawrence realize that the RAF lacked high-speed boats to reach a downed plane fast and save lives. Thus he found a cause, the development of fast, seaworthy craft, to occupy him.

Hythe

In March 1931, Lawrence went to Hythe for ten days' instruction in and testing of a new motorboat. The next month, he said, "My two-year war with the Air Ministry over the type of motor boats suited to attend seaplanes is bearing results now, and experimental boats are being offered by contractors."[23] The "two-year" war was overstated, but boats occupied, often consumed, Lawrence henceforth. Bucketing about in rough seas—the boats had to operate in all conditions—was tiring, the wind and spray hurt his eyes. Boat-testing nourished the "I am so tired" refrain in his letters.

As Lawrence grew more engaged in motor-boat trials, the settled routine at Mount Batten gave way to stays in a room near the Scott-Paine boat construction yard at Hythe, engine works in Wolverhampton, London offices, and RAF seaside stations. He might spend 12 hours daily at sea testing engines and boats, operating and maintenance procedures, target-towing, and delivering boats to coastal bases. In April 1931, he took a boat to Penzance; in June, to Plymouth; by November, he had driven 6,000 miles. In March 1932, he made a four-day, 740-mile trip from Calshot up the North Sea coast to Donibristle, Scotland, in very rough weather: the running time was only 35 hours.

The frequent moves made mail delivery late; reading, letter writing, and seeing friends grew difficult. "By evening my eyes are raw with salt-water and rheumy with wind, & I go to bed.... I have ... descended to *Tit-bits* and the *Happy Magazine*." "This work lasts till 8 or 9 at night. I then eat a little, and sit in a chair till 10:15, when I can decently go to bed. Letter-writing is not possible ... because I am dog-tired."[24]

Lawrence enjoyed working on these hard-chine boats that rose up and skimmed the water, handled and turned easily, and were stable in heavy seas. Quickly mastering the technicalities of boat and engine construction, operation, and maintenance, he suggested many mechanical improvements. An astonishingly detailed manual that he prepared on the boat's operation shows how completely he had grasped its components and vocabulary. Lawrence got on well with Hubert Scott-Paine, the boats' manufacturer, and used his contacts and manipulative talents to promote the boats' adoption by the Navy as well as the RAF. He was not, however, a designer or engineer and wrongly believed that large ships could be built on the same planning principle as these 37-foot craft.[25]

The *Odyssey* dragged. It was hard to find time and zeal for it, yet Lawrence would and could not give less than excessive attention to every word. "I never wrote (for printing) an easy line in my life. All my stuff is tenth-thoughts or twentieth-thoughts, before it gets out." Translation, he said, is "a feeling towards what the author would have said: and as Homer wasn't like me the version goes wrong whenever I let myself into it." By December 1930, he reached Book XX. "One grinds ... over each passage till the corrections begin to restore former readings."[26] All his spare time was spent on "fish-smelly Odysseus." He was fed up with "Homer's namby-pamby men and women." The crash inquiry interrupted work again. Would it never end? Bruce Rogers visited Lawrence in June, yet could not extract the last books. Lawrence apologized, but "I daren't skimp the last chapters.... It is better to be late than be careless."[27]

In July, he went on leave to the London attic where he had agonized over *Seven Pillars,* to rid himself of Homer. Working 17 hours a day, he finally finished and mailed the last two books. "I fancy that poor O-Homer threw his hand in at the end, rather as I did," he wrote Rogers. "So when you are disappointed with these two books, blame O-Homer as well as me."[28] Lawrence was still revising Book XXII in October. The revision might have continued if Emery Walker did not send whatever text he got to the Cambridge University Press for composition.

The limited edition *Odyssey,* issued in November 1932, is one of Rogers's most beautiful books. The pages have a clean, classical appearance and each chapter opens with Greek vase figures printed on a thick gold and black roundel. The chief failing is the inane lack of page numbers: Rogers said he could not think where to put them without spoiling the page! (He should have asked any schoolchild. None appear, either, in his two thin, lackluster volumes of Lawrence's letters.) Joseph Blumenthal, who was responsible for the 1973 Pierpont Morgan Library exhibition "Art of the Printed Book: 1455–1955," states: "During the several years spent in selecting the 112 books finally shown, I handled every title reputed ... to be among the finest volumes made ... since Gutenberg. I believe that the Bruce Rogers *Odyssey* is indisputably among the most beautiful books ever produced ... with a classic austerity..., Rogers created a masterpiece." Lawrence did not like it overmuch, preferring William Morris's richly decorated Kelmscotts. "The print [is] too delicate. The roundels neither true Greek nor new."[29]

Though refusing Cape's request for a British trade edition, Lawrence agreed to Oxford's U.S. trade edition and use of the name "T. E. Shaw" to help Rogers recoup his expenses on the limited edition. The full-page *Publishers Weekly* advertisement read "Translated by T. E. Shaw (Lawrence of Arabia)" and displayed a photo of Lawrence in Arab headdress. The *New York Times* headlined its full-page, lead review, "The Odyssey of Col. Lawrence."[30] Ralph Isham sent Lawrence an "I told you so" letter.

> The ODYSSEY is out and, God knows, so is your cherished secret regarding its translator. Of course it became obvious long ago that there was no secret.... Now, I notice, ... your name is prominent in every announcement and on every jacket of the book. I cannot pretend that I am not interested to know who brought about this change. It must have been some great master. Or was the whole idea merely the exercise of what someone has termed your "genius for stepping backward into the limelight"?

With surprising equanimity, Lawrence explained why he had allowed his name to be used. To the U.S. director of Oxford, he said, "I want you to realise that in accepting the use of my name upon your edition I am sacrificing what I regard as very important.... I shall be much more careful and exacting upon any future occasion."[31] Of course, no care would do. The quest for anonymity was a quest for *The Well at the World's End.*

In October 1931, Commander Smith was transferred from Mount Batten to Manston, the RAF base in Kent on the southeast coast. Clare Smith implored Lawrence to transfer with them but he declined. Her marriage was shaky and she loved Lawrence. He handled the situation well. Particular care was required at Mount Batten, where the two spent much time together. Upon Sydney Smith's departure, Lawrence gave him a copy of *Seven Pillars* inscribed "From T.E.S. to S.W.S. on dissolution of partnership."

Another Reprimand

Lord Thomson's death in an October 1930 air crash freed Lawrence from the restrictions on flying and meeting prominent politicians. Nonetheless his position as a humble yet influential airman who sought obscurity yet obtained and might solicit publicity remained equivocal and objectionable to many senior officials. In January 1932, a news story appeared on his boat testing. In March, he asked *Times* editor Geoffrey Dawson to send a reporter to write a story about the boats. "My name, of course, not to be mentioned." Two *Times* stories resulted. In August, *The Sunday Chronicle* ran a jazzier story headlined COLONEL LAWRENCE: MAN BEHIND BRITAIN'S PLANES, CARS, AND SPEEDBOATS. "Colonel Lawrence ... is now the uncrowned King of speed."[32]

This was too much for Air Ministry officials. Though not responsible for the story, Lawrence had prompted the *Times* reports and had pushed the development of high-speed boats for Air and Navy purposes: air-sea rescue, target towing, torpedo launching, ship-to-shore uses. Pulling strings, out-maneuvering bureaucrats, influencing the men at the top and their advisers was a sign of good health: and of conduct bound to aggravate Authority. Lawrence was ordered back to Mount Batten.

He got on tolerably well with but did not esteem the new station commanders (there were several in quick succession)[33] and regretted his removal from speed-boat work. The flu and other winter ailments increased his unhappiness. "*Very* tired again" with "fever and cold: and a sense of exhaustion," he did more reading, letter writing, and visiting friends.[34] He renewed contact with publishers (Cape, Greenwood, Frere-Reeves, Doubleday), urged Cape to publish Verner Von Heidenstam's novel *The Charlesmen,* wrote a jacket blurb signed "T. E. Shaw," edited a book of Middle East memoirs.[35]

He accompanied G. B. Shaw to see Shaw's comedy *Too True to be Good,* in which the character Private Meek is based on Lawrence (who had corrected the draft for accuracy). "I felt very nervous, until all was over, lest something in it should hurt," Lawrence wrote Walter Hudd, who played Meek. "I only wish nature had let me look half as smart and efficient as yourself. Only I get more gaiety out of my position. It's comic really, and I often see that."[36] Not enough gaiety at this period.

Robert Graves met Lawrence in London in September 1930, when he had just turned 42. His "accent was that ... one associates with men who drive lorries.... I commented on this, and he grinned, showing a row of gold teeth, which called for further comment. Common-clay vulgarity: no All Souls fellow could possibly have showed up with a mouthful of gold like that. He agreed, but said that gold was practical." Some of Graves's astringency reflected his disapproval of Lawrence's life in uniform, his extolling the military, machines, planes, and common men; some reflected Lawrence's aversion to Laura Riding, who accompanied Graves. Nevertheless, Lawrence liked her suggestion that he write a little book on speed for her and Graves's Seizin Press. He said that "speed, and especially the conquest of the air, was the greatest achievement of civilisation, and ... one of the very few subjects now left to write about."[37]

Two years later, Lawrence dismissed Riding's request that he reply off the top of his head to several questions in a kind of intellectual game. Graves was annoyed. "His reaction as of low-brow to highbrows surprised me." Graves charged Lawrence with "forced ingenuousness" in his new "low-brow" posture and "plainman tone." He replied, "Come off it, R.G....! I'm now a fitter, very keen and tolerably skilled on engines.... I live all of every day with real people, and concern myself only in the concrete. The ancient self-seeking and self-devouring T.E.L. ... is dead.... My last ten years have been the best of my life."[38] (They included the desperate time in Bovington, the suicide threat, and the vacant time in India.)

That was said in January 1933. In December, Lawrence said, "the only good thing I saw in 1933 was the weather."[39] Should he leave the RAF, occupy Clouds Hill, and take stock? After his mother and elder brother left the cottage for China in late 1932, he used *Odyssey* money to fix the roof wood-beetles were eating, make other repairs, erect book shelves, and set about installing a ram, a large pool for protection from heath fires, a boiler and bath for hot baths (the first, taken in December 1933). Collecting records and books dispersed among friends and camp, he found most of the records, poetry, and private press books, but 200–300 books were missing. Visiting used bookstores to replace missing volumes became a preoccupation.

Rearranging the cottage to suit his needs disarranged it for others, he warned his mother. "Arnie is not coming ... I ... told him the place was too unfinished.... The little room upstairs where you used to sleep is going to become a work-room."[40] In May 1934, he informed Charlotte Shaw, "My cottage is finished, inside and out.... I do hope you'll be able to see it ... some time soon." The same month, Henry Williamson, just returned from America, received a decidedly different picture: "[M]y cottage, ... that half-ruin and wholly unfinished place must be cleaned up enough ... to act 'home' to me."[41]

For half a year, Lawrence equivocated. "Do you get into places, sometimes, and doubt what road out to choose? I've been like that since October last," he said in March 1933. Camp chores had grown boring; his enlistment would be up in

1935: why not leave earlier? But the forced companionship eased, if it did not eliminate, loneliness; food, clothing, and shelter were laid on; the difficulty of being both Lawrence of Arabia and an aircrafthand was addressed, if not surmounted; the RAF lent a sense of purpose. Finally, on March 6, he applied for his discharge as of April 6. "It will be a ... large shock." He did not greatly want to go or to stay: let the RAF decide. "It shall be as they please."[42]

News of the impending discharge spread. RAF chief Sir Geoffrey Salmond promptly wrote. "I am alarmed to see in the Press that you are now proposing to leave." Lawrence went to see him and said he would not remain doing routine duties; he wanted more speedboat work or to take a long plane trip and write about it. Hearing nothing, he awaited discharge. On April 19, he was called to the Air Ministry. He would be posted to Cowes with 30 shillings a week subsistence allowance, visit builders' yards and prepare reports on boat trials and maintenance. "I shall try to take the boat work easier than I did last year," he told Nancy Astor.[43]

Reinstated

To avoid publicity, Lawrence was told to wear civilian clothes. But Lawrence and publicity were synonymous. Basil Liddell Hart now began research for a biography focussing on military aspects of the desert campaign and their significance for future strategy. When he broached the idea, Lawrence warned, "I dare not associate myself with anyone who brings out books or articles upon me.... Of course I'd do what I could, privately, to help you to avoid errors."[44] He cooperated fully, corresponded and met with Liddell Hart often, answered innumerable written questions, provided detailed comments on the draft, and was not modest about his military knowledge and talents.

> If you look at my article in the Pickaxe you will see how much I learned about explosives.... To use aircraft I learned to fly.[45] To use armoured cars I learned to drive and fight them. I became a gunner at need, and could doctor and judge a camel.... I have written only a few pages on the art of war—but in these levy contribution from my predecessors of five languages.[46]

In the fall of 1933, a story on Lawrence's part in developing target-towing boats appeared in a U.S. paper and was reprinted in Britain. As many facts were mangled, Lawrence liked Liddell Hart's proposal to write an accurate account, helped him, asked that he mention Scott-Paine and the British Power Boat Co. but "Please keep me out of it as far as possible."[47] The December *Daily Telegraph* article was well received by Air Ministry officials usually averse to publicity. Next month, *The Sunday Chronicle* began to serialize Liddell Hart's biography. Cape issued the book, *'T. E. Lawrence' In Arabia and After* (with quotation marks around the abandoned name), in March.[48]

"These people all exaggerate so, and make me more a mountain than a man," Lawrence told his mother. "I read his proofs and knocked out a good deal of stuff.... Unhappily I had to put in something, each time, to replace what I knocked out." Liddell Hart's recollection differed: "after approving, and suggesting numerous personal additions to, the first and second drafts ... he came to see me, began by suggesting radical modifications, went through it again pencil in hand, and ended up by deleting only one insignificant passage besides a few minor changes of phrase."[49]

Lawrence's circulation of *The Mint* led to more unwelcome publicity. Portions appeared in *The Legion Book* issued to raise charitable donations to the armed forces. Trenchard was angry. So was Lawrence. Thinking David Garnett responsible (he had had three typescripts made, for safe-keeping), Lawrence went to his Nonesuch Press office.

> He came in and looked at me with his eyes blazing, a man completely transformed by an internal force.... My astonishment must have shown him at once that I was innocent.... How then, I asked, in my turn, could *The Legion Book* Editor have got hold of *The Mint?* One of those to whom the book had been lent on ... [his] instructions, must be the guilty party.... He said ... it must have been a copy made by an officer in the R.A.F. to whom he had shown it ... he was convinced that I had told the truth.... But I was doubtful whether he had.

Lawrence later gave an explanation close to Garnett's. "An Irishman is lent the script by a friend of his to whom a friend of mine had without telling me lent it.... 'Hot stuff' says the Irishman and copies ... how much of it ... the *Legion* ... is then sent a précis of the last three chapters ... and comes out with a mash of it as an article by me."[50]

"There may be a masochistic strain in him," Liddell Hart suggested. It was exhibited anew in 1933 when his beatings by John Bruce grew more frequent. Lawrence (as "R") also sentenced himself to (to him) unpleasant horse-riding lessons in Southampton.[51] In the typescript of his biography, Liddell Hart asked "Whether it be true as he suggests, that [in 1933] 'genius has gone out' of him." Lawrence deleted *genius* and substituted *virtue*. Rejecting the role of hero that Lincoln Kirstein thrust upon him in a letter, he remarked, "The worst of being oneself is that one knows all one's vices too!"[52]

Speedboating again required Lawrence to move around; he often did so on his motorcycle. In May 1933, he went from his base at East Cowes on the Isle of Wight to Felixstowe, Hythe, Nottingham, and Manchester, back to Cowes, then to Hindhead, Bovington, and Cowes. When the Cowes work finished in July, he returned to the Hythe boatyard and Southampton lodgings. Many senior Air officials resented his activities. Recognizing "my present unpopularity in Air Ministry," he felt "the present direction of the R.A.F. is N.B.G. [no bloody good]"[53] But with his work sanctioned by the RAF chiefs (Geoffrey Salmond died unexpectedly and was succeeded by his brother John) and little time left in his enlistment term, he pressed on. Sydney Smith, now far off in Singapore, thought the RAF did not know how to make best use of Lawrence.

> "If I were at home, I'd make a big effort to get his time extended ... he's just drifting away from people and from everything. He's doing magnificent work where he is, but when that's done, he'll make no trouble to get anything else."
> [Clare Smith] "What about writing to someone?"
> "Letters are no use; you have to talk to Tes [T. E. Shaw]—it's his personality that's so convincing ... and yet no one will use him properly if he doesn't make them—and he won't trouble to make them!"[54]

Lawrence could still show his old assurance. "The Air Ministry ... get the boats and engines that I want, and not always what they want," he declared. He pushed Scott-Paine's boats upon the Admiralty, which was buying slower ones from another firm. "I ... thought it might be rather a rag to force one down their throats.... So I pulled string after string.... So Scott-Paine got the order for a new Admiral's Barge."[55] During pauses in his movements, Lawrence would write fifteen or twenty letters to friends; some he might visit unannounced. The friends were prominent military and political figures;

artists, poets, writers, publishers, editors, literary critics, booksellers; RAF and Tank Corps comrades; ordinary people. "See now," he told an admirer, "I am just an average chap.... We are all poor silly things trying to keep our feet in the swirl."[56]

After his death, some friends took a glowing view of Lawrence's RAF years, especially the period from Mount Batten onward. "In the last years ... he was perfectly happy," David Garnett said. Liddell Hart said that, working with Scott-Paine, "he was nearer being a happy man than I'd ever seen him."[57] In 1933, Liddell Hart asked Lawrence directly, "'Are you really happy?' After a moment's reflection, he replied 'At times. No one who thinks can be really happy' ... happiness was intermittent—it came in 'absorption'." "I see clearly that what I once took for contentment is resignation: and what I thought was happiness is sense of failure," Lawrence concluded. John Brophy, who met Lawrence in 1929, thought him "torn by an inward conflict. He never struck me as happy or fulfilled." To Arnold Lawrence, his later years "seemed negative, even futile, though he so filled his days with little things as to conceal their emptiness."[58]

Bridlington

In November 1934, not four months left to his RAF term, Lawrence was sent to Bridlington, on the Yorkshire coast, to put ten boats in running order. He lodged at the Ozone Hotel, a summer resort used as a winter RAF billet. H. E. E. Weblin, the officer under whom he worked, described him as "always smartly dressed and punctilious over saluting, showing the utmost respect to officers and N.C.O.'s." Lawrence's knowledge, bearing, and natural authority were such that, after two weeks,

"he said ... with a smile, 'they are all doing exactly as I tell them.'" At conferences, "he would listen quietly until everyone had said their say and then with a respectful 'If I might be allowed to suggest, sir...' he would present what was obviously the best solution of the problem ... [which] was invariably adopted." Weblin's picture contrasted with Lawrence's. "It is time I retired, for I'm becoming censorious.... I can see nothing that could not be better done, whether it is my own work, or another's."[59]

Lawrence felt too old to remain in the RAF. His letters refer gloomily—I have not noted one happy reference—to his impending departure. "I have a queer sense that it is all over—all the active part of my life, I mean." "I shall be 46 ... too young to be happy doing nothing, but too old for a fresh start." "How does one pass the fag-end of life? If there was any thing which I wanted to do, or thought worth doing, or seeing, or trying ... but I'm facing a vacancy. Indeed, yes, the machine is run down."[60]

In December, he sent John Buchan a "thank you" note. "If you meet Mr. Baldwin ... please tell him that the return to the Air Force secured me by him (on your initiation) has given me the only really contented years of my life...? You have me very hopelessly in your debt: and thank you both very much for it." He congratulates Liddell Hart on becoming military correspondent of *The Times*. "For myself, I am going to taste the flavour of true leisure. For 46 years have I worked and been worked [no childhood, college, Carchemish?]. Remaineth 23 years (of expectancy). May they be like Flecker's 'a great Sunday that goes on and on'."[61] March is "like a blank wall.... The R.A.F's solidity and routine have been anchors holding me to life.... I wish they had not to be cut," he says in early January; and at month's end: "After my discharge I have somehow to pick up a new life.... I can admit to being quite a bit afraid for myself, which is a new feeling."[62]

Though worried if his income would suffice even for his Spartan life, Lawrence did not wish to commit himself to a job or project. He wanted a period of rest, to do nothing but putter about his cottage, to think, to see how he felt. If money were short or his time too empty, he might do some editing or translating.[63] When Edward Eliot asked if he would accept a position as director of a publishing firm, he said, "Do you know, that sounds almost exactly right? ...But it must wait." Years before, the Bank of England had agreed to consider him for a night-watchman's job. Now the bank Governor, Sir Montague Norman, offered him the post of Secretary. Lawrence asked his banker friend Francis Rodd, who transmitted the offer, to "please say No, for me, but not a plain No. Make it a coloured No.... It is heartening and I am more than grateful."[64]

He wrote to service friends, Arthur Hall, Jock Chambers, and Arthur Russell. He asked Hall to find some good carpenter's tools for him in Birmingham pawnshops. Chambers, now working for the Post Office, planned to visit Clouds Hill in the spring. Lawrence's letter to Arthur Russell was precautionary.

> Do you think, if I came to Coventry, that you could find me some quiet place in which to settle for a little time, to make up my mind...? I may want to get away from myself...[!] I thought of getting a room, or a bed, anyway, with some working family; till I can pull myself together. I ... feel like a snail whose shell is being pulled off him!"[65]

At the end of January, he sent Pat Knowles, who forwarded mail from Clouds Hill, a batch of letters to local acquaintances and asked him to post them from Dorset. "If I send them from Brid-lington they may make efforts to see me ... and that is inconvenient."[66]

Early in February, Lawrence wrote what would soon become his own obituary. Asked to prepare one for *The Times*'s morgue, Robert Graves invited Lawrence to write it: "No one need know." Lawrence declined, but sent Graves a long letter reviewing his career. "[D]on't give too much importance to what I did in Arabia ... the Middle Eastern settlement ... should weigh more than the fighting. And ... this settlement should weigh less than my life since 1922, for the conquest of ... the air, seems to me the only major task of our generation." In mid–February, he invited half a dozen airmen to a motion-picture show followed by "a mild celebration" at the Ozone Hotel. A week later, a group of officers and airmen reciprocated with a party at a club (they drank gin, Lawrence ate cherries) and a Galsworthy play at the local theater.[67]

On February 20, Lawrence told Knowles to stop forwarding mail. On February 25, he sent RAF chief Sir Edward Ellington a short farewell note. "I've been at home in the ranks, and well and happy.... So if you still keep that old file about me, will you please close it with this note which says how sadly I am going?" A document in Lawrence's discharge file stated, "This airman has a habit of pushing any job too far. He can do rather too many things. He prefers a small job to a big one."[68] James Hanley's view of what the RAF meant to Lawrence reflected a 1933 conversation. "[H]e said he felt best when he was moving about amongst crowds, thinking of nothing in particular.... This merging of a single identity in the mass seemed to me a clue as to what he was after. He does not want to advance, ... but is slowly retreating.... [The RAF provided] a rhythmical, austere and ordered state of being that he hated to give up."[69]

On February 26, Lawrence got on a pedal bike he had bought, thinking the motorcycle would be too expensive in retirement. A photo shows him sitting on the bike, bareheaded, in a civilian jacket, wool scarf, and flannel trousers with bicycle clips on the legs. He looks downward, midway between the photographer and the ground—perhaps the sun is in his eyes. He squints and smiles (grimaces?) slightly, steadying himself with his right hand outstretched against the brick harborside wall. "He gave a half smile, and a half wave of the hand" and cycled off southward.[70]

10

The Last Twelve Weeks, 1935

Leaving Bridlington, Lawrence stopped at Cranwell, where he saw Rupert de la Bère, who taught at the Air Force College. Bère recorded: "He was untidily dressed in ancient flannels and a coat and muffler, ... had aged and lost much of his youth.... I felt sorry to see him so worn and, I thought, tired." Lawrence bicycled on to Bourne to visit sickly writer Frederic Manning, but, learning that he had died,[1] proceeded to Cambridge. "Manning had earned [his] ... release," he wrote Peter Davies, Manning's friend and publisher. "Yet his going takes away a person of great kindness, exquisite and pathetic.... I find myself wishing all the time that my own curtain would fall." "I cannot say how sad the news made me," he told William Rothenstein, his and Manning's friend. "He was a lovely person, and it is hateful to see him go out, unfinished.... It makes one feel as though nothing can matter very much."[2] In Cambridge, Lawrence stayed with his brother Arnold and his wife, spending much time playing and talking with their 8-year-old daughter, then bicycled to Oxford.

The day before leaving Bridlington, Lawrence had sent John Buchan *The Mint* typescript. "I suspect it is better writing than ... *Seven Pillars,* and if you could confirm that suspicion, I might be tempted ... to write something again." Sunday morning, March 3, Lawrence turned up and spent the day with Buchan, who thought him "extraordinarily happy ... he has become one of the most delightful people in the world. He has lost all his freakishness, and ... has become extraordinarily wise and mature."[3] Recalling the visit, Buchan said Lawrence

> looked brilliantly well, with a weather-beaten skin, a clear eye, and a forearm like a blacksmith's.... He had no plans ... [but] was looking forward avidly to leisure. He spoke of public affairs and his friends with perfect wisdom and charity.... I told my wife that at last I was happy about him and believed that he might become again the great man of action.... She shook her head. "He is looking at the world as God must look at it," she said, "and a man cannot do that and live."

Bère's and Buchan's accounts differ strikingly; Lawrence seemed a different man to each. Buchan has written perceptively about Lawrence but, on this occasion, his wife Susan was probably right.[4]

Damn the Press!

Replying to a letter from Tom Beaumont, a comrade from Arabian days, Lawrence had mentioned his forthcoming retirement. "My time runs out a month hence, and I shall be very sorry.... I may go there [Clouds Hill] for a while after my discharge." Beaumont sold the story to *The Sunday Express* which printed an article headed

LAWRENCE OF ARABIA
LEAVING THE AIR FORCE ON MARCH 1
'REALLY SORRY'

Lawrence reprimanded Beaumont and, with customary even temper, explained the difference between owning and publishing a letter. "If ... you got a good offer for my letters by all means take it! They are your property but the copyright (...the right to publish) remains mine always."[5]

The damage was done. At Bridlington, officials had warned Lawrence that pressmen were asking questions. Now, reporters and photographers stalked his cottage so that he forsook it, renting a room in Richmond as E. Smith. In six March 6 letters, he speaks of "a queer unrest," "aimless unrest," "this restless 'lost' feeling," feeling "lost," "quite lost," "lost and aimless and *cold*." The letter to Arthur Russell notes, "I have a long call to make in Scotland, before the summer visitors get there." Malcolm Brown suggests that this implies another projected chastisement by John Bruce.[6]

Herbert Baker had closed his Westminster office, but several friends offered Lawrence shelter: Winifred Fontana invited him to the Isle of Wight, Nancy Astor gave him her Plymouth apartment key, he could stay with H. S. Ede in London. He preferred the freedom and anonymity of rented rooms and hostels. Back at Clouds Hill in mid–March, he had a nasty encounter. Trying to drive him from the cottage for a word and a photograph, two pressmen shouted at him to come out, pounded on the door until it split, threw stones at the roof breaking several tiles, and trampled all over the place. Lawrence invited one inside and, "in a state of utter rage," punched him in the eye, hurting his hand (the man had to see a doctor). Shouting that they would sue for damages, the men left; Lawrence bicycled off to London.[7]

Many of his tormenters—today they are called *paparazzi*—were freelancers. Lawrence hoped to stop their harassment by talking to newspaper publishers directly. He appealed to Churchill to help arrange a meeting with Esmond Harmsworth, head of the Newspaper Proprietors Association. Churchill, who greatly admired Lawrence, asked him to Chartwell five days later. However, Lawrence did not wait, meeting Harmsworth and leaders of the Newspaper Society and press photographic agencies the day he wrote Churchill. A draft letter to Harmsworth, much crossed out and rewritten unlike most of his letters, is evidence of his anxiety. The meetings went well. "There are good hopes ... of persuading all [newspapers] ... to leave me alone, and to refuse to buy the stolen products of the freelancers."[8] Peace did not descend immediately. Lawrence was ousted from the cottage again and bicycled around the countryside. By April, the press hounds stopped baying and things quieted down.

Ennui

It would be good but untrue to say that his spirit lifted. He spoke of the beauty of the country, his satisfaction with the cottage, of looking forward to idleness and rest. He could fool Buchan and others about his state of mind. Or perhaps it

improved in their company so that he conveyed a sense of mastery and ease that
soon vanished. Alone (judging from his
letters), his overriding mood was one of
loneliness, despondency, listlessness,
weariness, purposelessness, aging, futility.
He could settle to nothing. "I putter about
all day, picking up jobs and laying them
down, to keep myself in an attitude of
busyness." An acquaintance who spotted
(but did not greet) him alone in a nondescript Italian restaurant in the Strand observed much the same man as had Bère.
"He looked tired and somehow shabby.
On his face was the deliberately imbecile
expression that he had never assumed with
me before."[9]

Offered many kinds of work, Lawrence equivocated. He did not know what
he wanted to do. A former Army colleague
offered a post at a new Penzance branch of
Devon Libraries. Peter Davies asked him
to edit Manning's unpublished writing;
Ralph Isham proposed a life of Mohammed that Simon & Schuster would
gladly publish. When Buchan suggested a
novel or biography, Lawrence replied that
a novel "would come very hard" as he was
given to exact description, not "invention"; a biography of Roger Casement that
he had contemplated required access to diaries the government had impounded.
Eric Kennington discussed a joint tour to
produce a book on English recumbent
effigies of 1200–1600; he would photograph and Lawrence would describe
them.[10]

Over the years, Lawrence made notes
for *Leaves in the Wind*, a book on man's
conquest of flight that would include *The
Mint*. He thought of taking up sculpture,
which had interested him since boyhood.
With help from Bruce Rogers, he planned
to set up a small hand press at Clouds Hill
by January 1936. A hundred copies of an
Augustus John drawing of him in uniform
were made for the first book, *The Mint—*

which would break his pledge not to publish it. He still tinkered with the text,
adding a note, "Alas: in March 1935 my
engagement ran out. J.H.R [John Hume
Ross]" Tom Jones, Assistant Secretary to
the Cabinet, wanted to involve Lawrence
in work of his Gregynog Press.[11]

After Lawrence's visit, Buchan said,
"he won't ever touch public life again." If
Buchan broached an idea Archibald
Wavell and Liddell Hart supported, this
implies that Lawrence dismissed it. The
idea was for him to lead, or front for,
"Lawrence's Bands," a youth movement
modeled on the Boy Scouts "to give a sense
of purpose ... to unemployed youths and
therefore prevent social unrest."[12]

Several friends promoted Lawrence
for an important national defense post.
Lawrence at times entertained it; informal
inquiries probably occurred; no evidence
points clearly to an offer or commitment.
Buchan thought Lawrence "might organ-
ise ... our imperfect national defences." In
March, Lawrence told Liddell Hart he had
been approached about a position with the
Committee on Imperial Defense; however,
"after oppressed hesitation he saw means
to avoid an active participation in the re-
planning of national defence."[13] On May
7, Lady Astor wrote, "I believe ... you will
be asked to help re-organize the Defence
forces.... If you will come to Cliveden ...
the last Saturday in May, you will never
regret it. Please, please come. Lionel [Cur-
tis], Pat [Mrs. Curtis], Philip [Lord Loth-
ian], and, for the most important, Stanley
Baldwin" (who soon replaced Ramsay
MacDonald as Prime Minister). Lawrence
replied promptly. "No: wild mares would
not at present take me away from Clouds
Hill.... Also there is something broken in
the works, as I told you: my will, I think.
In this mood I would not take on any job
at all."[14]

The rejection was consistent with the
depression that gripped him. "Consistent"

is a risky word, for Lawrence was anything but. Liddell Hart found him "curiously uneven" in his last year. "Talking in letter after letter of his desire to settle down and do nothing, yet every now and then suggesting that he might be coming back to do something bigger than ever before." In April, Lawrence "expressed [to Herbert Baker] with an unwonted enthusiasm a desire to serve in guiding" Britain's defense strategy.[15]

Nonetheless, Lawrence struggled under a leaden weight of ennui. He missed the subjection and order of military life; he could not adjust to, may have felt unworthy of, freedom. "I feel incredulous about it," he says after five weeks; "very empty in mind, tired out, and futile-feeling." After six, "I do not like civil life, nor leisure."[16] As John Mack observes, his letters "suggest a … progressive despair and emptiness. There is no relieving plan, nothing to suggest a … new interest in living." In May, his letters stay grim. "It gets worse instead of healing over." Thanking two officer friends for their farewell gift of candleholders, he says, "Life here is quiet and good enough but a very second best. I advise you all to hang on…. There's such a blank, afterwards."[17]

"At present the feeling is mere bewilderment. I imagine leaves must feel like this after they have fallen from their tree and until they die," he tells Bruce Rogers. In an oft-quoted letter to Eric Kennington, he says, "Days seem to dawn, suns to shine, evenings to follow, and then I sleep. What I have done, what I am doing, what I am going to do, puzzle me and bewilder me. Have you ever been a leaf and fallen from your tree in autumn and been really puzzled about it? That's the feeling."[18] It was May, not autumn, and the cottage rhododendron must have been blooming.

Young airmen had bolstered a reverie of continued youthfulness. But even a vigorous man—and, despite his laments about wounds, illnesses, and pains, Lawrence was strong and hardy—cannot defeat reality. The company of young men made him conscious of aging, as each new class of students can make a teacher feel old. Age was a prime reason for his retirement. "I must not … sign on again," he said in February, "as in 12 years time I should be too old to be efficient."[19] Jocular and serious comments show how much aging was on his mind in his forties, even thirties. "[E]very day I become more hopelessly decrepit and disgusting." "I'm gray-haired and toothless, half blind and shaking at the knees." "[A]lways there's a feeling that perhaps I'll miss old age by some happy accident."[20]

"The cottage has become quiet, now: except for a beastly tit, which flutters up and down one window-pane for six hours a day," Lawrence wrote a friend. "The bird continued this practice for some weeks," David Garnett explained, "until it was finally shot after Lawrence's accident."[21] The RAF had provided "companionship. A direct touch with men, obtained no other way."[22] The uniform, barracks, and mess made him part of a whole. Now he was an impoverished, aging bachelor in a small cottage on a large heath, intensely conscious of his loneliness and his technical celibacy punctuated by lacerating punishment with sexual release. Not the happiest way to live.

Lawrence invited some friends to stay at Clouds Hill, while pleading a lack of fit accommodations to others. Jock Chambers spent a fortnight there in April and May; H. H. Banbury visited in early May; G. W. Dunn and Posh Palmer were invited; Forster was to visit in mid–May, Wavell in June, Ede in August.

Upon reading *Revolt in the Desert*, Henry Williamson, the novelist and nature writer, felt that he *knew* Lawrence. When they met, Williamson felt happy, uplifted, instinctively understood. (Lawrence had that effect on others.) He hoped Lawrence would become "the friend I had always longed for," but his hope was stronger than his actions. They corresponded; Lawrence became a character in several of his books, but they met only twice; Lawrence had discouraged and later encouraged a visit. Williamson, 80 miles off in Devon, felt that they both wanted to be closer friends. Finally, Williamson resolved to visit Clouds Hill. Should he drop in unannounced (Lawrence's habit) or ask? He wrote that he planned to visit May 14 unless it rained. The letter arrived Saturday, May 11.

The Fatal 13th

On a bright, clear Monday, the 13th, Lawrence rode to Bovington on his Brough, which he had relicensed a month before, and wired:

11.25 A.M. 13 MAY 1935
WILLIAMSON SHALLOWFORD FILLEIGH
LUNCH TUESDAY WET FINE COTTAGE 1
   MILE
` NORTH BOVINGTON CAMP
        SHAW

Five minutes later, two boys, both 14, bicycling abreast on the straight, rising road north of Bovington moved to single file upon hearing a motorcycle behind them, Albert Hargreaves told Frank Fletcher, in front, to keep well in. In his garden across from Clouds Hill, Pat Knowles heard the familiar Brough sound. "I heard it rev-up as though he was changing gear, and thought 'Hullo, he's stopped to chat to someone....'" From the field to the east, Corporal Ernest Catchpole saw the motorcycle pass a black car coming in the other direction and immediately swerve to avoid the cyclists.

"Hargreave's bike hit my back wheel," Fletcher related. "As I was falling off I saw Lawrence go over the handle bars of his bike and land in a sitting position against a tree, at the same time I saw my mate lying in the middle of the road." Catchpole heard a crash. "I saw the bike twisting and turning over and over along the road." Fletcher got up and went to his friend, "but he never answered. He seemed to go to sleep. I waited a minute or two, being afraid to go to the man, because his face was covered with blood" coming from his nose and, profusely, from the top of his head. Catchpole arrived running and tried to wipe the blood away with his handkerchief. Lawrence lay on the other side of the road about ten yards in front of the Brough and twenty from where Fletcher had fallen.

A passing Army lorry took the unconscious Lawrence and Hargreaves to the Bovington hospital, where the boy, not seriously hurt, awoke. He remembered nothing of the accident, but the smashed rear wheel indicated that he had been thrown to the ground when the Brough clipped the back of his cycle. Tire marks showed that Lawrence had braked hard. The motorcycle was only slightly damaged but the footrest had cut a long, deep furrow in the road; fragments of Lawrence's clothing were imbedded in the macadam. Lawrence had worn no helmet. His skull had a terrible, nine-inch break; his brain was severely wounded, especially the right temple. Three eminent doctors who examined him in following days, a neurologist, lung specialist, and brain surgeon, agreed that nothing could be done.[23]

Reporters gathered at the hospital. Pat Knowles guarded the cottage; Stewart Newcombe and Lord Carlow stayed nearby. Lawrence's mother and elder brother were on the Yangtze; a cable with the news awaited them in Shanghai. Cambridge police phoned Arnold Lawrence, on holiday in Majorca with his family; he arrived a day later and stayed at Clouds Hill.

After six days in a coma, Lawrence died shortly after 8:00 Sunday morning, May 19.

Much nonsense has been written about Lawrence's death (and life!). It has been seen as a suicide: but a stranger form of suicide than clipping the rear wheel of a boy's bicycle can hardly be devised. It has been seen as murder "by agents of a foreign power," French, German, or Arab; or by British agents.[24] Some people believed that Lawrence lived: that his "death" was a cover for renewed secret activities. Some people believe anything they want and some writers and newspapers cater to their credulity.

Lawrence's disconcerting death fit few views of him. The accident was called "absurd," the death, "bungled." Knowing Lawrence's mastery of his Brough — George Brough, its manufacturer, said he was "one of the finest riders I have ever met" — admirers imagined small, ill-timed causes: that he was momentarily distracted by soldiers erecting tents nearby, blinded by an insect (he wore no goggles), or one bicyclist had swerved out.[25] Williamson mused, "if I'd turned up … without writing …he might be alive still." If I had remained at the cottage, Chambers thought, Lawrence would have worn his helmet—"I used to force him to put it on." If, after his discharge, he had gone away for several months instead of returning to the cottage, his mother thought, all might have been well.[26]

Such thoughts are understandable, if unconvincing. History is a global chronicle of accidents and deaths. Familiar habit, doing something routinely, without thought, causes constant accidents: a trivial happenstance intervenes and events too inconsequential to note are disastrous ("for want of a nail, the battle was lost"). Countless accidents occur at home, the most familiar place, when a foot placed automatically on what is always a solid surface finds a sheet of paper. Lawrence was so familiar with the short trip from Bovington, his actions were automatic: going up the rise, he accelerated; at a certain point, cut the motor and coasted home; on the 13th, that point was never reached. The weather was too good; rain might have slowed him. The road was narrow; as he approached the rise, the passing car (the bicyclists did not recall it; its existence is debated) made him move over; instantly the boys appeared; he put the Brough into second, jammed the brakes, swerved, and lifted off. On hedgelined rural British roads I drive in constant fear of hitting a cyclist beyond every bend and crest. A. L. Rowse said Lawrence "did not really want to live,"[27] but at that moment he wanted only to avoid the boys.

Eighteen years before, charging downhill at the Turks, Lawrence's camel collapsed. "I was torn completely from the saddle, sailed gently through the air for a great distance, and landed with a crash which seemed to drive all the power and feeling out of me."[28] Kennington drew a funny sketch of Lawrence high in the air, arm aloft scattering flowers in his descent. He had shot his camel in the head, yet landed safely. The landing from his motorcycle saddle was not funny. This time Kennington carved a headstone for Lawrence's grave and an effigy of him lying stone still in Arab robes.

The funeral was set for Tuesday afternoon, May 21. An inquest was held that morning. The coroner told the jury of seven that "what caused the Deceased to run into the pedal cyclist from the rear we shall never know, but the evidence would lead one to think that Mr. Shaw must have been travelling at a very fast speed…" The jury's verdict was accidental death. The death certificate of "Thomas Edward Shaw age 46 of Clouds Hill, Tonerspuddle, Wareham R.D., An Aircraftsman (Retired)" gave the cause of death as

"Congestion of the lungs and heart failure following a fracture of the skull and laceration of the Brain sustained on being thrown from his motorcycle when colliding with a pedal cyclist."[29]

Arnold Lawrence arranged the funeral at Moreton parish church two miles from Clouds Hill. The public was asked not to attend as the church held only 170; tickets were given to a hundred friends who came by special train from London. Three pallbearers, W. Bradbury, Arthur Russell, and Pat Knowles, represented Lawrence's time in the ranks and three, Stewart Newcombe, Ronald Storrs, and Eric Kennington, earlier years. Others attending were: Lady Astor, Jonathan Cape, Mr. and Mrs. Winston Churchill, Mr. and Mrs. Lionel Curtis, Col. and Mrs. Alan Dawnay, Mrs. Thomas Hardy, Augustus John, Capt. and Mrs. Liddell Hart, Mrs. Arnold Lawrence, Lord Lloyd, Bruce Rogers, Mr. and Mrs. Siegfried Sassoon, Air Vice Marshall Sir John Salmond, Major-General Wavell, Lord Winterton. Lowlier attendees included H. W. Bailey, Tom Beaumont, W. E. Beauforte-Greenwood, Robin Buxton, Alec Dixon, Philip Graves, S. C. Rolls, Raymond Savage, H. Scott-Paine. John Bruce claimed to be there but that is unlikely.

The previous day, *The Times* had printed Winston Churchill's tribute: "In Colonel Lawrence we have lost one of the greatest beings of our time. I had the honour of his friendship. I knew him well. I hoped to see him quit his retirement and take a commanding part in facing the dangers which now threaten the country. No such blow has befallen the Empire for many years as his untimely death." After the brief, severely simple service, Ronald Storrs, whom Lawrence had accompanied to Jidda on his first trip to Arabia, went into the mortuary chamber and looked at Lawrence until the plain oak coffin lid was screwed down.

[H]is injuries had been at the back of his head, and beyond some scarring and discoloration over the left eye, his countenance was not marred. His nose was sharper and delicately curved, and his chin less square. Seen thus, his face was the face of Dante with perhaps the more relentless mouth of Savonarola; incredibly calm, with the faintest flicker of disdain.... Nothing of his hair, nor of his hands was showing; only a powerful cowled mask, dark-stained ivory alive against the dead chemical sterility of the wrappings. It was somehow unreal to be watching beside him in these cerements, so strangely resembling the *aba,* the *kuffiya* and the *agāl* of an Arab Chief, as he lay in his last littlest room.[30]

Lawrence once hoped "not to have a grave: cremation, & the ashes into water." Nevertheless, he was buried in the cemetery near the Moreton church and his headstone bore the name "Lawrence" he had struggled to discard. "What about Westminster Abbey?" Bernard Shaw asked. "His country ... owes him at least a stone."[31] Instead, Eric Kennington's bronze bust was installed in St. Paul's crypt. At the January 29, 1936, dedication service, the organ played three pieces Lawrence liked: Purcell's Trumpet Tune and Air, Bach's Air on G String, and Beethoven's Funeral March on the Death of a Hero. Ecclesiasticus XLIV, 1 to 15, was the lesson selected: *Let us now praise famous men, and our fathers that begat us.* Not mothers!

Upon entering the great valley of Rumm, Lawrence wrote, "We looked up ... to a long wall of rock, sheering in like a thousand-foot wave.... The Arab armies would have been lost in the length and breadth of it.... Later, ... my mind used to turn me from the direct road, to clear my senses by a night in Rumm and by the ride ... up its valley in the sunset toward that glowing square which my timid anticipation never let me reach. I would say, 'Shall

I ride on this time ... and know it all?'"[32] In his address, Viscount Halifax, Chancellor of Oxford, who did not know Lawrence but had obviously consulted friends who did, remarked

> how strongly the personality of Lawrence has gripped the imagination of his countrymen. To comparatively few was he intimately known.... So true it is that men often admire most what they are least able to understand.... Lawrence himself was never free from the challenge of his nature's secret. Perhaps he came nearer to the answer when he lay in the uncharted land between life and death, and saw his life no longer in part, but whole before him.[33]

II

CHARACTER AND CONDUCT

11

Body and Appearance

Shortarse

The millions who know Lawrence only as the prancing, 6' 1½" Peter O'Toole in David Lean's 1962 film epic have been badly misled. His adult height was 5' 5½."[1] Surprise at finding Lawrence so short—heroes, it seems, should be at least normal height—and the fact that his large head sat on a small body made many think him even shorter.[2] Everyone noted his smallness. Geoffrey Dawson recommended "my little friend Lawrence" for an All Souls fellowship. Eric Kennington met "a small … kid"; E. M. Forster, "a small fair-haired boy." Bernard Shaw called him "very small"; Lionel Curtis, "tragic little being!" To comrades, Lawrence was "that little man," "the little chap," "little Lawrence," "the little fellow." At Farnborough, he was "Shortarse."

Though some writers insist that, being close to the 5' 6" average of British men at the time, Lawrence was *not* short, the average was heavily weighted by stunted, malnourished working-class men.[3] More important: Lawrence, shortest of the five brothers, *felt* short. He was keenly conscious of and despised his small body. At Carchemish, he noted with pleasure, most men were small, their height

"hardly more than mine." Held by three Turks at Deraa, "I cursed my littleness."[4] In 1919, when family friend Janet Laurie was getting married, she asked Lawrence to give her away (her father was dead). Just before the wedding, he backed out saying "he was too short and would look silly walking down the aisle with her." Robert Graves thought Lawrence looked better sitting than standing because "his legs were much too short for his body.[5]

A 1934 snapshot shows a smiling Lawrence standing on a bollard, his hair level with the top of Liddell Hart's hat. Thanking him for the photo, he said, "You and I get off about par." But he seldom joked about his size. "He had … a sense of humour about everything except the insignificance of his body … a strange neurosis prevented him from enjoying the comedy of his own smallness." He did not dislike his body; he hated it: "when … we did see our bodies, it was with some hostility, with a contemptuous sense," he writes of his Arab comrades, but plainly thinking of himself.[6]

Lawrence had the "power mania of the *small* man," Lawrence Durrell observed; Arnold "agreed that he had a marked Napoleon complex." As a boy, he boasted incorrectly that he was born on

111

the same day as Napoleon. "Lawrence's life," Auden wrote, "is an allegory of the transformation of the Truly Weak Man into the Truly Strong Man."[7]

Lawrence spoke of Churchill with warmth and admiration, but not the awe he showed for Allenby and especially Trenchard. Churchill's shortness and the commanders' commanding size affected his feelings. Allenby "was physically large and confident, and morally so great that the comprehension of our littleness came slow to him." "I love him as Petrie loves a pyramid."[8] Trenchard, 6' 6", who required a special bed, was "a magnificent, gigantic gorgeous man," "a sure, urging giant … immense."[9] Lord Beaverbrook thought he had "limited ability"; Lord Rothermere, who forced his resignation in 1918, thought this saved the Air Force. To Lawrence, "the awe of him … encompasses us."[10]

Most men Lawrence picked for his bodyguard were tall; John Bruce, whom he picked to beat him, was over six feet. William, the brother to whom he felt closest, was tall. Dahoum, whom he loved, was big and very strong. He preferred Feisal to Abdulla (who was shorter than Lawrence), one suspects, partly because, being taller, he better fitted his vision of a leader. There is some truth in Meinertzhagen's comment that Lawrence liked "big strong men" and "had little use for small men such as he was himself."[11]

Lawrence was stocky; exercise and repeated feats of endurance made him strong and muscular. John Buchan depicted him in 1920: "he looked slight, but, as boxers say, he stripped well, and he was as strong as many people twice his size, while he had a bodily toughness and endurance far beyond anything I have ever met." Eric Kennington, described him as "weighty from shoulders to neck … [In 1920, he was] the shadow of a burly youth … over 11 stone [154 pounds]. He must have once been as strong as a gorilla."[12]

Robert Graves suggests that Lawrence "idealized masculinity, partly perhaps because he knew that he was not conventionally masculine himself." A Bovington comrade mentions his "slight, almost girlish figure"; John Buchan, "his girlish face."[13] A. L. Rowse notes his feminine appearance in a photograph taken in India: "wide hips, slim waist, gesture of arm and hand held up to the face. Hence the constant and insane pressure to test himself physically … he could not and would not accept himself for what he was…. To these tensions he owed his genius."

"There was no flesh," Lawrence declares in "Myself," *Seven Pillars'* chapter of self-examination, meaning no sexual flesh, no holding, fondling, or being fondled. "To put my hand on a living thing was defilement; and it made me tremble if they touched me."[14] But there most definitely was flesh as muscle and body. Hyperconscious of his body, Lawrence exercised it to match or excel his classmates and barrack mates. "Mme. Chaignon … got a shock when she saw my 'biceps'…. She thinks I am Hercules," he writes from France as a boy of 18. The boast recurs in later years. "In 1914 I was a pocket Hercules, as muscularly strong as people twice my size, & more enduring than most. I saw all the other British officers' boots off in Arabia."[15] He could grasp a rifle by the end of the barrel and hold it out level at arm's length.

As a student, gym, exercise on the bars in the family garden, climbing, long walks, and fast bicycle trips enabled him to do 100 miles day after day in 1906.[16] Bicycling away from Bovington 29 years later, aged 46, he did 75 miles on the second day. Visiting Lowell Thomas in Wimbledon several times in 1919, he walked the twelve miles from Westminster. In India, he walked two hours a day inside the base. No one so small could handle a quarter-ton motorcycle as he did without being exceptionally strong. Once, when he broke his right hand, he operated it with his left hand alone. Comparing his body with his comrades', he explains, "I have to tell my body what to do and watch on it. They seem to obey their bodies…. They look natural."[17] His bodily movements were tightly controlled. "I never met a man whose body was kept in such perfect discipline," a friend who saw him in 1932 recalled.[18] Posing for a bust or portrait, he stood immobile for the entire session, as long as five hours.

Entering the RAF, he declares, "Till this year [1922], my insignificant body has met life's demands. If it fails me now I shall break it." One must pity a body so cruelly treated. He tells a friend he is so ashamed of his body, or its possible failure, he did not do a broad jump in front of other airmen but later "privily cleared over twenty feet." On another occasion, "Some demon of display took me. I jumped, suddenly confident, for the bar" and traversed "round the wall-girders on my wrists" while airmen watched. "I find myself higher in the general favour."[19]

"I can have but few more years of bodily fitness— … in the Service sense," he writes in 1928. "I shall so hate myself, when I prefer sitting to standing." He scorns Wyndham Lewis and Ezra Pound who are "flabby-faced and soft-handed, and pant when going up flights of stairs."[20] Unlike such aesthetes, he kept in trim and disapproved of airmen who did not. "I live in a society of men who take habitual care of their bodies, and temper them by games and exercise and diet … fifteen or twenty creatures with pendulous bellies and loose cheeks haunt the wet bar midday and evening…. But the 90% … are a satisfaction to watch. I like to see a man well in control of his limbs."[21]

Robert Graves spoke of Lawrence's "morbid horror of being touched." Nonetheless, Lawrence tested himself physically against others. He would provoke his schoolmates "till one of us would seize him and close in friendly wrestling, to feel … the strength of those iron wrists." At Carchemish, he tussled with Dahoum, who "wrestles beautifully."[22] In barracks, "we dog-fight promiscuously" and all combatants were not gentlemen. One airman tried to choke him, then "drove a knee into the pit of my stomach, suddenly, and shifted his other hand to that fatal 'bollock-hold'…. You bunch the things tightly and knead them. Not a brass monkey could resist such pain for sixty seconds."[23]

Lawrence was of two bodily minds in the ranks. In one, his aging body laments the pains and illnesses he has suffered. In the other, he triumphs over age and young airmen. "Physically I'm good enough to down any man of my weight in the hut." He reassures Charlotte Shaw, who expresses concern about his health. "…I'm of an almost inhuman toughness…. In the retreat from Moscow I should have put on weight!"[24]

A citizen who laid a hand on the small man could be sharply surprised. Leaving Jonathan Cape's office one day, Lawrence was getting on his motorcycle when Cape, remembering something, called out to a young apprentice, "Stop him! Stop him!" The apprentice ran out "and caught hold of the handlebar…. Next moment he had been sent flying by a punch on the jaw" and Lawrence rode off.[25] Working to salvage the crashed plane at Plymouth, Lawrence was pestered by a photographer on the salvage boat. Turning suddenly, he "tore the camera from his hands and pushed him over the side and into the very cold water." As noted, Lawrence punched a newsman in the eye. "It is twenty years since I last struck a man," he said,[26] which was untrue. In the military, perhaps, a push or punch was so customary it did not count.

Appearance and Manner

"[H]e was weighty from shoulders to neck, which jutted, giving a forward placing to the head, and a thrust to the heavy chin.... It was the face of a heavy-weight boxer." That was how Eric Kennington described Lawrence, then 32, when they met in 1921. Sculptor Charles Wheeler, who did a bust of Lawrence in 1929, wrote, "His eyes were small and seemed to be shrunken into his head.... His chin was large, but not so prominent as [Augustus] John portrayed it and there was a marked ridge of the frontal bone of his forehead running parallel to his eyebrows."[27]

Until roughened by wind and spray in the power-boat years, Lawrence's face was smooth. Light complexioned, the skin went red, not brown, in Arabia; in later years, it was ruddy or pink. Lawrence used no brush to shave, "only carbolic soap and a safety razor, suggesting that his facial hair was light-textured—and/or that he liked the resultant skin irritation. The frequency of shaving is in question. At Carchemish, it was three times a week. In the desert, he was clean-shaven when many British soldiers grew beards. "I shaved daily," he told Liddell Hart, but, queried—"I seem to remember your telling me that you did not need to shave so frequently"—retreated to "Regularly?"[28] G. B. Shaw said he "scarcely shaved."

At school, Lawrence's hair was trimmed like his brothers'; at Jesus College, he wore it long. At Carchemish, it was "always very long and in wild disorder—he used to say it was too long when it got into his mouth at mealtimes." It was too long for the taste of fellow officers in Cairo and Arabia. Upon first meeting him in Port Sudan, Colonel Pierce Joyce wanted "to tell him to get his hair cut."[29] In the ranks, he had a barber cut it regularly.

His eyes, observers said, were "startlingly blue," "an intensely deep, straight blue." Dissenting, Lawrence's armored-car driver S. C. Rolls said they were "steel-grey" and historian Arnold Toynbee, "grey," adding that "the moment he went into action" they "shone blue."[30] A friend said they were "normally ... dead as jelly: he became interested and life effervesced into them: he was angry, and they set hard." Though disparaging Lawrence as "a poseur," Beatrice Webb noted his "wonder-working eyes."[31] Others found them "piercing," "strangely penetrating," "magnetic," "blazing."

Eyes that do not look at you do not pierce or blaze. It was a matter of mood and the business at hand. "I never look at a man's face, and never recognise a face," he told Robert Graves. "Long practice has made me able to talk to whoever accosts me ... without betraying that I haven't a notion who he is." Graves remarked that, at Oxford in 1920, his eyes "never met the eyes of the person he was addressing but flickered up and down." Vyvyan Richards, a good prewar friend, also mentioned Lawrence's "reluctance to look others in the eyes." "Generally concentrated his looks on his feet," recalled a wartime colleague, "but when he did look up and at you, you wished he had not."[32]

David Garnett remembered "the long look, right into one's eyes, followed by a broad grin." Without the grin, it could be a contest of wills. "If I am angry, I can outface a man," Lawrence said.[33] "His most remarkable characteristic," Meinertzhagen wrote, "was the fire in his blue eyes, dormant if happy or dreaming, but sparkling with fire if roused." Depressed or apathetic, the fire was banked. In the ranks, Lawrence strove to stifle it; it was, of course, incompatible with the obligatory obedience to superiors. *The Mint* recounts his resultant humiliation by drill-sergeant Pearson. "'Look at me!' he yells: but I can't.... 'Look ... me in the face, you short-arsed little fuck-pig,'.... 'Funks looking at me, an' thinks his equipment's right."[34]

Lawrence's mouth was large, his lips full—writers who mistake physiognomy for character say "sensual." They expressed his mood: hard, sardonic, sad, kind, impish. In 1921, a hostile French observer saw "a fixed mocking smile" on his lips. French biographer Jean Villars describes his mouth as "sinuous, and in repose it had a disquieting curve, suggesting cruelty, irony, or deceit, but usually it was twisted into a tense smile ... often accompanied by a rather embarrassed giggle."[35] Many persons noted the giggle (a "cackle" to an enemy). A boyhood friend thought Lawrence "always wore a mask, the outer covering of which was ... that provocative ... curiously nervous smile." Liddell Hart thought his face "rather severe" in repose, but the severity vanished when he spoke and his smile was "utterly disarming."[36]

Lawrence spoke with a "slow deliberate intonation, ... exact and perfect elocution." His voice was "crisp and cultivated; the diction ... unstudied; his phrasing concise and expressive."[37] Friends from early and late in life say his voice had "singular charm"; however, Ernest Altounyan considered the "shut-up Oxford face, the down-cast eyes, the soft reluctant speech, courteous, impersonal" he observed at Carchemish "impressive, disturbing and disagreeable."[38] "He spoke in a low distinct voice—I have never heard him speak otherwise," an officer wrote. The soft, even tone reflecting his characteristic detachment could be present even under pressure. When, just back from India, he phoned Ernest Thurtle after midnight, Thurtle, ready for bed, was angry. "'Oh', I said rather savagely, '...I don't know you, do I?' 'No', was the soft answer, turning away my wrath, '...but you've been asking questions about me in Parliament'." By 1930, Robert Graves observed, Lawrence's speech had changed "from Ox-ford University to garage–English," yet, as they talked, the old accent returned, an example of Lawrence's native responsiveness to the manner of his companion.[39]

Lawrence's teeth were poor. His spare, at times semi-starvation, diet and taste for sweets cannot have helped, nor would some leading British dentists. (John Buchan, for example, had all his teeth extracted to treat a persistent stomach condition.) In 1922, six teeth were missing and two were defective. Some time thereafter, a prominent London dentist repaired the damage with gold teeth and fillings that Graves considered vulgar. Lawrence was pleased with them, asking his mother to tell the dentist "that his artificial masterpiece, my mouth, still stands superbly. It cracks nuts." Losing an eyetooth later, he felt that his face "seemed to fall in."[40]

As his eyes were dull or flashing, so were his face and appearance. "He looks like a mild bank-clerk," Kathleen Scott noted in 1921. "At times," Ralph Isham wrote, "people who expected to see a flaming personality found what seemed to be a second-rate person ... then his face took on the set, self-obliterated look of soldiers on review." "To the average person who met him," John Bruce said, "he was a dour fellow indeed"[41] (a posture very likely impelled by the role of Uncle R's incorrigible nephew). In engaging company he was composed, witty, entertaining, penetrating, provocative, impressive. In action, he led without commanding, knew immediately what to do, and showed it so clearly and confidently by manner, word, and act that others naturally followed.

The Lifelong Boy

Much of Lawrence's character and conduct can be better understood if he is regarded as a boy who never achieved a man's sexual, emotional, and social maturity or accepted adult responsibilities and moral compromises. Physically and psychologically, he looked and often acted more like a boy than a man.

In John Mack's view, Lawrence had "no real adolescence at all," physical or emotional, "his energies remaining in many respects those of a ... lively-minded schoolboy." Leonard Woolley, who knew Lawrence best from 1912–15, when he was 23–27, noted "his essential immaturity."[42] Whatever factors made him boyish in conduct also made him boyish-looking. Everyone was surprised at how young he looked. A doctor who met him in 1915, when he was 29, said he "looked about twenty." Wearing white Arab robes in Boulogne in late 1918, he looked like "a Catholic choir boy." When Eric Kennington got off the train at Oxford and first met Lawrence on the platform, he saw "a grinning hatless kid" who "giggled often."[43]

Detractors called Lawrence's smile a "smirk" or "sneer," his pranks "puerile." Kathleen Scott found him "Great fun..., this lad. He has an entrancing sense of humour, as subtle as the devil.... He's an entrancing child."[44] The "child" was then 32.

The word "lad" recurs often in *Seven Pillars.* Mohammed was a "hot-tempered lad of nineteen"; Abdulla "had a lad's supple body, and something of a lad's recklessness." It has a *Shropshire Lad* quality of youthful innocence, attractiveness, strength, and vulnerability against the background of war and death. The word was applicable to the man who used it. There was a schoolboyish quality to the disciplined military life he elected. Nearing 40, he acknowledged "my refusal to see that I'm too old to lead a boy's life much longer. They do not allow, in the Services, for grown ups ... the whole treatment and regimen is designed for the immature."[45] In one of several strange letters Lawrence, in the guise of an uncle "Edward Shaw," wrote to a Southampton swimming in-

structor in 1932–33, he called himself (then 44) "a young fellow" aged 28 or 29.[46]

Lawrence did not live long enough to lose his boyishness. "He did not appear to be a man; he was more like a boy" to Henry Williamson when they first met. "As usual he looked ten years less than his age" (42) when Robert Graves saw him in 1930.[47] "The very curious arrest of his physical development" puzzled Bernard Shaw; "at forty he still had the grinning laugh and artless speech of a schoolboy." Shaw thought that Lawrence "never grew up ... and also was mentally adolescent."[48] "His hatred for his body was a boy's hatred; his fear of women was a boy's fear" Ralph Isham, who wrote that, saw Lawrence last in March 1935, after a lapse of years. "[H]e seemed not to have aged a bit since ... I first met him, sixteen years before." Youth "seemed to be Lawrence's permanent possession."[49]

As a boy, Lawrence inhabited his body with ease and vigor. As he aged, the vigor diminished and ease could become strain. Especially during and after his time in India, "I am so tired" recurs in his letters. Though it refers, I think, mainly to his boredom and disinterest in almost everything, it was also physical. "I haven't the desire ... to do anything else but lie down flat on my back.... I don't think this exhaustion is laziness."[50]

Lawrence's boyish appearance went with boyish behavior—jokes, pranks, inventions, tall stories, leg-pulling. Indeed, many memoirs of Lawrence merely recite funny or outrageous things that he said and did. The great Howeitat warrior Auda Abu Tayi called him "world's imp"; Edward Garnett picked up the word; his friends thought it apposite. At Carchemish. "Lawrence cut a wind-vane from a biscuit-tin and fixed it with a rusty nail to my tent-pole; its grinding screech kept me awake ... all through the night." When Hogarth visited, Lawrence decorated his room with lace curtains, big pink satin bows, bottles of cheap scent, and "a very good Romano-Greek bronze strigil." Hogarth angrily threw out the decorations and took the strigil to the Ashmolean. Lawrence greatly enjoyed such practical jokes, Woolley remarks, but "hated being made ridiculous himself; if you laughed at him he would at once retire into his shell and very likely withdraw altogether from your company."[51] Lawrence did not like being made fun of and told no stories against himself.

Leg pulling was a Lawrence art. "I was never quite sure at any time ... whether he was pulling my leg or not," a college friend recalled; "nothing pleased him more than ... acceptance of one of his tall stories hook line and sinker." "[Y]ou are such a magician at leg-pulling," H. M. Tomlinson wrote, "that one is unaware that one's leg is off till you return that member with a non-committal air."[52] Lawrence admitted that, "When in fresh company, I would embark on little wanton problems of conduct ... treating fellow-men as so many targets for intellectual ingenuity: until I could hardly tell ... where the leg-pulling began or ended."[53]

12

Eating and Living Habits

At home in Oxford, where the food was ample if perhaps very plain, for three years Lawrence subsisted on vegetables, milk, eggs, cakes, and fruit. I have seen no explanation of this early vegetarianism; much later, Lawrence said that cereals were "a taste, not a principle, ... especially in hot places." Bicycling in Wales in 1907, he decided that "two meals a day with a glass of milk at one o'clock," were better than three.[1] In France the next year, he ate mainly bread, milk and fruit. He might skip a meal or fast; at college, he once went 45 hours without food. A college friend "never saw him eat a single solid meal"; at most, he would "nibble at a few biscuits, a piece of chocolate or a handful of raisins." Defending his brother Arnold, then 13, against their parents' concern about his poor appetite (Arnold's eating may have been influenced by T.E.'s), he writes, "Why not let him copy that very sensible Arab habit, of putting off ... bread till ... instinct makes it desirable. If we had no fixed meal-hours, and unprepared food, we would not fall into middle-age." Nonetheless, during digging seasons, Lawrence "liked good food and had a very critical taste in the Arab dishes ... and in Arab coffee he had the judgment of an expert."[2] Hiking around Syria, he easily returned to

the makeshift diet of boyhood trips, eating plain and little food.

In the desert Lawrence might set off without breakfast, while an English comrade had morning tea. He insisted, "it doesn't matter a straw what you eat or drink, so long as you do not do either oftener than you feel inclined." His wartime diet was flat bread, rice, dates, sweet coffee, sour water, and roast or cooked camel, sheep, or oryx. Like Bedouin and camels, he alternately gorged and starved. "I had learned to eat much one time; then to go two, three, or four days without food; and after to overeat.... I could go dry between wells, and ... drink greatly to-day for the thirst of yesterday and of to-morrow."[3]

At All Souls, he usually rose at 11 A.M., had no breakfast or lunch at the college and rarely dinner. His starving himself while writing *Seven Pillars* in 1922 has been recounted. In the ranks, it was hard for him to eat regular meals. "Distaste for the sight and feel of raw flesh has made me almost a vegetarian"; but gradually he ate the fare, skipping a daily meal. At Bovington, he seldom ate in the dining hall, preferring an evening meal in the camp restaurant alone or with one or two comrades. Back in the RAF, "I hate waiting more than 2 minutes for a meal: or spending more than 5 minutes on a meal. That's why I live mainly on bread & butter."[4] At the cottage, he stocked tinned or preserved food: biscuits, jam, honey, olives, almonds, baked beans, fruit salad, tinned milk, tea, supplemented by fresh milk, bread, butter, eggs, cheese. The association of tinned food with vulgar, lower-class taste did not trouble a man who, occupationally if not culturally, had joined the working class.[5] Cooked meals (the cottage had a fireplace but no stove or oven) were eaten in camp or prepared by his neighbor, Mrs. Knowles, who also made meals for his guests. He often picked up fish and chips, eggs, and bacon or chops for her.

As he aged, his ascetic diet eased. Nicolette Devas, who as a girl of 14 and 15 saw Lawrence when he visited Augustus John's Dorset home in the mid–1920s, was disillusioned to learn that he actually ate *food*. "Lawrence liked to tell stories of how he lived on a handful of raisins…. He impressed us until the day Poppet … sneaked into his [cottage] larder…. She had seen cold chicken, a joint, bread and butter and a pot of marmalade…. Lawrence came to lunch one Christmas Day … and … we counted his every mouthful of turkey. He was no ascetic that Christmas Day. He might still praise a minimal diet. "It is not as though we come to you starving," he assured Charlotte Shaw, who was moving to a new London apartment where the food served was reputedly poorer. "[Y]ou would be right to set before us a glass of water, & two water biscuits." RAF meals were a time-consuming nuisance. "I'll spend no more than ten minutes in the dining hall. If I haven't finished by then I … walk out."[6]

Not a year later, he confided to G.B.S., "I have begun to think with pleasure of the idea of eating … once or twice." Charlotte, of course, supplied a stream of delicacies; sharing them with airmen, he ate his portion, especially chocolate.

"Whenever I saw him [in India] he seemed to be eating chocolate," a comrade recalled. At Bridlington, his last station, "He enjoyed quite large meals, … always finished everything … drank nothing but water, tea, and coffee…. He liked fruit, especially apples."[7] In 1935, he had two meals at the Herbert Bakers and, to their surprise, enjoyed a second helping.

Lawrence denied being "ascetic." Coming late in life, the denial held a grain of truth yet was more obfuscating than clarifying. He said he "was 'not ascetic, but a hedonist'…. But his senses happened to be different … he found no pleasure in food or wine."[8] Henry Williamson suggested that "Much of his [later] despondency … came from … semi-starvation"; Malcolm Allen, that his view of food had the same roots as his masochism and abhorrence of sex.[9] If Williamson were right, Lawrence's despondency should have lessened, not worsened, toward the end; Allen's position seems sounder—until the later years, when eating better did not alleviate his masochism. If he felt hardier on a lean diet, a fuller diet could make him feel older, softer, more ordinary.

His avoidance of alcohol and tobacco requires minor qualification. At Carchemish, he "took wine seldom and spirits never"; but dining with Ralph Isham, "drank wine of various sorts freely." Lawrence tells of drinking a glass of port and refusing champagne; in Paris, Meinertzhagen "persuaded him to drink a little champagne to cheer him up."[10] Lawrence said he had never drunk a glass of beer and that water had more subtle and varied tastes than wine, an uninformed witticism, since he was no connoisseur of wine.

He rarely smoked. "Six months back, it was, my last cigarette," he said in August 1922. At Christmas 1923, he thanked the mother of his Tank Corps friend Arthur, for a present of cigarettes. "They made me break my … habit, of not smoking. Years ago in France we used to get nothing but those 'caporal' cigarettes, & so they brought back memories."[11] He smoked twice a year, he said, "just to show himself that he could smoke if he desired and also to feel the nasty taste again."[12]

As a youth, Lawrence slept as irregularly as he ate. While at Jesus College, he once went 45 hours without food or sleep. He slept after lunch until 11 P.M. and read all night. On his 1909 walk through Syria, he went to bed after 9 P.M. and woke at sunrise, about 4:30 A.M. At Carchemish, he slept from 11 or 12:00 P.M. to 6:00 A.M., seldom in bed preferring a trench or the mound. His claim that he learned to sleep through anything in his Polstead Road bungalow is implausible, as the sheathed rooms were unusually quiet. Upon entering the RAF he complained that he could not sleep; adjusting to the routine, he slept better. He said that, "when his own master," he avoided regular hours of sleep; in barracks, he slept from lights out (9 or 10 P.M.) till after midnight and dozed thereafter.[13]

Careless and Tidy

In dress, Lawrence was often untidy, even slovenly: and often tidy, clean, well groomed. His mother kept her brood clean and neatly dressed; however, a school photograph with most boys in well-pressed jackets shows his jacket wrinkled and his pants too long and baggy.[14] At University Officers' Training Corps, his uniform was always in disarray. On cycle and foot excursions, his kit and clothes were pared to an extra shirt and pair of socks, a cape (in rainy France), camera, and gun. At Carchemish, he dressed showily in "a blazer of French grey trimmed with pink, white shorts held up by a gaudy Arab belt with swinging tassels…, grey stockings, red Arab slippers and no hat."

But the archeologists' quarters were dirty: "we haven't any dusters, and … they wouldn't cope with a diurnal dust storm: one must just cultivate an admiration of grit."[15]

On map-making and intelligence duties in Cairo, Lawrence was usually scruffy, "part of a general refusal to comply with the … rules…. He 'forgot' to polish his buttons, … to put on his belt … [and] hat, … to salute." Ronald Storrs called him "the untidiest officer in Egypt."[16] On desert marches and raids, neatness was impossible, but visiting and receiving sheikhs, in Sherif Feisal's company, leading his ferocious bodyguard, and posing for Lowell Thomas's photographer, he wore the finest robes and headdress. No photos are more startling than those of him as a civil servant. In a dark suit, white shirt, and dark tie, he seems more constricted than in any uniform.[17]

In the RAF, he was initially untidy but soon dressed properly on duty, practically at work, casually—untidily, some said—off duty. Kennington saw him "neat, fit, and trim…. Every line always perfect, from set of hat to spacing of puttees, never a dull button, or speck on the boot, and … well-cut uniform." At Cranwell, his kit "was always scrupulously clean, brightly polished and neatly turned out." A 1930 photo shows him in uniform on his Brough talking with George Brough, its maker: both the machine (probably just cleaned) and he are shiny and well groomed.[18] A Bridlington officer called him "a model of correctness, always smartly dressed and punctilious over saluting." A more perceptive officer "sensed an impish quality in his outwardly strict obedient manner which bordered occasionally on insubordination."[19]

Wherever and whenever possible, Lawrence bathed. In India, after rigging up an electric water-heater, he took two baths a day. Hot baths were a lifetime addiction alternating with unkemptness and dirtiness. His interest in corpses, decay, garbage, filth, feces has been noted. Dirt, dirtiness, clean, and cleanliness run through *Seven Pillars* like a fugue; *the sword also means cleanness & death* is stamped on the cover. Presumably Lawrence felt cleansed after his compulsive baths, yet he slept in his clothes at the slovenly cottage. "I'm afraid Mrs. Shaw ... will find it unclean," he warned Bernard Shaw when inviting the couple to visit. Gilbert Spencer saw "endless dirty black cups and saucers—crumby." To be sure, the cottage was a wreck that he steadily improved, but it was never a tidy housewife's home. (After his mother lived there for a spell, he undid her handiwork.) Mrs. Knowles cleaned it and would spruce it up for special visitors. Nonetheless, a woman invited inside in 1935 "thought it looked a mess."[20] Lawrence didn't mind dirt.

If, to Lawrence, tidiness and discipline were marks of middle-class conformity manifest in his mother's home, he rebelled against them in his travels, his hostility to military conventions, and what he deemed to be short men's dress and manner. "Have you noticed how prim and conceited and touchy short men generally are?" he asked Charlotte Shaw. "They dress in silly neatness, hold themselves fully, as though they fear they have too little substance in hand to afford any negligence."[21] That was both a criticism and a confession. The masochistic and probable sexual element in his alternating states and feelings of dirtiness and cleanliness will be discussed in Chapter 21.

13

Possessions and Finances

A bachelor and loner, at periods a traveler and wanderer, Lawrence had little acquisitiveness and less possessiveness over goods, property or wealth. No wonder he preferred Bedouin to townsmen. "I do not know why people want to have & to hold," he said. "Possession frightens me as much as would being possessed."[1] What he nonetheless acquired is thus of special interest.

Possessions

His austere two-room bungalow at home was "hung from ceiling to floor with dyed Bolton sheeting and had no ornaments … save … a bronze head of Hypnos, cast from that in the British Museum."[2] The sitting room had a hearth rug, small oak table, books (history, archeology, classics, poetry, William Morris romances), medieval pottery and glass that he had found or bought from workmen for small coins, large brass rubbings of knights; the bedroom, a spring bed with hair mattress. Lawrence also had a late model racing bike with low handlebars and a .45 revolver. On his 1909 tour of Syria he took a heavy mauser, camera, and film. Going out to Carchemish in 1910, he bought a large £40 mahogany and brass archeological camera.

The luxurious Carchemish quarters he and Woolley furnished have been described. Earlier, at home and on trips to France and Syria, Lawrence was dependent on his father. Now he spent his own money on antiquities, crafts, rugs, exotic fittings, and his most persistent addiction, books, many brought or sent from England. He shopped, traded, and bargained with dealers, merchants, natives, and thieves for ancient seals and objects for the Ashmolean and British Museums and gifts for family and friends.

During the war, he acquired (bought, was given, or liberated) silk Arab garments threaded with silver and gold; silver and gold daggers (the latter made for him on a secret 1917 trip to Mecca); a cup and two bowls of silver; a diamond; gold ring with white sapphire inset; fine prayer rugs, station bells, rifles. The rugs and a bell went into his All Souls rooms with a large table, desk, and two heavy leather chairs, Augustus John's oil portrait of Feisal, a Kelmscott *Chaucer,* and "a four-thousand-year-old toy, a clay soldier on horseback from a child's grave at Carchemish."[3]

BOOKS, PAINTINGS, RECORDS

In the postwar interval before his enlistment, Lawrence had a good deal of money from his father, wartime pay, service with the British and Arab delegations in Paris, All Souls, and the Colonial Office. In 1919 and succeeding years, he bought 15 acres by Epping Forest, where he and Vyvyan Richards hoped to establish a private press. He bought costly Kelmscott, Doves, Ashendene, Golden Cockerel, and other private press books, limited and first editions, including a 1922 signed limited edition of Joyce's *Ulysses*. After he became famous, he received a constant stream of books, many in valuable editions and inscribed, from publishers (Cape, Doubleday, Nonesuch), poets and writers (Blunt, Doughty, Forster, Graves, Hardy, Sassoon, Shaw), and friends (Churchill, Edward and David Garnett, Edward Marsh, William Rothenstein, Charlotte Shaw). He commissioned from leading artists over a hundred paintings and drawings for *Seven Pillars*. Most of the art he gave to the artists, their subjects, and museums. "I'm too cluttered about with objects, & am going to get rid of them: especially the books & pictures ... when I give up All Souls ... I'm going to get down to the position in which I can carry all I have in my pockets."[4]

Few books could be kept in barracks where, borrowed freely, many disappeared. *Seven Pillars* was stowed in a box under the cot. Other books went into the camp library (Lawrence acted as librarian). Undistributed copies of *Seven Pillars* were put in an Ashmolean strong room; Vyvyan Richards kept many of the private press books at his home; twelve of the most valuable were kept, locked up, by Mrs. Hardy; Hogarth and Curtis stored things (some at Curtis's home were destroyed by fire). In 1933, when he almost left the RAF, Lawrence had bookshelves built at Clouds Hill to hold his scattered library. "I have now collected all my surviving books ... and am rather saddened at the gaps ... all the poems remain; only the prose has gone ... bit by bit I shall restore the missing ... books. There are only about 1,000 books surviving: so that 200 or 300 alone need be replaced."[5] At his death, 1,300 books were in the cottage, including some in French, German, Spanish, Greek, and Latin; a complete set of the Loeb Classical Library (32 volumes, Lord Riddell's gift); and at least 23 Kelmscotts, 8 Golden Cockerels, 8 Doves, 7 Ashendenes, 6 Gregynogs.

Lawrence constantly acquired records, despite the difficulty of housing and playing them in barracks; Charlotte Shaw and Robert Graves added to the stock. Lawrence bought good used records for half-price on Shaftsbury Avenue in London, discarding them when they grew scratchy. Many were left in Karachi when he moved to Peshawar. At Clouds Hill, he collected 225 compositions, the most numerous (in roughly descending order) were by Beethoven, Mozart, Bach, Schubert, Elgar, Brahms, Delius, and Wolf.[6]

DEADLY POSSESSIONS

Two death-dealing possessions Lawrence was seldom without: a motorcycle and a gun. He rode a motorcycle in Arabia in 1916 and bought an old Triumph in November 1922. Next month, he bought the first in a string of seven Brough Superiors, named George I-VII, powerful, heavy, expensive machines, the best in Britain. The first crashed when the front tire burst on a broken bottle; a comrade wrecked the second. "[I]t was indeed the safety valve I'd thought it," Lawrence told Robin Buxton, acknowledging the tension he was under trying to be a humble airman. "So I'm going to get a new one. It is absurd to spend so much [£150, but] ...

I'd rather want the money than get into trouble with authority in camp."[7] George III, acquired February 1924, was "a man-killer." George IV (cost £198) "will do 112 m.p.h. so long as the tyres will stand it." "Tremendous," he exclaimed when it arrived, with a specially lowered seat for his short legs.[8] After six months, he traded it for George V, which crashed twice. In December 1925, he skidded on ice, injuring his arm, leg, and knee. In November 1926, the wheels caught in greasy Islington wood paving; he hurt his knee and sold the damaged bike for £100.

Charlotte Shaw and several friends gave him George VI in February 1929, upon his return from India, but he insisted on paying for it.[9] In March 1932, he traded it for George VII, whose top speed of 90 disappointed him: "if only it was a bit faster." It was fast enough to lose police who chased him. "It looks as though I might yet break my neck on a B.S." (Brough Superior) he wrote a year before doing exactly that.[10] His letters to George Brough, the machine's manufacturer, show his close attention to every detail in the design, performance, and maintenance of the engine, body, and appendages. He repeatedly discussed improvements in George VIII that Brough was making for him in 1934 and '35.

During the war, Lawrence used a panoply of explosives, rifles, handguns, machine guns, mortars, cannon, swords, daggers. Thereafter, land, sea, and air vehicles and weapons were his natural habitat. He kept a gun at Clouds Hill; after his death, his brother Arnold's small daughter "found, and discharged a loaded revolver"[11] he had often practiced with. He could hit a half-crown tossed in the air; at Karachi, he practiced on the range; once he "picked up a pistol ... and put six 'bulls' on the target." At Clouds Hill, he set up a firing range so that he could practice when he pleased.[12]

CLOUDS HILL

The way Lawrence furnished, equipped, and used Clouds Hill, the only house he ever owned, offers clues to his character and the slowly changing nature of his largely vagrant life. Initially, the cottage served as a place to escape camp, to write or relax, to do as he pleased. Built in 1808, it housed a Moreton Estate laborer until 1914 or '15; unoccupied thereafter, the roof and floor rotted but the brick walls and chimney remained serviceable. In 1922, Tank Corps Sergeant Arthur Knowles rented the cottage and land across the road and began to repair the roof and floor while building a bungalow on adjacent land. After coming to Bovington in March 1923, Lawrence noticed the cottage, a mile from camp, and leased it and five acres that summer for 2/6 a week. To finish the repairs, he sold his gold dagger for £125 to Lionel Curtis (who gave it to All Souls College, where it can still be viewed).[13]

The house Lawrence once thought to build at Pole Hill was to have three-foot thick double walls, a ceilingless timber roof, and peat fire. "Clouds Hill," named after the hill it sits on, was at first as primitive, "very damp, and often cold."[14] Lawrence roofed the small, two-floor building with slates, put in a skylight, and removed a partition to enlarge the upstairs room. Soon the room—it had no ceiling and a steep timber roof—held a table, three chairs, leather settee, green carpet, a few books, records and player; lumber and firewood were stored downstairs. Lawrence would come out after duty, about 4:30 P.M., start a fire of rhododendron branches, work on a translation, write letters, revise *Seven Pillars*, or listen to music, and return to camp at 9 P.M. That December, he began using Clouds Hill as his mailing address. It had no kitchen, icebox, toilet, running water (a nearby spring supplied water for

Clouds Hill, Lawrence's cottage a mile north of Bovington Camp (courtesy of Malcolm Brown).

tea heated on the fireplace), electricity, gas, phone, or bed. When E. M. Forster visited in March 1924, Lawrence put him up at a Wool inn. In August, he added an iron cot, mattress, sheets, and blankets for an overnight guest; he himself used a sleeping bag on the floor. Though one or more Army friends might keep him company on an evening or weekend, he was often by himself and spent Christmas day 1923 and 1924 there alone.

Leaving Bovington in August 1925 for Cranwell 200 miles away, he considered dropping the lease but his brother Arnold and his wife Barbara wanted to use the cottage when they were in England between archeological expeditions. They occupied it from the summer of 1925 to January 1926, began negotiations to buy, and deposited £50 toward the £450 price of the land and building.[15] Then Lawrence de-

cided to buy it. Already in 1919, he had spoken of retiring to a cottage and writing a book. He did not want a substantial home and grounds requiring constant maintenance; the small, rough, secluded cottage set in untended bushes and oaks on an empty moor with a view of the sea from the hilltop suited him admirably. It was not intended as a full-time home, but, as E. M. Forster put it, a *pied-à-terre*. Not possessive, Lawrence shared it readily with comrades and family members. Upon renting it, he told Arthur Russell, "We've [not "I've"] got the cottage."[16] The mood of the place is caught by a verse:

If ye come thidder, ye must consider
When ye have lust to dine
There shall no meete be for to eate
Ne cake, ne ale, ne wine
Ne sheetes cleane to lie betweene[17]

When Arnold or Robert departed, keys were left with Knowles who was asked to let Tank Corps friends use it. In 1927, with Lawrence in India, Knowles installed a kitchen and it was rented for 7/6 or 12/- a week. Lawrence disliked the improvement, telling Knowles, "It's sad to think of that ... cottage being converted to Christian living! I did so much enjoy the savage feel. However I'm sure you will do nothing which cannot easily be ... broken away later."[18] James Lees-Milne, director of the National Trust that now owns it, called Clouds Hill "a pathetic little shoddy place." He was too accustomed to magnificent old mansions. To Patrick Knowles's suggestion that Lawrence get "a small, very modern house ... he replied firmly, 'No. I do not want anything that will last more than twenty years.'"[19] His feeling is expressed in the Greek motto *Ou phrontis*—"I don't care"—he carved over the door and his fondness for the cottage's defects, scars, and cobwebs.[20] When E. M. Forster, kept awake by a night-jar, threw a stone at it and broke a roof tile, Lawrence, delighted, would not replace it. He liked the defects of ancient statues, scars on new leather-bound books, and was untroubled by misprints.

By 1929, Lawrence had paid the last installment on the cottage. With money from the sale of his Pole Hill land and *Odyssey* translation, he had the bedroom walls plastered and a shed built for the Brough. Water still had to be brought by bucket sixty yards from the spring. There was no toilet.[21] A planned two-room addition proved too costly.

Back from China in the fall of 1930, Lawrence's mother and elder brother Robert moved into the cottage. They "converted the downstairs room into a living-room cum kitchen by fitting a cooking range into the fireplace ... it is probable that [Lawrence's] brothers and mother spent more time ... living in the cottage than he did himself!"[22]

Arthur Knowles, who with his wife had helped to rehabilitate and care for the cottage, died in April 1931. His widow, their son Patrick, and his wife remained as friends, caretakers, and occasional meal providers. After Sarah and Robert left in the fall of 1932, Lawrence started major improvements to turn the cottage into a home, "an infant palace," for his prospective retirement. To protect the site from developers, he tried to buy the land the Knowles rented. The Estate would not sell but, at Mrs. Knowles's request, transferred the £15-a-year lease to him. He removed his mother's kitchen, lined the walls with bookshelves, and installed a "window-seat, an affair six feet each way, built up of Bob's former bed and a big box-spring matttress."[23] Visiting Clouds Hill in 1960 to prepare for his role as Lawrence in Rattigan's *Ross*, Alec Guinness was puzzled by that "window-seat." "Why," he asked, "the vast bed for such an austere man?" But, to Lawrence it was a "lying-place" or "large couch." Using a sleeping bag stretched on the floor and keeping another for a guest, he insisted that he had "no bed.... I find the ruling-out of beds a great success."[24] Having no bed discouraged guests he wished to discourage and perpetuated a feeling of hardihood that was nonetheless yielding to selected comforts.

An oil-fueled water heater, tank, and bath were finally installed, the water fed by a small ram. To provide a steady flow and a reserve for fighting brush fires that threatened the cottage in dry seasons, Pat Knowles and two assistants laid a large concrete storage pool across the road; 40' × 7' and 5' deep, it took three months to fill with 8,000 gallons.[25] Water began flowing in August 1933; Lawrence took his first hot bath in December. To keep out leaves, the pool (also used for swimming) was roofed with glass that extended beyond the length to cover a space where he planned to fit a study, a hand-operated press, and intricately carved teak double doors he had bought in Jidda in 1921. In May 1934, he described the fittings thus:

> There are two sleeping bags, six loose blankets, and a shabby quilt. Many sheets. A large couch in the book-room, downstairs: enough cushions to pad a man's length of the floor, upstairs—and a narrow long floor-cushion in the food-room (ex-bedroom, upstairs). There are no cups or plates yet: but some are on order.... Six knives, six spoons, six forks. A small kettle: no pots or pans. Enough towels.... An axe: brushwood everywhere.[26]

The interior rooms had hanging cowhide curtains in lieu of doors; the steep stairs had pneumatic treads; the bookroom "lying-place" was covered with undyed leather. The cottage was as quiet as the boyhood bungalow where Lawrence had earlier practiced minimal housekeeping. The grounds were "an untended wilderness.... A bas gardens, I cry, if one has to care for them oneself."[27] A hidden path to the road cut through the back rhododendron enabled him to enter or leave unseen.

One writer observed the cottage's "cloistral, almost claustrophobic, atmosphere ... indicated by the windowless front...." The cottage was vintage Lawrence. "It is as ugly as my sins, bleak, angular, small, unstable: very like its creator. Yet I love it ... upon each visit I throw something out. Some day it will be bare walls and empty window-frames," he wrote Lady Astor, as if rehearsing the bareness theme would harden his softening taste. "[H]e became more luxurious as he grew older ... in the furnishing of his

The bookroom: Lawrence denied that the "window-seat" or "lying place" was a bed (courtesy of Jeremy Wilson and the National Portrait Gallery, London).

cottage his appetite for good things, and even for comfort, seemed to increase."[28]

As ten years before, Lawrence spent Christmas day 1933 and 1934 at Clouds Hill, the first with Jock Chambers and the second with Pat Knowles. The "lying-place" being too comfortable for his comfort, he built a "ship-cabin type" bunk with drawers in a dark "slip of a roomlet upstairs." A brass porthole inserted above the bunk enhanced the confined, shiplike motif. After attending Siegfried Sassoon's wedding in December 1933, Lawrence said, "If any of my generation has earned harbour after storm, it is S. S. and I am hoping for him."[29] The hope that Clouds Hill would become Lawrence's harbor was not fulfilled.

Finances

Lawrence is responsible for many biographers' mistaken notion of his family's modest means, writing this passage in Liddell Hart's 1934 biography: "The father's self-appointed exile reduced his means to a craftsman's income, which the landowning pride of caste forbade him to increase by labour. As five sons came, … the family's very necessaries of life were straitened. They existed only by the father's denying himself every amenity, and by the mother's serving her household like a drudge." He said his father had been "a spendthrift" whom his mother made "a careful spender of pence. They had … never more than £400 a year: and such pride against gain, and such pride in saving, as you cannot imagine."[30] Accepting these statements, biographers—Armitage, Knightley and Simpson, Stewart, Yardley, James—declared that the family had to live carefully on £300–£400 a year. Lawrence wrongly believed this. His father's income was closer to £1,500: £1,000 earnings on over £20,000 investments he received in

1888 in exchange for giving his brother Francis the Chapman family's Irish estates, a £200 yearly annuity received in the same settlement, and £300 a year from his sister Caroline.

Jeremy Wilson's exposition of these facts should correct misconceptions of the family's "straitened" circumstances. Arnold Lawrence recollected that the family took "a vast number of holidays, mostly in expensive hotels…. My father denied himself no amenities…. I emphatically deny that my mother served 'like a drudge'; she kept two maids, a charwoman, a gardener; … and seldom did any housework."[31] Arnold cannot attest to conditions he did not witness, say before 1904. His mother may have done more housework (she seems to have enjoyed it) when she had fewer children and was more fearful servants might discover her sinful state. However, his sense of the family's comfort is confirmed by other facts. The father rode and sailed, not penny-pinching activities; he bought expensive cameras and bicycles, built a sturdy, two-room bungalow still in use today, bought T.E. out of the military, paid the £65 cost of his 1909 trip to Syria. In March 1916, he gave his three living sons £5,000 each in treasury bonds yielding about £270 a year; the money came from a £25,000 inheritance from his brother. At his death in 1919, he left £17,800, his entire fortune, to Sarah. The £5,000 gift led Lawrence to say, "I'm now independent, so far as money is concerned, of any employment whatever."[32]

Lawrence seems to have been indifferent, even averse, to investing money prudently, let alone to maximize the return. Sending his father £300 to invest in 1917, he asked that he "put it in the most obvious thing, without troubling himself—or keep it." Taking payment for his Pole Hill land in 1930, he told Robin Buxton, "Don't take pains over the investment. Just whang it into anything." Later, he swore that "the best investment policy would be to stab the stock page of the Times from the back, with a pin!"[33] The remark reflected the merciless realities of the depression years as well as his obliviousness to investments.

Lawrence cared just as little about working for money, an attitude adopted from his father who, like other landed (or formerly landed) gentlemen, never condescended to earn any. "Poor Father!" Lawrence wrote in 1911, "his sons are not going to support his years by the gain of their professions & trades." After receiving his father's £5,000 gift, he expressed his intention of not having more than the £250 a year it yielded.[34] "I ... have never worked for it [money]: and won't." "There is nothing so repulsive as working merely for a living.... I refuse to do it."[35]

AN AFFLUENT PERIOD

From the war's end until his enlistment, Lawrence was more affluent than at any other period. In 1919, he had at least £7,000 in hand from his father, £2,000 from unspent 1915–19 military pay, and a £200 annual fellowship with free rooms and meals. He was widely dined, feted, and lodged in London and country homes. His pay and expense allowance with the Arab and British delegations in Paris are not established; for six weeks in Paris starting in late 1918, the Foreign Office allotted £1,000 for expenses.[36] His Colonial Office salary was £1,300[37] (in 1922, he stopped drawing it to induce Churchill to release him). Thus, in 1919 through 1921, his total capital and income were over £10,000. He gave away at least £3,300; much of the rest went into land, books, and paintings.

In October 1915, Will, his favorite brother, was shot down in France. Will and Janet Laurie were in love and hoped to marry. When Will asked T.E. to be his executor and, if he died, to give Janet any

money he left, T.E. cautioned that she might marry and "you cannot well leave anything ... to another man's wife."[38] After Will's death, he gave Janet the small sum Will had left. In 1919, Janet did, indeed, marry. The next year, T.E. did what he had told Will not to do. Hearing that Janet needed money, he secretly gave her £3,000, the amount Will would have received if their father's £15,000 had been shared by all sons. He did not want his family to learn of the gift because, holding Janet responsible for Will's death, his mother had broken relations with her.[39] The family "think I still have it," Lawrence wrote Hogarth, explaining the disposition of his father's £5,000 gift. "Two thousand was no good to me [!]: so I put £1000 into Epping [land] & £1000 into that book of mine [*Seven Pillars*]: pictures mostly."[40]

The gift to Janet Laurie was not the only one Lawrence made at the time. When Robert Graves owed £300 in 1921, Lawrence gave him £50 and three manuscript chapters of *Seven Pillars* that he sold for £200. He also contributed the largest portion of £400 to buy Charles Doughty's manuscript of *The Dawn in Britain* for presentation to the British Museum, a scheme he devised with Sydney Cockerell to relieve the aged poet's financial straits.

The cottage Vyvyan Richards rented stood on land at Pole Hill, Essex, adjoining Epping Forest. Since their college days, Lawrence and Richards had spoken of establishing a press to print fine books in the William Morris mode. In 1919, Lawrence's architect friend Herbert Baker inspected the site preparatory to designing a building for the press. Lawrence bought five Pole Hill acres that year and ten more subsequently at a total cost of about £4,000. For unclear reasons, the building was not constructed.[41] The land may have evoked, to a modest degree, feelings more appropriate to the landed gentry. Lawrence knew of his father's former Irish estates and, with doubtful seriousness, declared that if he had the money, "I shall ... buy myself some yards of County Meath ... and squat on it for a while."[42] In 1930, he sold the Pole Hill land for £3,500 to the Chingford Council, as an addition to adjacent Epping Forest, rather than to a builder who offered £7,000. He had swayed back and forth about profiting from the sale. At first, he considered selling to cover "most of the [*Seven Pillars*] overdraft." Offered £1,550 for part of the land, he put the builder off, noting "The value rises year by year." Eventually, he resolved that "dealers are barred."[43]

Lawrence devoured books as a youth and read constantly as an adult. Books occupied three walls of his cottage. Kennington's stone effigy shows three books beside his head. In 1919–21, he may have spent £600–£800 on books: £15 ($75) for a signed, limited edition of *Ulysses,* an unknown amount for a Kelmscott Chaucer, £80 for the Kelmscott *Water of the Wondrous Isles,* £12 for an Ashendene *Boccaccio.* Prices fell in the 1930s; still, the books represented a significant asset[44] readily convertible to cash. He almost sold them in 1925, but halted when Cape advanced £3,000 on the *Revolt in the Desert* contract. *Ulysses* was kept "wrapped away ... ready for sale in an emergency."[45] At various times, Lawrence sold a Shakespeare Fourth Folio for £80; seven Melville firsts for £120; a Dante (Ashendene?); Galsworthy and Hudson firsts. "[T]hirty pounds is a very good return for the thirty shillings ... I paid ... a few years ago," he wrote a bookseller after an unidentified sale. However, he denied the "yapping of some idiot about my ... living by selling the books decent people gave me."[46]

After 1926, valuable copies of *Seven Pillars* were at hand for gift or sale. "I'm relying on them to buy me a super motorbike [upon returning from India]. They represent my only ... realisable asset."[47]

He asked F. N. Doubleday for a few copies of the rare U. S. edition published to preserve copyright (and priced at $20,000 to prevent sale); these were given away, not sold.

Lawrence commissioned so much art for *Seven Pillars* Jeremy Wilson claims he "was becoming one of the most significant private patrons of contemporary art in Britain." Counting 118 works of art plus a complete set of initial letters, Valerie Thompson terms the subscribers' edition "a time capsule of 1920s art in Britain."[48] Commissioning art became a mania, a hobby enabling Lawrence to meet artists, conceivably a way to counterbalance with genuine art writing he increasingly denigrated. The quantity went far beyond the purpose of illustrating the text and the chief figures in the revolt. It cost about £3,000: £600 alone for Augustus John's portrait of Feisal, £1,920 for Kennington's work.[49] Unlike the excess royalties from *Revolt in the Desert* (which, after the bank loan was repaid, went to a charitable trust), Lawrence regarded the art as his, paid for mostly "out of my own money ... years before the financing of Seven Pillars."[50] That meant assuming, instead of passing on to the *Revolt* trust, the loss of about £2,000 incurred in disposing of the art.

Lawrence was generous to the artists. He gave hard-up William Roberts £120 for four portrait drawings and helped him to sell them, retaining only their copyright.[51] He paid Wyndham Lewis for a portrait Lewis never supplied (nor did he return the money). "Lawrence is of the salt of the earth and I know he's doing much of this simply to help painters who find a difficulty in *affording* to paint," said Paul Nash, who did five landscapes. When seventy-five works were put up for sale in 1927, Lawrence told his attorney, "I'd be delighted if you give away any balance remaining.... Please regard them as entirely yours, and rid me of the whole lot."[52]

"It's been seven years, living on my hump, and the hump has melted into my ribs!" Lawrence wrote in 1923, meaning that he had drawn down his capital. That was and was not true. During this period he received £2,000 in unused military salary, £600 from All Souls for three fellowship stipends (he did not draw the last four), at least £1,000 for expenses in Paris and £1,300 from the Colonial Office—all told, at least £4,900; his mother may have given him another £4,000 from his father's bequest.[53] However, he was as scornful of money as of his body, so that in mid-1922 he was hungry, emaciated, and virtually deranged. Thereafter, his main assets were his Pole Hill (later, Dorset) property, books, and, more valuable than both, two assets he would not use: the *Seven Pillars* copyright and his name.

FINANCES IN THE RANKS

Though Lawrence's pay and living expenses in the ranks were small, his fame, tastes, and excessive generosity kept his finances precarious. At All Souls and the Colonial Office, money passed freely through his hands to friends, artists, and bookdealers. He did not deposit a £17 check until asked to do so. His dealings with Cape over translating *The Forest Giant* showed his indifference to money (also, perhaps, his guilt at having rejected the contract for an abridged *Seven Pillars*). He told Cape to deduct the cost of having the manuscript typed and asked for less money. "I think 12/- a thousand a very high rate. Make it ten." When the check arrived, he found it "too large ... I'll hold it till you reconsider."[54]

At Bovington, his pay was 2/9 a day— £51 a year. Yet he paid John Bruce £3 a week; bought motorcycles for £150–£200 (minus the trade-in value); insured and maintained them; leased and began to repair a cottage; and displayed a general's generosity on a private's income. In India, he earned 3/3 a day—£60 a year. This was supplemented by fees of four guineas for the *Spectator* reviews, a pound a week for the rent of his Epping property, and 12 shillings a week for that of Clouds Hill when family members or friends did not use it: about another £100. His depleted investments also generated income. However, during the first months in Karachi when half of his pay was withheld in London, he complained that he could not afford postage for his letters and, refusing to pay the duty, rejected parcels from unknown admirers. In Britain, he bought the cheapest tea—"it is better to pay 1d than 2d for a cup.... It makes a bit of a difference!"—and rode miles out of the way to avoid tolls. Promoted to first-class aircraftman in 1927, he declared, "that means fourpence a day [£6 a year] extra money, for which I'm grateful." He had no overcoat, pronouncing it "a wicked waste of 3 or 4 pounds, for a mere month."[55] The chilblain-breeding cold of damp English winters makes that "month" preposterous. Lawrence was especially sensitive to cold; for him to wear no coat was another masochistic exercise.

"Brick by brick I have sold or given away or lost everything I possessed. The course cannot proceed much further, or I will be naked in the world," he told Edward Garnett in 1927 with his usual mix of truth and exaggeration. Invited to see Feisal, now King of Iraq, in the summer of 1930, he wired, "Give him my deepest regards regret I am ... financially unable visit London often as it costs fortnights pay."[56] He had tea with a Persian government minister at Lyons Corner House, a mammoth, tasteless London eatery. Anticipating lower income and higher expenses in retirement, he proclaimed his poverty. "I cannot answer your wires," he protested to Lady Astor, "because often I have not a shilling to spare" and warned Charlotte Shaw, "Next year I am going to draw in my ink-horns: for this year I have tried—vainly!—not to spend more than 2/- a week on post [he spent 5/-]. After February ... I shall not spend more than three pence weekly."[57]

Lawrence gave money away rather than using, saving, investing, or earning it. He offered the Ashmolean expensive seals at half-price. His gifts to Doughty and Graves have been noted. Eating in the Bovington restaurant with one or two comrades, he paid the bill. Visiting Clouds Hill, E. M. Forster stayed at an inn as Lawrence's guest. When Jock Chambers visited from London, Lawrence paid the rail fare. He gave a comrade his fee for translating *The Forest Giant*. He paid a London surgeon £50 to repair the lamed ankle of a hostile Tank Corps sergeant. He gave Herbert Hodgson, who helped print *Seven Pillars*, £10 at Christmas and apologized that he was short of cash. He gave Posh Palmer a rare proof of *Seven Pillars* and arranged for Ralph Isham to buy it for £400.

The "clean money" from the 1927 sale of *Seven Pillars* art was divided 50/50 between Palmer and Manning Pike, the prime *Seven Pillars* printer, who were both in need of money (who is not?). Running into Ronald Storrs in London, Lawrence took him to Jonathan Cape's, "where, walking around the room, he picked out half a dozen expensive books, and, as though he were the head of the firm, made me a present of them."[58] When Alec Dixon wired from the Straits Settlements asking for money, he sent £40. When a friend faced bankruptcy, he borrowed £200 from his bank to lend him.

Taking all circumstances into account—his tiny salary, limited reserves, and refusal to profit from the fame of "Colonel Lawrence"—he was decidedly heedless of money. In Jordan in 1922, he

mislaid £7,500 later found in a safe. Twice, he gave a Bovington garage owner about £50 in bills and cash, asked him to put it in his account, would not count it or take a receipt, but sometimes asked him for £5. Acknowledging a £30 check from Herbert Samuel for a copy of *Seven Pillars*, D. G. Hogarth wrote: "...I shall pay it in to ... the Bank of Liverpool ... against T. E.'s return from India.... I shall not tell him ... for ... [he] would at once ... squander it on a friend! He takes no thought of the morrow."[59] But Lawrence usually managed for the day: he kept a few hundred pounds in a checking account, paid bills for cottage work promptly, and had a stock of half-crowns in the petrol filler cap of his motorcycle.

"I'm going to swear never to run into debt again," he said in mid–1927, when the end of his overdraft was in sight,[60] but by 1930, he had built up a £600 overdraft. Though he cleared it with the Pole Hill proceeds, his financial situation had worsened. The price he accepted for the land meant a loss of £500 capital and perhaps £1,000 in income the £4,000 investment might otherwise have earned over the years. The £450 cost of Clouds Hill land and more than twice that spent on the cottage, motorcycle, books, gifts, etc. reduced his reserves. The depression reduced the value of, and the return on, his investments. Against these losses, he could put only the £800 *Odyssey* fee and £450 royalties on American sales; he gave Bruce Rogers the translator's copyright. By mid–1934, his savings were under £2,000. He accepted checks from his mother—she sent him two £50 checks a year (one, on his birthday)—but refused money Robert Graves, H. S. Ede, and other friends offered.

RETIREMENT

In the 1920s, Lawrence had set a target income of £300 a year. In the 1930s, he lowered his sights to £50–£100, at most £150, partly out of necessity (dividends were lower), partly to escape income tax,[61] but mainly, I think, to gratify his urge for self-abasement. His name, even the name "T. E. Shaw," was still gold. Cape and other publishers would gladly pay to add it to their board of directors. His letters sold for £20; in 1927, he was offered £5,000 for a copy of the Oxford Text. Compunctions and uncertainties attending his impending departure from the RAF immobilized him. Arnold Lawrence attributed his penurious life style to a fear that John Bruce might blackmail him. Arnold did not sufficiently credit his brother's ability to handle a dangerous man. Lawrence kept an iron hand in a soft glove. His generosity, careless prodigality, and determination to live on little began well before he met Bruce.

In February 1934, he expected a retirement income of £100—or so he told his mother. Two months later, he asked Faber chairman F. V. Morley to keep him in mind for future work. In June, he hoped that, by rearranging his securities, he would not have to work. By November, that hope had gone with the collapsing market. His prospective income was down to £65, enough to live at the cottage but not for travel, visits, and restaurant meals. In early 1935, interest fell further and he expected only £52 a year. "Instead of trying to make more, I am going to try to need less."[62] He reckoned he had enough money to live without working for six months.

He managed well enough to put the motorcycle back on the road. "My true living expenses the last three weeks have been 22/- weekly," he boasted in April. But the cottage was "the only spot, apparently, where I can afford to live."[63] How long would he be content to live there, forsaking the larger world, his friends in London, and (a more expensive trip) John

Bruce in Scotland? To hibernate for ten or twenty years was not his style.

POSTHUMOUS INCOME

The gross value of Lawrence's estate was £7,441: investments, £2,576; books and paintings, £726.10; current account, £200. Allowing, say, £300 for the furnishings and damaged motorcycle would leave £3,600 as the value of the cottage, land, and the lease of 17 acres across the road. Arnold Lawrence, chief heir in Lawrence's will[64] and (with Oxford solicitor John Snow) one of its two executors, initially wished to leave the cottage and its contents to his daughter, bequeathing it to the National Trust after her death. Changing his mind, he gave it to the Trust in 1938, possibly because some of Lawrence's friends wanted an immediate transfer and (rightly or wrongly) felt he was putting money-making before other concerns in his handling of Lawrence's estate.

Many people made money out of Lawrence's name and work after his death. Ten weeks after, on July 29, Jonathan Cape issued the first trade edition of *Seven Pillars*. Priced at 30 shillings, four times the usual price of a novel, over 100,000 copies were sold by Christmas; by April 1939, there were fourteen printings; a new edition in 1940 was reprinted eleven times. The book remains in print and has been translated into more than thirteen languages; over a million copies have been sold. Lawrence had written the introduction to Cape's first title, *Arabia Deserta;* in 1927, *Revolt in the Desert* increased Cape's yearly profit from £2,000 to £28,000. "Always, from the very beginning, Lawrence was the key to our success," said Cape's partner Wren Howard.[65]

The *Revolt in the Desert* Trust will be discussed shortly. Arnold Lawrence assigned to The *Seven Pillars of Wisdom* Trust, formed in March 1936, all benefits from the Cape publication and £10,000 of the £13,000 he received from Doubleday, Doran for the U.S. copyright. In exchange, the Trust reimbursed various expenses including £2,000 for Kennington's Lawrence effigy, and put £10,000 into a trust for his daughter. Additional *Seven Pillars* income went to various charitable purposes.[66] The Letters and Symposium Trust, formed in April 1936, received royalties from David Garnett's edition of Lawrence's letters and *T.E. Lawrence by his Friends* and payments for the right to print Lawrence's writings. Its grants were generally smaller than those of the *Seven Pillars* Trust, with which it merged in 1986; upon Arnold Lawrence's death in 1991, the unified trust held the copyright to both brothers' work.

The sale of film rights, personal papers, manuscripts, and inscribed books can be more lucrative than royalties. Arnold Lawrence, who retained the *Seven Pillars* film rights, received £25,000 in 1960 for use of the book in David Lean's 1962 film *Lawrence of Arabia*. He forfeited another £5,000 because, displeased with the portrayal of Lawrence as a sadist, he refused permission for it to be titled *Seven Pillars of Wisdom*.[67] In 1959, Robert Graves remarked that "ever since his [Lawrence's] death there's always been something coming from him to help me…: sale of his MSS letters in 1936 for £2000…; money for *Lawrence and the Arabs* film rights, twice…: £1000 and £3000."[68] Liddell Hart received £3,000 for his help in a 1955 Lawrence documentary and £3,000 plus 1 percent of box-office receipts for use of his biography in Terence Rattigan's play *Ross*.[69] He, Eric Kennington, and others received unknown amounts for Lawrence letters and papers now lodged at the University of Texas. Large sums have been paid by dealers, collectors, and archives for Lawrence's letters, papers, books, and other possessions.

Legally, a trust is supposed to be in-dependent but the founder can often influence, if not control, its policies. Of the three *Revolt* trustees, solicitor Edward Eliot was most active and knowledgeable about the trust's legal obligations. As Lawrence explained, Eliot "is the only Trustee, really; but I added Hogarth and Buxton so that I could carry any point against him … if I wished it deeply."[70] Trust funds were to be devoted to the education of the children of disabled or deceased RAF officers, not servicemen, because most flying was done by officers who suffered heavy casualties. During his life, the trust paid £4,142 in school fees; in 1935, thirteen children were being educated.

Lawrence was no enthusiast for trusts. "Charities are not any good," he felt, "unless they are individually given."[71] Nor did he aim to earn as much money as possible for the trust, which was established to clear his debt and demonstrate that he was not making money from *Revolt* sales: "if … there was only 5/- over for charity, my eyes wouldn't be wet with tears!" In his self-contradictory manner, he also hoped "there will be thousands of pounds. The more, surely, the merrier."[72] He told Buxton, "I want your Trust to be a sleepy comfortable body, meeting every ten years or so for lunch: not a white-hot money-making corporation." He did not even like writing to Eliot, who would bill the trust for his time: "making Eliot write me letters … [is] like sitting in a taxi, & hearing it tick—at R.A.F. Fund expense."[73]

"It was in the deed that they [the trustees] should not consult me upon the disposition of balances. I heard a vague suggestion … of using them in an educational scheme," Lawrence misinformed Trenchard. The information was not "vague"; if trustees were not to consult Lawrence, he was free to consult them—and did. "[I]f a bright idea occurs to me I won't hesitate to send it in to Eliot."[74] He suggested that the trust help fund a swimming bath on the

Karachi base, then wrote, "No swimming-bath please. They muddled the plan."[75] He also solicited funds for the needy widow of an RAF sergeant.

Lawrence's attitude toward money passes my understanding. He did not, as some suggest, emulate his father, who did not live beyond his means, spend his capital or incur debt to help others. Lawrence's deliberate deprivations began in boyhood; in adulthood, they marked the same downward urge as his enlistment.

As billions know, poverty is a great leveler. Was his generosity "saintlike," as John Mack, among others, says? We are unaccustomed to saints in our midst and would not credit them if they walked among us, let alone a saint in military uniform tending the weapons of war. Saint and sinner, sane and mad, Lawrence was an unusually compassionate man who gave money away so freely he endangered his prized freedom to live as he pleased.

14

Parents

Father

Thomas Chapman's Protestant ancestors left Leicestershire for Ireland where, in the 16th and 17th centuries, they received large tracts of land from courtier-adventurer Sir Walter Raleigh, a cousin, and Oliver Cromwell, Ireland's conqueror and devastator. Thomas was the second of three brothers (William was older, Francis, younger) and a sister, Caroline. Educated at Eton, like his brothers, he led a country gentleman's life, hunting, riding, sailing, entertaining, drinking, marrying, and siring four daughters. Everyone describes him as a gentleman, meaning well-mannered and living on unearned income.

No one calls him strong-willed, the most frequent characterization of Sarah Lawrence and T.E. Both his wife Edith and common-law wife Sarah dominated him. Edith, called "the holy viper" and "a religious maniac," made him visit his club in Salvation Army uniform and locked him out for taking their eldest daughter to a Dublin theater.[1] Edith drove him to drink, Sarah, to abstinence. Col. Magan, an Irish neighbor, said Thomas was "a good fellow" who "hadn't a brain in his head." Lord Stamfordham, the King's secretary,

said he was "an eccentric old man, half sportsman and half idealist."[2]

His boldest act was to leave his estates for the anxious life of a counterfeit husband in staid, middle-class Oxford. Though the settlement he made in 1888 upon assigning his estates to Francis enabled him to live comfortably without working, he forfeited his social position and great wealth. Upon Francis's death in 1915, his estate was valued at £120,000, "equivalent in today's terms to … more than £3 million."[3] Thomas became the seventh and last Chapman baronet in 1914, but never assumed the title.

In contrast to their criticism and condemnation of their mother, T.E. and Arnold Lawrence speak of their "ever considerate and loving father" with warmth and admiration. "T.E.'s words … 'I liked him so much', apply to me too," Arnold wrote.[4] Red-bearded, tall, thin, "completely the aristocrat," he is described as courtly, grave, reserved, shy, "sometimes brusque," and, rather contradictorily, as having a relaxed, friendly manner. Arnold recalled his firm authority in quieting unruly students and family disputes, though usually he deferred to Sarah. Physically, he resembled G. B. Shaw. Lawrence thought him the "walking image" of

Walter Raleigh, adding, "I'm not like that side of the family."[5] At home and on excursions and holidays, he spent much time with his sons and passed on to them many of his interests, sports, and hobbies. He taught T.E. carpentry, photography, church architecture, a close appreciation of the countryside, yachting, snipe and pheasant shooting. A strong cyclist, Thomas often rode 100 miles a day and each fall bought the best next year's model; the summers of 1905 and '07, he and T.E. took bicycle tours of English and French castles. Like most gentlemen, he was no scholar or intellectual: "Never read a book till late in life," T.E. said. However, "He knew French grammatically, and in old age quoted Horace to express his own sentiments, and a line of Homer for its metrical felicity." Arnold Lawrence declared, "His influence can scarcely be overestimated."[6]

Lawrence's remarks to his father in his letters are kind, solicitous, respectful, and obedient; he requests and accepts his father's judgment and does not question it. "If you feel able to give me long enough to finish my ... survey of the country I would be delighted," he writes from Syria in August 1909. "But if you think I have done enough I will come back direct from Damascus."[7] His father approved the extension. In 1911, he asked his father for money to erect a building for the press he and Vyvyan Richards wanted to operate. The money posed little difficulty, but Mr. Lawrence had already built T.E.'s bungalow; two buildings for one son were an overindulgence and the parents disliked Richards, a homosexual. The decision, T.E. wrote, "is entirely for ... [father's] judgment: if he feels inclined to do it, ... it would make matters much easier.... If not we will have to wait."[8] They waited. The press was never established.

Few letters from Lawrence's correspondents have survived, as he discarded most. His mother and brothers, especially Will, seem to have written most, his father less often. "Tell Father not to write overmuch: it is no great pleasure for him," Lawrence wrote in 1911. A letter from his father to Carchemish with a £20 check "was most welcome," but a forthcoming trip to Ireland provoked T.E.'s only known rebuke. "Don't go to Ireland.... I think the whole place repulsive historically: they should not like English people, and we certainly cannot like them." Very likely, the rebuke arose from Lawrence's knowledge of his father's other family. Palliative remarks followed quickly. "You would feel a certain pleasure out here, shooting.... I counted 30 wild-duck ... swimming about the river."[9]

His father accepted T.E.'s infatuation with the East and the prospect of his remaining there; during the entire war, he did not visit home. His parents, who had lost two sons, naturally worried about him. He seldom wrote; at times, Hogarth's wife and E. T. Leeds of the Ashmolean passed along news. In November 1917, Lawrence was awarded the *Croix de Guerre* for the capture of Akaba. Seeing Mr. Lawrence in the Union Society smoking room, Leeds congratulated him. "I can see him now shaking with pride, speechless until at last he rose to his feet saying 'I must tell his mother', and hurried away."[10]

At the Paris Peace Conference in April 1919, Lawrence received a telegram from Arnold, FATHER HAS PNEUMONIA COME IF POSSIBLE. He flew back but, two hours before he arrived, his father died. When they were alone, his mother gave him an envelope with a letter to "My dear Sons" his father had prepared confessing what T.E. already knew, that his real name was Thomas—"now Sir Thomas"—Robert Tighe Chapman and that he and Sarah had never married. "You can imagine ... how yr Mother & I have suffered all these years, not knowing what day we might be recognised by some one and our sad history published far and wide … there never was a truer saying than 'the ways of transgressors are hard' … there is no happiness in this life, except you abide in Him thro' Christ & oh I hope you all will." As this letter indicates, Lawrence's father was as religious as his mother, though his religion may have been more heartfelt, hers, more doctrinaire. It was the father who conducted the family's morning prayers and who, Arnold Lawrence said, "was more religious-minded."[11]

Mr. Lawrence remains a fainter figure than Sarah, the woman for and by whom his life was cut in two. Dying before Lowell Thomas made his son famous, he was not visited by biographers; living until 1959, Sarah was inspected by Lawrence's friends and chroniclers. Lawrence remembered him as "on the large scale, tolerant, experienced, grand, rash, humoursome, skilled to speak, and naturally lord-like. He had been 35 years in the larger life, and a spend-thrift, a sportsman, and a hard rider and drinker. My mother … [made] him a teetotaller, a domestic man, a careful spender of pence."[12]

Lawrence was very aware of the Chapmans. From the letter his father left at his death, he had some reason to hope his father's sister Caroline might bequeath him £6,600, but she did not.[13] Occasionally, his letters mention his father's Irish family and former estates. In 1933, he asked his father's Dublin solicitor to check on a Dublin widow who might need assistance, starting his letter, "I believe you used to act for my father, Thomas Chapman of Southhill."[14] By a strange coincidence, Clouds Hill and thousand-acre Bovington Camp had been part of the Frampton estate, whose owner, Henry R. Fetherstonhaugh Frampton, was a distant relative of Thomas Chapman. "[Q]uaint how these people are settled all about here," Lawrence wrote his mother. "The

daughter of the rector of the Southhill parish it was who knew all about us. She … is living in [Bovington] camp, being the mother-in-law of one of our officers."[15]

Lawrence's affection for his father has an undercurrent of compassion and regret at his capture by and submission to Sarah; pride at the brave forfeiture of his social position; and agonized emotions—purported indifference, bitter pain—at the illegitimacy he imposed on his sons, a heavier penalty for T.E. than his brothers. "If my father had been as big as you," he wrote Trenchard, "the world would not have had spare ears for my freakish doings." He gave Lady Scott an unflattering picture of his father. "Had a drunken father. Whilst drunken, first, dull, son born. Reformed; and had had then another."[16] From boyhood on, he sought to escape his father's fate: Sarah's domination.

Arnold Lawrence criticized biographers who suggested "that his father was spineless and his mother dominant. Both parents had strong personalities."[17] However, the father lived falsely and fearfully, and T.E. did not depict him as strong. In Lawrence's "exposed detachment, one … sees the image of his father. The old landowner … must … have been something of a spectator in his own family…. The fates of father and son have curious resemblances. We also have the not uncommon sight of passionate elders using up a family's erotic capital, leaving the children with little or none."[18]

Mother

Sarah's early years are poorly documented; even her surname is uncertain. She was born August 31, 1861, in Sunderland, on the coast not far from Newcastle, the illegitimate daughter of Elizabeth Junner, a Scottish servant in the home of surveyor Thomas Lawrence, and John

Lawrence, his son, a ship's carpenter, who was probably Sarah's father. (He was 18 and Elizabeth, 28 at Sarah's birth.) After her mother's death from alcoholism, Sarah lived with her grandparents near Perth and then with an aunt married to an Evangelical rector on the Isle of Skye. Around 1879, she was recruited to serve as governess to Thomas and Edith Chapman's daughters in Delvin, Ireland.[19] Thomas was not the only Chapman to love energetic, efficient, pretty Sarah; his daughters all loved her and, when she left, Mrs. Chapman gave her a locket with their pictures.[20]

Short like his mother, T.E. had her blue eyes, straight nose, determination, thoroughness, and remarkable memory. He resembled her in physique, face, and character. Like all the sons but Arnold, he was breast-fed at least a year. A sequence of nannies and governesses cared for him under Sarah's close supervision. In later years, Sarah spoke proudly of his precocity, strength, fearlessness, and (more problematic) happiness. Robert, her first-born, almost three years older, conceded his leadership in intellect, games, and action. Will, her third son, may have been her favorite though John Mack, who thinks so, adds that T.E. "was the child in whom both parents had the most important emotional investment. He was treated differently, as if he were special, and ... would do something important with his life."[21] Robert was obedient; Will, obedient and/or indulged.

T.E. challenged Sarah's authority and was often whipped for it. "I never had to do it to Bob, once to Frank and frequently to T.E.," Sarah said. Will was unmentioned; Arnold was beaten once. "The beatings seem to have been brought on by ... routine childhood misbehavior ... they seemed to be given for the purpose of breaking T.E.'s will." Sarah could not break it. The whippings (when did they

Sarah Lawrence, T.E.'s mother, ca. 1910 when she was 49 (courtesy of Jeremy Wilson and the National Portrait Gallery, London).

end?) set the pattern of an enduring contest between the mother's demand for submission and the son's refusal to yield. If T.E. saw his father's love for Sarah as another form of submission, that would help to explain his inability to love. Sarah submitted only to God. Constrained by her improper liaison and working-class origin from proselytizing her middle-class neighbors, she consecrated her young sons to God. She wanted them to become missionaries. T.E. "took part in the family Bible readings, attended faithfully ... sermons at St. Aldates, and even taught Sunday School classes."[22] His gradual breach with his mother was accompanied by a breach with her fundamentalist faith.

The conflict reached one climax in 1905, when T.E. ran away and enlisted. A second break occurred in 1908, when he left the family home for his bungalow. His letters show that the withdrawal from his mother's embrace took many years and was completed—as far as it ever was completed—only during the war. In successive summer 1906 letters to his mother from France, he says, "Love to yourself. (Don't do any work at all)." "DON'T WORK TOO HARD … you are worth more than the house…. Love. love. love. love. love. love." That does not sound like a son who is cool to his mother, unless one reasons that distance engenders a loving relief. Two summers later, he writes "Dear Mother" from France, "I wish you were here." "We must return there [to Chartres] … and spend a fortnight in pure happiness."[23] These are not representative passages. The long letters are full of unbelievably technical descriptions of the layout, construction, and embellishment of fortresses and churches intended for use in his thesis. Their number (at least 8 in the summer of 1908, 14 the next summer), length, and manifest enthusiasm attenuate the impersonal content. The 1909 letters from Syria express his excitement at the new country, people, and customs; some have Biblical references bound to please his mother. He tells 8-year-old Arnold "take great care of Mother: I want her to get quite strong, so as to be able to come out here for a trip with me in a couple of years."[24]

Growing Detachment

Lawrence's fascination with the East and his detachment from his mother grew simultaneously. Instructing her in missionary politics, he explains that, as Moslems cannot be converted to Christianity, the American Presbyterian mission set up schools throughout Syria and Palestine; its Beirut college has educated the country's leaders who promote political reforms. "I will have such difficulty in becoming English again, here I am Arab in habits."[25] On board ship to Syria in 1910, he is again the dutiful son who writes because, if she received no letter, "Mother would no doubt feel unquiet." His criticism of two French priests seems applicable to others "too narrow to get outside their own civilization." He asks, "Is civilization the power of appreciating the character and achievements of peoples in a different stage from ourselves?" His many letters— 29 from December 1910 to July 1911— lively, full of encounters and adventures, are now directed to his brothers as well as parents. August 1910 is the last to "Dear Mother," though next January a letter goes "particularly to Will … with Mother perhaps as principal listener"[26] and her August 1912 birthday is noted. His signature changes from "Ned," last used in August 1910, to "N.," often no signature at all, occasionally "L.," with no "love" but, at times, "Salaam" or "Salaamat."

Dangers from robbers or illness Lawrence plays down or conceals. "Anxiety is absurd: if anything happens you will hear it by wire: I am well known in this district." He mentions two broken ribs, but "They were not important … [and] are mended up." To his mother's protest upon learning that Friday was the Carchemish Sabbath, he responds, "would it be quite considerate to make 200 workmen miss their day for the sake of the two of us?"[27]

When war broke out and Lawrence headed for Egypt in late 1914, his mother almost accompanied him. During the next two years, his letters are brief and barren except for a 5,000-word May 1916 opus, composed on a ship bound for Cairo, describing his visit to Mesopotamia. The usual signature is "N.," three times "T. E. L."! No letter has a salutation, save one to his mother upon news of Frank's death. Lawrence's first response was silence; his subsequent response, almost brutal. Informed by wire, he did not answer.[28] After two letters from his father (highly un-usual), he writes, "The only thing I feel a little is, that there was no need surely to go into mourning for him...? [A]t this time it is one's duty to show no signs that would distress others: and to appear bereaved is surely under this condemnation." Finally, when his anguished mother writes, he replies:

Poor Dear Mother

I got your letter this morning, & it has grieved me very much.... *Don't* you ever feel that we love you without our telling you so?—I feel such a contemptible worm for having to write this way.... If you only knew that if one thinks deeply about any-thing one would rather die than say any-thing about it. You know men do nearly all die laughing, because they know death is very terrible.... There, put that aside, & bear a brave face to the world about Frank.[29]

Was Lawrence thinking of men going into battle—whom he had yet to see? None of a dozen men I have seen die laughed, smiled, or smirked; dying is a desperately serious business. Plainly, he would rather die than say anything loving to his mother.

Succeeding letters are uncommu-nicative. "[A]nother week gone, & nothing has happened." "There is of course, noth-ing happening here.... I can't think of any-thing else to say."[30] August 31, he remem-bers, "is Mother's birthday." As he grows engaged in the revolt, his letters take on life with a strange mix of emotion and im-personality ("one has become monoma-niac," "one's thoughts"). He seldom ad-dresses a family member directly: it is "tell Mother," "ask Father," "tell Arnie." De-spite the uncertainties of wartime mail, censorship, and his frenetic, exhausting activities, Lawrence wrote 21 letters to his family (more precisely: his family received, preserved, and published that many) be-tween October 1916, when he visited Jidda,

and July 1918: 10 from Cairo, 11 from Ara-bia. Most are signed "N."; one, "T. E. Law-rence." Central features of *Seven Pillars* emerge: his preference for Feisal over Ab-dulla, train smashing, the uncertain future of Syria and Palestine, the wonderful, bar-baric Bedouin.

The Lawrence who returned home in October 1918, who had dealt with generals and princes, led and killed men, endured terrible ordeals, was not the man who left home four years earlier. Little information is available on his relations with his mother in the ensuing years until his Au-gust 1922 enlistment. Only four letters to his family from this period survive and the little that his mother and brother Robert wrote about him dealt mainly with his boyhood. The brief April 1919 visit home from Paris upon his father's death must have stirred deep feelings in mother and son, but the son concealed his. His mother acknowledged her great sin; he, having long known it, let the revelation pass as inconsequential.

With her common-law husband and two sons dead, Sarah turned increasingly toward Lawrence for solace, but he would not give it and had his own wrenching problems. During the 1919–20 winter, Sarah reported, he "would sometimes sit the entire morning ... in the same posi-tion, without moving, and with the same expression on his face." "I can't live at home...," he said, "the place makes me ut-terly intolerable."[31] All Souls was scarcely better; the academic ambience did not suit his mood, nor, one suspects, did the close-ness (a 15-minute walk) to home. He did little work there, escaping to Baker's Lon-don loft for serious writing.

The wish to escape his mother must have played a part in his enlistment. Richard Aldington, a hostile biographer, sees little good and much falseness in Law-rence. Nonetheless, his comments on the enlistment are worth attention: "having triumph in his grasp he throws it all away, to escape the mother who now turned instinctively to the brilliant son for comfort. Let him be ... ruler of Egypt, she could still follow and madden him with female efficiency and prayer. There was one place where neither she nor any woman could follow him—a barrack-room." Lawrence acknowledged that, "One of the real reasons ... why I am in the service is so that I may live by myself"—meaning, *away from his mother*.[32] Like virtually all of Lawrence's friends, his mother did not approve or understand his enlistment. Expecting a great future for him, the decision left her—the words are E. T. Leeds's—sad, bitter, and numbed; "he had passed beyond her comprehension.... 'Mr. Leeds [she said], I think Ned is mad!'"[33]

The Polstead Road home was sold in late 1921. Mrs. Lawrence lived alone on the outskirts of Oxford, Robert having gone to China as a medical missionary. In 1923, she joined him, traveling by ship via Vancouver and Shanghai. Writing to her in Paoing in November 1923, Lawrence is depressed. "I hope not again to do anything of my own." He hopes her journey was not wearisome, "yet, you know, these journeys don't really end, till we do." His brief next letter is no more cheerful. "It isn't much good my writing frequently, since I have nothing to say."[34] Nothing, that is, to say to her. The same day, he prepares a statement for *Seven Pillars* subscribers; the next day, he writes G. B. Shaw a long, good-humored letter and invites him and his wife to visit Clouds Hill.

The Tank Corps cannot be the cause of Lawrence's depression. Back in the RAF in mid–1925, he attacks his mother and himself savagely, despairingly, punishing her for having borne him, for tormenting him and refusing to leave him alone. She asks to share his life; he slaps her down: "that I won't allow. It is only my business. Nor can anybody turn on or off the tap of

'love' so called. I haven't any in me, for anything." As he prepares to depart for India, she suggests that he leave the RAF and live quietly somewhere. "Thank you...," he replies, "but ... the bustle and enforced duty of the R.A.F. is good for me." They dance a minuet. She wants to send him money. He says, "No thanks." She sends a check anyway. He says "many thanks," but it is too big.[35]

The exchange is typical of what has gone wrong between mother and son. She knows and does what is right for him regardless of what he says. In her letters, she pleads for love "and points us to Christ"; he and Arnold turn their backs on her and her God. "It is a dreadful position for her, and yet I see no alternative ... we would never give any other human being the pain she gives us ... and yet we give her the pain." His mother declares her love and asks for his; he would not acknowledge his if put to the rack. He rebukes her for expressing her feelings. "Airmen ... dislike mention of love and God ... because they care about these things and people should never talk or write about what is important"! He dreads her "harrowing" letters; they "make me want to blow my brains out."[36]

"Her care for my finances is of course touching," he tells Charlotte Shaw. "Touching is very well: but being touched isn't ... we do rub each other up the wrong way." Plainly they did: financially, religiously, intellectually, in their style of life, their ways of dealing with people, in half a dozen other ways. About the ways Sarah brought her son into the world, Lawrence professed indifference to his illegitimacy and confessed aversion to copulation. "Knowledge of her will prevent my ever making any woman a mother,"[37] he said, without making clear exactly what knowledge he had in mind. Her domineering nature was not characteristic of all women, though he may have feared it was; perhaps he feared most the hidden sexuality that had seduced his father and produced child after child.

"Fitted Only to Dictate"

Friends draw a kinder picture of Mrs. Lawrence than does her son: she had not whipped them or told them how to live. Lawrence recognizes her admirable qualities—"mother is rather wonderful: but very exciting.... She by dint of will raised herself to be his [father's] companion ... she is ... an extraordinary person." But, in his eyes, her faults greatly outweigh them; the will that can impress others is, to him, insufferable. "She is fitted only to dictate in a *small* world."[38]

When Mrs. Lawrence and Robert stayed with the Kenningtons, Mrs. Kennington writes, "I just handed my will completely over to her ... hers was a world of dazzlingly white whites, and intensely black blacks, ... no shades of grey existed." She was "dogmatic about all kitchen affairs. Apples should never be peeled or cored but wiped and cut in quarters and then stewed.... Porridge must be cooked overnight." In the summer of 1940, Mrs. Lawrence lived with and helped care for Lady Kennet (Kathleen Scott), who was ill in bed. Every time the anthem sounded on the radio, she stood to attention. Unable to endure her unalterable habits yet unwilling to evict her, Lady Kennet moved out of her own home.[39]

Victoria Ocampo, who met Mrs. Lawrence in 1946 and repeatedly thereafter, was impressed by her puritanism, her fortitude in disregarding a broken leg and chilly room, her uncomplaining acceptance of her frugal lot, her "contempt for money," her "vitality and ... integrity," clear, "inexhaustible memories," the way she controlled her "intense emotions" about T.E., of whom she spoke "with passion." Because of its obscenities, neither

she nor Robert had read *The Mint,* and Robert asked Ocampo, who had translated it into Spanish, not to mention it to his mother.[40] Mrs. Lawrence read *Seven Pillars* and was much troubled by T.E.'s pain and suffering; she read with more pleasure Graves's and Liddell Hart's biographies and reviews and letters of praise that T.E. sent her.

Sending his mother some books and a *Times* subscription, he adds one to the *New Statesman,* "which does not instantly condemn an idea" for being new.[41] She regrets his inability to worship Christ; he disapproves of her and Robert's missionizing and of foreigners patronizing the Chinese. "So long as she [China] permits outsiders to teach or preach in her boundaries, so surely is she an inferior nation. You must see that" he tells his mother who sees no such thing.[42] Leave China, he urges in February 1927, but recognizes the futility of saying so: "it is no use talking these things over again. The difference of opinion is too fundamental."[43] As it happened, his mother and brother came back that year, but returned to China later.

Lawrence writes his mother at intervals of months. "She writes often and at length, and cries out for letters."[44] The time it takes a letter to reach her and the occasional loss of a letter are to him reasons for writing less often. "[W]hen we do not write so rapidly, our letters have time to reach their destinations ... so that we do not need to repeat everything many times." "Your letters take about two months.... There is no reality in the exchange of only three letters in a year. All the news in them is stale." "[W]e will have to send a telegram to each other, once a quarter, saying 'Well' and no more: indeed, reduced to its essences, there is no more to say."[45] His letters are flat, detached, cool; his mother's, affectionate, warm, worried. She is concerned about his mode of life, his finances, his happiness; he wants to be left alone. She sends parcels and checks; he asks her to send neither, but accepts both. "Please let me off parcels. The [Indian] duty makes them a real inconvenience. Books come free … but I get so many that I cannot read the half of them."[46] He doesn't write that way to Charlotte Shaw, Jonathan Cape, Edward Garnett. Addressing the ostensible problem directly, his mother sends him £1 for the duty. In 1929, she sends two £50 checks, one for his birthday, one "to help with [work on] the cottage." In 1933, she sends two more; "please do not bother yourself…. It is never hard for me to make money," he says untruthfully after receiving the first; after the second, "I am sorry you made them so big." Next year, she sends £45.[47]

His mother aggravates Lawrence at a distance; nearby, she aggravates him more. Yet he does his filial duty, helps her find lodging, visits, introduces her to several friends. Herbert Baker lets her use his Westminster flat, where Lawrence visits her often in late 1922. In the fall of 1929, she moves to London rooms to be near him: "There I am, beset," he complains—and lunches with her. In the fall of 1930, his mother and Robert occupy Clouds Hill for almost two years, declining Florence Hardy's invitation to stay at Max Gate. "I think they would be better off at Max Gate: but they would not be convinced," Lawrence explained.[48]

His mother loves Clouds Hill; if she cannot possess her son, she possesses his place. She cleans it furiously, to his distaste, and installs a cooking range he later removes. She and Robert settle in contentedly, befriend the Knowles, attend morning and evening service at Moreton church. The daffodils and primroses his mother plants offend him. "I hate flowers round a house…. Unreasonable beings, mothers, aren't they?" he writes Mrs. Knowles (who, a mother herself, would

not fully agree). "She knows I can't stand any sort of garden or plants…. Yet she would cheerfully spoil the place for me!" His mother knew he would be angry, but she liked flowers. "I brought these pretty things from the woods," she said. "I expect Ned will be very cross with me."[49]

Mount Batten and Hythe, where Lawrence was then stationed, were not far, but he discourages visits. "[O]ur day is full from 7 A.M. till 10 P.M. So I do not want you to come here. Nor can I come to Clouds Hill." Lacking the frequent contact she wished, Mrs. Lawrence pressed her feelings on his friends. "I have only had the briefest notes from him," she informed a comrade who wrote to Clouds Hill. "I fear he is very worn out with the hard work. I wish he would get a good rest. You know he never spares himself."[50] After his mother left the cottage, Lawrence asked Mrs. Knowles to take some flowers and told his mother that repairs required their removal.

From China, his mother persists in being—his mother. "My dearest Ned, I hope you had a very happy birthday…. With much love to you dear Ned, Your loving Mother," she writes in August 1929. "My dearest Ned," she writes in 1934, detailing the familiar household articles that have just arrived in Mienchu: "my own bed with Fathers [sic] Vi spring mattress, & … the spring part of your own bed & your hair mattress … & the book case you carved for Father."[51] She wants to preserve a world she cherishes; he wants to obliterate it. She worries about him; he worries about her. He would like her out of China, settled peacefully in Britain. "Mother needs a little garden, for flowers, and somewhere to walk in; and a house (not too big) which she can polish with her own hands."[52]

In February 1935, she says, "I hope a letter will come from you to tell me if you went to Clouds Hill at Christmas."

Communist armies are on the march. "I am worried now about Mother and Bob.... The troubles are touching their area," he writes shortly before his death.[53] He wants to hear they are safe. Scanning the morning mail, he tells Pat Knowles, "Nothing from China." In her last letter, his mother, as usual, tells him what to do. Knowles's mother had just died. Should Pat leave, "You will have to get someone [to replace him].... You can't do every thing for yourself. It would be too much for you & tiresome stupid work, even if you go out for all your meals."[54]

So things stood relatively unchanged between mother and son near the end. Arnold Lawrence believed T.E. was emotionally damaged by their mother's determination to subdue him, as she had sub-dued their father and Robert. "He was afraid, I believe, even of her influence when they were not together," Celandine Kennington thought.[55] Lawrence said the same. "I have a terror of her knowing anything about my feelings, or convictions, or way of life. If she knew they would be damaged: violated," Yet, especially after Thomas Lawrence's death, mother and son were drawn to each other: "we ... so hanker after one another," he said.[56] He identified with her and, lacking them himself, scorned and admired her moral assurance, her absolute convictions. He was repelled by and sought to break that identification, but it was too deeply engrained. For all his harsh words, he could not sever the cord that bound him to his mother.

15

Brothers

Lawrence's mother drew an idealized picture of her sons as "a most happy band of brothers" and T.E. as "a most loving son and brother." Ernest Cox, Assistant Master of Oxford High School, called them "an ideal family of boys."[1] Whatever truth such remarks convey could only be true of the family's early years—the earlier (the more innocent T.E. was), the truer. In later life, he could be astringent about the family. "[I]f we could choose, we would probably all of us vote to remain strangers to our blood-or-family-relations. There is no sense in making a fuss over a physiological bond." "No wonder all her [his mother's] children are queer. With such a father ... and such a mother, we have no chance of being useful citizens."[2]

"None of us can ever afford to keep a wife," he declared in 1911, projecting his idiosyncrasies on his brothers. Years later, Arnold rejected a similar statement attributed to T.E. "Will was on the verge of marriage...; Frank had quite normal views on girls, I married at twenty-four."[3] Robert was the only other brother who chose not to marry and his mother may have broken up a romance. I will discuss T.E.'s brothers in the order of their death, roughly the same order as the amount of information we have on each.

Frank

Frank Helier Lawrence was born Feb. 7, 1893, in St. Helier, Jersey (hence his middle name), where his mother had gone from Brittany so that he might escape French conscription. Four and a half years younger than T.E., far less bookish, only 22 when he died, his life was the briefest and he was the least traveled of the brothers. In 1910, at 17, he joined T.E. in a bicycle tour of French castles. "Each time I have a bath," Frank wrote, "he goes and buys a book instead." A devout believer and diligent churchgoer, Frank attended a series of church summer camps. Addressing the 1913 camp, he said, "Each Camp should give us more ... of the grace of God to enable us to lead the life which Christ would have us lead."[4] Unlike T.E., Frank liked team sports, captained the high-school football team and miniature rifle club, was vice-captain of the cricket team and first in the school gymnastic competition three successive years. His letters show affection and concern for every family member; he also writes to Janet Laurie, her mother, and former governess Florence Meesham.

After a brief spell at Jesus College, Frank enlisted as a 2d Lieutenant at the

The Lawrence brothers, 1910, left to right: T.E., Frank, Arnold, Robert, Will (Bodleian Library, University of Oxford).

war's outbreak in August 1914. The officers' "abominable" language and the "terrible curse" of drink shock him. Intercepting a soldier bringing beer to camp, he pays him for it and pours it on the ground. "I never thought such a state of things could exist anywhere," he writes; "there is no-one left here like people I have been accustomed to." Yet he likes the Army and, recognizing that it suits men who want to "walk pleasantly through life," wants to make a career of it. "I very much like the life I am leading now, out of doors all day long."[5]

Visiting home, Frank stays in T.E.'s bungalow, the choice accommodation at Polstead Road. He asks T.E. why his Colt does not function properly; T.E. explains the mechanism; Frank expects him to get a D.S.O. He and T.E. are affectionate, but not on the same wavelength. When, at 18, Frank proposes an Army career, T.E., the only brother to pursue a military career, opposes it. "Has he considered what an officer is when he retires? The narrow specialisation makes him quite unfitted for anything else ... he will lose some of his originality in the mill." (Frank had less originality to lose.) Raising the idea again in 1915, Frank asks Will, not T.E., for advice. "I know you like the Army, and ... Ned does not. But Ned is so very different from me that I am not putting too much weight on his opinions in this matter."[6] The photos of dead men T.E. sends home appall him.

Of the ten officers in Frank's battalion in September 1914, four were dead by January, four wounded, one missing. Germans targeted officers, who modified their uniform to look more like enlisted men; some wore metal plates in their breast pockets. It did not help much. Frank was killed by a shell on May 9, 1915. In a letter to his parents prepared earlier, he said, "Do not grieve for me ... whatever happens will be with His foreknowledge and by His orders in accordance with His plan ... the parting will not be for long.... I can never be sufficiently grateful for having been given such parents.... In these last three months I have gone through indescribable depths of infamy.... Goodbye, till we meet again not on this earth."[7]

Jeremy Wilson thinks Frank was his mother's favorite (others have said Will). "The last letter my darling wrote," she wrote on the letter he sent just before he died. The attack in which he was killed was unsuccessful. T.E. wrote Will, "Frank's death was as you say a shock, because it was so unexpected. I don't think one can regret it overmuch.... The hugeness of this war has made one change one's perspectives."[8]

Will

Born in Kirkcudbright, Scotland, Dec. 10, 1889, 16 months after T.E., William George was closest to him in age and intimacy. They were the best-looking brothers. T.E., more complex, had a stronger will and more independent, wide-ranging mind; Will, tall, athletic (he set the school record for the mile), affectionate, loving poetry, nature, and God, was better balanced and more immediately attractive. A friend called him "an Adonis, beautiful"; Ernest Barker thought him "the most winning" of the brothers; T.E. said he was "very remarkable."[9] Understandably, Janet Laurie preferred him to T.E. Hating his own smallness and convoluted conflicts, T.E. must have admired and envied Will's poise, his ease with women, his ability to love.

As boys of 8 and 7, T.E. and Will shared a hut at the end of the garden long before T.E.'s cottage was built. They dug a barrow, explored the fields, played games, read much poetry, and must have shared confidences and discussed issues weighty and light. T.E. could be big brotherly. He sent Will precise instructions on how to dig a mound and how to proceed with his studies. "[R]ead a little Rabelais.... The Scaligers don't touch. What is a nympholeft? ... don't use these words.... You are going to too many lectures ... give him [Ernest Barker] up after the first term." Study European history from the French point of view—"it will be fresh and valuable."[10] Winning a better scholarship than T.E., Will went to St. John's, a more fashionable college than Jesus.

His letters home are more demonstrative than T.E.'s and he writes their father more often. Where T.E. drops salutations and closes with a bare "N." or "L.," Will addresses "Dearest Mother," "My Darling Mother," "My Dear Bob," and closes "your loving," "Love to you, all of you" and "Will." His letters have less technical detail and more personal feeling than T.E.'s, give his impressions of the country and individuals he meets, express interest and concern for each family member. It is hard to imagine T.E. telling his mother, "Here's a saying of Mohammed's for you, 'Heaven lieth at the feet of Mothers'."[11]

Will took bicycle and walking tours in France and Spain, but did so to enjoy himself. In August 1911, he hiked from Calais to the Ardennes, walking 360 miles in 17 days, and one has the feeling he walked more casually than T.E., with a midday read and less intense observation of every building, hill, and stone. At Oxford, T.E. impressed others by his knowledge, mind, memory, determination and fortitude; Will impressed by his character and grace. Once, Will invited Ezra Pound to talk about the troubadours to a college society. Pound was taken with him and, months later, invited him to his wedding.

In September 1913, Will sailed for India to teach history at St. Stephen's College, Delhi, visiting T.E. at Carchemish en route. Ned is "a great lord in [Aleppo] ... known by everyone, and their enthusiasm over him is quite amusing" he told the family. Some letters to T.E., he said, might not be delivered because "Various people ... probably bear him a grudge.... At the same time he is such a king ... a great power ... for good: the Kurds apply to him continually, as arbitrator in tribal difficulties, and he has contrived to keep his village ... sober."[12]

Will's experience in India contrasts with T.E.'s in Syria. India was a vast colony where the proper sons of Britain found instant rank, adventure, money, and comfort. Years later, a depressed Lawrence found India too vast to contemplate. When Frank contemplated a military career, T.E. urged him to go to the Sudan, Nigeria, or Malaysia, not India. They were cheaper, better for exploring and shooting, with "a chance of advancement," "less 'white glove' nonsense." "In India he is always dancing on the skirts of society: out in the wilds he has a chance to do something."[13] That shrewd assessment may have been influenced by his knowledge that their parents were not married and "white glove" society did not favor bastards.

Will did well in India. A friendly, handsome Oxonian "said to be a great favourite with the ladies," he soon knew "the richest man in ... Delhi, ... a tremendous grandee," tutored his 17-year-old son and managed his wedding entertainment, met "all the richest men," medieval Maharajas with great estates, retinues, stables, hawks.[14] He renewed an acquaintance with Rabindranath Tagore, whom Pound had introduced him to at Oxford—"a poet no doubt but only half a man"—who had just received the 1913 Nobel literature prize. Visiting Indian homes he wore a white Indian dhoti and khurta, "because I like them." He met prominent compatriots: the Viceroy, the Commander in Chief, Lord Islington, head of the (Indian) Public Services Commission, Labor leader and future Prime Minister Ramsay Mac-Donald, "an immensely fine fellow."[15]

Deeply religious, Will perceived (better, evidently, than Robert and his mother), the difference between genuine belief and doctrinal conformity. He would not teach scripture or religion, because "many … students read only to find avenues of attack." The Delhi church struck him as "lifeless," with a dull chaplain "who talks of unimportant things in the superlative." Missionaries, he observed, were often unpopular; the ideals of many "seem doubtful: young ordained men getting prestige by serving … abroad, and … making money by exploiting their converts.… Mission work is a method by which poor men at home may become important abroad."[16]

Will disliked the lines drawn between English and Indians, the airs British "nobodies" assumed. Many of the Delhi English had a "fairly low-class appearance," yet snubbed distinguished Indians who had been their friends at Eton and Oxford; "there's great social bitterness between European, Eurasian and Indian." If he were Indian, he, too, would be bitter.[17] India was fascinating and sickening; at times it seemed a volcano ready to burst, at times, a rotting pool. "Delhi is like the decaying carcase of an Empire." Hindus would not eat meat, yet let a dog with a broken back lie in pain rather than mercifully kill it. India was a land of fat men, child marriages, cruelty to animals.[18] Will tried to avoid politics, but it surrounded him: police spies watched student radicals and opened mail at his school, there was a riot in Calcutta, three men were sentenced to death, the loyalty of Sikh troops was questioned, an uprising was feared.

In Syria, T.E. could befriend the natives, oppose their Turkish rulers, escape English society, yet serve Britain's political interests. In India, Will could not escape English society or carry his friendship with Indians to the point of opposing British rule—nor did he wish to. Proud of being English and Christian, he believed Indian religions were "diabolical at times" and "we're a little better … thanks to Christianity." He liked "the old India" some Rajahs cherished, where "Englishmen were perfect." In one fortified preserve, he rode "the fastest horse in the south Punjab"; the Rajah's men bowed, kissed his hand, and touched his knees. Here, General George Lawrence was still honored; "possibly my name was the main cause of my royal treatment."[19]

What might have happened if Will had remained in India? Admired and respected in influential British and Indian circles, honest and able, he might eventually have risen to a high post. A peacemaker, he stood for reform, not rebellion; if he led troops, he would put down an uprising. His illegitimacy could not have helped his career.

Will discussed T.E.'s activities with the family. He is "a royal benefactor as it were and … making a great name" in north Syria, Will wrote. "And it will all come out of him in a book someday that will make him known." "[H]e's going to be quite famous." "[H]e's got the gift of seeing the whole campaign as well as the detailed manoeuvres, so never fear for him," he remarked about T.E.'s March 1914 foray with Dahoum at Akaba.[20]

When war broke out, T.E. was in England. "What will Ned have to do, stop at home or go East again and steer his country into safe waters?" Will wondered. Hoping a naval victory would end the war quickly, he was inclined "to … get in with Frank." Did his parents think the war or "the education of India on Christian lines" was more important? On October 15, he heard that Turkey had declared war. "That will give Ned employment." Young Moslem men in Delhi wore the "Enver Bey" fez in support of Turkey.[21]

"I don't think you will have difficulty getting a commission...," Frank told Will. "Ned would ... get you in anywhere. The casualties among officers are very great." Robert also advised Will "to go to Ned," but Will thought it useless because he knew no Arabic and nothing about Egypt. His mother wanted him to stay in India; his father was noncommittal. Finally, in January, he applied for a commission. "I'm sorry for Mother's sake," he wrote his father. "Still ... if it's anyone's duty to fight it is mine.... I'm sorry to have had to act without taking your advice." His father had not said "no."[22] His mother held Janet Laurie responsible for the decision, but there was equal ground to blame Will's father.

The brothers tried to meet in Port Said, but Will's ship was delayed and T.E. returned to Cairo leaving a letter and presents. When the ship arrived, Will phoned. In the Mediterranean, he struck up a friendship with Lady Evelyn Cobbold. Her husband, Lord Methuen, was Governor of Malta, which she and Will drove around in his car.

Will enlisted as a Second Lieutenant, transferred to the Royal Flying Corps as an observer in August 1915, and went to France in mid–October. On October 23rd, he was shot down and killed.

Robert

Montague Robert ("Bob"), conceived while Sarah was governess to Thomas Chapman's daughters, was born in Dublin, December 27, 1885. The birth certificate registered him as "Chapman" and his father used that name for him in his will.

Robert and Frank, the least bright, least intellectual, most conformist brothers, paired off. Though 2 years 8 months older, Bob accepted T.E.'s leadership in their games. John Mack, who met him several times in 1964 and '65, says T.E. "played the role of oldest brother oftener than Bob." A schoolmaster describes Robert as "conscientious, solicitous, always kind." In Mack's view, Robert "was so overprotected and stifled" by his mother, "he was unable to deal directly with any of the emotional issues that arose within the family." When, in 1906, he visited a Brittany castle T.E. had earlier inspected, T.E. taunted him for his silence about its "beautiful" latrine. "What could he have been thinking about not to mention these most attractive domestic conveniences?"[23]

Robert entered St. John's College, studied medicine under the renowned William Osler, and twice failed his exams before finally becoming a doctor. His mother broke up a budding romance with a nurse, destroying her letters unopened. She wanted Bob to marry Janet Laurie, but Janet found him "so terribly good" that he even objected to her saying "pub"—"Pub is not a nice word." During the war, he was a doctor on the front lines in France. "I was never wounded though I should have been killed eight to ten times," he wrote decades after. "Even now I can hear the whine of the shells as they passed over.... The Lord was very good to me."[24]

In 1921, Bob went to Szechuan as a medical missionary in the Church of England section of the international, interdenominational China Inland Mission. His mother joined him in 1923 and the two lived together, in China and England, until her death in 1959. Bob died in December 1971, shortly before his 86th birthday.

T.E. was caustic about Bob's religiosity. "I have a brother who is a saint, and so I know how baffling saints are!" In 1931, when Robert wanted to return to China, T.E. wrote Arnold, "Bob babbles again of China this year. He is a very tiresome creature with his 'call'."[25] The death of Frank and Will, T.E. remarked, left "gaps in age over wide for sympathy to cross" between him and his remaining brothers. But death widened no gap between him and Bob; there had always been one in temperament and outlook. Nonetheless, T.E. tried to help Bob (and his inseparable mother) find suitable work and lodging in Britain. "My brother must find some altruistic work, in doctoring, to content his conscience. If he can do it in a decent place, where my mother can live with him? He is capable of slumming, or fever-hospitalling, or other impossibility."[26]

A conforming, deeply religious man who would not read *The Mint* or have a laudatory biographer mention it to his mother could not understand his brilliant, anarchistic, nihilistic brother. Until 1955, Robert did not understand his own illegitimacy. His incomprehension shows in his saccharine 1937 account of family happiness and T.E.'s happiness at school. His brothers' letters, he said and doubtless felt, "to me … are sacred." He spent twenty years preparing them for publication. Yet their sacredness did not keep him from removing many passages he disagreed with or deemed offensive or improper.[27]

When Victoria Ocampo visited Robert and Sarah Lawrence in the late 1950s, they were living in a two-story boarding house outside Oxford, Bob in a ground floor room, his mother directly above. If Sarah wanted Bob, she knocked on the floor and he ran up. "The Lord was very good to me," he wrote, "preserving me so that I was able to be with my mother for forty years after my father passed away." He and his mother "seemed completely at one. They shared the same religious convictions … the same evangelistic language … the same pleasures; walking, gardening, woodcutting."[28]

Robert believed God had "raised up [T.E.] for the magnificent work he did in Arabia." He wished the Aldington and

Nutting biographies could be removed from a library and burned, and that sensational Sunday papers could be eliminated. T.E.'s portraits by Augustus John and William Orpen and Kennington's "excellent" bust, he said, "do not bring him back. Life is very short and is a preparation for Eternity. I wish people would give themselves to God by accepting the sacrifice of the Lord on Calvary."[29]

Arnold

Arnold Walter, Thomas and Sarah's last child, was born May 2, 1900, four years after the family moved to Oxford. The only son born there, he may have represented his parents' hope, after at least six homes in fourteen years, to settle down and pass for a normal family. Seven years younger than Frank, their last son, he was the family pet. T.E. liked looking after him. At about 3, he took him to the Ashmolean. Fearful of the statues, the child clung to his brother's neck and asked, "Are they all alive?" T.E. carved a stone face and gave him a hammer to break it with "so that he would not be afraid."[30]

Arnold was much influenced by T.E., who took him on bicycle trips, gave him pottery shards, taught him to rub brasses. "I slept in a room papered with his black rubbings of knights, and I read … [his] story-books." T.E. encouraged Arnold to develop "wider and deeper" interests than those acquired in school, emphasizing a self-directed, adventitious approach even to school athletics. "Arnie must not run to win the Cup…: the things you get by trying after are never worth the things that, if too set on the end, you will pass over by the way."[31]

Will's letters pay "Arnie" special attention; he is sent stamps, given a quaint description of an animal, told to find a city in the atlas. Will may have copied T.E., who wrote that way earlier. Singularly good with children—half a boy himself—T.E. poured on Arnie endearments he seldom offered other family members. He addresses him, aged 12 or so, as "Dear Worm," "Ancient beast," "puffet," "tumult"; writes "TO BE READ ALL BY HIMSELF SPECIALLY WELL WRITTEN"; explains Arabic words—"Euphrates is Frat ... canoe is shahtur"; sends him stamps and coins; hunts for a dried jackal's tail for him; "I have got you such a glorious spider." Who would not love such a brother?

In the fall of 1917, Arnold asked T.E.'s help in getting to the Near East. "It is looking too far ahead" (of Arnold's 18th birthday), he replied, "but should there be opportunity I would much like the arrangement." Securing approval would be easy; Arnold should work in the Arab Bureau "till *au fait* with the situation," then go into the field. To prepare, he should learn Syrian Arabic and French; learn to shoot a revolver and rifle, to fire explosives, operate a mortar and machine gun, fuse and aim artillery, drive a motorcycle and cars. "Bomb-throwing is a very handy thing."[32] In February 1918, T.E. thought General Clayton had wired for Arnold; in July, a request was made, but not acted on.

In 1919, Arnold, not Bob, wired T.E. in Paris to come home, FATHER HAS PNEUMONIA. It was Arnold, not Bob, whom T.E. told about their illegitimacy,[33] urged to leave home and escape their mother, and named executor in his will. Despite marked differences—in height and marriage, in preferring scholarship to action and a car to a motorcycle—Arnold was, of the brothers, "perhaps the closest in temperament" to T.E.[34] Both flouted intellectual orthodoxy, were outspoken, provocative, even outrageous. Arnold pursued the archeological career T.E. abandoned. After studying classical archeology

Arnold W. Lawrence (1945): T.E.'s youngest brother and literary executor (Museum of Classical Archaeology, University of Cambridge).

at New College, he went to the British schools at Rome and Athens, excavated in Greece 1920–21, and at Ur under Leonard Woolley. T.E.'s mentor D. G. Hogarth may have helped him get a travel scholarship for research on Hellenistic sculpture. After Arnold spent a week at Clouds Hill in 1924, T.E. said, "I like him.... He's original, & strong-flavoured, & intelligent, with a great deal of humour & self-sufficiency. Altogether a very complete & excellent person.... It comes rather as a shock to find him quite mature in every way."[35]

ARNOLD'S WIFE

Such praise was subsequently tempered, partly because of T.E.'s dislike of Barbara Thompson, whom Arnold married in 1925 despite his mother's strong disapproval. Starting in July, the couple stayed at Clouds Hill for half a year. Arnold sought to buy the cottage and made a down payment of £50; then T.E. intervened. Arnold considered a publishing job, so T.E. wrote to Jonathan Cape. "He is adventurous, opinionated, intelligent, and pleases people. Wants about £300 a year, to begin with.... Can you give him any advice?" Though no job eventuated, Cape published Arnold's first book, *Later Greek Sculpture,* in 1927, when T.E. wrote, "If you'd cast an occasional kindly eye on ... my little brother you'd gratify me much."[36] Cape accepted Arnold's proposal for a book on *Classical Sculpture,* published in 1929, and offered to employ him, but Arnold continued his scholarly career, becoming Reader in Classical Archeology at Cambridge in 1930.

In April 1926, T.E. informed his mother, "Arnie is somewhere in or near London, with his wife. She is expecting a child of some sort soon. That is a pity, but perhaps it won't come off." This was one of many nasty comments about Arnold's wife, in whom, it was later said, "he was very fortunate: besides charm and intelligence, she had a less insistent conscience."[37] Gratuitously harsh, they counter the impression of Lawrence's compassion, but are consistent with a report that his unpublished letters to Laurie Hallsmith are "very cold and harsh."[38] The reality of a sexually active woman invading the family and breeding a baby was abhorrent. "If you come to England," T.E. wrote his mother, "you will find Arnie & his queer little wife apparently contented at Highgate. You & she will not hit it off ... however there is no reason why you should. I'd suggest that you & Bob settle somewhere not too far off them, so that Arnie may ... see you without her." T.E. hoped Arnold would leave Barbara. "I wish there was some way of securing him £500 a year, extra. Then he would be comfortably able

to leave his wife. At present he is tied to her: all well while they like each other: but sooner or later they will get tired of liking—and then they must have enough money to live apart."[39] The prophecy was wrong; the marriage lasted sixty years until Barbara's death in 1986.

"[I]t doesn't matter a snip whether I like her [Barbara] or not: or how she behaves to me," T.E. wrote Charlotte Shaw. "If my brother likes her (and I'm sure he does) & she isn't nearly an idiot as she looks:—then there's a reasonable chance of their union lasting for quite a while, say till one of them, or their child, grows up." After Mrs. Lawrence returned from China and inspected Barbara, she fully shared T.E.'s condemnation. "Arnie's wife seems to have upon you the effect she had upon me," he said. "Never have I met a human being less comfortable to have in the same room with me.... She does not want us, and has not the courage to say so.... I cannot be bothered to open an oyster, when I do not much care for oysters."[40]

Perhaps this disparagement led T.E. to criticize Arnold, whom he now charged with "a ... ruthless incuriosity.... He gets enthusiastic never, except in denunciation: and he has ... so little breadth of judgement. He condemns the man [unidentified], without asking the circumstances of his home-life, or generation: as if all men were born equal ... he has actually produced a book on Greek sculpture.... Yet ... never had a chisel in his hand.... If he has not qualified in the activity, how can he judge it?" "Arnie is not an easy person to help," T.E. informed Hogarth. "His deserts appear to exceed his qualifications."[41]

Despite T.E.'s talent for masking his feelings, Arnold must have at least partially discerned them. He did not worship T.E. and could see weaknesses others missed. His feelings about their mother may have been harsher than T.E.'s. When she would not give Robert Graves information about T.E. for his biography, he apologized "for her inevitable connection with us."[42]

Dislike of Barbara did not keep T.E. from seeing and helping Arnold. In 1930, he suggested him to David Garnett, who was looking for a scholar to prepare a Nonesuch edition of Herodotus; Arnold's revised, heavily annotated edition of Rawlinson's translation appeared in 1935. After Arnold moved to Cambridge, T.E. spoke well of him to Sydney Cockerell: "what I did see of him was impressive. He was angular, decided and frank: I doubt his settling smoothly into any common room." He defended Arnold against their mother. "You are inclined to persecute him, you know.... I think Arnie does not want to see too much of us."[43] That "us" and "we" reflected a rare concord between son and mother.

Literary Executor

T.E.'s death gave Arnold, as his executor, control of his copyrights and papers. Over the years, he oversaw publication of Lawrence's writings and access to his letters. He cannot be accused of scholarly detachment. Scholars and writers he distrusted were barred from the Bodleian collection; manuscripts were scrutinized and changes required before copyright permission was granted.

Upon Lawrence's death, Jonathan Cape began a new printing of *Revolt in the Desert*, regarding the sales ban as applicable only during his life. Knowing how much T.E. had disliked *Revolt*, Arnold insisted that the printing be stopped and replaced by the full *Seven Pillars*. Cape agreed; by heroic measures, 60,000 copies were published at the end of July; the book became a best seller in Britain and the United States.

Arnold asked those with letters from

T.E. to let him make copies for a contemplated book; profits would go for purposes "T.E. himself would have approved" as determined by a Trust composed of Lord Carlow, Col. Alan Dawnay, Edward Eliot, and himself. Letters omitted from the book "will be ... accessible only to persons authorised by the Trustees, until the year 2000."[44] This restricted access bred speculation about national, personal, and sexual secrets the letters, deposited in the Bodleian Library, held. Having examined the collection, I doubt it holds great revelations, though careful study may illuminate obscure features of Lawrence's life. Papers that might sully his reputation were destroyed or not deposited. Arnold Lawrence "used to grin like a kid while telling people that he had burned 'thousands of pounds' worth of documents."[45] The 870-page selection of Lawrence's letters that David Garnett edited after E. M. Forster dropped the task appeared in 1938. A year earlier, Arnold edited *T. E. Lawrence by His Friends,* insightful recollections by 80 friends from all phases of Lawrence's life.

Robert Graves had proposed that he and Liddell Hart relate their experience writing their Lawrence biographies. Arnold approved the project "provisionally" in August 1935, "but insisted that the completed book be submitted to him and the other trustees ... before ... permissions could be given." Before long, the trustees began "to prevaricate" and Arnold, perhaps fearing competition with Garnett's forthcoming letters collection, proposed that the book be a limited edition. Not pleased, Graves wrote Liddell Hart, "Your letters and mine from T. E. are essential to any collection they make: so though Arnie has the *veto* as executor, we have the power of being nasty and withholding our letters. And very nasty, if we care to sell our letters in America." Initially, the trustees withheld permission to publish Lawrence's letters even in a limited edition. Graves was "so incensed" he half-seriously thought of pirating the letters in the U. S. Eventually, permission was granted and, in 1938, limited editions of *T. E. Lawrence to his Biographers* were published in Britain and the U. S.[46]

Meeting Arnold in 1944, James Lees-Milne noted, "a slightly contemptuous, slightly mocking smile. He answers abruptly, deliberately, as though to assert his disrespect for people and authority. Not good looking; a lean face, clear skin, but dark and swarthy. Not like his brother in appearance. He stares at you with penetration while he speaks."[47] Later that year, Arnold returned to Cambridge as professor of classical archeology and a fellow of Jesus, T.E.'s college. He was said to be "a good judge and adviser of students but at first an appallingly bad lecturer, though ... he eventually became more than competent."[48] Many were surprised that, in 1951, he resigned and moved to the University College of the Gold Coast (it became Ghana in 1957). Arnold said, "It is partly to be less surrounded by cleverness."[49] Another explanation may be that, in Cambridge, he could not escape being "Col. Lawrence's brother." In Ghana, "he became fully his own man," established an archeology department, the national museum, a research program, studied and restored coastal forts, and "got along better with the illiterate tribesmen in the bush than with the officials."[50]

From Ghana, Arnold supported Liddell Hart and Lady Astor's efforts to stop English publication of Richard Aldington's denigrating biography of Lawrence that had been published in France in 1954. Aldington complained of "the threat of censorship [i.e., of denying permission to quote copyright material] from Prof. A. W. Lawrence and the literary Trustees, who write menacing and truculent letters the moment this topic [homosexuality] is hinted at!"[51] Some—very far from all—

misstatements in that unpleasant, wrong-headed work stem from Aldington's paraphrasing copyright sources.

Arnold faced the problem of censorship himself in publishing *The Mint*. Cape had considered publishing it in 1940, but the Battle of Britain made that inopportune, if not unpatriotic. Herbert Baker, who thought it revolting, hoped Trenchard would prevent publication. Cape dropped the project. In 1949, publication was again postponed for fear of libel to the still-living Uxbridge commandant. Pseudonymns and the deletion of obscenities were necessary in the 1955 trade edition; an unexpurgated trade edition waited until 1973.

Arnold's 1957 retirement was another surprise, but he had not, like T.E., given his patrimony away. T.E.'s valuable copyrights, papers, and possessions were a ready source of funds; upon his death in 1991, his estate was appraised at almost £500,000.[52] He built a small modern house in Highgate where he wrote *Trade Castles of West Africa,* a 1963 work that inevitably recalls T.E.'s interests in medieval forts and his *Crusader Castles* thesis, whose 1936 publication Arnold had arranged. The fortress theme persisted in his *Greek Aims in Fortification* (1979).

In 1959, Arnold was involved in a controversy over Terence Rattigan's play *Ross,* with Alec Guinness playing Lawrence. Before licensing the performance, the Lord Chamberlain, "the great guardian of the British stage," asked him to approve the script. Robert Graves and Basil Liddell Hart participated in ensuing negotiations as friends and authors of copyrighted biographies that Rattigan might have utilized. (Another view of these events is that Arnold asked Graves to persuade Rattigan and Guinness to alter the script or he would ask the Lord Chamberlain to bar the production.) The basic issue was Rattigan's depiction of Lawrence as homosexual.

Graves suggested removing certain lines; Liddell Hart thought only a few cuts and word changes were needed. Arnold would not discuss the matter with Rattigan lest he seem to cooperate with him. The threatened ban dissipated when Rattigan declared that, in that event, he would televise the play or put it on in the U. S. *Ross* opened at the Haymarket in May 1960; the play and Alec Guinness's performance were widely praised.[53]

Many proposals to make a film about Lawrence and the Arab revolt had been rejected by T.E. and, later, Arnold. Finally, in 1959, Arnold sold the *Seven Pillars* film rights to producer Sam Spiegel for £30,000. "Spiegel," he said, "has done a first-class ... abridgment. It's the only really accurate film script of the book I have ever seen." That opinion was based on an early script later replaced by Robert Bolt's. After reading the latter, Arnold told Spiegel, "I am extremely disappointed ... almost every event ... is either fictitious or fictionalised." Viewing half of the film, he declared, "I can see very little consistent with my brother, and an overwhelming amount utterly inconsistent with him." Liddell Hart termed the film "an appalling perversion of history"; David Garnett, "an outrage." Arnold withdrew permission for it to be titled *Seven Pillars of Wisdom* (legally, it appears, the title could have been used anyway), forfeiting £5,000, and gave much of the money he had received to the Lawrence trusts.[54]

Stanley Weintraub's study of Lawrence's relations with Bernard and Charlotte Shaw, *Private Shaw and Public Shaw* (1963), was constrained by Arnold's scrutiny of the manuscript. "AWL charged me 11 percent of my royalties...," Weintraub wrote, "and retained a veto over what [copyright material] I used.... And he wanted to see the whole text—not just the quotes."[55]

The *Sunday Times* had serialized *The Mint* in three installments early in 1955. In June 1968, it ran a series of four articles by Colin Simpson and Phillip Knightley on "The secret life of Lawrence of Arabia";[56] the third, "How Lawrence of Arabia cracked up," revealed that, from 1923–35, Lawrence had periodically had himself severely whipped by John Bruce. Arnold had long known of this unhappy practice and referred to it obliquely as "his subjection of the body ... by methods advocated by the saints,"[57] but did not explain the "methods." They were too painful, too hard to understand, too amenable to journalistic sensationalism. To this day thoughtful observers disagree about their meaning. However, punishment for insufferable conduct, not a saintly wish for suffering, was the reason Lawrence gave John Bruce.

The *Times* articles were prompted by a letter from Bruce. Reporter Colin Simpson interviewed him and checked his story. Arnold acknowledged the beatings, interpreting them as an attempt by T.E. to subdue his body. To convince Simpson of this interpretation and put the beatings in a fuller context, Arnold gave him access to the Bodleian collection, and he agreed to treat the beatings "with sympathy and understanding." Simpson tried to comply but headlines sell papers and editors determine them and the final text. Arnold was double-crossed.[58] The *Times* declined his request that it run an accompanying story by psychiatrist John Mack, who had begun research for his Lawrence biography.

The details, emphasis, and tone of Bruce's story dismayed Arnold. Upon publication of the first installment, publishers bid over $100,000 for rights to publish in eight languages a book based on the series. To placate Arnold, Harold Evans, chief editor of the *Sunday Times,* invited him to review the manuscript to "ensure that the tone was sober and scholarly." Arnold adopted the opposite course of shunning responsibility. The contract specified that he would provide no help or consultation and this would be stated in the book; he would approve all references to himself; at most 4,000 words would be quoted, respectively, from copyright material owned by Arnold Lawrence and the *Seven Pillars* Trust; quotations from Lawrence's letters to Charlotte Shaw would be confined to those already printed in the *Sunday Times*; matters that might distress the Altounyan family and others would "be slurred over"; no mention would be made of Clouds Hill as a site of beatings or of an act of sodomy by a British soldier related in the Oxford Text; Simpson's access to the Bodleian would be extended until the book's publication; John Mack would receive a copy of all information provided by Bruce; the Lawrence trusts would be paid £3,000 plus 2½ percent of net earnings.[59]

By the end of 1975, few persons had seen the Bodleian papers: John Mack, Colin Simpson, Arabella Rivington (assisting Simpson), and Jeremy Wilson. Refusing access to Desmond Stewart, a widely published writer on Islam, the Arabs, and the Near East, Arnold apologized but said he was "precluded from following my inclination" by the recent designation of an official biographer (Jeremy Wilson).[60] However, the next year H. Montgomery Hyde received access. Stanley Weintraub, Jeffrey Meyers, Michael Yardley, and Lawrence James, among others, were refused. Trust solicitors reportedly "told Stewart's publishers, Hamish Hamilton, that unless certain changes were made ... they would revoke copyright permission to quote from Lawrence's works. They later withdrew this condition but urged that the passages be modified if not deleted. Hamish Hamilton refused."[61] A novelist as well as a scholar, Stewart invented episodes about Lawrence's flagellist sexuality. Nevertheless, Arnold did to other scholars what would have outraged him, had it been done to him.

To counteract Knightley and Simpson's account of Lawrence's beatings with a more sensitive, scholarly interpretation, Arnold gave psychiatrist John Mack every help in conducting his research. Mack's careful, sympathetic but candid recital of the facts distressed him. At the last minute, publication of *A Prince of Our Disorder* was held up by a threatened denial of permission to quote copyright material. Negotiations ensued between Trust lawyers and publisher Little, Brown until a tempered version of the beatings was agreed upon.

After contracting for Jeremy Wilson to write Lawrence's authorized biography, Arnold's relations with him deteriorated. Wilson recalls "a deepening hostility to the biography project and perhaps to me personally." At one point, Arnold wanted to break the contract; Wilson threatened legal action; for more than ten years, the two did not meet. Long delayed (the work took 14 years), Arnold thought the biography would never be completed. After its 1989 publication, he wrote Wilson "praising the book very generously." However, the "very wide rift" between the two was never fully bridged.[62]

As he aged and relinquished more control over Trust decisions, a more liberal access policy was adopted and the Trust no longer used its control of copyright to review and seek to modify manuscripts. Jeremy Wilson states that he worked on the authorized biography in complete independence; Malcolm Brown, who edited the 1988 collection of Lawrence's letters, also states that Arnold Lawrence "has not attempted to influence or censor me."[63] Neither Wilson nor Brown dwelt on Lawrence's sexuality. Like Arnold, both believed that he was a lifelong virgin, not homosexual, and that detailed discussion of sexuality was unwarranted in writing for a broad audience.

After his wife's death in 1986, Arnold

"went into a visible decline, but ... was rescued from his desolation by a friend of many years, Peggy Guido, who gave him companionship and scholarly support during a remarkable Indian summer." As late as 1989, he might respond to scholarly inquiries about T.E. At 90, he was reworking his 1935 edition of Herodotus. He died March 31, 1991, a month before his 91st birthday.

"I do not believe that any brother has understood his brother better than A.W. has understood T.E.," Victoria Ocampo wrote. Returning the compliment, Arnold praised Ocampo for seeing "with equal clarity" T.E.'s "virtues and his faults, his successes and his failings, his wisdom and his silliness."[64] Arnold's view of T.E. was balanced, yet pessimistic for, as a married man and a father, he regretted his brother's view of marriage, sex, and procreation, his asceticism, masochism, and abdication of normal life for a punishing military regimen.

Arnold wearied of the endless questions and approaches by those who saw him only as a source of information about his brother. Living twice as long as T.E., he could no longer regard him as his protective older brother. Death had taken T.E. while boyish traces remained. Time reversed their childhood relation. Seeing more clearly the marks of immaturity, weakness, and failure in T.E.'s character, Arnold served as protector of his now younger brother's reputation.

Friends

Lawrence could not love or form a deep affection; something was missing in the strength, candor, and intimacy of his feelings. Friends often wanted more than he could give. He understood quickly and was generous with praise, sympathy, and help but not with his time and affection. Thus, a one-way relationship tended to develop, friends wanting to draw closer and Lawrence holding back. They could not penetrate and he could not abandon his reserve. His most satisfactory friendships may have been with older persons who, adopting an indulgent, parental role, did not press for closer intimacy; with them, he could relax and behave like a bright, respectful, entertaining boy.

Merely to name Lawrence's friends would fill several pages. Some he met at school, college, or in Syria; many were wartime colleagues, civilians, officers, soldiers. After the war, he met leading political and social figures, officials, publishers and editors, artists, writers, poets, service men. Almost everyone, it seems, wants to meet a famous man, to talk to or observe him. Lawrence traded on his fame to meet many writers and poets; thus, he arranged to be introduced to Siegfried Sassoon and Thomas Hardy and might write to authors he did not know (e.g., Laurence Binyon, C.

Day Lewis). He had a very large correspondence. Though he discarded most letters strangers addressed to "Colonel Lawrence," replying to friends and acquaintances, dealing with practical matters, writing at odd hours in barracks and rented rooms could be quite burdensome.

I will review Lawrence's relations with eleven friends: Robert Graves, E. M. Forster, Thomas and Florence Hardy, Vyvyan Richards, D. G. Hogarth, Bernard and Charlotte Shaw, and three service comrades, Chambers, Palmer, and Guy. Lawrence met all but Richards and Hogarth after the war. Hardy, Hogarth, and the Shaws belonged to a decidedly older generation; Graves and the servicemen, to a younger one; Forster and Florence Hardy were nine and ten years older. The selection of so many writers is due partly to Lawrence's choice of friends and partly to available sources.

Robert Graves[1]

Lawrence was 31 and famous, Graves, 24, an impoverished poet, father, and veteran, when they met at Oxford in late 1919. Absorbed in literature, trying to purge their war experiences and decide how to live, they became good friends. Lawrence overvalued art and artists, especially poets. He gave Graves detailed comments on his poetry. Graves valued his "keen eye for surface faults," thought him a great man, introduced him to other poets, dedicated three books to him, felt closer to him than to any other man. Lawrence, he told Mrs. Hardy, "is as unquestionably the greatest of our generation as Mr. Hardy is of his."[2]

Lawrence set the emotional limits of their friendship but gave Graves unstinting financial and practical help. "[H]e stood as a sort of guardian angel over me; if anything went wrong he was always at hand to help," Graves recalled. "You know you have my help and fellowship whenever you need it, in any direction I can reach,"[3] Lawrence pledged and kept that pledge. Starting when he had a good Colonial Office salary, his generosity continued into the years when he was far poorer than Graves. In 1921, Graves owed £300 and faced bankruptcy; Lawrence gave him £50 and three manuscript chapters of the Oxford Text, which he sold for £200. He tried to get Graves books to review and a job writing an RAF history, helped him secure a £1,500-a-year appointment as professor of English in Cairo, gave him a copy of the subscribers' edition with a note "Please sell when read"—it netted £330. In 1927, Lawrence got Cape to commission Graves to write his biography, insisting that Graves not be told about his role. Graves received a £500 advance and, for a time, royalties of £350 a day.

Some years later, Lawrence mentioned that declining interest rates would halve his anticipated £2/2 weekly retirement income. Graves asked if he could send him £55 to make up the difference for a year: "may I? I don't think you'll refuse me that."[4] Lawrence refused, as he had refused before. A generous giver, he was a poor taker, but he accepted books and records from Graves and asked him

to screen his mail, discarding fan letters before forwarding the rest to India.

The early years of their friendship were the closest. Like most of Lawrence's friends, Graves disapproved of his enlistment and tried to induce him to leave, inviting him to go with him to Nepal for a free sojourn as the foreign minister's guest. But Graves understood Lawrence's sexuality so little he believed "S.A." was a woman and that Lawrence should settle down with a woman. "He ... does not know too much about me: will think out some psychologically plausible explanations of my spiritual divagations," Lawrence remarked as Graves was working on his biography.[5] Often changing ideas, Graves wrote quickly and carelessly, yet frankly and perceptively. A close reading shows veins of criticism in his laudatory biography. Lawrence, he observes, keeps his friends "in watertight compartments.... Toward each friend he turns a certain character.... He has no intimates to whom the whole might be shown." Graves says he prefers the Oxford Text to the subscribers' edition on which Lawrence labored so mightily. "It should somehow, one feels, have been a little more casual." Stung, Lawrence countered, "Edward Garnett, whose competence as a critic I vehemently admire, ... says that my revision has done wonders." But Garnett was (with E. M. Forster and Frederic Manning) one of what Graves called the "spavined team of T.E.'s literary friends."[6]

Lawrence detested Laura Riding, Graves's enamorata, for using her body to dominate and humble men and, for all her intellectual conceits, did not think her very intelligent. When she asked him for a quick list of historical figures he liked, he declined—not to her but to Graves. This angered Graves. "[Y]ou had only to write to Laura & excuse yourself. Instead, you wrote a long chatty letter to *me*.... The protest I registered did not convey anything to you.

You merely wrote to *me* again, and your whole tone conveyed the sense of Laura as a sort of intellectual freak … having no status of her own."[7]

Graves complained that Lawrence had forsaken the serious world of cultured men for the vulgar world of mechanics. "Honestly, R.G.," Lawrence replied, "you have been so drastic in your condemnations of ordinary people, of late, that I've been afraid to stay near you." He charged Graves with prostituting his talent for money from the "unrelieved crime and horror" of *I, Claudius,* "a grim tale … too grim." "[C]ome home," he urged, "at least for a while, and meet [ordinary] people.… You are losing your englishry."[8] "My Englishry was never more than my affection for the English temper and … language," Graves rejoined. "And it might improve things if you left 'home' for a time & came here." When a pirated section of *The Mint* appeared, Graves accused Lawrence of writing "recruiting propaganda for the Air Force" and declared, "the situation between us is unsatisfactory."[9] Plainly, it was. Nonetheless, a bond remained and neither took what would have been a comparatively small step to break it. However, Lawrence refused to lend (give?) Graves any more money. In January 1935, Graves asked him if he wanted to write his own obituary—"No one need know"—that *The Times* had commissioned him to prepare. Lawrence's statement was published four months later.

After Lawrence's death, Graves and Liddell Hart came to believe that Lawrence had demeaned each of their biographies to the other. "T. E. in my opinion was at the end treacherous to you as a friend, & not very faithful to me as his friend," Graves wrote Liddell Hart; Lawrence lacked "coherence." Courageous, generous, intuitive, charming, good-humored, he was also cunning, with vivid, ugly, even "diabolical" fantasies.[10]

E. M. Forster

After meeting Lawrence at a 1921 London luncheon, E. M. Forster wrote "how glad, how proud, I had been." Lawrence did not reply. (After Frederic Manning expressed "a sense of pride" at meeting him, Lawrence did not resume contact for eight years.) Praise closed his heart. Upon reading the Oxford Text, Forster took a different tack. "I thought it a masterpiece, but to have said so would have been fatal. I restricted myself to detail, and analysed particular sentences and paragraphs, chiefly from the point of view of style." This time Lawrence replied, offering the kind of fulsome praise Forster had prudently avoided. "Writers & painters aren't like other men … meeting them intoxicates me." Forster was "among the elect"; Lawrence was "abnormally grateful" for his "extraordinary" criticism; etc.[11]

The friendship was launched—on Lawrence's terms. "I had to figure as a great artist and he was a bungling amateur. This did not suit me in the least, but protests were useless," Forster recalled. He visited Lawrence in Dorset in March 1924 and again in June; "the talk was decidedly sticky" at first. "I like Lawrence though he is … odd and alarming."[12] Forster sent him *A Passage to India,* published that June. It shows "you are a very great writer," Lawrence responded, whereas *Seven Pillars* "stinks of me"; he was a "flea," Forster, a "lion." On leaving for India, Lawrence gave him "a gorgeous copy" of the subscribers' edition. Forster was moved. "I used to think him incapable of affection, but have changed my opinion."[13]

Each put the other on a pedestal; each jumped down and humbled himself. "[Y]ou are a 'greater genius than myself,'" Forster insisted. "Don't contradict me— only wastes time." Lawrence rejoined, "I feel inclined to say Cher Maître, and stop making a fool of myself.... Don't laugh at my writing, by telling me that it's better than yours." "I'm not ... fit to read your writing."[14]

When Lawrence contemplated writing an article on Forster (never finished), Forster offered to send him *Maurice*, the 1913 novel on homosexual love published only in 1971, a year after his death. "I suppose I am elusive..., but there are one or two people ... to whom I'd like to be clear. I haven't any secrets from you ... there's no question you asked which I wouldn't answer. But this is ... not what you want, alas." Lawrence declined. "I wanted to read your long novel, & was afraid to. It was like your last keep ... and if I read it I had you: and supposing I hadn't liked it?"[15] That made explicit what others had to deduce: a certain distance would be maintained that Lawrence alone defined and understood. It fluctuated; it could include intimate confessions, yet something was always held back. Thus, confessing his rape at Deraa, Lawrence warned that he would say no more about it, "for it will be hard to speak of these things without dragging our own conduct and bodies into the argument: and that's too late, in my case."[16] What did he mean by his "conduct" (Bruce's beatings?) and "that's too late"?

Forster knew that Lawrence suffered. "You seem nearly always ill.... I can't guess what you feel like, except that it is necessarily lonely.... I ... often wish I could help you." "Most certainly he did not always speak me the truth, though did it matter?" he reflected. "I seldom asked questions because they involved ... answers, and though I was frank with him he was never equally frank in return." "I shouldn't have said ... I was very fond of him," Forster said shortly after Lawrence's death, "now it seems to me that I have been."[17]

Thomas and Florence Hardy

Max Gate, Thomas Hardy's home, was nine miles from the Bovington camp where Lawrence arrived March 12, 1923. Eight days later, he asked Robert Graves, "do you think old Hardy would let me look at him...? You know the old thing, don't you?"[18] The "olds" may seem demeaning, but Lawrence was unusually sensitive to the end-of-life waiting of aged people. Graves extolled him to Florence Hardy as "unquestionably the greatest of our generation.... Don't be surprised in whatever guise he appears, as a boy selling papers ... or a gypsy girl: he is like that." Lawrence appeared at Max Gate on March 29 in a private's rough khaki. Hardy, 82, struck him as "incredibly old";[19] Florence, his second wife, was 44; Lawrence, 34.

"It sounds greedy, always to come when you ask," Lawrence wrote Florence after his third visit. "Mr. Hardy ... has seen so much of human-kind that he must be very tired of them." Before long, Hardy read the Oxford Text (the small type strains even young eyes) "& made me very proud with what he said of it." In September, Lawrence sent Graves a wonderful description: "Hardy is so pale, so quiet, so refined into an essence ... [with] an unbelievable dignity and ripeness ... he is waiting so tranquilly for death, without a desire or ambition left.... Then he is so far-away. Napoleon is a real man to him.... He feels interest in everyone, and veneration for no-one."[20]

Hardy and his wife were much taken with Lawrence, who became one of their closest younger friends. They hung a photo of his bust on the wall; the maids were told to admit him without query, but if someone was present he did not want to see, he would not enter. For Nellie Titterington, the Hardys' maid, his visits lifted the "noiseless gloom" of the place. "He had a wonderful sense of humour.... I always chatted with him when he came." Once, dropping in to avoid the rain, he stayed three hours "keeping us ... almost spell-bound with his conversation.... I never saw T.H. so utterly captivated by anyone before," Florence reported.[21] Lawrence arranged for Augustus John to do Hardy's portrait, accompanied the Hardys to performances of Hardy plays, gave Florence a ride in his motorcycle sidecar. The Hardys visited his cottage and Florence asked him to edit the Hardy "biography" she had ostensibly prepared (Hardy wrote it). She deemed him "one of the few entirely satisfactory people in the world ... so very kind."[22]

In November 1926, Lawrence saw Hardy for the last time, managing the long ride from Lincolnshire with one hand, his broken right wrist being still unusable. As he stood by the motorcycle, Hardy went indoors to fetch a shawl against the afternoon cold. Without a "goodbye," Lawrence wheeled the cycle into the road and departed, "so that no possible reproach might lie against me for having helped him into ... a chill." "I have never known my husband grow so attached to anyone in such a short space of time, as he did to Lawrence...," Florence said. "I consider him the most marvellous human being I have ever met. It is not his exploits in Arabia that attract me, nor the fact that he is a celebrity: it is his character that is so splendid."[23]

Hardy died January 11, 1928. Four days later, a Sunday, the news reached Lawrence in Karachi. He was listening to Beethoven's last quartet and waited until it was finished—"because all at once it felt like him"—to write Florence. "It was only you who kept him alive.... And now, when I should grieve, ... almost it feels like a triumph. That day we reached Damascus, I cried, against all my control, for the tri-umphant thing achieved at last, fitly: and so the passing of T.H. touches me. He had finished and was so full a man.... Oh, you will be miserably troubled now, with jackal things that don't matter.... I am so sorry." Many visitors disliked Florence Hardy and thought her unworthy of her husband. She and Sydney Cockerell, Hardy's joint literary executors, quarreled. Lawrence's letter shows his native ability to understand and sympathize with almost anyone. Florence replied, "You say the news struck you as a triumph.... [A]fter he had been laid out ... [o]n his face was a radiant look of *triumph*.... He was devoted to you. Somehow I think he might have lived had you been here.... You seem nearer to him, somehow, than anyone else."[24]

Charlotte Shaw sent Lawrence a copy of the Westminster Abbey funeral service and an evocative account of the ceremony. "The clergy ... shocked me. All except one looked full of worldly pomp & ... disdain." Writing William Rothenstein three months later, Lawrence expressed views that would have deeply offended his mother and missionary brother. Hardy "would have smiled, tolerantly ... but I grow indignant for him, knowing that these sleek Deans and Canons were acting a lie behind his name.... I wish these black-suited apes could once see the light with which they shine."[25]

Lawrence and Florence met occasionally after his return from India. "I feel very much for Mrs. Hardy who remains like a plant which has grown up in a pot, from which the pot is suddenly stripped," he wrote Sydney Cockerell. "She will find it hard to begin life again."[26] Florence offered Lawrence the use of Max Gate, servants and Hardy's study included (she would use the occasion to get away). He declined. She consulted him about a memorial sculpture of Hardy; at his suggestion, the commission went to Eric Kennington. She sent him posthumous

Hardy publications and rhododendrons for Clouds Hills; he gave her an *Odyssey* and used her carpenter for work at his cottage.

Florence attended Lawrence's funeral at nearby Moreton. Afterwards, she told a friend, "T.E. was the truest friend.... Just to have known [him] ... made life worth living.... I have no words to say how fine he was. But I think his life was over. He didn't seem to know where to turn next."[27] Two years later, her life was also over.

Vyvyan Richards

While living at Jesus College in the summer of 1908, Lawrence returned to his room one night, noted an invitation to visit Vyvyan Richards, a senior classmate, and went upstairs. Richards saw a "slight figure with longish flaxen hair and an unforgettable grin." They sat by the fire talking late into the night. Two years older, with an inventor-businessman father and an American mother, Richards was studying logic and metaphysics. Though he scorned archeology and architecture and Lawrence's military interests were "strange and uncongenial," Richards succumbed to "the intoxication of his dear companionship."

The two became close friends. They talked and talked, boated on the Thames, experimented with medieval crafts such as beating and enameling copper, bicycled to churches and earthworks, visited a Broad Campden home with William Morris tapestries, chintz, a hand-press, and a collection of Kelmscotts including the prized Chaucer. They spoke of establishing a press to print fine books. Lawrence's enthusiasms infected Richards, "One of the dearest things about him was the eagerness to get a companion, too, on fire about a cathedral ... or a poem of Christina Rossetti's." Lawrence's friendship was "enchantment ... magic ... the whole of a rich personality opening warmly upon a friend."[28]

Richards fell in love with Lawrence: "it was love at first sight.... He received my affection, ... eventually my total subservience, as though it was his due." Presumably the "subservience" was Richards's posture, not Lawrence's demand; it contradicts the "strong sense of ... equality" in Richards's depiction of Lawrence's "gift of friendship."[29]

After Oxford, Richards taught history at a Woodford Green school and lived nearby at Pole Hill, where he and Lawrence thought to house their press. Writing from Carchemish in 1911, Lawrence asked his father for a loan for the building, but did not get it. His parents disliked Richards, because of his homosexuality or for that and other reasons.[30] Lawrence saw Richards's limitations, yet conveyed only affection (was he more reserved after the war or did love blind Richards?) and, making him feel accepted and understood, retained and used his friendship. This strategy (to use a word that is not quite right, because the conduct was more natural than contrived) is clearly conveyed in a letter to his brother Will. "Richards is extremely narrow in his outlook and interests.... He has said things to me of an intimacy & directness which are beyond anyone else I have met. Altogether though he is a most complex and difficult personality.... But he will do his best for the press, ... so that only a little savoir vivre is necessary to make a very satisfactory partnership."[31]

Lawrence grew cold and hot over the press. Back in England for two weeks in the summer of 1913, he did not see Richards and, months later, said he could not print with him. Carchemish was too enticing and "after that I'll probably go after another and another nice thing." Could Richards print by himself? In 1916,

Lawrence hoped Richards would do something about the press. He expected to remain in the East, but wanted "a niche" when in England. He had enough money to cut a fount.[32]

Lawrence carried a letter from Richards with him for a month in Arabia and, in July 1918, sent him an absorbing, prophetic reply. "Whether we are going to win or lose, ... I cannot ever persuade myself.... Achievement, if it comes, will be a great disillusionment.... I hate being in front, and I hate being back, and I don't like responsibility and I don't obey orders.... [We] pounce on unsuspecting Turks and destroy them in heaps: and it is all very gory and nasty.... When they untie my bonds I will not find in me any spur to action."[33]

When his bonds were untied, a private press again seemed inviting: a tie to past dreams, a sober craft in the mad world of diplomacy and Lowell Thomas. Richards lived for a time with Lawrence in the Westminster loft. Long before, they had resolved that "if either of us ever found anything really worth doing he would wire the other." In 1919, Lawrence wired that he had bought Pole Hill, the 300-foot high land Richards had rented, where he had built a cottage, pool, and garden. Now they planned a great hall with an open roof spanned by salvaged beams; three-foot thick double stone walls with a space in between for insulation; the lawn would be scythed. It came to nought, Richards thought, because Lawrence resolved to make no money from *Seven Pillars.*

Lawrence described Richards as "an unworldly sincere, ill-mannered Welsh philosopher.... An interesting man." He felt indebted to him; named his "cousin" Richards his next of kin upon entering the RAF, stored at Pole Hill valuable books and the Jidda teak doors, and left the property to Richards in his 1926 will.[34]

Richards perceived Lawrence's vanity and megalomania. "There was ... an almost sinister side to his sense of his own power. Throughout his life he must be supreme on all occasions." Lawrence never told a story or joke against himself, "must never appear put down in any way," enjoyed the admiration of "a little private gallery." He was not cruel: the hardness of his mouth was directed at himself. However, like any good military leader, he could be hard when necessary. Richards appreciated the unique qualities of *Seven Pillars,* but judged the prose and appearance of the subscribers' edition artistic failures. *Seven Pillars* was "a work of will not of art"; inspiration could not be commanded. The endless rewriting to obtain a solid page of type was "absurd." There was more "creative originality" in William Morris than in "the purple splendour of ... *Seven Pillars.*" For all his prodigious talents, Lawrence was too divided, too self-conscious to find fulfillment: "not in satisfied love, nor ... at Damascus, nor in his book."[35] Richards conveyed his criticisms of the Oxford Text to Lawrence in a long letter. They "miss their aim," Lawrence replied. "I have made them all (& many others) in a far stronger sense, to myself."[36] If he agreed, why did they "miss"?

Richards went to Lawrence's funeral. Lawrence had intended to leave Richards his books, but for some reason he received a £300 check instead. Richards also believed he had a claim to Clouds Hill. After Lawrence's death, he sold *Seven Pillars* and Lawrence's letters, bought a house with the proceeds, and wrote two largely laudatory books about Lawrence. Writing Basil Liddell Hart twenty years later, Richards was more critical. "[A]part from his magnificent reporting, he failed on paper— even some of his letters have turns of preciosity which ... leave a bad taste.... In the man himself & his straight reporting I find only integrity of the highest order: personally noble."[37]

In 1968, a *Sunday Times* interviewer spoke with Richards at least twice. The first time, his memories and love poured out. The second time, he dried up. Lawrence had had enough attention; a sick old man of 82 in a nursing home, he now had other things on his mind.

David Hogarth

A fatherly figure, David George Hogarth played a critical role in Lawrence's career. They met in January 1909, when Hogarth, 46, became Keeper of the Ashmolean and Lawrence, 20, planned a summer trip to inspect crusader castles in Syria. Hogarth, a seasoned Near East scholar-traveler, reported their conversation:

> "This is the wrong season to visit Syria: it is too hot...."
> "I'm going."
> "...You'll want a guide and servants to carry your tent and baggage."
> "I'm going to walk."
> "Europeans don't walk in Syria, it isn't safe or pleasant."
> "Well, I do."[38]

Hogarth was "a man of the world ... deft and sensitive in the handling of men ... an excellent scholar of the Middle East, and a careful, creative archeologist."[39] Lawrence saw him often at the Ashmolean and his home a block away on St. Giles, where he became almost an adopted son and an older brother to the Hogarths' young son William. Impressed by Lawrence's bravura hike across Syria and his thesis, Hogarth arranged a four-year fellowship for him to join the Carchemish dig in the spring of 1911. He met Lawrence in Lebanon, took him to the dig, and initiated him into the work. "Mr. Hogarth ...

has been most exceedingly good to me ... taught me a tremendous lot about everything from digging to Greek erotic verse."[40]

Hogarth gave Lawrence part-time work sorting shards at the Ashmolean; introduced him to Charles Doughty, the great Arabian traveler; coached him on Near East history and peoples; pressed him to learn and improve his Arabic and archeological techniques; sent him to Egypt in 1913 to learn from Flinders Petrie; arranged for his and Woolley's 1914 Sinai archeological survey and for his military map-making position in London; served as his director, colleague, and adviser at the Arab Bureau and as his liaison with London officials.

Hogarth recognized Lawrence's wide-ranging talents: piecing together fragments of pottery and sculpture, scrounging bazaars for stolen antiquities, befriending villagers, getting the best out of workmen, sensing the living past in present ruins, the political and military realities of the region's peoples and geography. He gave Lawrence the freedom to do what he did best, rather than, like many remote administrators, delegating his supervision to the resident director. He corrected and directed Lawrence "when he thought he was being silly or ... 'a bloody nuisance.'"[41] Lawrence was more exuberant and expressed his emotions more freely at this period than any other; at times, he was bawdy.[42]

If Hogarth was angry at a Lawrence prank, it was the brief anger of a father at a mischievous son. His sympathy, understanding, and diplomacy in dealing with his extraordinary protégé is shown by his handling of a dispute between the British Museum, which financed the Carchemish excavation, and the Ashmolean, to which Lawrence gave his primary allegiance. Hogarth and British Museum director Frederic Kenyon had agreed that all finds or purchases within ten miles of Carchemish should go to the Museum, whereas Lawrence, the expedition's best purchaser, felt the rule should apply only during digging seasons. Kenyon objected: by financing the dig, his museum had brought the archeologists to the area and fueled the local antiquities market. Hogarth concurred, but observed that Lawrence's enthusiasm and "elaborate scheme of deception" had surmounted difficulties and risks; "the natives deal more readily with him than with Woolley" and he "is the cheaper and better buyer." Kenyon would get more good objects if he did not suppress, but utilized Lawrence. Indeed, Hogarth suggested, Lawrence might circumvent a rule he considered unfair.[43]

The war, Lawrence said, stopped his development "into a sort of Hogarth: a traveled, archaeological sort of man, with geography and a pen as his two standbys." That is conceivable but unlikely. Archeology has a portion of scholar adventurers. A concise and fluent report of perceptive, hands-on observation, his *Crusader Castles* is an example of advocacy, of observation in the service of an idea, not dispassionate scholarship. That was characteristic of Lawrence's thinking. Elie Kedourie contrasts Hogarth's balanced writing on Turkish affairs with Lawrence's impassioned slant: "Hogarth was not an advocate.... Even when he defended a political interest ... he would not evade or gloss over points detrimental to its case.... Where Hogarth argues, ... hesitates, contrasts and compares, Lawrence [in *Seven Pillars*] lays down the law, categorical and pressing."[44] I doubt that Lawrence would, absent the war, have settled into a regime of digs, assembling shards, and scholarly reports. Had he entered seriously upon a scholarly career, he would have been a different kind of scholar than Hogarth: perhaps his own version of Richard Burton or Thor Heyerdahl.

During the war, Hogarth served as Arab Bureau director and *Arab Bulletin* editor. In mid–1916, Lawrence lived with him for a time on an island in the Nile. "*Mentor* to all of us" (British partisans of the Arab Revolt in Cairo), Lawrence called him, "our father confessor and adviser, who brought us the ... lessons of history, and moderation, and courage. To outsiders he was peacemaker (I was all claws and teeth, and had a devil)."[45] Hogarth saw Lawrence's parents in Oxford and kept them informed of his achievements. After the war, Hogarth helped to word the liberal provisions of Lawrence's All Souls fellowship. Upon losing the draft of *Seven Pillars,* Lawrence "joyously" told him, "I've lost the damned thing." Angry, Hogarth demanded that he write it again. About this time, Hogarth drew a brilliant sketch of Lawrence:

> The things he wants not to be are quite numerous; but things he could be, if he wanted, are more numerous still.... He makes fun of others or kings of them, but if anyone tries to make either ... of him he runs away. Pushing ... he finds more congenial than leading.... To think as fast or as far as he thinks is not easy, and still less easy is it to follow up with such swift action ... when he is not bluffing, he has a way of holding the aces: and he can be ruthless.... He should go far; but it may be in driving lonely furrows where at present few expect him to plough.[46]

In Palestine in 1921, Lawrence again bought antiquities for Hogarth—bronze axes and daggers from Philistine tombs. Unhappily, he was driving an unexpected furrow toward an unattainable obscurity. "Lawrence is not normal in many ways, and it is extraordinarily difficult to do anything for him!" Hogarth told G. B. Shaw who was brashly trying to help him.[47] Why had he enlisted? Lawrence gave Hogarth several answers: security; politics wearied and worried him; "I've finished with the 'Lawrence' episode ... —not the sort of man I'd like to be!"[48]

Lawrence consulted Hogarth about publishing Edward Garnett's abridgment of *Seven Pillars*. "I don't like the notion of doing that. It's a favourably false impression, you see." Hogarth approved the abridgment, but Lawrence drew back. Shouldn't he publish the whole thing in a limited edition? "It's pitiful to have a mind so feeble in purpose. What am I to do?"[49] Publish, Hogarth said; a headless mouse would have said it: any positive decision was better than perpetual indecision. Finally, Lawrence agreed and designated Hogarth his literary executor.

Hogarth, he said, is "very kind, very wise, very lovable." He was also ill, suffering from diabetes and related ailments; "he is now feeling fully his age."[50] "I hope you are fit again," he writes Hogarth, but the letter tails off. "Writing to people I have known is becoming difficult for me." For gloomy stretches, he falls silent. Hogarth complains, "I can't get any replies out of T.E."[51]

Eventually, the "damned thing" was re-revised, proofed, printed, bound, distributed. Hogarth became a member of the trust that received *Revolt in the Desert* royalties. Before proposing Robert Graves to Jonathan Cape as his biographer, Lawrence asked Hogarth if he would do it. The timing was bad. Hogarth, trying to finish his Doughty biography, told Lawrence, "My heart goes on bothering and I don't feel at all fit…. You ask 'Will I have two years?' I too ask that."[52] Next month he was dead. Lawrence was "benumbed…. Hogarth was the man I liked best. He was so full of understanding, that he did not exact explanations, ever." "He was like a great tree … and till he fell I hadn't known how much he had served to harbour me"; "the best friend I ever had."[53]

"I know you will miss him, more than perhaps anyone else except Billie and me," Mrs. Hogarth wrote. Some months later, she asked, "Some day will you do David's life for us? There is *no* one else. I ask this very seriously."[54] I have not seen Lawrence's reply, but guess he dodged a direct answer. He never undertook the work; to this day, no Hogarth biography has appeared. Lawrence expressed his real feelings to Charlotte Shaw in words that, asked to write a life of Christ, Judas might use: "as for D.G.H. and Doughty; do you really think I would foul them with trying to draw my slime across their track? Oh, they are much too good!"[55]

Bernard Shaw

Lawrence met the Shaws in March 1922. After lunching with Lawrence one Saturday, Sydney Cockerell, head of the Fitzwilliam Museum, was to collect a portrait that Shaw was giving the museum. Assured that the Shaws would be away, Lawrence accompanied him to their London apartment. They had not yet left. The playwright and the hero talked warmly for half an hour. In mid–August, Lawrence asked Shaw to read the Oxford Text—"it's long-winded, and pretentious, and dull." Save for the March encounter, "we are utter strangers, and likely to remain so," Lawrence wrote in one of his poorer prophecies.

Send it, Shaw said, he would read it but not immediately. "You need not stand on any ceremony with us. You are a privileged soul, and can deal with both of us as with old friends."[56] While he was teaching in Yorkshire and campaigning for Labor in the fall election, Charlotte devoured the book and thought it magnificent. Hearing nothing, Lawrence joshed Shaw. "I'm afraid you are either making a labour of it, or you don't want to tell me that it's rubbish." "Patience … I haven't read it yet…," Shaw replied. "I estimate the number of words as at least 460,000." He invited Lawrence to visit.[57] Contrite, Lawrence "remembered that it was the longest book written…. Please don't, out of kindness, bore yourself." He couldn't visit, because he was now in the RAF. "You have no idea how repulsive a barrack is." Shaw was now quick. His publisher, Constable, would be "honoured" to publish the book. Exactly *what* was Lawrence doing in the RAF? He sympathized with the poor officers commanding "Lawrence the great, the mysterious…. The thing is ridiculous."[58] It certainly was.

That set the tone of their relation, which changed little as they grew better acquainted. Shaw's habits, his rambunctious, outrageous wit, his *persona* were too firmly established to change. He and Charlotte acted almost like foster parents and Lawrence, almost like an adopted son. The childless Shaws appreciated Lawrence's assumption of their name. Tall, thin, gentlemanly, G.B.S. is said to have resembled Lawrence's father, who, however, lacked his wit, learning, creativity, provocativeness, and could not have emulated his opinionated intrusions into Lawrence's affairs.

Lawrence praised Shaw's work to the skies. *Methusaleh* was "unearthly"; *Saint Joan,* "pure genius"; *Heartbreak House,* "The most blazing bit of genius in English literature"; *The Intelligent Woman's Guide* (which he labored to finish), "a very great book"; *Too True to be Good,* "magnificent … priceless … terrific."[59] He offered less extravagant comments, even corrections, on details, but lavish praise predominated. When his first letters to "Dear Mr. Shaw" earned Mrs. Shaw's rebuke—"don't call him 'Mr.' Shaw!"—he shifted to "Your lordship," "My Lord," or "Dear G.B.S." The "constant deferential praise" in his letters and conversation annoyed Shaw.[60]

To others, Lawrence drew a more balanced picture of Shaw. "Very bracing, though such sureness of success has closed his pores." "He is beclouded … with works which tend to live more intensely than their creator." "G.B.S. … must have been wonderful … fifty years ago," he told novelist James Hanley. "Now he is pedestalled, and not so good as you."[61]

Shaw was impressed by Lawrence's exploits, *Seven Pillars,* his mind and knowledge, technical and mechanical ability, his gift of command. But he was not captured by Lawrence, nor did he (like Hardy) accept him and his indentured service without rebuke. He called him "Colonel Lawrence" and wished he would act the part.

Shaw interfered with Lawrence's affairs incorrigibly. In May 1923, he asked Prime Minister Baldwin to award him a pension, terming his service as a private soldier "a scandal" and "shocking tomfoolery." "[H]e is determined that you shall confer this pension on him, but solely in order that he may refuse it."[62] Four years later, Shaw vainly renewed the request. Undoubtedly he sought to help Lawrence; undoubtedly, he enjoyed thrusting himself upon the Prime Minister's attention. Lawrence was unenthusiastic: "really you should not. If I won't to do that sort of thing for myself, other people should not do it for me." "What a troublesome chap you are!" Shaw later expostulated.[63]

Shaw offered to guarantee Lawrence's overdraft, rewrote libellous passages of *Seven Pillars,* and (wrongly, in my opinion) induced Lawrence to drop the introductory chapter. Lawrence thanked "Mr. and Mrs. Bernard Shaw for countless suggestions of great value and diversity: and for all the present semicolons."[64] Shaw revised the publication contract for *Revolt in the Desert.* He sent Edward Garnett's alarmed report of Lawrence's suicide threat to the Prime Minister, warning about the "possibility of an appalling scandal."[65]

In 1927, Shaw wrote publicly, "Any country with … a spark of gratitude would have rewarded ... [Lawrence] with a munificent pension and built him another Blenheim."[66] "G.B.S. suggests my being offered Bachelor quarters in Blenheim, and other sad things," Lawrence (misinformed by Karachi newspapers) wrote a friend. "It's a pity people don't generally realise that I can make the most lovely bubble and squeak of a life for myself."[67]

Shaw considered *Seven Pillars* "a masterpiece" and Lawrence, "one of the greatest descriptive writers in English literature." *The Mint* he judged "unfit for publication"—at the time, this was legally true. "It was a description of barrack life in which no detail was spared. Its obscenities, its drunken vomitings, ... its coarsest sexual songs.... It is ... priceless as a document, but not for the entertainment of the common reader."[68]

Soon after they met, Shaw threatened to put Lawrence in a play; nine years later, he did. Private Meek in *Too True to be Good* is a good-humored portrayal of a knowing private who commands from the bottom, an idea with some merit that Shaw repeated rather too often, blocking more painful truths with a laugh. Stanley Weintraub suggests that Lawrence can also be seen in the more tragic figure of *Saint Joan*, written while Shaw was getting to know him.

Lawrence often spent the night in "the Lawrence room" at Ayot or stopped unannounced for an hour or two. Janet Dunbar says Shaw "inevitably took the floor, and Lawrence felt overshadowed." That does not ring true. Lawrence could be silent, respectful, depressed, but not permanently overshadowed by anyone—not Churchill or the King. Osbert Sitwell gives what seems a truer account, that, with the Shaws, "there was ... a sort of audacity of mischief about his attitude and conversation."[69] Lawrence remarks on "the intellectual delight of fencing with a real swordsman." On one occasion, "G.B.S.

couldn't edge in a word ... while I maundered."[70] Shaw was kind to Lawrence, gave him an overcoat (a foot too long), tickets to, and inscribed copies of, many of his plays, an *Intelligent Woman's Guide to Socialism and Capitalism* with a specially printed title page inscription. He got Yeats to invite Lawrence to membership in the Irish Academy of Letters. Luckily, Labor Air Minister Lord Thomson refused his unsolicited request that Lawrence travel on the maiden voyage of the dirigible R-101, for it crashed killing all on board.

Shaw liked Lawrence, valued his friendship, respected his intellect and his powers as a leader and man of action. He recognized Lawrence's essential immaturity, "maddeningly intense conscientiousness," and "perfectly ridiculous adoration of literature and authors." He could not understand or approve his immersion in the ranks. Lawrence was, he decided, "a born and incorrigible actor. Being in that line myself, both professionally and naturally, I was not taken in."[71] "You and I," Shaw told him, "are worse than characters: we are character-actors." "You have read too much of yourself into me," Lawrence rejoined. "Your advice would sink my ship." Asked "whether Lawrence was a genius or a phoney," Shaw answered, "Both."[72]

In South Africa when Lawrence died, Shaw said, "He died at the right moment.... I cannot imagine how he could or would have supported himself in civil life." Shaw survived Lawrence 15 years and Charlotte, 7. During his long life, he had met many great figures yet "Lawrence lurked ... often in the corridors of his consciousness."[73] He was surprised to discover how much Charlotte had confided in Lawrence; reading their correspondence, he learned things about her that he had not known, "for she poured out her soul to Lawrence." Once, Stephen Winsten woke Shaw (then 90) from a nap.

"I was talking Chinese with T.E. Lawrence.... He made himself perfectly clear to me and ... laughed at all my jokes."

"How do you know it was Chinese?"

"I took it to be Chinese.... Only ... the last person I want to talk to is Lawrence. Oscar Wilde, yes; Chesterton, yes, but not Lawrence."[74]

Charlotte Shaw

Charlotte Townsend (her mother changed the family name to Payne-Townshend) was born January 1857 on her father's estate in Derry, County Cork. She early learned the ways of the Protestant Anglo–Irish landlords who, like Lawrence's father in Delvin, spent much time socializing; managing their lands, tenant farmers, and servants; and outdoors with their horses and dogs. Privately tutored, she read literature, history, and political philosophy in her father's library. Marriage into the gentry had spurred her middle-class mother's social ambitions. To her husband's displeasure, she left Derry for, successively, Cork, Dublin, and London, taking Charlotte, her sister, and their father with her; preferring Derry, he returned there often. Charlotte loved her gentle father and hated her domineering, nagging, social-climbing mother. When both parents had died, she was 34. Attractive, intelligent, and wealthy, she rejected many marriage proposals. Only once was she in love, to the famed Swedish doctor Axel Munthe, "a tall man with a personality so powerful that he seemed to bewitch even those who disliked him."[75]

Charlotte's lifelong problem of what to do with her life resulted partly from her wealth, which freed her from the need to work. She did not want to be merely a wife. The idea of sex was unappealing, the idea of having children, revolting; she sought serious, socially useful activity, but lacked the ability or urge to work independently. She envied the productive intellectual comradeship of Beatrice and Sidney Webb, contributed £1,000 to the London School of Economics they established, took a flat in Adelphi Terrace above LSE, became involved with the Fabians, and thereby met Bernard Shaw. Nine months later, he asked his actress friend Ellen Terry, "Well, shall I marry my Irish millionairess? She ... believes in freedom, and not in marriage; but I think I could prevail on her.... I am really fond of her and she of me."[76] Even before they married, Charlotte was typing Shaw's plays. After, she tended his health, spirit, and work. Being a celebrated writer's companion, helpmeet, goad, hostess, and promoter, she could still feel lonely and dissatisfied.

Lawrence aimed his initial letters at Shaw. His aim was good; he got pretty much what remained for him in the aging Shaw, more than he expected from Charlotte Shaw. Three months after reading *Seven Pillars,* she could contain herself no longer and, when Lawrence pressed G.B.S. for his opinion, she gave him hers. "I have met all sorts of men ... that are called distinguished; I have read their books ... but I have never read anything like this."[77] Her signature, "C.F.S. (Mrs. G.B.S.!)," produced a "Dear Mrs. 'G.B.S.'" reply signed "'T. E. Lawrence,'" a name he was using rarely.

G.B.S. gave Lawrence his advice on publication and tried to give him his publisher; he gave the Prime Minister and, indeed, the public his advice freely or for the price of a theater ticket. But he was too busy to write Lawrence often. Charlotte was not. Before long, the two became hyperactive correspondents. Each wrote more than 300 letters. Charlotte saved Lawrence's; he destroyed most of hers.

Initially, his letters appear fashioned for G.B.S., with extensive comments on

Shaw plays that he saw or read. Soon he wrote about events and feelings he confessed to few others. In March 1924, he told Charlotte as much about Deraa as he told anyone. In June, he expressed the disapproval of "bringing children into this misery of a world" and of sexual intercourse—"I hate and detest this animal side"—that he and Charlotte shared. Readmittance to the RAF made him feel "like a ship getting into harbour at last." Thoughts of suicide were set aside: "I may be living on for years now." But his depression did not lift; he was as gloomy with Charlotte as with his mother. "Do you know what it is when you see, suddenly, that your life is all a ruin?"[78]

Charlotte began sending packages of goodies—cookies, sweets, luxury foods from swank shops—records, books, book reviews, *The Times Literary Supplement*. The stream followed Lawrence from England to India and back. Lawrence accepted Charlotte's offer to proofread *Seven Pillars;* thereafter, he sent her everything he wrote, in draft or proof, for correction and comment. To compensate for her largesse, he gave her some of his most valuable manuscripts and publications.

Charlotte's letters and gifts could become burdensome. Lawrence noted "your weekly toil, of choosing, packing, posting, writing. Not anybody can feel, every week, in the mood to send or give." He sought to staunch the flow. "You must spend too much of your very scanty leisure on them [clippings of reviews and news]. Please do not over-do them." Barely arrived in India, Lawrence burned most of Charlotte's letters and told her, "It's vandalism."[79] The excuse that she would not want strangers to read them could not cushion the blow. Yet two weeks later, Lawrence proceeded to new and deeper confessions.

Both he and Charlotte sensed the mother-son aspect of their relationship.

Lawrence showed her praise of *Seven Pillars* to his mother—"She likes you now, because you praised my work." He asked Charlotte to meet his mother and related his feelings about her with painful honesty: how he shrank from her demands for love, from her wish to understand him and determine how he should live.[80] Charlotte responded in kind.

G.B.S. had little interest in her early life; "he had listened politely but ... made bantering, paradoxical remarks which dried up any more words." Charlotte told Lawrence things she had never before disclosed. "I had a perfectly hellish childhood & youth.... My mother was ... managing and domineering.... My father ... was a marvel of patience ... she ought to have been *beaten!*" Charlotte condemned herself for not standing up to her mother. "[M]y own home life made me firmly resolve never to be the mother of a child who might suffer as I had suffered."[81] The parallels with Lawrence's childhood and adult feelings are plain.

"You remain the solitary woman who lets me feel at ease with her," Lawrence said. Mrs. Shaw "is quaint and comfortable, and fresh, and kind," he told F. N. Doubleday. "G.B.S. is exciting, per contra. Together they are like bacon and eggs." Michael Holroyd suggests that "Lawrence had approached the Shaws' marriage like an undercover agent, the kindred spirit of each partner separately and the ally of both."[82]

Returned from India, Lawrence's correspondence slackened. The Shaws often traveled abroad (Charlotte had a wanderlust) and Lawrence was preoccupied with power boats. For long stretches, the Shaws did not see him. Probably at this period, after Lawrence had not visited for an unusual length of time, G.B.S. asked Charlotte, "whether there was any quarrel—any unpleasantness. 'No. No quarrel. No unpleasantness. But he is such an IN-

FERNAL liar.'"[83] Shaw does not explain what caused the outburst. Very likely, it was an occasion when Lawrence's manipulativeness, so engrained he practiced it unnecessarily, was unexpectedly revealed.

Janet Dunbar says that, "for Charlotte, at least, the bonds of friendship were loosening a little. It was inevitable that sooner or later she should become impatient with Lawrence's deviousness, though she still kept her admiration and affection for him." Shortly after his death, Charlotte said, "I somehow cannot feel he is really gone—he seems to be here in this little house [at Ayot] he came to so often."[84] She refused David Garnett's request to include her Lawrence letters in his collection. Upon reading it, Jeremy Wilson thinks she was "very hurt to discover that Lawrence had been close friends with so many other people, and had told them things she had previously believed he had confided exclusively to her." To a friend, she expressed puzzlement. "He was an inexpressibly complicated person. In a sense he was tragically sincere. But, also, he always had one eye on the limelight … in the end, he was very dreadfully lonely. The strangest contact of my life."[85]

Three Service Friends

Three of Lawrence's good service friends were A. E. "Jock" Chambers, "Posh" Palmer, and R. A. M. Guy.

JOCK CHAMBERS

Eight years younger, yet with prior Navy and Army service, Chambers was an orderly in Lawrence's Farnborough barracks. He noted Lawrence's tricks to reduce his movements in drill and to dodge spud peeling, but nonetheless admired him: he backed the men against harsh punishments, got a non-commissioned

officer transferred, was good for a half-crown loan, sported a massive Brough. Lawrence instructed Chambers in literature and music, lent him books, and paid for his membership in the London Library. The two kept in touch after Lawrence moved to Bovington and Chambers became a postal sorter in London. "[D]on't hesitate to write if … I can ever be of use to you," Lawrence said. He helped Chambers get payments from the services, paid his rail fare to visit Clouds Hill, arranged for him to sell his letters. Confidences about Deraa, his illegitimacy, and the tribulations of fame balanced any patronizing element in his friendship. "Jock," he pleaded, "I'm very weary of being stared at and discussed and praised. What can one do to be forgotten?"[86]

"The cottage will never be *less* than partly yours, whenever you want it," Lawrence wrote Chambers early in 1935, adding, "I don't like women in my place … but am too perfect the little gent to refuse them." The cottage was available, but not necessarily its owner. In April, Chambers spent two weeks there. During the years that denigratory biographers impugned Lawrence's character and achievements, he stoutly defended his friend. "He was one of the finest men who've ever trod the globe, better than Christ."[87] Chambers died in 1987 at 91.

E. S. PALMER

Private Palmer worked with Lawrence in the Bovington quartermaster's stores. Meeting him at Clouds Hill, E. M. Forster also befriended him. Transferred to Cranwell in August 1925, Lawrence sent Palmer several long letters describing his new life and asking him to do a number of errands. "I remembered Clouds Hill, and you, … and I … wept." On a Sunday, Cranwell was "Heaven"; on Tuesday, "not heaven." "I wish there was someone like yourself in camp."[88] In 1927, Palmer asked Lawrence to buy him out of the Army. Lawrence got Ralph Isham to buy his proof-copy of *Seven Pillars* for £400 and Forster bought Augustus John's portrait. In two years, Palmer was again in financial trouble. Later, marital troubles were added. Though Lawrence had his own troubles, he invited Palmer to visit. "Many people oh excellent P, would like to make a complete break with the past—but pasts are unavoidable facts. You can (by the aid of a gas oven) make a complete break with your future ... at Clouds Hill there are no gas ovens, so I shall look forward to seeing you this summer."[89]

ROB GUY

Lawrence was much taken with Robert ("Rob") A. M. Guy, whom he met at Farnborough. Guy, he said, "embodies the best of the Air Force ranks as I picture them." He was short, "beautiful, like a Greek God," but had a "vile" Birmingham accent.[90] We have no direct information about their friendship at Farnborough; what we know comes mainly from letters Lawrence wrote after leaving the camp bemoaning his expulsion and separation from his friends. He addresses Guy as "My rabbit" and "Dear Poppet," refers to his "exquisite letter," and says "it would give me contentment to see your queer but jolly face again." Soon after, he sent Guy a Savile Road overcoat and cashmere suit that cost £33.[91] For Guy's birthday in September, Lawrence sent him his fee for translating *Le Gigantesque*. The translation, he said, "was done on your account, for I had the ambition to send you a trifle for your birthday. My pleasure in the R.A.F. was partly, largely, due to the pleasure I got from your blue & yellow self: and I owe you a deep debt for many happy times." At a guess, the fee was £20. "I made it in less than a month, so that it is no great gift.... I wish we could meet again."[92]

Lawrence was famous; Guy, unknown. He must have been flattered by Lawrence's attention, not to mention his presents, knew that he was in touch with Trenchard, G. B. Shaw, and other notables, and wished to maintain their friendship. Near the end of the year, Lawrence said, "This is the last [letter]." When Guy protested, Lawrence replied:

> Letters don't work, nor do casual meetings ... we're very unmatched, & it took ... the barrack-room communion to weld us comfortably together. People aren't friends till they have said all they can say, and are able to sit together ... hour-long without speaking. We never got to that, but were nearer it daily ... and since S.A. died I haven't experienced any risk of that's [sic] happening.[93]

Guy left Farnborough for the aircraft carrier HMS *Hermes,* stationed in Portsmouth; visited Clouds Hill in October 1924 and perhaps other times; married; half-faded from Lawrence's life, but continued to correspond. When Lawrence did not reply for a period, Guy complained. Lawrence wrote, "Old thing, I write to nobody: and everybody writes to me.... I would like to see your funny face too: ... in September [1929]? Man, I've said that to 50 people." In 1930, Guy asked for £350. Lawrence replied, "I can't afford that sort of thing." Next year, Guy asked to use Herbert Baker's loft. "Baker will not let anyone else occupy the attic.... I wish I could help you, but I haven't an idea," Lawrence replied. He kept in touch with Guy and, in November 1934, wrote that, when he retired, "I shall ... let alone the people I used to know. I mean the important people.... My sort seem to be the plain sort, for with them I can chat away and reach common ground."[94] Dubious; to W. E. Jeffrey, he said, "My friends are writers and artists."

Desmond Stewart states that Lawrence wrote to Guy "ecstatically" (in 1923) and that his "pet names" and presents show "he had become strongly attached" to him. Jeremy Wilson responds that the letters were merely friendly, the "pet names" were camp nicknames, Lawrence was no more generous to Guy than to other friends. "None of the evidence cited as proof of a homosexual affair between Lawrence and Guy stands up to examination."[95] I agree. Wilson may protest too much, as Stewart does not explicitly make that charge, though some readers may infer it. Nevertheless, it was plainly Guy's physical appearance, not character, intellect, or conversation, that appealed to Lawrence. It was the same kind of aesthetic, vaguely erotic appeal that Sherif Ali and the supple, "clean" Arab men had in *Seven Pillars*. It was Lawrence's misfortune that he could not become "strongly attached" to anyone.

17

Illegitimacy and
Pseudonyms

The value of knowledge can be much exaggerated. Scientists and scholars think it far better than ignorance, but the knowledge that Thomas and Sarah Lawrence were not married is a contrary case. Knowing that their seeming propriety was a sham tormented them. Were the truth known in the Oxford of their day, they could not have remained respected members of the Evangelical church that was so important to them and might well have had to move again to escape their intolerable ignominy. Ignorant of the truth, Will and Frank felt part of a normal family and community. So did Robert until his late sixties.

Arnold also enjoyed the feeling of normalcy and, learning the truth at 23, laughed it off: "illegitimacy ... never worried him."[1] Why was his reaction so different from T.E.'s? Less prominent, he had less to lose or to fear from disclosure. More mature than T.E. had been when he learned, he found the truth disturbing. Arnold was more stable and less self-conscious than his brother. The discovery that his fundamentalist mother was hypocritical struck him as funny; the same discovery made T.E. feel tricked and trapped.

Learning the Truth

Brightest of the brothers, T.E. did not simply accept what he was told or take appearance for reality. He thought for himself and had his own astute methods of inquiry. At 4½, he "began to discover ... the situation" from a conversation between his father and a solicitor about an Irish estate. By the time he was 9 or 10, he had solved the puzzle. "I knew it before I was ten, and they never told me." "The fact that T.E.'s parents never told him...," John Mack reasons, "served to underscore the deception and intensify his resentment of them for it." Lawrence's knowledge enabled him to expose his parents, confide in them, or become their secret accomplice. He took the last course with a bitter feeling at having been put inextricably in a false position. The feeling was directed mainly at his mother, the dominant parent whom he held responsible for capturing—seducing—his father "whom she kept as her trophy of power."[2] (That she could not have been solely, and may not have been primarily, responsible did not alter his feelings.) His knowledge strengthened his resistance to his mother, his emancipation from his parents' religiosity, his resolve to become independent. It underlay his boyhood flight into the army and, probably, his leaving the family home for his garden bungalow.

Some acquaintances suspected the parents' impropriety. How could they not? Thomas and Sarah's manners and speech differed strikingly and in Britain manners and speech betray one's social position. Basil Blackwell, a Polstead Road neighbor and T.E.'s classmate, said the Lawrences were ostracized: "there was something odd" about them, "they were so punctilious, churchgoing, and water-drinking." However, their position was not that black. Many acquaintances accepted the Lawrences as a proper, if peculiar, family. When, decades later, Aldington revealed the facts, they were shocked. Arnold Lawrence thought "no one in Oxford suspected my parents of not being married." Hearing the story in 1937, Ernest Barker did not credit it. "Barker ... would certainly have heard if it had been current either in town or in university circles."[3]

In 1914, T.E. evidently told Stewart Newcombe "his parents were not married and he 'had no right' to the name Lawrence." If so, this was the first known time he disclosed his illegitimacy. It was, of course, known to members and friends of the Chapman family in Ireland and Britain;[4] happenstance may have spread the story here and there in the East as in England. It became more worthy of gossip when Lawrence became famous. From 1919 to 1955, two streams of information flowed in opposite directions: one, with Lawrence himself a prime source, conveyed the truth to friends who spread it to wider circles; another, fed by writers and biographers, led the public to assume that Lawrence's parents were married.

In early 1919, Lawrence dealt with world figures in Paris. In April, as his father lay dead, his mother revealed her shameful liaison to him alone, whereupon

"something I said showed ... that I knew, and didn't care a straw."[5] He cared a great deal, but did not care to show it. Thus, evidence can be presented of both his indifference and bitterness.

Robert Vansittart, Lawrence's second cousin via Thomas Chapman, believed he was not embittered. "He was immensely sure of himself, and the two traits rarely mix." David Garnett agreed: "the fact that he should ... joke about calling ... [his *Odyssey* translation] *Chapman's Homer* seems to me a proof that he was not worried by the fact of illegitimacy."[6] Garnett referred to a conversation late in Lawrence's life, when the crisis of discovery had passed and he handled it wittily. Vansittart was right about Lawrence's self-confidence, but he was the rare case who was also bitter. "[H]e could not face it, even as a grown man ... he lied to the historian Namier about it ... he felt himself branded," his All Souls colleague A. L. Rowse said. "Although he usually made light of his illegitimacy, he could occasionally speak of it with great bitterness to close friends," Jeremy Wilson writes of the 1921–22 period; "he seems to have regarded both his illegitimacy and his short stature as real handicaps, which would in some way prevent him from taking a more prominent place among the ruling élite." "[I]t appears to have embittered their lives," Lord Stamfordham said rightly of T.E., if not his brothers.[7]

The practical consequences were exclusion from certain social circles (or admission with private condescension) and positions where correct birth was essential. The personal consequences of adding a large weight to an already heavy sense of worthlessness were greater.

Disclosing the Truth

Lawrence's colleagues at All Souls knew about his illegitimacy. After he dropped the name "Lawrence," he began to explain that his unmarried parents had adopted it. He gave newspaper editor R. D. Blumenfeld a good hint in 1922. In 1923, he told Leo Amery and the Hardys; in 1924, Jock Chambers, Robin Buxton, and Harley Granville-Barker; in 1925, E. M. Forster. It is hard to chart the flow and ebb of Lawrence's confessions, to understand why, in 1923, he told First Lord of the Admiralty Amery, a mere acquaintance,[8] and the Hardys, new friends, yet waited until 1927 to tell his closer friends David Hogarth and Charlotte Shaw. Lawrence was moody, his talk and letters were unpredictable, he might tell a stranger a secret he kept from friends. Alone with his thoughts in India, while publication of *Seven Pillars, Revolt in the Desert,* and Graves's biography renewed his fame in Britain, a confessional dam seems to have burst. In addition to those mentioned, he told John Buchan, A. E. Cowley, F. N. Doubleday, Robert Graves, Ralph Isham, his solicitor Edward Eliot, and no doubt others.

Almost the first thing Lawrence did upon returning to England in 1929 was to visit Ernest Thurtle, the M.P. who had questioned his use of "Shaw" in the RAF, and explain the illegitimacy of "Lawrence." He talked a good deal about his illegitimacy to the Lionel Curtises; many friends now knew of it. Upon seeing Liddell Hart's biography in typescript, Edward Garnett asked Lawrence if he had approved the account of his father's Irish family. Lawrence had: indeed, he wrote it: "The friends of his manhood called him 'T.E.,'…to show that they recognised how his adopted surnames—Lawrence, Ross, Shaw…—did not belong…. T.E.'s father's family seemed unconscious of his sons, even when … recognition of their achievement might have done honour to the name."[9]

This rather unrealistic wish for "recog-nition" from distant relatives (whom? his half-sisters?) he never knew is another sign of Lawrence's affection for his father. At least once, he wrote to his father's Dublin solicitor; he expressed a wish to buy land and live in Ireland; and, an unusual act for a man who routinely declined invitations to join anything, accepted W. B. Yeats's 1932 invitation to membership in the Irish Academy of Letters. There is no sign of comparable interest in his mother's lowly relatives. Yet more perplexing for a former intelligence officer, Lawrence never bothered to look at his birth certificate and mistakenly thought "Chapman" was entered on it.

At Polstead Road in April 1919, his mother gave him an envelope on which was written, "To my Sons, (But not to be opened except Mother & I are dead.)—OR when Mother desires to." Removing the letter, he read. "My dear Sons, I know this letter will be a cause of great sorrow & sadness to you all, as it is to me to write it. The cruel fact is this, that your mother & I were never married." Other cruel facts followed: he had left four daughters; "There was no divorce"; "I drank." Happier facts were presented at greater length: "My real name … was Thomas Robert Tighe Chapman … & … I am now Sir Thomas Chapman Bart but … have never taken the Title." No apologies were offered, no sense of guilt expressed beyond "'the ways of transgressors are hard'. Take warning from the terrible anxieties & sad thoughts endured by both yr Mother and me for now over thirty years!" Lawrence also read that "*men* are valued for *themselves &* not for their family history, except of course under particular circumstances"; *except* was no doubt incised in his memory.[10]

Illegitimacy is not, like shortness or an Oxford accent, openly manifest and Lawrence could hardly walk around with a sign proclaiming I AM A BASTARD. He was in the unhappy position of unintentionally misleading friends and companions by passing as what he was not or making an open declaration that might make them uncomfortable or elicit embarrassing sympathy. His honesty was not the only consideration: a confession meant a condemnation of his living mother.

Death resolved his problems but not his mother's. Those in the know spoke more freely. "Had long talk with General Grant about Lawrence who is said to be dying now," Bruce Lockhardt jotted in his diary on the deadly Sunday. "He is of illegitimate strain. His mother or grandmother was poor Scottish governess in Irish family of Chapman. Old Chapman lived with her (leaving his family) and had four children by her." The truths and near-truths are a pretty good record for gossip. The same day, Thomas Jones wrote, "He was born out of wedlock and became aware of the fact when he was nine and this was an element in his various complexes."[11] An accurate, succinct analysis for so early a date.

The public remained ignorant for another twenty years. Preparing a short biography of Lawrence for the *Dictionary of National Biography*, Ronald Storrs sounded Arnold Lawrence out on the illegitimacy matter. Arnold told his mother, who wrote Storrs, "Would it be possible for you to say that his father was Irish & his mother Scotch & give no further particulars history of his antecedents [sic]. If you can do this you will make an old woman of 85 most grateful." Discontent with this course, Storrs appealed to Arnold, who replied, "I'd not blame you at all for ignoring her."[12] Storrs, an experienced diplomat, eventually wrote: "His father, Thomas Robert Chapman (who had assumed the name of Lawrence), the younger son of an Anglo-Irish landowning family, ... lived on private means.... His mother, Sarah Maden, the daughter of a Sunderland engineer, was brought up in the Highlands." Chapman's first family, Sarah's family background, where and how the parents met, why Lawrence was born in Wales, when and why the family moved to Oxford are a few points he diplomatically overlooked.

Storrs's account was published in 1949. A fuller and clearer account, based on information supplied by Arnold Lawrence and Stewart Newcombe, appeared in France in 1941, but Aldington's 1955 biography first made it widely known in Britain. To shield Sarah Lawrence, then 95, friends tried to keep her from hearing a BBC discussion of the book. "But Robert ... led her straight to the room where the program was on the air. Mrs. Lawrence sat through it stoically, without moving or speaking.... At the end she got up and walked stiffly out of the room without comment. At the end of her life she admitted—the confession gave her visible relief—that she had had a responsible part in T. E.'s 'nervousness.'"[13]

Countless Names

Name changes are common in Britain and the U.S. Many women use their maiden names at work, their married names at home, and each remarriage can generate a new name. Hyphenated names displaying a prominent ancestral surname are common; a new name and mode of address accompanies elevation to the peerage. Each name represents a different status, role, or stage of life. For Lawrence, it represented a new identity, an effort to become a new person. During his life, he used an astonishing number of names, pseudonymns, and initials: all have probably not been identified. If each represented a different phase or aspect of his life, he was a most multifarious person. Each was a mask he wore or removed for a purpose. With so many masks, things could, at times, become quite confusing. Just as his interest in guns and the military was manifest before the war, so was his predilection for pseudonyms and anonymity.

"L ii" and "Lawrence ii" on high school pieces designated his place in the file of brothers; "Two Calcotripticians" (brass-rubbers) on a piece written with a friend was an effort at schoolboy humor; "C.J.G." on a more serious sketch published in 1913 has yet to be deciphered. To ensure his family saw it, he told them, "by the way I did write something (I have forgotten what, [!] but something very short and simple) for … a Jesus College magazine."[14]

Submitting his report on the Sinai survey, Lawrence asked Hogarth to omit his name. As Hogarth disregarded this request, *The Wilderness of Zin* (1914) became the first book bearing his name. His *Military Report on the Sinai Peninsula* (1914) and *Handbook on the Turkish Army* (1915) were, like most government reports, unsigned. When *The Arab Bulletin* (1916–19) was "strictly secret," his many contributions were unsigned or initialed "TEL"; as the circulation broadened, Lawrence and other contributors were often identified.

The "Colonel Lawrence" Era

After the war, until 1921, Lawrence exploited the publicity value of his name and the value of anonymity, which enabled him to say what he pleased without clearing it with officials, as the occasion warranted. In Paris, he publicized himself and Feisal to the world. In Arab robes, he stood out like a nun in a men's club; was interviewed, photographed, painted; met with journalists, publishers, experts, advisers, officials, diplomats, anyone who

might be useful. Contrariwise, he wrote anonymous articles on the revolt and Mideast policy for *The Times* and *Round Table*. That was the practice of these publications and also necessary to dodge Army clearance. A 1919 *Daily Telegraph* article was signed "Perceval Landon." To any authority too dim to perceive the author, he volunteered help. "Lawrence claims that he has written all the recent articles in the press … on the Syrian question including no less than twelve contributions to *The Times*," G. K. Kidston of the Foreign Office noted.[15]

After leaving the Army July 31, 1919, "T.E.," "Colonel" (or, more rarely, if more accurately, "Ex.-Lieut.-Colonel") Lawrence appeared on a dozen letters and articles in newspapers and magazines. For six months starting August 1919, Lowell Thomas's London performance broadcast Lawrence's name to millions. His newspaper articles fiercely attacked official policy; his longer articles in *The Army Quarterly* (1920) and *The World's Work* (July–October 1921) began the rich torrent of prose that eventually became (or was extracted from drafts of) *Seven Pillars*. Paying Robert Graves for the articles Lawrence gave him to sell, the American magazine *The World's Work* bought not just the text but the famous name "Colonel Lawrence." Lawrence was far more relaxed, often affected not to care about, American publishers' use of his name.

In July 1920, to persuade Lee Warner and Jonathan Cape to republish Charles Doughty's 1888 *Travels in Arabia Deserta*, long out of print, Lawrence agreed to write an introduction. Warner and Cape would not publish without it. Lawrence's name greatly helped—to this day, helps—sales. The new firm of Cape opened for business January 1, 1921, with Doughty as its first title. Its listing expatiated, "This reprint has been issued under the supervision of T. E. Lawrence, Fellow of All Souls,

Oxford, who acted during the War as Chief Liaison Officer with the Emir Feisal on the Staff of Lord Allenby." More people undoubtedly read the introduction than the enormous work that followed; the 500 copies sold out in three months at 9 guineas, a high price, and had to be reprinted. "T. E. Lawrence" also wrote a preface to the October 1921 catalog of the Leicester Galleries' exhibition of Eric Kennington's Arab portraits.

Even in this period when he made most use of the name and fame of "Col. Lawrence," he disappeared for stretches and lived as "Ross" in London. "I am changing my own name to be more quiet, and wish I could change my face," he said in February 1920. In April, he advised Ezra Pound, "Here in Oxford I'm still Lawrence…, but in London I've changed it for peace and cleanliness, and I couldn't dream of printing anything over it."[16] That was untrue. "It isn't that I hate being known—I'd love it—but I can't afford it: no one gets so victimised by well-meaning people as a poor celebrity," he told F. N. Doubleday.[17] That was also untrue—he would not love it—but convenient.

"Ross"

The August 1922 transformation of "Colonel Lawrence" to "Aircraftman John Hume Ross" was a limited success. "Only by hiding that past identity can I get squarely treated like the plain run of men,"[18] Lawrence imagined, but hiding was futile. Uxbridge officers knew about Ross before he arrived. For some months, comrades, perhaps Lawrence, were fooled. Necessarily, high RAF and government officials knew; necessarily, Lawrence told certain friends. Word spread, the secret was too intriguing to keep. Suddenly, everyone knew it.

Like "Thomas Edward Lawrence,"

"John Hume Ross" was tripartite, but single-syllabled. The names, Lawrence said, "seem to me to fit my length & breadth; also I could drop the Ross & sign … 'John Hume' without its seeming odd." Bearing a different name on each shoulder posed problems. "The difficulty is about cheques…. Can I draw on J. H. Ross? and pay in cheques made out so to me?" Lawrence asked his banker. (A collector has a check made out to "J. H. Ross" and signed "T. E. Lawrence.") Other authors get paid in their pen-names—but I'd like to use the old 'Lawrence' as a pen-name, & live under the new one."[19] Not what he told Ezra Pound!

The dilemmas of one person with two names and titles were aggravated by the difficulties of deciding which should be used with each old and new friend, acquaintance, and stranger and how each should be asked to address him. Lawrence knew too many people, it took too long to instruct them all, all did not learn. His attempts to cope, David Garnett thought, had "a childish air of make-believe"; he "played a game of psychological hide and seek, and a physical Box and Cox performance, which is hard to understand."[20]

While "Ross" to his barrack mates, he remained "T. E. Lawrence" in his letters to RAF Vice-Marshall Swann, Trenchard's aide T. B. Marson, Churchill, the Shaws, Mrs. Hardy, Charles Doughty, Jonathan Cape, and others. He was "T.E.L." to Robin Buxton; "E. L." to his friends Baker, Edward Garnett, Graves, Hogarth, Kennington, and Richards; "T.E.S." to his old friend Stewart Newcombe; "J. H. Ross" to H. W. Bailey and B. E. Leeson, comrades from Arabian days who had written to "Colonel Lawrence." Early in 1923, ousted from the RAF and not yet installed in the Tank Corps, he notified Lady Scott, "This self lacked courage to tell you that it has changed its name … and now answers to Mr. J. H. Ross." Below the "JR" signature he remembered, "My mother sends her kind regards. She is called Mrs. Lawrence."[21]

"Shaw"

Though Lawrence became "Private Thomas Edward Shaw" on March 12, 1923, it was hard to drop "Ross" instantly. Explanations can be more troublesome than inconsistency. So he signed "R" in letters to recent RAF friends; once, writing Robert Graves, he started an "R" before changing it to "T.E.?" "R" was the initial of the "uncle" who prescribed Bruce's lashings. The tormented 1923 letters to Lionel Curtis were initialed "R.," "E.L.," "L.," and "E." For airmen Guy and Chambers, "R" persisted until at least December 1923. For others, the extraordinary little man was still "T.E. Lawrence," "T.E.L.," "E. L.," or "L.," even as "T.E. Shaw" and "T.E.S.," sometimes "E. S.," emerged and the all-purpose "T.E." grew more frequent. Gilbert Spencer received a letter signed "Shaw" with a request from Colonel Lawrence to do a drawing for *Seven Pillars* and a £5 check, signed "Ross," as a deposit. On checking accounts and hotel or room registrations, "Ross" persisted for years.[22] Often the name problem was resolved by omitting any signature.

By 1924, "T.E.S." had become common even for old friends like Richards, Hogarth, and Dawnay. Thereafter, it or "T. E. Shaw" was fairly standard, sometimes "T.E." or "Shaw," rarely "S." For Trenchard, "Lawrence" was retained until 1925 when "Shaw" was announced:

> Yours very apologetically
> T E Shaw
> Ex. TEL)
> JHR)[23]

Jock Chambers was introduced to the new initials with a letter signed "TES (ex J.H.R. ex T.E.L. ex E.C.)." "C" stood for "Chapman." In a second letter signed "TEL," "S" was scrawled over the "L" and "Slight confusion: tried to sign all my names at once."[24] As his names multiplied and the conditions of their use became more complex, so did his instructions to friends.[25] The likelihood of mistakes grew.

Anticipating his legal adoption of "Shaw" by deed poll in 1927, Lawrence declared, "I've now legally abandoned the name Lawrence, so there can be no question of my ever using that again."[26] He repeated this declaration on other occasions: "I gave up the name of Lawrence ... five years ago, and am not legally entitled to use it now.... I haven't used it once since, and never again will," he said in June 1927. The name "Lawrence," he insisted in 1933, "will never be resumed by me in any circumstances."[27]

Neither before nor after 1927 did or could "Shaw" entirely abandon "Lawrence." In 1925–26, "Shaw" instructed subscribers to the limited edition of *Seven Pillars* to make their checks out to "T.E. Lawrence." Sometimes, "Lawrence" or "L" seemed to slip in from forgetfulness, as in a 1926 letter to Edward Garnett signed "T.E.L." Sometimes, "(Colonel T. E. Lawrence)" was written beneath "T. E. Shaw" to explain why a strange man was answering a letter addressed to Colonel Lawrence. Sometimes "Colonel Lawrence" was employed openly, as in a 1926 statement sent to George Brough for use in promoting his motorcycles. The catalog of the February 1927 exhibition of art "Illustrating Col. T.E. Lawrence's book 'Seven Pillars of Wisdom'" announced that "Colonel T.E. Lawrence's book Revolt in the Desert will be published on March 10th." T. E. Shaw advised Ernest Thurtle how to use "Colonel Lawrence" in the cause of abolishing the death penalty for cowardice: "I should introduce it neatly by saying Col. L. *on his return from Arabia* said...."[28] "Shaw" allowed Peter Davies to use "Colonel Lawrence" in a 1930 pamphlet promoting Frederick Manning's novel *Her Privates We.*

His birth certificate said "Lawrence"; it was his mother's and brothers' name, his name in Arabia, in Paris, and as His Majesty's Minister Plenipotentiary. "Colonel Lawrence" and "Lawrence of Arabia" were known throughout the world, in newspaper headlines, the *Encyclopedia Britannica*, the biographies of Thomas, Graves, and Liddell Hart. "Lawrence" had entered history and history cannot be undone. As George Bernard Shaw warned when headlines proclaimed that Colonel Lawrence was hiding in the RAF, "It is useless to protest that Lawrence is not your real name ... you masqueraded as Lawrence and didn't keep quiet; and now Lawrence you will be to the end of your days ... you created him, and must now put up with him."[29]

Toujours Colonel Lawrence

The fact is, people were more interested in and pleased to know Colonel Lawrence than John Hume Ross or T. E. Shaw. Lawrence might cajole his family and many friends; he could not control what anyone said in private or what newspapers printed. "I know you hate titles, but I must be allowed to keep Colonel and D.S.O. in your Address," Charles Doughty admonished. At the Hardys, he "was introduced solemnly as Mr. Shaw, and addressed as Colonel Lawrence."[30] Beneath the inscription to "Colonel Lawrence: from Thomas Hardy" in *The Dynasts* a second hand wrote, "To T. E. Shaw for his comfort in camp from Lawrence." In 1929, years into the putative era of T. E. Shaw, *The World Crisis* was inscribed "To Colonel Law-

rence, from his friend Winston S. Churchill." When Private Shaw dined at Chartwell, he might even be required to wear the Arab roles he had once given Churchill and again play the part of Lawrence of Arabia.[31] Lady Astor called him "Colonel"; friends who might say "Shaw" or "T.E." to please him would say "Colonel Lawrence" when talking about him to others.

Of course, the press knew and often reminded readers that "Aircraftman Shaw" was Colonel Lawrence. Thus, in February 1931, a paper reported the role played in the Plymouth flying boat rescue and inquest by "Aircraftman Edward Shaw, the name by which the famous Col. Lawrence of Arabia is known in the Royal Air Force." Discussing Liddell Hart's draft biography with him, Lawrence put a cross against the sentence, "In concluding the book [*Seven Pillars*] he closed his life as T. E. Lawrence" and remarked "that he might reassume the name of 'Lawrence'."[32]

What are we to make of this profusion and confusion of names? No single explanation suffices and as the explanations (ours or Lawrence's) mount, they lose their cogency, become farcical, somewhat mad.

The multiple initials on schoolboy essays and the pseudonym under which Lawrence presumably enlisted as a boy show a continuity with his adult inventions. They began a lifelong array of postures, poses, and roles, never long one unaccompanied by another that he could quickly assume if the first proved uncomfortable. After 1919, any name he used for a while might prove uncomfortable, like shoes that do not break in. "There was a special attraction in a new beginning ... to free my personality from its accretions and to project it unencumbered on a fresh medium, that my curiosity to see its naked shadow might be fed.... Whence came our pleasure in disguise or anonymity."[33] That

passage was written while "Colonel Lawrence" lived anonymously, or as "Ross,"
in London, before enlisting. It shows Lawrence acting as many parts as Alec Guinness in *Kind Hearts and Coronets,* uncertain of who and what he really is, searching
for and failing to find a stable inner self.

The name "Lawrence," which he
vainly tried to discard, represented the colonel with bloody hands, Lowell Thomas's
saccharine hero, and his parents' illicit, fe-
cund union. It was apparently the name
of Sarah's unmarried, youthful father
(John Lawrence). In rejecting "Lawrence,"
T.E. continued the course of rejecting (or
striving to reject) his mother's demanding
love that marked and marred so much of
his life. He never showed the same hostility to his father's birthname, Chapman.
On the contrary, he thought of publishing as "Chapman," even of adopting the
name, and signed a 1931 article "J.C."[34]

Though he could not stop those who
knew from thinking "Colonel Lawrence," a
pseudonym enabled him to pass unknown
in the nondescript rooms, hostels, and inns
where he often stayed. In such places,
"Shaw" or "Smith," which he used increasingly late in life, protected his anonymity.[35]
His attention-getting Brough and cultivated
speech were more likely to betray him.

Ultimately, only Lawrence could (if
even he could) understand the rationale
for each use of each name. He outfoxed
himself. His explanations became incom-
prehensibly convoluted. He would not
write anything as "Shaw," he told F. N.
Doubleday shortly after legally adopting
the name, "for that has been my name for
five years now, & is well known!" When
Raymond Savage suggested he write something pseudonymously after leaving the
RAF, he got so carried away that his
thoughts cancelled themselves out. "I, too,
have thought of trying some day ... to
write something, and put it through pseudonymously. Only suppose the bally thing
succeeded! We should be in the soup then.
It therefore seemed to me an impracticable plan. I could only publish it if I could
find ... some poor wretch who would acknowledge it as his."[36]

At August John's Christmas dinner
around 1934, Lady Pansy Lamb met "a little bright-eyed man in a white sweater:
"we all had our places marked with our
names and my younger sister found herself next to the stranger.... He picked up
his name ticket and said, "Ah—Shaw—I
wondered what name they would put." My
sister ... thought he was joking, and asked,
"Have you many aliases?" He replied,
"Quite a few." "And many nationalities?"
"Always Irish," he answered firmly.[37]

18

Sociable and Solitary

"I like to live alone for 80 percent of my days, and to be let alone by 80 percent of my fellow-men, and all my fellow-women below 60," Lawrence remarked late in life.[1] The alternating urge toward sociability and solitude is common. If Lawrence's case is at all distinctive, it is in the public recognition his fame imposed, the many people he knew in many reaches of society, and the resultant difficulties he experienced in keeping and/or avoiding the friends, acquaintances, and strangers who might recognize him. How he handled these difficulties provides much insight into his character.

Lawrence's mix of sociability and aloofness was evident in childhood. Assigned to a group game at school, he would drift away and watch the others play: the role of detached observer was easier than that of hearty participant. Boating with Janet Laurie, he put a friend with her in one boat and followed in a second, observing. His photographic perception and recall reflect the disposition of a writer who remains detached the better to observe and mentally record events and their setting. It contributed to Lawrence's grasp of the forces and terrain in Arabia, to his calculating coolly amidst turmoil and danger. It was part of his talent for leadership, a talent not of demanding obedience but of knowing instantly what to do.

Shyness and intellectual independence made him prefer his own reading to school classes and college lectures, though he liked the give and take of conversation with a friend or tutor. The major feats of his youth were solitary excursions on bicycle or foot; for one in a family of seven, he lived a relatively solitary life in his bungalow. "Why does one not like things if there are other people about?" he asks.[2] The emptiness of the desert appealed to his solitary, nihilistic nature; solitary reading and writing occupied him much of his life. He disliked addressing a group. "To one person I can talk honestly. To two with some circumspection. To three only from behind a mask. To four hesitatingly.... Seven means silence."[3] Yet his soft-spoken lucidity impressed his occasional audience.

Shortly after the war he agreed to tell a group of [Oxford] undergraduates about the Arab revolt. The largest private room in Christ Church was packed.... Punctually at the appointed hour Lawrence crept in, ... shyly sat down on a sofa and without a note told the whole story in exactly an hour, never moving a muscle.... Every

186

sentence was simple, clear and perfectly phrased. Had anyone taken his talk down in shorthand, the uncorrected transcript would have been a literary and historical masterpiece.[4]

Of Lawrence's prime periods of public activity, the earliest, in Carchemish and Arabia, were most successful. His ability to lead bands of men from whom he was parted by language and culture attests to his insight and resourcefulness. The failure of his diplomatic efforts (despite a personal triumph) in Paris and, even more, his resultant depression attest to his megalomania and naiveté in imagining that his will and wiliness could overcome patent political realities. The retreat from All Souls to a London attic foreshadowed his retreat into the military. The Colonial Office months appear as an interval of settlement and preparation for life in the ranks, whose ambivalent quality of companionship and isolation is well caught by Montgomery Hyde's title *Solitary in the Ranks*.

The descent from high social, political, and cultural circles to the company of humble men, some nasty and brutal, was a flight from the freedom to live anywhere, meet anyone, and do what he wished to regimens, orders, regulations, uniforms. Lauding Lawrence as representing "the Spirit of Freedom" in "a world in fetters," Liddell Hart forgot that self-evident fact.[5] In uniform, Lawrence abdicated much, but not all, of his freedom. He continued to see and correspond with friends he wished to keep and made new ones. The military was an obstacle to visiting outside of camp—and a splendid excuse for not visiting.

Everything depended on his mood. Confined to base each day, the cottage and motorcycle restored his freedom after hours. A motorcycle is made for one driver; to carry a comrade pillion is the driver's choice. On the cycle, he was alone with his thoughts; often he drove around just to be alone. He did so after a Dorchester performance of *Tess of the D'Urbervilles* in November 1924: "when it was over, at midnight on a stormy night, I rode to Southampton & back round the forest till dawn."[6] "When my mood gets too hot … I pull out my motor-bike and hurl it top-speed through these unfit roads for hour after hour."[7]

No Appointments

Advance engagements were the exception; Lawrence preferred to knock at a friend's door as the route and spirit moved him. He might pass nearby without stopping, stop and find no one in, knock at the door in a dirt-spattered uniform and be sent away. One friend, another, or none seemed satisfactory. "It will be nice to see you: but I will not gnash my teeth, if I find you not there." "I did not know I was going to call … until my bike passed a labelled door." "So far I've only missed you three times, and Wavell … twice. Some day you'll be there."[8] Lawrence gave twenty reasons why appointments were impracticable. "My mobility depends on Boanerges [his motorbike], and the weather, and my energy." The bike might be laid up; the Air Ministry might require him. "I never decide 24 hours ahead."[9]

A butler might deny entry because he would not state his business, looked too common, or said "Shaw" when "Lawrence" was expected. Usually, he would leave but he might storm in. Calling at E. M. Forster's London rooms, he "stood patiently outside … for hours until I returned."[10] Admitted with other guests present, he might leave or sit quietly for an hour before leaving. If his friend was alone, he stayed only an hour or two, not more than three at Hogarth's. If he wanted a meal or a night's lodging, he would say so, perhaps adding that, if it were inconvenient, that was all right. "London is full of beds for me: so don't bother to arrange for … lodging. Let's be like crows in a field." "I plan … to stay with you a night or two … possible?"[11] He could spend a night at friends when they were away or sleep in Lionel Curtis's rooms at All Souls. Lady Astor was glad to have him stay at Cliveden, where he kept some books; he declined keys to her London flat.

Lawrence admitted being "unclubbable…: meaning one who took everything, and returned nothing."[12] True, but harsh. Friends could not drop in at Clouds Hill: Lawrence was seldom there; it was isolated, ill-stocked, and ill-equipped, with no toilet, running water (until 1933), phone, stove, ice-box, or, at times, bed. It was designed for Lawrence, not guests. He would have liked a phone as mail took time and telegrams required a trip to Bovington, but only a line out, not one enabling others to call when they pleased.

Fixing up the cottage to suit his retirement, "It will be difficult even to put up a visitor, the place is so 'one-man' now," he pointedly informed his mother. "Probably when you come … I shall give you the cottage, and camp myself in the little work-room by the pool." He tried (unsuccessfully) to forestall a 1933 visit by Arnold and his wife—"there being no bed or food-preparing place."[13] His invitation to Henry Williamson was not entirely inviting: "bring your own food. I shall have no cooking. It smells in so small a house…. No water near, alas!" Inviting himself to the Kenningtons, he quickly disinvited them to stay with him. "[H]ow on earth I'll ever be able to put anyone up baffles me. There cannot ever be a bed, a cooking vessel, or a drain."[14] Having completed most of his improvements, he could still pronounce the place uninhabitable: "do you [Evelyn Wrench] ever travel (not that I can put anybody up: I camp out

amidst the ruins!)" "I cannot put you [Bruce Rogers] up. My activities have reduced the cottage to chaos!"[15]

After sending these messages, Lawrence prepared to receive E. M. Forster and told Posh Palmer, "I shall look forward to seeing you this summer." It is not easy to explain such inconsistency, but, at the time, he was turning somewhat away from his cultured friends towards military comrades. "The place is not very comfortable, I fear … so he [Forster] cannot dare stay long," he told Palmer. "You will be a marvellously welcome person"[16] Lawrence's Tank Corps and RAF friends were important to him. Jeremy Wilson reasons that they were so obviously inferior that he could relax as he might not with men of higher birth or achievement. If he imagined that they judged him solely as one of them, not as Colonel Lawrence, he was, of course, wrong.

"The Children"

Lawrence was paternalistic towards his service friends: Jock Chambers, R. A. M. Guy, Arthur Hall, Arthur Russell, Posh Palmer, A. Pugh, Alex Dixon, W. E. Jeffrey. He referred to them as "the children"; one said, "He fathered us."[17] He took them on motorcycle rides; welcomed them to Clouds Hill; gave them advice, help, and money; introduced them to Hardy, Forster, G. B. Shaw, to literature and music—he "saw himself as a cultural missionary to the working class," Lawrence James suggests.[18]

But these friendships should not be idealized. Lawrence used his service friends as readily as other friends. To G. B. Shaw, "he looked very like Colonel Lawrence with several aides-de-camp"; Russell cleaned his motorcycle and acted like an orderly.[19] Transferred to Cranwell, Lawrence asked Palmer to send his helmet and leggings from the cottage; a housewife[20] from the Bovington canteen stamped with his new RAF serial number; and broken-in boots. "Does Willis wear sixes in boots? I want someone with feet that size to break in a pair of boots for me ... and then to have them soled with rubber by Tangay."[21] David Garnett tells a story showing the ease with which Lawrence both helped and used people. They were on a Southampton ferry, Garnett with a rope in hand for tying down his light plane.

> On board were two ... young aircrafts-men. Shaw ... began talking to them, telling them that two boats were being sent up to Scotland soon and there would be a chance for them to be part of the crews. They were ... breathless in grati-tude. Quite suddenly Shaw ... took the rope out of my hands and asked one of the men to splice an eye at one end, and the other to work a backsplice at the other. They set busily to work.... 'They like being asked to do something,' said Shaw. It was obvious that they did. As I very much liked the beautifully finished off picket rope, it was a magical arrangement.[22]

The fiasco of Lawrence's initial en-listment—the press brouhaha and his re-sultant discharge—led him to rethink his tactics. During his thirty months at Bov-ington, his friends knew his identity. Re-instated in the RAF, he made no effort to conceal it. In any event, his age, military experience, cultivated speech, and com-posed, confident manner, not to mention his gleaming motorcycle, books, and fancy gift packages made him a singular oddity. Many airmen obeyed him or, rather, fol-lowed his lead as if he were an officer. De-spite his "quite unassuming" manner, one said, "his bearing, coupled with his repu-tation, almost compelled me to call him Sir." A companion detained by two mili-tary policemen for improper dress called out, "Sir, sir, I'm being arrested." Law-rence (in dungarees) said quietly, "Oh it's all right, Corporal, he's with me," the po-licemen saluted, and all was well.[23]

Friends and strangers importuned Lawrence for money, jobs, advice, auto-graphs, pictures. He was the object of flat-tery, adulation, observation, gossip, per-petual interest, interruptions, intrusions. He could not walk in London without six or seven people stopping him. At Bridling-ton, strangers sought to talk to or look at him. A woman he had met at Oxford begged an autographed portrait for her son. A New Zealand woman chastised him: "It is sinful to let your great brain lie dormant." A wealthy woman asked his help in finding a new chauffeur.[24] A woman to whom Lawrence had shown his cottage wrote: "Please try and forgive my disgraceful behaviour of yesterday. Was suddenly overwhelmed by a fit of abject humility—thinking what a pitiable igno-ramus I am ... by side of all you can do and what a lot you must know if you have read all those books." A demented woman pleaded, "You made me your wife and did not put the ring on my finger.... I will forgive you if you return to me Dearest."

Lawrence was solicitous and gener-ous to his new friends. When Manning Pike, the American who hand-printed *Seven Pillars*, fell into depression and idle-ness, Lawrence asked Jonathan Cape to give him work, which Cape did. Nonethe-less, Pike's case was difficult. "Pike is his own enemy.... Will you ... try to chase away his clouds?" Lawrence asked Vyvyan Richards from India. "Sex-troubles are at their source." Pike's troubles persisted. "I'm afraid he is bound to go down, even-tually: but I'd like to feel that I'd tried to do something to prevent that."[25] Lawrence sent money, persuaded the head of a print-ing firm to interview Pike, urged him to accept any job that was offered, no matter how junior, and wrote him an unduly frank letter:

I have my R.A.F. pay of about 26/- a week, and about £70. a year of private means. This suffices for me, normally ... but occasionally ... I have, very unwillingly, to capitalise some of my past reputation.... It's a sort of prostitution.... You must, however, put up a scheme.... Buxton will lend me something ... upon my promising to pay it back within the year.... I'll have to take on another foreign translation.... I am asking W_____ to do paymaster for me meanwhile to the extent of £5. Do look round ... and find some sure way of doing something.[26]

Some people cannot be helped. A year later Pike was no better off. "Pike is difficult," Lawrence wrote Wren Howard. "He said the U.S.A. trip was essential. I paid half of its cost: and it proved ... only a joy ride ... at last [I] said it couldn't go on.... You can draw on me up to £20 to keep him alive.... He has no intention ... of doing anything except martyrise himself."[27] Pike eventually comitted suicide.

In the 1930s, Lawrence met a young discharged sailor at the London Union Jack club. They became friends, sometimes lodged in the same house, and Lawrence helped him get a messenger job in the Foreign Office.[28] During the 1930s depression, many acquaintances turned to Lawrence for help. Bookseller K. W. Marshall lost his job. "Do let me know if ever there is anything that you think I could help in," Lawrence wrote.[29] He invited Marshall to stay at Clouds Hill, sent him a few pounds several times, offered to borrow money for him in an emergency, asked Henry Williamson to talk with him, asked a publisher friend to suggest a bookshop job. "Do you think that a small subsidy would persuade some bookseller to give Marshall a trial?" For this purpose, Lawrence proposed to sell his limited edition of *Ulysses*.[30] Marshall eventually found work with Boriswood publishers.

Many who asked for help had to be turned down. Lawrence explained the reasons forthrightly. To a man who asked him to contact Trenchard, then head of the British police, about a job for his nephew, he replied, "Out of the question." When W. E. Jeffrey, whom he had met at Bovington, asked for help in finding a job, Lawrence sent him an informed, well-reasoned letter of discouragement. Secretarial jobs require 80 words a minute; "women are cheaper than men"; higher secretarial jobs go to boys from lesser public schools. "My friends are writers and artists, semi–Bohemian people.... They do not employ anybody."[31]

Detached

Arnold Lawrence said his brother's friendships "were comparable in intensity to sexual love, for which he made them a substitute."[32] Unlikely: intensity was what was most lacking in his feelings. Perhaps Lawrence made up in the number of his friends what he lacked in strong feelings for any; and his feelings were so well camouflaged no one could vouch for them.

"I do not love anybody and have not, I think, ever—or hardly ever.... Altogether I am a bad subject for feeling." "This Christmas [1933], there has been an epidemic of love [declarations] amongst my friends, male and female. It makes me feel all shuddery, to be so cold and hostile to it. What can I do? If I turn hard they mope ... and if I talk gently they beg for more."[33] It was not just love that Lawrence did not feel, but real emotional commitment, even real hate. His reserve took two forms: avoidance of sociability, social engagements, and close friendship; and a shyness, emotional restraint or aloofness. Both forms were present much of his life.

A friend criticized his refusal to socialize at Jesus College. "To be self-sufficient ... was his ideal, though I felt ...

he deprived himself unnecessarily of many pleasant contacts ... by holding aloof from men. It was a constant source of argument between us." At All Souls, he was equally unsociable: "I'd rather be a prig than be sociable." In the RAF, he avoided the mess and convivial groups. "He was ridden with friends and yet he tried to be isolated," an airman observed.[34]

"[O]ne hears of his thrusting away approaches of friendship with some rudeness," Lady Gregory noted in her 1923 diary. "After I had enlisted, my need ... of friends much declined," Lawrence declared.[35] Were the Shaws, the Hardys, Lady Astor not friends or not needed? His comrades? "One doesn't make real friends after twenty-five. The shell hardens," he remarked in 1933.[36] Lawrence was 26 in August 1914. If we were to take that remark seriously, Edward Garnett, Kennington, Graves, Forster, Doubleday, Curtis, almost everyone of note in his postwar life but Hogarth and family members, were not "real friends." That is hard to credit, yet something was missing in the quality of his friendship: a normal degree of relaxation, unselfconsciousness, and warmth. "[N]ever could I open myself friendly to another. The terror of failure in an effort so important made me shrink from trying." "You can hardly conceive the thousands of people I know: from tramps to Air Marshals.... I like nearly everybody.... But I don't think I have an intimate."[37]

Even during Lawrence's enthusiastic days in Syria, Leonard Woolley felt "he was frightfully reserved about himself and in all our long talks seemed detached from what he said." Winifred Fontana noted his "absorbed and discomforting aloofness" in her Aleppo home, but found him much more relaxed at Carchemish. After the war, she complained that his letters "are as perlite and non-committal as pressed ferns."[38] In the small Cairo intelligence group, "where we all knew each other fairly well, ... Lawrence remained always aloof," rarely mentioned his family, and kept his feelings about about them "almost savagely to himself." At Akaba in September 1917, a British soldier recorded, Lawrence "has never been unfriendly; rather he has been detached."[39]

Talking with Lawrence, Eric Kennington observed that his face was "removed from me as a picture or sculpture. However gracious, ... it remained distant." When David Garnett joined him for a speedboat trip, Lawrence "turned himself into a pedantic guide, speaking very precisely about what interested me not at all. He was something between a scoutmaster or a curate and an Oxford don, rather shy and celibate." After they got into a launch and he started the engine, the scoutmaster vanished and "an eager, confident, weather-beaten mechanic" emerged.[40] Lawrence gave an eerie picture of his detachment. "Do you ever feel that there is a wall of glass between you and the streeet? You see the people scurrying and waving their arms—but no noise, no eddy of air and no touch?"[41] Robert Graves sees detachment as central to Lawrence's character, his powers, the impression he made. "It is this extraordinary detachment ... which makes him the object of so much curiosity, suspicion, exasperation, admiration, love, hatred, jealousy, legends, lies. He has ... adopted the attitude towards organized society, 'you go your way and I'll go mine.'"

E. M. Forster attributed Lawrence's leadership power partly to his detachment—his ability "to reject intimacy without impairing affection."[42] Detachment enabled him to analyze a strategy, tribal altercation, battle, plane crash, or person dispassionately, without distracting, confounding feelings. The normal run of feelings may have been present (not, I think, love or hate), but weakened, encapsulated, controlled, overridden by a rapidly calculating intelligence.

"The fear of showing my feelings is my real self."[43] Even alone, Lawrence seldom experienced prolonged pleasure (though he experienced prolonged depression). "I find it difficult to go on 'feeling' for more than a few minutes. At a concert, … I get two minutes exquisite pleasure every half-hour or so…. The same in Brough riding, and in talking, and in seeing pictures. In reading, by much practice, I can draw out my pleasures to a full half-hour or more."[44]

Detached insight, the ability to read expressions and gestures, to put himself in another person's skin and grasp their feelings gave Lawrence unusual empathy and understanding. "When he had just been with someone he tended to take on the characteristics of that person." When writing about Hardy, his handwriting might resemble Hardy's; writing to Henry Williamson, it resembled Williamson's. Lacking strong feelings of his own, he more readily sensed the feelings of others. He was a chameleon who could assume a friend's mood and thought. He himself used the word; Trenchard called him "a 'chameleon' [who] took on quite honestly the colour of his surroundings."[45]

Acerbic

Lawrence's aloofness made some complain of his coldness. Aloofness led him to make surprisingly critical remarks about friends, though to him they may merely have been neutral facts. For example: "poor silly little [King] Abdulla"; "Hogarth, and Lady [Kathleen] Scott gossip too freely"; "Woolley is … good company: but not right, fundamentally."[46] Of Ronald Storrs, he wrote, "his eyelids were heavy with laziness, and his eyes dulled by care of self, and his mouth made unbeautiful by hampering desires." The *Seven Pillars'* description of Storrs Lawrence termed "loathesome … put in out of

spite."[47] Of Storrs's "falseness," he said, "Oh yes, I saw it: but because … he knew that I knew it, it had no share in our relations…. Storrs could retort about the falseness of me." Storrs called Lawrence "a loyal, unchanging and affectionate friend." Nonetheless, his feelings were mixed and, during the controversy over Aldington's biography, he did not immediately rally to Lawrence's defense.[48]

Lawrence took pains to ensure that Ralph Isham, who had initiated his *Odyssey* translation, received a copy of the limited edition without knowing that he had sent it. Weeks before his death, he visited Isham in London. However, "I don't trust the man or like him, to my regret."[49]

Lawrence's candor or, it may be said, tactlessness, prompted G. B. Shaws's admonishment about libelous passages in the Oxford Text: "the blow below the belt, the impertinence, the indulgence of dislike, the expression of personal contempt … are not and should not be privileged."[50] Aware of his tendency to jab his friends— "It's not in me to praise without a twist of the lip"[51]—Lawrence asked a number to comment on their depiction in the Oxford Text. Thus, he asked Robin Buxton, who led the Imperial Camel Corps in Arabia, what he thought of the ICC account. "I have a censorious devil within me … [but I] will alter to please your judgement, so far as I can." Others had no such opportunity. "You will not be moved to pleasure by the things I have said of you: but … I cannot help hurting the feelings of people," he wrote P. C. Joyce after *Seven Pillars* was issued. "In many ways I'm hardly responsible."[52]

"[S]ome of the hatred he has drawn upon himself he deserved," Arnold Lawrence remarked, "for he had a very sharp tongue, he was sometimes a 'showman', and he annoyed people unnecessarily."[53]

Understanding

To Lawrence's friends, his charm, self-deprecatory humor, wide-ranging and penetrating mind outweighed any critical remarks they heard or overheard. Something in his manner, directness, and freedom from conventional opinion and conduct made them pleased and proud. "When he came to a house," Robert Graves recollected, "he made everybody feel good. It was his proudness, the sense of extraordinary physical health and wellbeing, and the sense of ... 'Oh he's a lovely man!'" When he visited, Henry Williamson thought, "what a marvellous person. And I began to feel very big and strong and happy and confident."[54]

Lawrence must have read facial expression instinctively, though he claimed to disregard it. Friends noted his "ability [in Arabia] to sense the feelings of any group," "to read your thoughts—you felt it was silly to hide things from him although you felt he was hiding things from you."[55] "[N]ow that T.E. is gone, I shall never be understood by a living soul," Ernest Altounyan lamented. Celandine Kennington related how, ill and depressed after a miscarriage, Lawrence came into her room, looked at her and began to talk. "'[Y]ou must be feeling you are utterly no good and nothing can ever be worth while...' On and on he went, ... clarifying all the nightmare fears ... and doing it all from the woman's point of view."[56] Friends felt a mesmeric quality in Lawrence. In almost identical words, several said they could have followed him anywhere he led.[57]

Lonely

His countless friends served to emphasize that none was of special importance, that he had no intimate, loved no one, and rejected love that was offered. "I think ... solitude ... the prime condition of welfare." "Sometimes I think it impossible for one live thing to touch another live thing."[58]

Lawrence chose the ranks to escape total loneliness, to be "one cell in a honeycomb."[59] Comrades could not dissolve the layers of kindness, courtesy, reserve, and coldness under which he hid. *The Mint* ends with a paean to brotherhood, to merging jagged individuals in a harmonious mass. Lying on the grass in the sun with fellow airmen, there was "Everywhere a relationship: no loneliness any more." That was Lawrence's hope, not achievement. This section of *The Mint* "was vamped up ... to take off the bitterness," he admitted. "I have never been really one with my fellows."[60]

"[I]t is not wholesome for a man to live too much by himself," Lawrence reflected. "Celibacy overturns a man's balance: for it throws him either on himself (which is unwholesome, like sucking your own tail, in snakes) or on friendship ... and such friendship may easily turn into sex-perversion. If I have missed all these things, ... well then, I'm barrenly lucky. It has not been easy: and it leads, in old age, to misery."[61] Arnold Lawrence and those who accepted his view that Lawrence's beatings were sexless acts of penance could not think of them as "sex-perversion." Lawrence was bolder. In my reading of this letter, he neither betrayed nor deceived himself.

"I had hoped, all these years, that I was not going to be alone again," Lawrence said, preparing to leave the RAF. On an early *Seven Pillars* page headed "Detachment," he refers to his "feeling of intense loneliness." On a late page, the muezzins' last call to prayer at the end of the day he entered Damascus "showed me my loneliness."[62] Altounyan perceived his "utter loneliness." Simpson and Knightley declared, "No one could read the complete [Bodleian letter] collection ... without recognising how desperately lonely the man was."[63] A sense of his isolation and immaturity led friends to adopt a protective posture towards Lawrence. At Farnborough, "gradually we all seemed to gather round him and sort of look after him." His friends "felt noticeably protective ... as though recognising a persistent youthfulness that occasionally lapsed into immaturity."[64]

As Kathleen Scott was seeing David Hogarth off at Victoria in 1920, "a little man" gave him some papers. Hogarth introduced Lawrence. After the train left, she offered him a ride. "I asked him where I should drop him ... he replied 'It doesn't matter where I go.'...fifteen years later ... I was seeing him out of my garden gate— he turned to the left which goes no where of account. I said 'Why where are you going' & he replied 'Oh it doesn't matter where I go.'"[65]

Political Outlook

George Orwell called Lawrence "Perhaps the last right-wing [British] intellectual." Perhaps he meant nothing more by "right-wing" than Lawrence's war and postwar service to the Empire, Churchill, and the RAF at a time when many British intellectuals were communists, socialists, or pacifists, critics of the Empire, the aristocracy, the Conservative Party, and the "ruling classes," many of whom were Lawrence's friends. Many were also his enemies and left-wing writers—Shaw, Forster, the Garnetts, Tomlinson, Sassoon, Day Lewis—were his friends. Orwell adds a point that helps to explain why Lawrence found the RAF so much more attractive than the Tank Corps:

> Since the [18]'fifties every war in which England has engaged has started off with a series of disasters.... The higher commanders, drawn from the aristocracy, ... have always clung to obsolete methods and weapons, because they ... saw each war as a repetition of the last ... the navy and, latterly, the Air Force, have always been more efficient than the regular army. But the navy is only partially, and the Air Force hardly at all, within the ruling-class orbit.[1]

It is hazardous to judge anyone's political outlook from their wartime activity.

In World War I, men of many viewpoints served in the military and thereby served "the Empire." What else could they do? The only alternatives were flight, prison, or conscientious objection (which David Garnett chose). After being badly wounded and decorated for bravery, Siegfried Sassoon barely escaped court martial for issuing "Finished with the War, A Soldier's Declaration" defying military authority. The vast multitude enlisted. In 1914, age 11, Orwell wrote a poem calling young men of England to enlist or be labelled cowards.[2]

As a young man, Lawrence was a Conservative, like his father. At Carchemish, he played the part of Lord of the Manor that his father had played in Ireland—his own kind of lord who (unlike his Eton-educated father) went to no public school and disliked "the type they produce." *Seven Pillars,* he said, "would never have been written by anyone properly imbued with the public school spirit."[3] During the war, his primary policy was the same as that of every officer and soldier: victory, to which he added a goal, at the least cost in lives, unknown to many generals. The goal of Arab "freedom," repeated often in *Seven Pillars,* was secondary both to British victory and to

Britain's keeping its diplomatic "word," whatever that meant. In diplomacy, no single "word" but many words with different meanings and nuances are spoken. Of course, Lawrence sought victory *and* to fulfill *his* word, but, faced with a choice, "better we win and break our word than lose."[4]

Elie Kedourie, who called Lawrence "a liberal and a romantic," thought his policies largely vacuous. "He believed neither in the Sharif [Hussein], nor in Faisal, nor in the Arab national movement…. Ultimately, he was not interested in ideas."[5] The second sentence is true, especially of Lawrence's later years; of the revolt, he said, "We were wrought up with ideas inexpressible and vaporous, but to be fought for." He also said, "Arabs could be swung on an idea as on a cord…. One such wave [of Arabs] … I raised and rolled before the breath of an idea, till it … toppled over and fell at Damascus."[6] But he did not say what that idea was besides ending Turkish rule.

The first sentence is also true. Lawrence judged Hussein useful only for a short time;[7] Feisal, a weak man yet a convenient tool for the advance on Damascus and, later, for British control of Iraq; and the Arab "movement," discordant factions fit at most for separate states, not one nation. He said, "I meant to make a new nation"[8] and helped to make three while the French made two more. Lawrence was a liberal imperialist favoring self-governing states within the British commonwealth rather than colonies like India in an enlarged Empire. He aimed "to save England … from the follies of the imperialists…. I think, though, there's a great future for the British Empire as a voluntary association."[9] The "freedom" of Arabs meant to him their rule by Arab kings under British control. To George V's remark, "This is a bad time for Kings: seven new republics were proclaimed yesterday," he re-

sponded, "Courage, Sir, I have made three new Kings in the East."[10]

The idea of rallying Arabs to help defeat Turkey succeeded; the establishment of Jordan and Iraq with Sharifian kings succeeded until the Iraqi regime was overthrown in 1958. The conception of guerrilla warfare persuasively elaborated in *Seven Pillars* and validated by the Turks' expulsion is Lawrence's intellectual legacy. His unrealistic hostility to French interests and misreading of Ibn Saud's position in Arabia were major policy errors. His three successes and his failure to keep the French out of Syria were policies in which he was an active, influential protagonist. Where he succeeded, it is difficult or impossible to separate the merit of a policy from his effectiveness in advancing it. His genius in action and manipulation is indisputable; the closer he came to the levers of power and to "hands-on" action—to Allenby and gelignite—the more likely was his success.

Lawrence's ideas for a Middle East settlement did not go far beyond the broad conception of a British commonwealth and the boundaries drawn at the 1921 Cairo Conference. He favored Jewish settlement to improve the Palestine economy, so long as Jews remained a minority. In Syria, he preferred gradual, indigenous development to more rapid change spurred by foreign investment.[11] He supported the use of planes instead of soldiers to control Iraq. Then he lost interest in the area and turned his attention to writing, illustrating, and producing a book and to obliterating the public image of Colonel Lawrence.

Lawrence was interested in military strategy and tactics, methods of attack and defense between states and of rebellion and the maintenance of internal order. He had little or no interest in domestic politics or economic and social issues. He could be greatly interested in individuals, be they national leaders or servicemen and citizens. At Bridlington, "He seldom discussed social problems, and when he did it was with detachment, for he seemed to be strongly opposed to any kind of organized social reform. But for the underdog, as an individual, he had the keenest sympathy." He believed "It is not possible to change the organic structure of society: or at least it would be easier to reform the single man of his kidneys, leg, or hair."[12]

In a period when many of his friends liked Russian communism, Italian or German fascism, or Labor reforms and socialism, Lawrence stood aloof from politics. At Churchill's request, Ralph Isham tried, in 1920, to persuade him to join the Colonial Office. He declared, "I like Winston.... But he's a politician. I'd rather be a chimney sweep than a politician.... Too much necessity for compromise. All ours that I know, are honest and devoted—but they have an eye on the weather and they reek of red herrings." G. B. Shaw thought he had no interest in politics. "I have talked to him on every subject on which he could be induced to talk ... but they did not include politics.... [T]hough ... people of all political complexions question me eagerly about [the Russian Revolution] ... because I have visited Russia, Lawrence never once mentioned it to me ... he showed no consciousness of the existence of Lenin or Stalin or Mussolini ... or Hitler."[13]

Meeting Lawrence at the Shaws in November 1926, Beatrice Webb formed a poor opinion of his mind and politics. "He was more interesting to look at than to listen to ... vivid but shallow in thought, with wit and sensitivity but without knowledge or reasoning power ... delighting in cheap abuse of democracy and dogmatic assertions on matters about which he knew nothing." (Did they discuss social or legislative issues with which she was engrossed, was she appalled at Lawrence's

witty dismissal of her ardent concerns?) Reading *Revolt in the Desert* a few months later convinced her that Lawrence detested "the common civilized man, more especially the bourgeois democrat." She termed him "the perfect A—Aristocrat, Anarchist, Artist, ... Ascetic."[14]

"I have ... no sense of public spirit," Lawrence said. He was not interested in the daily affairs of government, politics, business, reform. Politics, Labor M.P. Ernest Thurtle observed, involves "contact with the sordid, the petty and the mean. T.E. would have had the contempt of a Coriolanus for these things."[15] Referring evidently to his work at the Colonial Office, Lawrence said, "The life of politics wearied me out by worrying me too much. I've not got a coarse-fibred enough nature for them.... It's not good to see two sides of questions when you have (officially) to follow one."[16]

Lawrence wanted no revolutionary change and had no interest in the slow process of reform. "Politics in England means either violent change ... or wasting 20 years of one's time and all one's strength on pandering to the House of Commons."[17] "The ideals of a policy are entrancing, heady things: the translating them into terms of compromise ... is pretty second-rate work.... I'd rather be dustman [than politician]." He dismissed political panaceas like Social Credit or socialism. Accepting no political doctrine, he could not safely be identified with any party. "The Labourites think I'm an imperial spy, & the Die-hards thought I was a bolshie."[18] To Ezra Pound, smitten by economic nostrums, he protested, "I don't care a hoot for economics, or our money system, or the organisation of society ... what time I have for thinking ... goes ... upon themes within my governance."[19]

G. B. Shaw was wrong to say Lawrence was unaware of Lenin, etc. Perhaps, knowing Shaw's glib infatuation with communism, he simply avoided the subject in conversation. When the Shaws were en route to Russia in 1931, Lawrence wrote Charlotte Shaw, "There is a lack of commonsense about Bolshevism which will hurt his [G.B.'s] sense of fitness: yet it is a noble effort." The goal of "the Soviet experiment" was right, "but the means might spoil my faith." To C. Day Lewis, then an avowed communist, he said, "The trouble with Communism is that it accepts too much of today's furniture. I hate furniture."[20] I take that less-than-clear remark to represent disapproval of the Soviets' industrialization, which Lawrence, like William Morris, disliked.

Lawrence regarded Lenin as the greatest man of his time for having designed a theory, "carried it out, and consolidated." He thought Napoleon "a very great man—he remade Europe," but had a low opinion of Mussolini, who had arranged for no successor, had no intellect, had practical sense but "no capacity for abstract thought." He wanted Trotsky given asylum in England—"he's so much one of the big figures of the world that I'd like England to have the honour of housing him"—and berated the Labor Government for barring him.[21]

As these examples may indicate, Lawrence's judgment reflected his assessment of a leader's achievement in gaining and holding power and implementing his program, not the nature of the program. He was more interested in a nation's military status than its political character. Thus, he wished for a Chinese communist victory and consolidation. "It is the only hope I can see, as against Japanisation."[22] He cautioned Churchill (via his private secretary Edward Marsh) against attacking Russia. "It's hard to attack, for its neighbours, except Germany, aren't very good allies for us. We can only get at her, here [India], through Turkey, or Persia, or Afghanistan, or China, and I fancy the Red Army is

probably good enough to turn any one of those into a bit of herself." In 1934, he did not favor increased RAF appropriations. "Our present squadrons could deal very summarily with France. When Germany wings herself—ah; that will be ... our signal to reinforce.... All we now need is to keep in ourselves the *capacity* to expand the R.A.F. usefully."[23]

Much nonsense has been written about a proposed meeting between Lawrence and Hitler and the prospect of his joining Oswald Mosley's fascist movement. I have noted only one reference by Lawrence to Hitler, made in the course of commenting on F. M. Ford's *It was the Nightingale*, "where he tries to blacken Lloyd George and Hitler—far be it for me to defend those two great ones. They can forget people like him and me."[24] In 1932, Nazi foreign affairs emissary Kurt von Lüdecke evidently contacted Lawrence, who rejected the overture; nothing more is known of what transpired.[25] While this episode has been ignored by most biographers, excessive attention has been given to a non-event. Writer Henry Williamson admired Hitler, considered Lawrence "our nearest approach to Hitler," and resolved that the two should meet. "I wrote thus to him, shortly after he had left the R.A.F. He replied immediately by telegram, asking me to come the next day."[26] Lawrence's Monday, May 13, 1935, telegram agreeing to lunch with Williamson on Tuesday was the last thing he wrote. Neither the telegram, nor Williamson's May 10 letter about the visit, nor Williamson's diary contain any reference to a meeting with Hitler. Examining the story in detail, Anne Williamson pronounces it a fiction invented by Williamson after Lawrence's death.[27] Another possibility is that Williamson wrote such a letter but did not post it (something he often did).[28]

Mosley supporters approached Lawrence who rebuffed them. Former M.P. Sir

Oswald Mosley launched the British Union of Fascists in 1934. Capt. Lloyd-Jones, a Mosley backer, invited Lawrence to a BUF dinner. Declining, he said, "I want your movement to … put an end to the license of the daily Press. It will be glorious to dance on the combined cess-pit that holds the dead *Daily Express, Daily Chronicle* and *Daily Herald.*"[29] Often harassed by the press, Lawrence was only half-joking. If Mosley gained power, he told Liddell Hart, "he would agree to become 'dictator of the press'—for a fortnight…. Would stop all mention of anybody's name except public servants. I said that he was going against his own principle of freedom. He said it would do no harm to suppress the cheaper press, save the decent three."[30]

Deeming Lawrence's letter equivocal, Lloyd-Jones wrote again. This time, Lawrence said, "I suppose Mosley is doing his best. He is daemonic, and a leader of conviction … but the Staff work very patchy…. These Jews, Diehards, Liberals are like wet brown-paper. What faces you, actually, is the machine of government; and what ails you is that you don't know where the keyboard is…. No, please don't make me any part of your Club."[31] Liddell Hart spoke to Lawrence about "the many people who were approaching me to seek him as 'dictator'…. T.E. said there was no doubt there was a big call for a new lead…. Mosley was suffering from megalomania … and wouldn't tolerate any decent good chief of Staff. But his chance might come if somebody big took him under their wing."[32]

Other friends also thought Lawrence might succumb to the fascist temptation. "[I]f he had lived…, there is no doubt that the Fascists would have tried to use him as a mascot," E. M. Forster wrote. Robert Graves believed Lawrence "played with the idea of … becoming a dictator. If he had not been killed … he would have found the temptation to strong political action almost irresistible."[33] I think Liddell Hart, Forster, and Graves were wrong. Lawrence was not a man who cried easily. No matter how depressed, he put up a good front, especially to note-taking writers. But a man whom "wild mares would not" drag to talk informally with the incoming Prime Minister would not take on the hazards and obloquy of campaigning for a questionable cause. He had never engaged in public campaigning—serving as staff to a leading politician was no way to escape the merciless press—or shown any inclination to do so, least of all during his last, unhappy years.

Nor had he ever joined a political organization. He was a loner, not a joiner, a rebel against government, society, organized reform, organized charity. "I am … a philosophical anarchist, if you need a label." However, he was critical of any formal ideology. "After [reading] Oil, I rose up a capitalist, sympathising … utterly with the victims of Upton Sinclair's attack…. I'm like an Irish pig whom someone has tried to drive down a particular road."[34]

Contrariwise, he did not hesitate to criticize the sacrosanct Royal Family. His conduct in refusing honors King George proffered had few defenders. The excuse that he refused in a private audience was unsatisfactory. Churchill told him to his face "that his conduct was … grossly disrespectful … monstrous." The Prince of Wales declined to meet him, insisting that he *had* embarrassed his father. "Don't you like the idea of royalty?" Ralph Isham asked. Lawrence replied, "Yes, I think it is very valuable for Boys' Books."[35] Lawrence was particularly harsh about the Queen, who, he said, had been "very huffy" about his conduct. "I resent any politeness shown to the Queen. A disagreeable woman. The whole Royal Family would be the better of a little wholesome neglect."[36]

"I'm an anarchist, and want to avoid using or coming under any courts or authority, for or against. Why try to make a bad thing tolerable?" Why not? Though a developer threatened to impinge on his Pole Hill property, he said, "in no circumstances would I take legal procedures against anyone. Governments are things with which men should have no dealings." "I grudge every penny any government extracts from any worthy citizen. They waste it so on policemen and customs and navies and airforces and prisons and politics," he counseled Lady Astor in 1934, when the issue of government military expenditures was of growing urgency.[37] Was the RAF financed by charitable contributions? Did he oppose paved roads, traffic lights, and driving licenses?

It is impossible to force everything that Lawrence said and did into a consistent mold. "Consistency," Emerson said, "is the hobgoblin of little minds." At any rate, Lawrence was consistent in keeping his income low enough to escape taxation.

Independent, rebellious, anarchistic, Lawrence immured himself in the uniformed, obedient military. The military is a mass of disciplined men who obey commands and use weapons to protect, threaten, capture, destroy, and kill. Keenly conscious of death, Lawrence was unusually solicitous of elderly friends and their widows. Yet he did not shrink from killing: it was a mission of the military, where he chose to spend most of his adult life. In peacetime, the military may be regarded as a (temporary) deterrent to war. After the grisly experience of World War I armies, the RAF could be viewed as an instrument of mercy. "I sometimes think people do not realize that I do not want to use the Air Force for killing only: ... [it] should in time ensure that we may not continually go on the warpath with as many casualties as we did in the past," Trenchard told Lawrence, who concurred.

"We are doing what you'd like out here [India]. Flying over a civil war, and persuading them, without using violence, to be good. Doves, in fact, not eagles."[38] Lawrence's left-wing friends disagreed. E. M. Forster called Trenchard's letter "a gem" of chicanery. H. M. Tomlinson saw the RAF "as an institution deliberated for the destruction of the innocents—its wings are the dark pinions of Ahrimanes, coming by night to breathe into sleeping children the vapours of the pit."[39]

A realist, not a pacifist, Lawrence justified the bombing of Arab villages: "There is something cold, chilling, impersonally fateful, about air bombing.... The R.A.F. ... bombs only after 24 hours notice given.... It is ... infinitely more merciful than military action, as hardly anyone is ever killed." "Every true pacifist supports the R.A.F.," Lawrence assured Ernest Thurtle sardonically. "In case of war we will destroy (1) fleets (2) civilians (3) soldiers in that order!" Maybe he was not sardonic, for he expected planes to render capital ships obsolete and thought bombers "the only democratic weapon!"[40]

Penetrating and detached, Lawrence could reach chilling conclusions that flouted common sensibilities. He could also accept foolish ideas of his time and place. Thus, it "hurt" him that "tom-tom playing" negroes "should possess exact counterparts of all our bodies." He believed "Red-haired men are seldom patient" and "petulance often accompan[ies] curly hair." There was a "Jewish aptitude for languages" and a "Jewish odour." Arabs were "a limited, narrow-minded people"; Syrians, "an ape-like people"; Turks, a "child-like people." A "blend of native intelligence and vigour ... often comes in a crossed stock" (to which he assigned himself). Nonetheless, he repudiated the "suggestion that one race is better than another."[41]

Lawrence was an extreme individualist who set his own standards of eating and living, thinking and acting, disregarding those of his wealthy, middle-class, poor, and bohemian friends. He was not a political or social proselytizer. He did not want to change society; had he wanted to, he would, like William Morris, have changed it backwards toward the bucolic, romanticized Middle Ages. He most wanted to be left alone to live as he pleased. He had a remarkable mind set in a still more remarkable character, but both his mind and character could leave the realm of reality for one of the utmost folly.

20

"My Name Is Legion"

The artists who painted and sculpted Lawrence portrayed different persons: romantic, tough, emaciated, brooding, bland. He conveyed no single dominant, consistent mood. "Cockerell declares that he is fifteen different men," G. B. Shaw told Prime Minister Baldwin, "and that you never know which one will be on duty in any given emergency." Lawrence himself said, "Lots of people ... go about saying they alone understand me. They do not see how little they see.... My name is Legion!"[1] He was a confident leader and fawning adulator, vain, megalomanic, humble, astonishingly frank and needlessly devious, self-assured, self-doubting, kind and rude; he sought renown and obscurity; he loved and despised himself. To inventory all his contradictions is difficult, to explain them, impossible. "Lawrence ... wanted me to ... give some coherence to his diversities. But he had ... fought coherence. I could not ... do for him what he had set his face against doing for himself," Robert Graves regretted. Writer John Brophy believed "he did not understand himself."[2]

This chapter will review some major schisms in his nature. Two passages convey the theme. Brophy sees duality as the central feature of Lawrence's life.

Duality marches through his career.... He was successively the most famous colonel and the most famous private soldier in the British Army. He was a contemplative and a man of action. He was classic in his taste and interests, and romantic in the impulses ... of his active years. He was an ancient, in love with Greece and ... archaeological remains...: yet he was also a modern, deeply interested in ... contemporary literature, and ... rapid travel.... All this suggests a man at variance with himself, torn by an inward conflict.[3]

In a penetrating sketch of Lawrence's character, John Buchan discerns "contradictions which never were ... harmonised.... He had moods of vanity and moods of abasement, immense self-confidence and immense diffidence ... though the gentlest ... of human beings, ... he could also be ruthless. I can imagine him, though the possessor of an austere conscience, crashing through all the minor moralities to win his end." Contrasting his English and Arab selves, Lawrence senses the near madness of a man "who could see things through the veils at once of two customs, two educations, two environments." His bifurcation was native, not a product of Arabia. "There was a fissure in him from the start ... [a] crack in the firing."[4]

The Elements of Genius

Despite occasional fear and caution, his strongest critics (Aldington, Yardley, James) do not question Lawrence's bravery. Jaafar Pasha, commander of the Arab regulars, called him "the bravest man he knew."[5] Repeatedly he led men in raids and battles; repeatedly, disguised, he spied in Turkish-held territory. He could enter the camp of a two-faced sheikh and turn him in the right direction. Thus, he advised Trenchard on how to deal with Feisal-el-Dueish's Wahabi who were raiding Iraq in 1928: "my instinct would be to walk without notice into his headquarters. He'd not likely kill an unarmed solitary man ... and in two days guesting I could give him horizons beyond the [Wahabi].... He would make a wonderful border-warden.... I've done it four times, or is it five?"[6]

Lawrence kept his ear to the ground and knew how to use what he learned. The ideal "was perfect intelligence" of both Turk and Arab. "The enemy I knew almost like my own side. I risked myself among them a hundred times, to *learn*." Seeing a prospective attack as the enemy would see it, he could introduce the surprise—"the kingfisher flashing across the pool"—that brought victory. "My business was to see every one with news, and let him talk himself out to me, afterwards arranging and combining ... these points into a complete picture." En route to the Hauran, he added three local peasants to his guard; "there was need ... to learn its [the Haurani] dialect, the construction and jealousies of its clan-framework, and its names and roads. These three fellows ... would teach me their home affairs imperceptibly, as we rode ... chatting."[7]

Lawrence read the mood of a man instinctively and addressed his concerns directly. He "was the first officer we'd ever had who took his troops entirely into his confidence," a British soldier remarked. His wartime memoranda are astonishingly direct. The "Twenty-Seven Articles" on managing Arabs display his forthrightness and guile: "The beginning and ending of ... handling Arabs is unremitting study of them. Keep always on your guard; never say an unnecessary thing: ... hear all that passes, search out what is going on beneath the surface, read their characters, discover their tastes and their weaknesses, and keep everything you find out to yourself."[8]

He was adept at eliciting bits of innocent information that, pieced together, disclosed a secret; at withholding damaging information and using partial truths effectively; at protecting his secrets with indistinguishable truths, half-truths, and lies, correct and misleading clues. "I must have had some tendency, some aptitude, for deceit, or I would not have deceived men so well." Deceit, disguise, and duplicity are essential in intelligence work and he was a born intelligence officer. When the revolt broke out, Arab Bureau members broke the code Hussein used to communicate with his Cairo liaison, monitored the messages, and conducted covert surveillance in Arabia. Learning of Auda and Mohammed el Dheilan's treasonable dealings with the Turks, Lawrence rode to see them. "I played on their fear by my unnecessary amusement, quoting in careless laughter, ... actual phrases of the letters they had exchanged. This created the impression desired.... Finally I suggested that Auda's ... expenses in hospitality must be great; would it help if I advanced something of the great gift Feisal would make him, personally, when he arrived?"[9] Lawrence told Cairo "the situation ... was thoroughly good, and no spirit of treachery abroad.... [T]he deception was mine, and I regularly reduced impolitic truth in my communications." He reported favorable truths and half-truths and withheld facts that might hurt Feisal's cause. "I began in my reports to conceal the true stories of things, and to persuade the few Arabs who knew to an equal reticence." Hubert Young rightly said, "As a statesman, T.E. possessed all the qualifications for success, including ... calculated unscrupulousness in the interest of his main object."[10]

In 1918, Feisal was, with his knowledge, replying to Turkish overtures. In time, he pursued the negotiations secretly without informing Lawrence, who, nonetheless, monitored them (via one of Feisal's staff). When Hussein insulted Jaafar Pasha and, in a telegram, called Feisal "a traitor and outlaw," both resigned just as the final advance was to start. While Allenby sought to temper Hussein's temper, Lawrence "had undesirable passages [in his telegrams] mutilated ... before handing them in code to Feisal." Eventually, Hussein wired "a lame apology and ... a repetition of the offence." Lawrence gave Feisal only the apology. Knowing his father's manner, Feisal knew Lawrence had doctored the message. "I offered to serve for this last march under your orders: why was that not enough?" "Because it would not go with your honour," Lawrence replied (nor with his avoidance of direct command), and Feisal, "You prefer mine always before your own."[11]

Before the war, he had walked over much of the battleground in Syria, Palestine, and Sinai, and his photographic memory kept it vivid. When W. F. Stirling set out to blow up a bridge, Lawrence told him, "'a whole series of stone blocks has been missed out right across the [third span] ... this [is] an excellent place for laying the charges....' Lawrence had seen this bridge once ... before the War." A sheikh swore that he "had only to pass a place once, and it became part of his mind. He knew all the wadis, wells and hills between Azraq and Aqaba."[12] He could correct the tone or color of a print from memory without having seen the original painting for six months. His memory for the friendships, feuds, and scandals of the tribes was prodigious. His mechanical ability and interest in technical detail enabled him to see how a weapon or machine operated and to dismantle, repair, and reassemble it.

Lawrence was a brilliant amateur at guerrilla war, with an amateur's originality and capacity for mistakes. George Lloyd learned that his "navigating skills left much to be desired." On one raid, he led the band too close to a station and then missed the railway. On a nighttime demolition excursion, "My guiding fell through. We wandered for three hours ... not able to find the railway ... nor our starting-point."[13] His maverick methods, slovenliness, and disdain for standard military methods evoked many officers' enmity.

For their utility and the respect they earned, Lawrence used the best camels and weapons, a gold dagger made in Mecca, powerful field glasses, white silk robes, gold-braided headdress. His feet were hardened to hot sand, his body withstood repeated long rides with little food, water or rest. Beneath his soft-spoken manner was an unfathomable will and, if needed, ruthlessness. You would not want him as your enemy. Guile, courage, insight, imagination, resourcefulness, and remorseless determination all made for his success.

Vanity

"I was very conscious of the bundled powers and entities within me." Lawrence was indeed, far too conscious far too constantly. "Yes, there is too much ego in my cosmos: in fact it would be true to say that all my cosmos was ego." Overly interested in what others said about him, he strained for "the oblique overheard remarks" in his "eagerness to overhear and oversee myself."[14] Closely involved with Lowell Thomas, Robert Graves, and Basil Liddell Hart during their writing of his biographies, he told the first two to say nothing about his involvement, leading them to make false disclaimers. "I cannot help scanning ... anything that appears in print about myself,"[15] he admitted. Charlotte Shaw dutifully sent him batches of reviews and clippings. Though scoffing at Thomas's performance, he saw it at least five times, visited him often, and posed in London in Arab robes for his camera man.

Seven Pillars and *The Mint* were supposedly closely-held works, the former because of its shameful confessions, the latter because publication would break Lawrence's pledge to Trenchard, betray his comrades, and hurt the RAF. Yet he circulated both works ceaselessly, displaying his tormented self for admiration, condemnation, pity, or astonishment. It is not clear what he really sought other than viewers for his private exhibition; he rejected praise and criticism alike yet continued to solicit opinions. Asked (indelicate question) what he thought of the Deraa episode, Jock Chambers could only say "Poor old chap."[16]

Distrusting direct comments he sought indirect ones. "I'm absolutely hungry to know what people think of it [*Seven Pillars*]—not what they are telling me, but what they tell to one another," he beseeched Lionel Curtis. He asked Edward Garnett to transmit any "private verbal opinion" he heard of *Seven Pillars* or *Revolt*. "Things they tell the author, or the Press, aren't ... honest. I like to overhear my verdicts."[17] He asked Kathleen Scott to find out what G. B. Shaw really thought of *Seven Pillars* and Garnett, what Trenchard thought of *The Mint*.

Over the years, he posed for many artists, sculptors, and photographers. This was courtesy, not vanity, Jeremy Wilson contends, because he never "actually asked anyone to paint his portrait or to photograph him."[18] That superlative courteousness extended to a photographer who accosted him on the street. Some view his posing as a kind of research, part of his effort to learn what sort of a person he really was. There is no obvious conflict between these explanations: courtesy, self-examination, and vanity can easily intertwine.

Lawrence prized his talents and watched their effects. Aaron Aaronsohn thought him "infatuated with himself."[19] At Tafileh in 1918, "bad temper and conceit" made him show "my power ... to the enemy and to everyone." *Seven Pillars*, he complains, "is not good enough to fit my conceit of myself."[20] Villars notes his "pathological vanity ... a vanity that never slept" and "increased with age." David Garnett agrees that "with the passage of years, his vanity became more fastidious."[21]

Humility

There is much evidence of Lawrence's shyness, mingling with and trying to lose himself in crowds and the ranks, befriending sympathetic comrades and treating them as equals: of an effort, as Robert Graves put it, "to become ordinary" or, as Lawrence said wryly, to join his mother's class. Some thought him modest—"extremely modest," said Bruce Rogers. But modesty is not the right word. "I was not modest," Lawrence insisted, "but ashamed."[22] A modest man can, unlike Lawrence, respect himself. The wish to humble himself, to obey orders and perform menial and humiliating tasks had other sources.

"'Mr.' please on envelopes." "Please not 'Colonel'" he had to say when the transition started: but it never ended.

Years later, the plea continued. "You mustn't call me Sir.... A.C.1 [Aircraftsman] now!"[23] The humble posture he assumed intermittently is illustrated by his servility to Sydney Smith, his commander-friend at Mt. Batten: "I hope you will forgive me, Sir, for worrying you for advice ... _____ has asked my advice about getting married ... and I don't know what to say.... Do you think, Sir, it would be all right for me to tell him to get the necessary formal permission from the C.O. and carry on quietly...?"[24]

A key feature of Lawrence's humbling himself in the ranks was its public character. The job of nightwatchman or lighthouse keeper, which he contemplated, lacked that feature, unlike that of doorporter or chauffeur, which he also considered. On base and in barracks, he was on display, fled from display to his cottage, motorcycle, London streets; and also relished it to gratify and affirm his humiliation. Lewis Namier offers a convoluted analysis of Lawrence's convoluted behavior. "He had to rise above others and then humble himself, and in his self-inflicted humiliation demonstrate his superiority." In Isherwood's analysis, his "humility ... could hardly be distinguished from the extremes of arrogance."[25]

Assurance and Doubt

During his years in Syria, Arabia, Paris, and the Colonial Office, Lawrence had a purpose and confidently pursued it. He saw what should be done, conveyed his view with assurance, and acted upon it forcefully. His grasp of practical alternatives, articulateness, and decisiveness made him a formidable advocate. To Wavell, he gave "the impression of steady enduring strength," a "general air of decision." A college friend sensed "a sureness and completeness about his whole being."[26] Assurance, even arrogance, might emerge at any time, as a bird puffs its feathers. But it was purer before the war, until perhaps mid–1917 when it fought visibly with self-doubt. With his enlistment, self-doubt grew, though he was good at disguising it.

Lawrence told Kennington his 1926 bust was, "a most convincing portrait of a person very sure of himself who had entirely convinced the artist that he really was sure of himself." Hardly: in the last of five half-hour sittings Kennington saw his eyes in "turmoil, a vibration of the head.... He shivered ... hands on knees, trembling."[27] In later years, friends saw his fluctuating confidence and doubt. David Garnett thought him "supremely self-confident at moments, and rather shy and self-conscious at others." He struck Liddell Hart as "Superficially, ... very confident. But underlying this there was this undoubted lack of self-assurance."[28] Rejecting a job Ralph Isham offered in 1927, Lawrence wrote, "Do realize that I have no confidence in myself." Yet when Isham asked "how he happened to do what he did in Arabia," he answered with a madman's assurance, "I felt it as something already *done* and therefore unavoidable." Frederic Manning received quite a different version of his feelings, or retrospective feelings, in Arabia. "Things happen, and we do our best to keep in the saddle."[29]

Arnold Lawrence recognized his brother's "inner lack of confidence," "a diffident, perhaps weak core, so controlled by his colossal will-power that its underlying presence was rarely suspected." Jeremy Wilson thinks "a deep sense of insecurity" drove Lawrence into the ranks "where his intellectual superiority would be effortless and unrivalled."[30] I doubt it. Lawrence was insecure about his sexuality and literary artistry, not his intellect. In the ranks, his intelligence remained engaged in *The Mint*, the *Odyssey*, improving boats, corresponding and conversing with high-brow friends; he readily challenged ideas, but not artists.

Megalomania

That is the only word for Lawrence's overweening sense of personal power. "Always I grew to dominate those things into which I had drifted.... Indeed, I saw myself a danger to ordinary men, with such capacity yawing rudderless at their disposal."[31] *Always?* Not as a loner at school and college. Not during two years in Cairo or the months in Arabia before the capture of Akaba. Nor was he at *anyone's* "disposal." He chose Feisal, Feisal did not choose him. Allenby accepted him; Churchill had some difficulty inducing him to serve. Thereafter, it was almost impossible for anyone to get him to do anything.

Meeting General Chauvel, commander of the Australian troops, in Damascus, Lawrence felt "a little bitter ... to waste my powers playing down to [him] ... I grudged lavishing my brain on men who had not earned my respect." In Damascus, "The lone hand had won against the world's odds," yet Damascus was a small prize. It "was to lead to ... Anatolia, and afterwards to Bagdad; and then there was Yemen."[32] In rallying the Arabs to fight despite his knowledge of duplicitous secret treaties, "I presumed ... that I would ... be able to defeat ... my own country and its allies in the council-chamber. It was an immodest presumption."[33] Not immodest: unrealistic, grandiose.

One explanation he gave for enlisting was "to wipe out my inconvenient power of doing things at other people's bidding." "The terror of being run away with, in the liberty of power, lies at the back of these many renunciations of my later life," he explained to Charlotte Shaw. "I am afraid, of myself. Is this madness?"[34] It certainly is.

In India, the theme of transforming Asia recurred. "Do you know," he informed Edward Marsh, "if I'd known as much about the British Government in 1917, as I do now, I could have ... radically changed the face of Asia?"[35] Did he think Britain would go to war with France over Syria while fighting Germany? That the United States, France, Germany, Russia would stand idly by while Britain "changed the face of Asia?" Or that the Near East outweighed Russia, India, China, and Japan on the scales of Asia?

In 1934, Lawrence told Liddell Hart that using the RAF to control the Near East was his idea. "As soon as I was able to have my own way in the Middle East I approached Trenchard on the point, converted Winston easily, persuaded the Cabinet swiftly into approving." After his death, Liddell Hart discussed the claim with Trenchard, who agreed that "T.E. was unbalanced at this period; he said that T.E. had certainly got much saner, but had I noticed that ... his conceit of his powers had grown.... He said, not long ago, to T. that the Air Force owed him a lot; T. agreed, but T.E. then went on to say quite calmly, 'I made the Air Force'."[36]

Lawrence's aspirations for *Seven Pillars* exhibit more than a little megalomania. He aimed to write not a good or important book but a "Titanic" work to stand beside the greatest ever written— *The Brothers Karamazov, Thus Spake Zarathustra, Moby Dick, Leaves of Grass, War and Peace, Rabelais, Don Quixote*. Peculiar models: not memoirs of travel, history, or war, but works of literary imagination.

What is left by and about Lawrence on paper supports the vein of megalomania. But Lawrence in person was not Lawrence on paper: he could persuade,

impress, move. Impressed by his power—
"I was under his spell"—Winston Churchill
credited his fantasies: "if the Great War
had continued … he might have arrived
at Constantinople in 1919 with most of the
races and tribes of Asia Minor and Arabia
at his back.… Napoleon's young dream of
conquering the East … might well have
been realized by one in whom one can
hardly see lacking any of the qualities of
which world conquerors are made."[37]

Fawning

In someone so strong-minded, vain,
and resourceful, so insistent on the equality of man, Lawrence's tendency to fawn—
to praise and flatter beyond measure—is
odd. It betrays an emotional sickness, a
conviction of his inner baseness and
worthlessness that was most manifest in
his posture toward some men he served
and many writers and artists.

He fawned upon Allenby and Trenchard, not Feisal or Churchill. Feisal he
patronized. He was "a good looking but
not seaworthy ship," "a brave, weak, ignorant spirit.… I served him out of pity."[38]
Churchill he considered a worthy leader,
not an idol. "Winston [is] … a great man
… as brave as six, as good-humoured,
shrewd, self-confident, & considerate as a
statesman can be."[39] Allenby "came nearest to my longing for a master, but I had
to avoid him … lest he show feet of clay."
His greatness lay in his character, which
"made superfluous … intelligence, imagination, acuteness, industry.… He dispensed with them by his inner power."
Great praise with great barbs that ignore
Allenby's less admirable traits. "With sub-
ordinates he was brusque, even rude; he
was a stickler for protocol.… The absence
of creases in a uniform, or a split infinitive
in a military report, were grounds for ag-
gressive reprimand."[40]

His groveling to Trenchard betrays
his sick, masochistic side. Expulsion from
the RAF did not alter his view of Trenchard as "one of the really great people."
"[W]hat can you do when your execu-
tioner is a magnificent, gigantic, gorgeous
man…?" he laments to Edward Garnett.[41]
Gigantic was correct—Trenchard was 6'
5"—but Garnett did not share Lawrence's
admiration. After meeting Trenchard, he
wrote, "I liked him on the whole but I
shouldn't care to be under him. He might
sit for a picture of Mars. But then your
feminine side has a passion for being
under these heavy military men."[42]

Size and simplicity, which he lacked,
enhanced Lawrence's esteem for Allenby
and Trenchard. Trenchard "is as simply
built as Stonehenge, and serves equally as
well as a temple … he misunderstands me,
often. Not that any such tiny detail could
… blot his greatness, in my eyes."[43] Lawrence flattered Trenchard embarrassingly:
"you have done the biggest and best thing
of our generation" "the R.A.F. is the finest
individual effort in British history … it's
thanks to your being head and shoulders
greater in character than ordinary men."[44]
Trenchard disliked his adulation in *The
Mint,* which strengthened the widespread
belief that Lawrence served as his spy.

Lawrence's fulsome praise of writers
and artists was unwelcome to those who,
admiring him and *Seven Pillars,* wanted to
praise *him* or to establish a friendly relation. However, it gratified Lawrence's need
for self-depreciation and kept friends at a
prescribed distance. Artist Gilbert
Spencer, who lived at Clouds Hill for some
months in 1924–25, said Lawrence "gave
me the impression of thinking that I had
opened the final gate and gone through.…
Almost the only conversation I really ever
had with him … all seemed to steer toward
this sort of adulation. Frankly, I thought
this was rather sad." In the 1920s, Nicolette Devas (born 1911) lived in a large

Dorset ménage managed by her father and Augustus John, whom Lawrence visited periodically. Lawrence, she remembered, "had a rather cringing, obsequious admiration for Augustus and called him, 'Master' much to our astonishment."[45]

Lawrence called Emery Walker, Bruce Rogers, Edward Elgar "public monuments." He told Elgar that his 2nd Symphony "moves me more than anything else—of music—that I have heard ... the mere setting eyes upon you is a privilege." He told W. B. Yeats, "I set eyes on you once, in Oxford, ... and wanted then to call the street to attention (for lack of the power to make the sun blaze out appropriately, instead!)." While worshiping others, he denigrated himself. "You have had a lifetime of achievement, and I was a flash in the pan," he tells Elgar; and Yeats, "I'm afraid the truth ... would destroy the flattering picture of myself that I have put about."[46] Bernard Shaw is "great and I'm worthless." He tells E. M. Forster he is "a very great writer, & ... it's irredeemably weak of me to envy you.... [*Seven Pillars*] stinks of me: whereas [*A Passage to India*] is universal." Forster's *Aspects of the Novel,* which a light breeze lifts, is "superb."[47]

Lawrence thanks Frederic Manning for writing *Her Privates We,* "the best book I have read for a very long time." Something "makes you as satisfying a writer, to me, as anyone who has ever written." A sickly recluse, Manning wanted Lawrence as a friend but got an apprentice. He "preferred ... to see Manning as his master."[48] Again, "master." A servant, slave, or dog has a master. Lawrence demanded a servile role: "voluntary slavery was the deep pride of a morbid spirit." He offered extravagant praise to many, measured praise to more, yet rejected any praise he received: "he could accept only unfavourable judgments upon his work."[49]

Abasement and Filth

From fawning to abasement is a small step, part of the masochistic syndrome discussed in the next chapter. Lawrence yearned to subject himself to someone strong enough to deserve his subjection. "I was always hoping for a master whom I could have fought till I dropped at his feet to worship.... I used myself as I would have let no man use another, but needed over me one yet harder and more ruthless.... To him I could have given such service as few masters have had." He never found such a master; "they were all nice to me ... and gave me licence, which I abused to raise their anger—but always reached insipid indulgence."[50]

Enslavement in the ranks was a public abasement. Of his private abasement less is known, but a wish to dirty himself and enter lower human depths is evident. "The lower creation I avoided," he writes, and quickly contradicts himself: "I liked the things underneath me and took my pleasures and adventures downward. There seemed a certainty in degradation, a final safety. Man could rise to any height, but there was an animal level beneath which he could not fall." The passage affirms Irving Howe's observation that, as autobiography, *Seven Pillars* "is veiled, ambiguous, misleading: less a revelation than a performance from which the truth can be wrenched."[51] What pleasures, what degradation did Lawrence seek—and find? The company of paupers, thieves, drunkards, villains, perverts might yield insight and painful comradely feeling, but degradation involves more than talk. Lawrence never explained what he meant.

His affection for blackguards is exhibited in his account of his bodyguard, "lawless men" without family, "helots" whose "extreme degradation was a positive base on which to build a trust." Their jokes were "lewd or lurid." Abdulla's humor was "sardonic, salacious, lying," his "foul mouth … a maw of depravity which had eaten filth in the stews of every capital in Arabia." The "perfect retainer," Lawrence "engaged him instantly" as head man who ruled the bodyguard with "unalloyed savagery." "[A]dolescents full of carnal passion…. These lads took pleasure in subordination; in degrading the body … [in] abasement." The characterization is transparently confessional: no one can speak for other men as surely as for himself.[52]

"The war was good by drawing over our depths that hot surface wish to do or win something," he wrote a friend. "So the cargo of the ship was unseen."[53] Presumably, "the depths" and "the cargo" were animal thoughts and acts unfit for clearer depiction.

Just as *clean,* one of Lawrence's favorite words, betokens *virtuous,* so *dirty* and *filthy,* which he also uses frequently, imply moral as well as physical squalor. He called British and Arab "lads" (*not* himself) *clean.* He says, "partly I came in here [the RAF] to eat dirt, till its taste is normal to me."[54] That *dirt* signifies more than a humble life, something closer to moral and sexual degradation, letters to Charlotte Shaw indicate. "I want to dirty myself outwardly, so that my person may properly reflect the dirtiness … it conceals…. Normally … the Puritan, is in firm charge, and the other poor little vicious fellow, can't get a word in." And when all is not normal? He is never explicit; he edges back from and toward the sexual implication. "Please do not believe that I like this dirt. It hurts me … for … the only difference between me and the worst of them [his comrades] is that I keep a closer guard on my lips. We are all alike as animals: and while the exercises and excitement of a puppy are beautiful, the same conduct in an old dog is horrible."[55] Plainly, he is the "old dog."

The references to castle toilets and latrines in Lawrence's letters from France must have dismayed his family. His bungalow held the brass rubbing of a corpse worms were eating. He is morbidly drawn to filth, decay, death. He straightens huddled heaps of "wonderfully beautiful" Turkish corpses. The Damascus hospital stone floor is strewn with dead bodies, "some stark naked … crept with rats, who had gnawed wet red galleries into them…. Of some the flesh, going putrid, was yellow and blue and black. Many were already swollen twice or thrice life-width, their fat heads laughing with black mouth across jaws harsh with stubble…. A few had burst open, and were liquescent with decay." On RAF "shit-cart" duty, Lawrence spoons binfuls of rotting filth with his hands. "My overall-legs are getting stuffed from the bottom with ordures…. Something bubbly and soft is working up into my crotch. Too smooth for a rat, anyway."[56]

The Mint's photographic, phonographic transcription of the basest barrack life, "everything hard, cold, metallic, and cruel," shows Lawrence's obsession with scatology, carnality, brutality, corruption, putrefaction. "When you turn over an aged stone, all manner of feeble, pale-coloured things scrabble away in search of cover. I am like that, with *The Mint.*"[57] This was the RAF he loved. The army was worse. The army confirms "my … conviction of the irremediable filthiness of myself and most people."[58] Yet he entered the army voluntarily; at some level, he must have relished its animality as he had relished his bodyguard's savagery. His sickening record of seasick women's defecations in a stuffed toilet "fairly takes the breath away by its sheer brutality." At the Karachi air base, he lies upon the earth "like a crust of dung."[59] At Mount Batten, an officer saw him "scraping up the grease and filth from the bottom of a boat …

[whose] engine had been removed. 'Do you have to do that, Shaw?' I asked him.... 'Somebody has to do it, sir.'"[60]

Rebecca West, who met Lawrence several times in the summer of 1923, perceived his split personality, narcissism, and attraction to filth in a remarkable portrait:

> Lawrence ... was a schizophrenic and might well be represented by two men. You feel that ... [he] might be a great man, but his disciple is a shoddy fair-barker who adores him and lies about him and is his 'manager,' and it does not seem possible that ... [he] would have such an uninviting companion if he were not unappetising himself, and the suspicion grows. That was always the feeling that Lawrence gave me—two men in one skin, and why had the one given the hospitality of his body to the other little horror.[61]

In the ranks and at Clouds Hill, Lawrence befriended good-hearted men with little education. Their names are known; some bore his casket; their recollections have enlarged our knowledge of him. But he had companions whose names, other than John Bruce, are unknown. Something rootless, rebellious, base, dangerous, but closely held and controlled, drew him to them. When Robert Graves called them men "with a criminal tendency," Lawrence changed the words to "mildly a ruffian" and acknowledged a "special tenderness for ruffians." In polite discourse, "ruffian" is about as far as one can go in the range from unblemished virtue to unspeakable degeneracy. "By some odd kink I easily forgive ruffians," Lawrence told Charlotte Shaw, *kink* implying an ingrained moral defect; with visible longing, he noted that, "In fine weather tramps have an ideal life."[62]

E. M. Forster, with a policeman lover and some familiarity with working-class men, used other words for Lawrence's odd companions. "At the bottom of our social ladder," they were "the unprintable scamps who enjoy degradation." "There was a chance encounter in Queen's Hall, where he was with some men whose faces I instinctively distrusted. (All his friends will agree that he had some queer friends.)" Forster did not refer to his good service friends, some of whom he knew and liked. Drawing upon Forster's reports, Jean Villars says, "People came across ... [Lawrence] with strange companions ... and one whole side of his life seems to have remained secret."[63] Until John Bruce's secret was disclosed.

Pat Knowles called Bruce "a nasty fellow with a lot of queer habits. He was dirty."[64] Arnold Lawrence called him "a swine," perhaps because he tried to extract money from him, because he menaced T.E.'s reputation, or because Arnold could not understand or control him. Arnold was not T.E. Where Arnold was abrupt and arbitrary, T.E. was easy, persuasive, if necessary sudden and effective. Arnold resorted to lawyers; T.E. handled Bruce himself, held his trust and admiration, was godfather to his son. If Bruce was a "swine," there might be something swinish in T.E.; but he would have called Bruce a ruffian.

Self-Hatred

Upon reading the Oxford Text, Vyvyan Richards advised Lawrence to "Cut out all suggestions of self-depreciation." He replied, "But I really do cut myself down, in all sincerity. I've been & am absurdly over-estimated."[65] In their conflicting biographies, Liddell Hart and Aldington both see self-depreciation as the obverse side of Lawrence's vanity. Lawrence excoriated the part he played in the revolt, the quality of *Seven Pillars*, his translations and reviews. "He seemed to be pleased by nothing which he did, unless it was an act of kindness … [or] some simple ingenuity," an RAF friend writes. Lawrence himself says, "It does not seem … as though anything I've ever done was quite well enough done."[66] He was pleased with "influencing my fellow airmen towards a pride in themselves" and with helping to develop high-speed boats. But he could not endure praise, admiration, or honor. "Whenever I hear praise I say 'Ah, they can't know me very well.'" He had "a profound dissatisfaction with what I am."[67]

Especially after the war, Lawrence hated, despised, loathed himself. At college, he urged Vyvyan Richards to read, "a dozen, fifteen times," Christina Rossetti's Martyr poem with the lines:

> Now I am tired, too tired to strive
>   or smile;
> I sit alone, my mouth is in the dust:
> Look Thou upon me, Lord, for
>   I am vile.[68]

As a young man, his self-criticalness was borne jauntily, but at 45, when he said "this vile body," he meant it. In 1924, he declares, "I hate & despise myself more & more for the part I played in" the revolt.[69] But the revolt was more an excuse than a cause of his hate. Irving Howe notes "the merciless guerilla [sic] raids Lawrence conducted against himself" in Seven Pillars. Noel Coward discerns in his writing "a bitterness directed against himself, a contempt for his smallness."[70] Not just smallness: his illegitimacy, inability to love, inability to be unselfconscious, his animal pleasure at being raped. Recollecting Deraa, he cries, "Unclean, Unclean…!" There's not a clean human being into whose shape I would not willingly creep." Meeting him in 1924, Apsley Cherry-Garrard thought he "considered himself not only unworthy but sometimes unclean."[71] That feeling persisted till the end of his life,

as letters written in the guise of "the Old Man" show.

Will

A central feature of Lawrence's character was his will: the determination and perseverence with which he pursued his objectives. It was manifest in his walk through Syria, his encounters with Turkish officials in Syria and Sinai, his mastery of workmen at the dig. In the ranks, it only occasionally burst forth. During the revolt, it overrode obstacles that would stop most men and reached his goal of Damascus.

Churchill recognized Lawrence's "imperious will." Aldous Huxley calls his will "of heroic, even of Titanic, proportions. "To Elie Kedourie, Lawrence is "a symbol of … the constant irruption into history of the uncontrollable force of a demonic will exerting itself to the limit of endurance."[72] His will went with self-confidence, decisiveness, and instant action in emergencies. Lawrence says less about it than we might expect. "I had found…. Will a sure guide to some one of the many roads leading from purpose to achievement" expresses the confidence that, one way or another, he could achieve his objective. "Collapse rose always from a moral weakness eating into the body, which of itself … had no power over the will" expresses his brutal disdain for his body.[73]

He says little about what fired his will. "Into the sources of my energy of will I dared not probe." The sources may be the drive to overcome his small, illegitimate body and his strong-willed mother's domination. War, patriotism, his brothers' deaths, the common rewards of uncommon men ("to be a general and knighted when thirty") spurred his exploits. He adds, without explaining, elusive personal motives: a "longing to feel myself the node of a national movement"; "historical ambition"; "The strongest motive throughout had been a personal one ... present to me ... every hour of these two years.... It was dead, before we reached Damascus."[74] The last motive is widely taken to refer to his love for Dahoum. Is it credible that he led a revolt for the sake of a young man?

"The very accident that normally I am empty of motive, helped make the rare motive, when it finally came, overpowering. Now [1927] ... I am ... an empty room."[75] In Arabia and the Colonial Office, he wanted and got big political things. In Paris, he lost and fell into depression. He wanted to be a great writer and became a very good, very tortured one. He wanted to develop motor boats and did. He obtained most small things he wanted: a plain uniform, poverty, a cottage, small RAF reforms. The biggest thing he wanted, to be at peace with himself, willpower could not achieve. The moment he enlisted was the moment he sought to abdicate his will. It burned low, at times it flamed; it was never extirpated.

Powerful masochistic thoughts and acts preceded enlistment: reliving the agonies of the war and of Deraa, starvation, sleeplessness, overwork. A paper by Freud, "Those Wrecked By Success," points to another possible cause of enlistment. "Always in working I had tried to serve, for the scrutiny of leading was too prominent," Lawrence wrote.[76] Lowell Thomas had made him too prominent. He could not stand the constant limelight which forced him to act a costumed part he knew to be false. A psychiatrist describes a parallel case:

> The masochist Waldemar led a dangerous life, full of difficulties and privations, which he bore perfectly well ... until the day ... he found himself face to face with a business opportunity which ... would bring a fortune his way involving a complete change in his material circumstances

... he was seized with anxiety, which grew until it became intolerable, reaching a point at which he felt an imperious need to do something immediately to rid himself of the opportunity.... That done, he breathed freely again.[77]

Once settled in the RAF as a private, Lawrence breathed more freely.

Near Madness

In a memorable passage of *Seven Pillars*, Lawrence writes that "madness was very near" when his "body plodded on mechanically, while his reasonable mind ... looked down critically on him." The passage acknowledges his near madness (albeit in an acceptable context, battling exhaustion). Col. Edouard Brémond, head of the French military mission in Arabia, called Lawrence a case for a psychiatrist.[78] Lawrence often feared for his sanity. "I was a very sick man, again [in early 1918], ... almost at breaking point." Note *again*. Before the war ended, he "came a frightful crash." He "cackled" hysterically amidst the putrescent bodies in the Damascus hospital.[79] After Paris, he was in a deep depression; some who saw him sitting silently in the All Souls common room thought him "off his rocker." During the 1921 Hejaz negotiations, he was under great strain; the ensuing ordeal of finishing *Seven Pillars* left him near "complete breakdown."[80] Lawrence was scarcely better after entering the RAF. Ejected, he sank to another low, wandered the streets penniless, slept on the Embankment, on Paddington station benches, in Salvation Army hostels. In the Tank Corps, his distress persisted; "sometimes I wonder how far mad I am, and if a mad-house would not be my next (and merciful) stage."[81] "He thinks ... his family will die out because they are all mad," G. B. Shaw said. Lawrence speaks of madness as "the other fate I'm always fearing" (other than death in a motorcycle crash); "I am hardly sane at times."[82]

"I have been damaged ever since" being evicted from the RAF, he says in mid–1928. Why should the insult of eviction persist three years after reinstatement? Did each affront to his sense of mastery scar him permanently? "It would be so easy and so restful just to let sanity go and drop into the dark."[83] At Bridlington, his last station, where he was supposedly content, "something, or maybe someone, was haunting [him]." Near the end of his life, he says, "I am always aware that madness lies very near me, always."[84]

Nihilism

After rejecting his parents' religiosity, Lawrence was a nihilist acutely conscious of death's omnipresence and the futility of human effort. "The practice of our revolt fortified the nihilist attitude in me."[85] Following that consuming experience, he was involved in international politics and in writing *Seven Pillars*. Thereafter, nothing absorbed him so fully. Testing and improving high-speed boats seems comparable, emotionally, to endlessly rewriting *Seven Pillars* or revising and clean-copying *The Odyssey* translation. Regarded as a quest for perfection, these were also ways to consume time that, absent more compelling activities, yawned emptily.

Visiting Clouds Hill early in 1924, Eric Kennington was appalled by Lawrence's condition. "He was … visibly thinner, pale, scared and savage … nihilism … was his recurrent curse." Usually hidden, it once burst forth. "Everything was attacked. Life itself. Marriage, parenthood, work, morality, and especially Hope." "I fall … into the nihilism which cannot find … even a false god in which to believe," Lawrence avowed.[86] If dates and occasions must be given for the fall, they may be the summer 1917 depression preceding his perilous ride into Syria, the November 1917 events at Deraa, and the desperate depression preceding his enlistment. We have no accounts that might document boyhood bouts of nihilism or depression. If the ranks, imposing companionship and a daily routine, were his way to doctor loneliness and depression, his boyhood enlistment might have had a similar function.

John Mack detects "an increasing nihilism" during Lawrence's time in India. Work of compelling importance might have shaken that mood, but

Lawrence's tombstone, Moreton, Dorset: his mother inscribed her faith on the stone (courtesy of Malcolm Brown).

Lawrence shunned it. "A decent nihilism is what I hope for, generally, ... an established land, like ours, can do with 1 percent ... nihilists."[87] That was his mood toward the end of his life. His nihilism was accompanied by a sense of life's futility, even a hostility to life and, above all, to procreation. This hostility was turned and twisted into self-disparagement, self-hatred, and an abhorrence of intercourse and birth. The next chapter discusses Lawrence's masochism, sexuality, and inability to love. Lawrence writes of his "contempt, not for other men, but for all they do" and "a contemptuous sense that they reached their highest purpose, ... when ... their elements served to manure a field."[88] The line between "men" and "all they do," between others and himself, wavers and vanishes. Nihilism becomes contempt for life, pessimism, ennui, the futility of action in the face of death and oblivion.

Lewis Namier saw in Lawrence "a deep neurotic negation of life.... It was this deep negation of life which drew him to the desert, and ... the sterility of garrison life." David Garnett judged him "sometimes ... an enemy of life."[89] To Lawrence, heterosexuality and childbirth were repulsive. Interrupting Auda embracing his young wife, "I asked if he had found life good enough to thank his haphazard parents for bringing him into it?" "[M]ankind will be at its zenith the day it determines to propagate its species no more."[90]

"He has ... no use for the human race ... or interest in its continuance ... he despises the works of men, as Swift did," Robert Graves wrote. Lawrence demurred at "despises" but did not disagree. "I think the planet is in a damnable condition, which no change of party, or social reform, will do more than palliate insignificantly. What is wanted is ... birth control ... to end the human race in 50 years." When a friend protested his refusal to have children, he replied firmly, "don't you think it's time to close down?"[91] That pessimism—the word is too cheerful for so bleak an outlook—was personal. It did not prevent, it may have spurred him to help others, to try to cheer them up and feel better about living.

The barrenness of Bedouin life and of the desert matched Lawrence's outlook. "Semitic creeds" preached "world-worthlessness ... bareness, renunciation, poverty.... The Bedouin ... haunted starvation and death." In an almost incomprehensible episode, Lawrence urges a camp of tribesmen to battle not for victory but failure and death. "To be of the desert was ... to wage unending battle with ... hope.... Death would seem best of all our works.... To the clear-sighted, failure was the only goal."[92] Years later, the desert retained its hold on his memory. "I wake up now, often, in Arabia: the place has stayed with me much more than the men and the deeds." "Whenever a landscape or colour in England gets into me deeply, ... often ... it is because something of it recalls Arabia." He rode his motorcycle over the sand dunes at Poole—"They remind me of the desert."[93]

Hatred of Thought

A rapid, omnivorous, retentive reader, Lawrence's wide-ranging knowledge and vocabulary, and unusual modes of thinking and feeling are evident in *Seven Pillars.* Ronald Storrs called him "supercerebral"; Robert Graves, comrades, and correspondents used him as a handy reference tool. Yet, despite his education, several languages, All Souls fellowship, and friendship with scholars, writers, and intellectuals, Lawrence lacked a scholar's temperament and passion for ideas. He challenged accepted ideas to show their failings and for the fun of it. His forte was to grasp a concrete situation and, perceiving how its technical elements articulated, know how they could be rearranged or disarticulated. This grasp of both detail and structure made the field of action his natural domain.

Never content to live only with books and ideas, he grew more critical of intellectuals, ideas, even thought itself. He prized art and beauty above scholarship and truth; saw the gaps, weakness, and ignorance underlying scholarly claims to knowledge; and rejected the leadership claims of intellectuals.

Overwhelmed by Chartres as a young man, he defended the medieval mind "in spite of ... [its] narrowness and ... ignorance of the truth ...: the truth doesn't matter a straw, if men only ... believe something." Doesn't matter to how well we live and behave. Knowledge afforded no guide to living. "We know too much, and use too little knowledge."[94] "To acquire more and more knowledge becomes a craving, like drink: with the same hopeless end, for one can no more learn everything than drink Rheims dry." "I can't feel that knowledge matters at all ... one can spend the few active years one has so much more enjoyably out of doors on practicalities."[95]

A sometime student of history, Lawrence attacked historians' claims to knowledge. "[H]aving helped to produce history bred in me a contempt for our science, seeing that its materials were as faulty as our private characters, which supplied them." "The historian ... learns to attach insensate importance to documents. The documents are liars."[96] Explanations of the Arab Revolt were after-the-fact rationalizations. Liddell Hart's biography "makes it all fit in: ... it didn't happen like that: but who will believe it now?"[97]

His attack on the value and ascertainability of knowledge developed into an attack on thought itself—or on his own thinking. Thinking too much of himself, he condemned thinking, as if his mind, rather than his whole nature, governed his thought. Lawrence's "chief curse," Robert Graves says, "is that he cannot stop thinking." Colin Wilson, also, sees "his inability to *stop thinking*. Thought ... is an unending misery." What holds the *Seven Pillars* reader, V. S. Pritchett observes, is "the extraordinary spectacle of a brain working the whole time."[98]

Lawrence tried futilely to stifle his corrosive self-contemplation. "I envy everyone who doesn't think continually." "I haunt ... [his comrades'] company, because the noise stops me thinking. Thinking drives me mad."[99] The pain of whipping and injuries, the fatigue of long work and exercise, the maniacal motorcycle rides brought relief from thought. "[W]hy I joined [the ranks]? Mind-suicide." War only "delayed me from mind-suicide, some slow task to choke at length this furnace in my brain." The hours of peace as a clerk, floor cleaner, mechanic, and motorboat operator were times he did not think of himself. "No one who thinks can be really happy."[100] Work, not thought, is his prescription for living: "a simple healthy person has little need of brains. The curse of our age is this thought-maggoty caries of the head from which the high-brows suffer." He could not speak for high-brows; he was cursing himself. To Ezra Pound's wild exhortations, he rejoined, "many of us go wrong by being too exclusively cerebral.... Old Gandhi would prescribe for you a daily wrestle with the spinning wheel, to grow contentment.... Abstract ideas are another name for maggots of the brain."[101] His spinning wheels were the texts, motorcycles, and motorboats he tinkered with endlessly. "It's no good thinking any more. One must do things with one's hands.... Thought is only good when it precedes action. Thought without action is frustration."[102]

As a boy, Lawrence attended church faithfully and taught Sunday school. From Chartres and Palestine, at 20 and 21, he wrote letters home that, while not declarations of faith, evoked warm Biblical themes. However, any Christian faith he retained was burned out by the war and his comradeship with Moslem men. He opposed missionizing and often rebuked his mother and brother for their work in China. He characterized Aquinas as "the founder of European dogmatic Christianity" and Christ as "its rather pitiful eponym." "What was his God?" Eric Kennington asked, and answered, "process without aim or end, creation followed by dissolution, rebirth, and then decay.... But not a hint of a god, and certainly none of the Christian God."[103] Once, Lawrence said he believed in God.[104] What kind of belief in what kind of God, he did not say. Not one offering consolation for grief and mortality. He never wrote his proposed "Confession of Faith," but, to judge from what he wrote, he had more faith in machines than in man or God.

21

Masochism and Sexuality

That Lawrence was a masochist admirers and detractors agree. As a youth, he punished his body. Breaking his ankle wrestling in the school playground, he said nothing and returned to class though the break kept him at home for a term. The diary of his 1911 walk in Syria shows him "less interested in unknown cities than in his ... capacity to stand pain." Near death, he tells his family he is very well. Breaking two ribs, he says, "They were not important ribs, only the little measly ones low down."[1]

Seven Pillars displays Lawrence's masochism with painful frequency. Battles with the elements are bouts of pleasure. A painful scorpion bite kept him awake "to the relief of my overburdened mind." Spreading his toes to hold a muddy path "was exquisitely painful." "My body's reluctance to ride hard was another (and perverse) reason for forcing the march." Arabs covered their heads in a sand storm, fearing "the sand particles which ... open the chaps into a painful wound: but ... I always rather liked a khamsin ... it was pleasant to outface it." Feverish, sleepless, exhausted on the march, "approaching ... insensibility ... [seems] delectable."[2]

Much that Lawrence wrote about the Arabs is scarcely concealed introspection:

The Bedouin "hurt himself ... to please himself. There followed a delight in pain." To his bodyguard, "Pain was ... a solvent, a cathartic, almost a decoration." Reviewing *Seven Pillars*, V. S. Pritchett deemed it "a kind of flagellation" and noted, "Lawrence could not bear to be touched unless, one supposes, he was hurt."[3] Lawrence Durrell thought the book "epic," but Lawrence "disgusting ... [for] ripping and goring his body because he loathed it so." David Garnett called *Seven Pillars* and *The Mint* "the record of self-mutilation."[4] The words are well chosen. To Lawrence, "The most beautiful parts of all the best Greek statues are their mutilations." Garnett's edition of his letters showed Herbert Read that Lawrence's nature was "masochistic; a psychological state of which we find, not only the overt symptoms, but also the secondary characteristics. Everything in his life fits the interpretation."[5]

"I had strung myself to learn all pain until I died.... Pain of the slightest had been my obsession and secret terror from a boy," Lawrence writes. Terror? Do you embrace what you fear? "What is it," he asks Edward Garnett, "that makes me ... so ready to cry out, and yet so ready to incur more pain?"[6] He was silent when Bruce whipped him; pain gave him physical and

218

emotional satisfaction. He tells Charlotte Shaw, "I'm always afraid of being hurt" and Lionel Curtis, "my masochism remains and will remain, only moral."[7] They believed him. Mrs. Shaw thought, "He always dreaded pain" and Curtis, "I have never met anyone more entirely devoid of vice."[8] But an "obsession" that has become an addiction is not "dreaded." Lawrence did not tell Mrs. Shaw of his zest for pain and he lied to Lionel Curtis, deliberately misleading two close friends.

Lawrence filled his life with physical and moral suffering. "The desire to suffer ... [was] the most abnormal feature of Lawrence's character."[9] Many of his injuries, ailments, and pains were inescapable; others were avoidable. He need not have bared his face to the sandstorm or his feet to hot sand and rocks, have pushed companions beyond their preferred pace or gone forth in near-impossible conditions. He could have treated his ailments instead of suffering them like a wounded animal. He need not have entered the ranks, competed physically with younger men, endured the brutalities related in *The Mint*, driven behemoth motorcycles at lethal speeds. But this amounts to saying he need not have been who he was. His whole style of life—eating quickly and little, sleeping on the floor or a chair, tearing into the wind and rain—was a form of self-punishment.

When, in 1919, the plane in which he rode crashed in Rome, killing the two pilots, he suffered "a cracked shoulder-blade and ... other minor injuries. To these he paid no attention while busying himself with the victims." Out riding, he was asked to help start a car's motor. As the motorist left the car in gear, the starting handle flew back and broke his right wrist. Without complaint, he asked the driver to put the gear in neutral and turned the handle with his left arm. Asking a bystander to start his motorcycle, he rode off steering with his

left hand, "his right arm dangling." The camp doctor ordered him to hospital for an operation; he refused, had the wrist bound, and returned to work.[10] David Garnett called this behavior "ridiculous and a sign of abnormality."[11] Running with Lawrence to catch a London bus, H. S. Ede "noticed that [he] ... was a little slow ... [he] had broken three ribs; he was doing nothing about it, they would float into place in time."[12]

Whippings

Three sets of beatings illuminate Lawrence's inner life. As a boy, his mother often beat him for unclear reasons. Arnold Lawrence said it was for such misbehavior as refusing to learn the piano. That seems inadequate cause to cane a boy severely and repeatedly on his bare bottom.[13] As Robert was goody-good, T.E. was the first and most punished son. A loving, strong-minded mother, Sarah punished to gain obedience. T.E. was not stupid. The first whipping might have surprised him but thereafter he knew what to expect and how to avoid or secure punishment. His repetition of whatever conduct occasioned the beatings initiated a pattern of severe whippings and a lifelong contest for domination and independence between mother and son. An erotic element may also have arisen with Lawrence, like Rousseau, deriving pleasure from being beaten.[14]

Biographers recognize the importance of the November 1917 episode at Deraa but disagree on exactly what happened. Struggling to say something new about a man whose life has been combed clean, Desmond Stewart and Lawrence James contend it never happened, that it was an imaginative or coded account of a wish to be sodomized or of another sexual encounter in which he acquiesced. I think they are wrong. Lawrence envied creative writers but lacked their rich imagination. A descriptive, not creative writer, he could not invent such a gruelling, gripping story nor do those who say he did explain why he should "encode" an event he never otherwise mentioned or lie about Deraa in confessional letters to Charlotte Shaw and E. M. Forster.

Seven Pillars relates that, in disguise on a spying mission in Deraa, Lawrence was detained by Turkish guards and taken at night to the Bey's bedroom. The Bey grasped him; he resisted. Summoning four men to grip him, the Bey said, "You must understand that I know: and it will be easier if you do as I wish." Lawrence refused; the Bey told the men "to take me out and teach me everything." They lashed him cruelly until he felt "a gradual cracking apart of my whole being by some too-great force." They took turns whipping, then would "ease themselves, and play unspeakably with me ... when I was completely broken they seemed satisfied." Kicked, Lawrence smiled, "for a delicious warmth, probably sexual, was swelling through me." Thereupon, a guard "hacked with the full length of his whip into my groin. This doubled me half-over ... trying impotently to scream.... Another slash followed. A roaring, and my eyes went black: while within me the core of life seemed ... expelled from its body by this last indescribable pang." He is beaten further; two men "split me apart: while a third ... rode me astride." He is then brought to the Bey, who "now rejected me ... as ... too torn and bloody for his bed." Left in a shed, he escapes, with "the burden, whose certainty the passing days confirmed: how in Deraa that night the citadel of my integrity had been irrevocably lost."[15]

This account was rewritten many times, yet important points remain obscure. If "the citadel of my integrity" is Lawrence's chastity that the guards repeatedly violated ("ease themselves" and "rode me"), why must days pass before its loss is "confirmed"? If he was beaten so savagely, how could he ride for four days to Azrak and Akaba immediately after? In a June 1919 memorandum, Lawrence states he was "not as hurt as ... [the Bey] thought."[16] This explains his ability to ride to Akaba, but, then, why did he falsely describe a monstrous beating? Was it to conceal voluntary submission?

Lawrence told Charlotte Shaw, "I wanted to put it plain in the book" but "my self-respect ... wouldn't, hasn't, let me" ("hasn't," because the 1926 version was no plainer than the 1922). "[T]o earn five minutes respite from a pain which drove me mad, I gave away ... [my] bodily integrity ... and it's that which has made me forswear decent living."[17] In short, cruelly beaten, he submitted to rape and, despising himself for doing so, sentenced himself to the ranks. Some have interpreted this letter to mean that Lawrence yielded to the Bey, but the guards are more likely. On one occasion, he reputedly said "they all had a go."[18]

He told E. M. Forster, "The Turks ... did it to me, by force,"[19] which conflicts with the idea of voluntary surrender. The line between forced and willing sex is often an issue in rape cases; Lawrence was quick to condemn himself; brutal force and pain are involved in every rendition of Deraa. It is too much to expect every word Lawrence uses on different occasions to be in precise agreement and to convey precisely what happened. My opinion (it can be no more than that) is that he was beaten severely and raped by the guards (or, raped by one, yielded to the others), but could not acknowledge it to Stirling; he made the painful journey to Akaba to punish himself for yielding and for his sexual pleasure. One report that, after Deraa, a doctor made a sling for his very swollen testicles, confirms an awful beating.[20]

The Oxford Text version ends on a different note:

> I was feeling very ill, as though some part of me had gone dead that night in Deraa, leaving me maimed, imperfect, only half myself. It could not have been the defilement, for no one ever held the body in less honour than I did myself: probably it had been the breaking of the spirit by that frenzied nerve-shattering pain which had degraded me to beast-level when it made me grovel to it, and which had [*has*] journeyed with me since [*ever after*], a fascination and terror and morbid desire, lascivious and vicious, perhaps, but like the striving of a moth towards its flame. [The bracketed words were used initially in the manuscript.][21]

The meaning of that "striving" became clearer with the revelation that, from at least 1923 through 1935, Lawrence subjected himself to vicious whippings and other masochistic ordeals.[22]

John Bruce, then a hefty Scots youth of 19, arrived at Bovington in March 1923 three days before Lawrence. Some months later, after extensive preparation, Lawrence arranged the first in a series of beatings by Bruce at Clouds Hill. The preparation involved recruiting the gullible Bruce as an aide and bodyguard for £3 a week and relating an elaborate story about nasty offenses for which a fictitious relative, "The Old Man" or "Uncle R," demanded that he be punished. The story was a nightmarish invention. R, a member of his father's Irish family who inherited his father's wealth, despised him and his father. "How he must loathe us, for my father's sins."[23] Lawrence had disgraced the family by forsaking God, leaving the Colonial Office, insulting the King, going deeply into debt, borrowing from "the damned Jews." To escape exposure as a bastard—"I have my mother to consider"—he must now obey R, who ordered him whipped.[24]

The first whipping was unsatisfactory. The birch R sent had no effect through Lawrence's trousers, so R insisted they be removed. His letters gave Bruce precise instructions and questions. Needless to say, Lawrence wrote and delivered the letters and read Bruce's replies, thus prescribing his punishment, directing Bruce's attention to his reactions, and reading Bruce's observations: a prize example of narcissistic self-contemplation, his "eagerness to overhear and oversee myself."[25] R asks minute questions about his behavior: After the flogging, did he "stand quite steadily, or did he show any signs of trembling...? Did his face remain pale...? Is he sorry...? Does he feel justly treated?"[26] They resemble questions Lawrence asked Oxford Text readers: "[H]ow does it strike you as history?" "[I]s there any style in my writing at all? Anything recognisably individual?"[27] They are the questions of a self-absorbed man who, distrusting his own judgment, forever seeks and dismisses the judgment of others. Uncle R treats Lawrence as a boy, calls him "Ted" and "the lad," speaks of "these schoolboy measures," and says Ted "should be ashamed to hold his head up amongst his fellows, knowing that he had suffered so humiliating and undignified a punishment."[28]

Bruce recalled seven to nine floggings over the years at Clouds Hill, Barton Street, and (Bruce returned to Scotland in 1925) Edinburgh, Perth, Aberdeen, and Collieston. At least four were given by an unidentified man; a third man also administered beatings. At several sessions, a companion observed the punishment and replied to R's questions. The beatings grew more severe: initially, 12 strokes with a birch; later, 30 to 75 with a metal whip. From June to October 1933, there were five floggings. "They were brutal, delivered on the bare buttocks." According to an observer, "Lawrence submitted to them 'like a schoolboy,' registered obvious fear, … but did not … cry out."[29] In 1934, he was flogged in Edinburgh; letters mentioning a prospective trip to Scotland may point to another flogging planned for mid–1935.

Some writers believe the floggings—a number, on the Deraa anniversary—served to expiate Lawrence's submission at Deraa. Arnold Lawrence said that his brother "rebelled unceasingly" against sex, adopting "methods advocated by the saints" (which could yield sexual pleasure).[30] Psychiatrist John Mack, who has conducted the closest study of the beatings, writes that "Lawrence was trying … to destroy his sexuality," had no other conscious purpose than penance, and did not "seek or even experience pleasure in these episodes." Mack expresses concern "lest this most tortured aspect of his life be given too great an emphasis," yet recognizes that "Perhaps some readers will choose to go further than I will in their own formulations."[31] Though rejecting the idea that Lawrence sought and obtained sexual pleasure by being beaten, he states that Deraa "led to the permanent welding for Lawrence of sexual pleasure and pain," a desire to repeat the experience, and "He required that the beatings be severe enough to produce a seminal emission."[32] A draft said "ejaculation." Colin Simpson, the *Sunday Times* reporter who interviewed John Bruce repeatedly, states that "the first stroke or so generated an erection and the beating stopped once he had ejaculated."[33]

In the foregoing two paragraphs, Lawrence reportedly prescribed a set number of lashes, yet the lashes stopped upon ejaculation. That inconsistency aside, the linkage between whipping and sexual pleasure seems clear and any remaining uncertainty is resolved by Lawrence's clear statements that in Deraa "a delicious warmth, probably sexual," swelled through

him and evoked a "morbid … lascivious … striving" to repeat the experience.

Lawrence and his alter ego "Uncle R" arranged an inventory of other physical and emotional punishments or "training" sessions: riding horses, swimming, boxing, physiotherapy, dietary regimes, gym sessions, "remedial" Swedish massage, and "medical electricity." R would write and request training for, and a report on the performance of, "a recalcitrant nephew for whom severe discipline was necessary." Thus, Uncle R—in this case, his name was "Mr. E. Shaw"—wrote a Southampton riding school, "I want my nephew taught to ride … [in] private lessons … : not a road or public park … he will not be an easy pupil, but I can help you … with my authority."[34]

Swimming sessions "Edward Shaw" arranged for his nephew "Ted" in 1932–34 had practical as well as disciplinary purposes. Lawrence swam long distances and underwater, useful skills while testing motorboats. By letter, Shaw asked that swimming coach Abrahams not talk or say "please" to Ted, but order him about. "Keep him hard at it all the time." Abrahams was asked to record Ted's progress in a diary that he periodically took to his uncle. Ted (then 43), his uncle said, was "28 or 29." Some instructions were designed to conceal Ted's identity, but Abrahams and his staff could not take seriously the idea of an uncle managing the lessons of a middle-aged nephew and quickly identified Lawrence from newspaper photos. They played along with, but only Lawrence was taken in by, the charade. As a swimsuit involved the display of whipping bruises, Abrahams was advised that "Ted" had received painful "correction" by "old-fashioned methods" and that, if possible, his lessons should be given in off hours when few people used the pool.[35]

The best documented episode of punishments occurred near Collieston, north of Aberdeen, in September 1930. The Old Man asked Bruce to hire three horses and a groom and rent a cottage on the coast where Lawrence spent a week's leave swimming in the sea and riding two hours each morning and afternoon. The week ended with a beating so severe that the groom, who witnessed it, became sick. Bruce told some fanciful stories, but his account of this episode is convincing and his astonishment at Lawrence's contrite obedience to Uncle R's dictates lends it credibility. "For Lawrence to agree to all these suggestions of The Old Man was madness—he detested horses.... The water was freezing cold and very rough.... To try to understand Lawrence is near impossible."[36]

Lawrence described his stay at Collieston in a long letter to F. N. Doubleday that so impressed John Buchan he said Lawrence "never wrote better prose." He names his companions as "Jimmy who ... jobs horses in Aberdeen" and "Jock [Bruce], the roughest diamond of our Tank Corps," describes the cold, three-room cottage, the "maddened North Sea," and other details broadly corroborating Bruce's report.[37] Read together, Bruce's frightful and Lawrence's cheerful version bolster the evidence of Lawrence's split personality, one half coolly monitoring how the other half writhes. Colin Simpson termed Bruce a "sinister and pathological liar."[38] Yet Lawrence picked him, managed him artfully, and traveled far to retain his services. That they reached one climax in 1933 and continued thereafter shows that they did not merely recapitulate Deraa, but had become an independent, gratifying ritual.

Trying to understand Lawrence better, I read some of the psychological literature on masochism. Thomas O'Donnell did the same. It is not an overly satisfactory procedure, for one inevitably selects passages that fit Lawrence's case and such

selectivity holds little explanatory weight. It would be easy to select passages that, applied to Lawrence, are obviously wrong.[39] Nonetheless, for what it is or is not worth, I will summarize a few germane observations.

Havelock Ellis thought male flagellation the most common English sexual perversion; the French call it *le vice Anglais;* in Australia, *english* is prostitute slang for a whipping. The typical male flagellant is spanked or whipped moderately by a woman. If Lawrence's syndrome originated in childhood beatings, that, too, is common. Among middle- and upper-class Englishmen, the beater is often a lower-class nanny, beating being a common working-class discipline that, as a child, Sarah Lawrence would have learned and may have endured (did she beat the Chapman daughters?). Theodor Reik might interpret the meaning of severe whipping by a man as "being used as a woman by a man." In the large literature on Victorian flagellation, Steven Marcus says, "the figure being beaten is ... always a boy" who, submitting to a beating, "has transformed himself into a girl." The fantasy is homosexual: "a little boy is being beaten—that is, loved—by another man."[40]

While the interpretation of such fantasy can be questioned, some analyses of masochism seem pertinent to Lawrence's condition. Masochists "cannot stand praise and have a strong tendency to self-depreciation," are "characterized by total inhibition in the face of pleasure" and "forced into unconditional obedience, dirtied and debased."[41] The "meaning of the masochistic inclination is: 'If you oust, humiliate or kill me—yet I will do what I want.'...Prometheus, fettered, ... still refuses to bow to the gods." The masochist manifests "inflexible ... will power.... He has an inexhaustible capacity for taking a beating and yet ... is not licked.... This ... combative energy ... makes him as unmanageable ... as a ton of iron ore."[42] Contrariwise, the masochist's fantasy "is a feeling of being putty in the master's hand, ... being absolutely subjected to another's domination ... the satisfaction he seeks seems to be the ... extinction of his individual self." To those who cannot comprehend the pleasure Lawrence derived from pain but know the pleasure desert heat and hot baths gave him, Wilhelm Reich's insight may be helpful: in beating and making the skin bleed, "the patient wants to feel the warmth of the skin, not pain ... the pain is taken in the bargain because of the 'burning.'...Cold, on the other hand, is abhorrent."[43]

The masochistic ritual must be performed precisely as prescribed (in Lawrence's case, the naked buttocks, type of whip, and number of lashes were prescribed in writing, a merit of the "Old Man" invention). An observer may be present to ensure that the instructions are followed. Despite the appearance of craven, childlike submission, it is the masochist, not his beater, who directs the terms of the engagement. Robert Stoller, who conducted insightful field studies of sadomasochists, stresses the importance of trust in the ritualized encounter. The "players negotiate the 'contract' ... so that ... absolute limits will not be exceeded.... [They] all appreciate sophisticated partners who know ... the rules of the game." By his private explanations, The Old Man's instructions, and an observer's presence, Lawrence tried to limit the danger. But Bruce was unsophisticated. As time passed, he threw himself more ardently into his assignment, once apologizing to The Old Man "for ... overdoing the beatings." Mack speaks of Lawrence's "distress at and fear of the severity of the beatings."[44] But he would not have made the long trips to Scotland if, taking all factors into account (maintaining secrecy, obtaining the requisite punishment and report), Bruce's services were not the best he could arrange.

Stoller discusses the masochist's effort "to master the traumas and frustrations that emanate from the 'sadists' of infancy and childhood: our parents ... the details of the adult script tell us what happened to the child." If "Perversion is hatred, erotized hatred,"[45] Lawrence's Turkish captors, his mother, perhaps his father, and mainly himself would be those he hated. Marcus observes "how truly and literally childish" is the flagellation of Victorian gentlemen, "how deeply sad ... it is ... an imprisonment for life." That was true of Lawrence. Nevertheless, the beatings brought temporary peace, physical and moral relief, "the overwhelming cleansing effect of severe corporal punishment, that leaves you feeling the debt is paid, the slate wiped clean."[46]

Sexuality

"I'm so funnily made up, sexually," Lawrence wrote E. M. Forster in 1927.[47] He certainly was and writers continue to spar about his sexual nature. One group has portrayed him as a homosexual; another has denied it. Virtually all of Lawrence's friends, including some homosexuals who sought his love, are in the second camp.

Not attending a boarding school, Lawrence was spared the homosexual experience and beatings that boys from the best families often received there. At Oxford, Vyvyan Richards, fell in love with him. "He never gave the slightest sign that he understood ... my desire. In return for all I offered him—with admittedly ulterior motives—he gave me the purest affection, love and respect that I have ever received from anyone."[48]

At Carchemish, Lawrence was in love or came closer to love with Dahoum than with anyone ever again. *Seven Pillars'* dedicatory poem to "S.A.," who seems to represent Dahoum, opens, "I loved you."[49] Leonard Woolley reported the Arabs "tolerantly scandalized by the friendship," especially after the dig closed in 1913, when Dahoum moved into the house with Lawrence and posed for a naked figure he sculpted. "The scandal ... was widely spread and firmly believed"—but, Woolley adds, "quite unfounded. Lawrence ... was in no sense a pervert ... he had a remarkably clean mind."[50]

Hostile French observers suggested that Lawrence was homosexual; "unkind rumours were continually circulating."[51] Some feminine mannerisms supported the supposition. Alec Kirkbride remarked "how feminine" were his "likes and hatreds." If he liked you, "he was charming, but if he disliked you he was spiteful and malicious." Upon first meeting him, S. C. Rolls "heard a soft, melodious voice, which sounded girlish." When Lawrence entered a British officer's tent "dressed in spotless white," he "stared ... at the very beautiful apparition" and asked, "Boy or Girl?"[52]

Lawrence's warm acceptance of Arab homosexuality in Seven Pillars and disgust at their heterosexual concourse sets forth feelings that, with little change, he held throughout his adult life. He contrasts the "raddled meat" of the "public women of the rare settlements we encountered" with the "clean bodies" in which "our youths began indifferently to slake one another's few needs ... —a cold convenience that, by comparison, seemed sexless and even pure."[53] At Akaba, he puts a guard over the prostitutes "because they were so beastly that I could not stand the thought of their being touched by the British: even though deprivation drove the men into irregularities." He scolds Auda for taking "unhygienic pleasure" with his new wife. Were the homosexual "irregularities" hygienic? Discussing intercourse and procreation

with another newly married chief, he asks how Arabs "could look with pleasure on children, embodied proofs of their consummated lust?"[54] While thus condemning intercourse with both prostitutes and wives, he speaks sympathetically of homosexual gratification, be it solely physical or loving. He retains a homosexual pair as servants, though he did not need them, because "they looked so young and clean." Genuine love of woman is, he says, "impossible" for Arab men, who use women as "a machine for muscular exercise"; "man's psychic side could be slaked" only with other men.[55]

Seven Pillars is primarily a story of guerrilla war, an elemental desert, and a man; sex plays little part in it. The Mint has almost no story; it is a slight work, snapshots of reactions to the brutalities of military life. Yet sex looms larger in it; it is full of obscenities (there are none in Seven Pillars) that had to be expurgated in the first trade edition. It conveys the animality of male bodies mingled in barracks and drill, latrines, roughhouse, mess. Lawrence painstakingly records the "sensual cauldron" of his barracks.[56] He sees the "lust" of officers' sadistic arousal: "evident through their clothes is that tautening of the muscles ... which betrays that we are being hurt ... to gratify a passion." He observes an airman's electric sexual experience: "I met a girl ... and we ... clicked and went off together ... like two hundred volts. I wondered if we'd go up in flames."[57] Yet his womanless airmen engage in sex far less than they talk about it.

Lawrence's private life—what he thought and felt when alone, what he did when he entered the lower depths— will never be known. It probably held fewer sexual acts than thoughts and was unquestionably womanless. There is no evidence that, as a boy and youth, he engaged in any sexual activity.[58] Indeed, his boyishness was so pronounced and protracted, the physical signs of immaturity (girlish giggle, dubious beard) so suggestive, one suspects a physiological cause. Richards thought him "sexless [at college]—at least he was unaware of sex"; Robert Graves and Henry Williamson thought the Deraa whipping made him impotent.[59] Lawrence himself "emphasized his 'sexlessness,'" meaning that he was "devoid of sexual appetites;"[60] but, in view of the sexual element in his beatings, this cannot be literally true.

There is ample evidence that he had no love for or sexual interest in women; avoided or rejected any sexual opportunity with or overture from a woman; abhorred the congress of man and woman. Mack has documented the sole possible exception. In 1965, he interviewed Mrs. Janet Hallsmith, then 79, who, as Janet Laurie, was a childhood friend of the Lawrences in New Forest and Oxford, where she saw the brothers often during their high school and college years. Alone with Janet once after a family dinner, T.E. suddenly asked her to marry him. She laughed. "He seemed hurt, but merely said, 'Oh, I see,' ... and spoke no more about it." Though they had spent much time together on outings and playing games, T.E. had never expressed his feelings, had never kissed or touched her affectionately. Two years older, Janet felt like his elder sister; she wanted to marry tall Will, not short T.E. A friend said that T.E. had "adored" Janet. But, Mack concludes, "he was unable ... to communicate these feelings ... or to change the relationship to an adult one ... his essential immaturity prevented his courting a woman successfully."[61] Some question Mrs. Hallsmith's memory of what happened 55 years before; I tend to credit it; it furnishes further evidence of Lawrence's incapacity to love.

If Janet Hallsmith's story is correct, it was the only known occasion Lawrence showed serious affection for a woman. The women to whom he was closest, Charlotte Shaw and Lady Astor, were 31 and 9 years older, respectively, and married. Women closer to his age whom he knew well, like Celandine Kennington and Clare Smith, were also safely married. Seeking an acceptable explanation for why T.E. never married, Arnold Lawrence said he "had no ... opportunities to meet women of his own age and ... interests."[62] Everyone, especially Lawrence, makes opportunities to pursue their goals. Lawrence liked the ranks, in part, because women were excluded from them. "Women, when we want them, we can encounter: but of our own will, only. They cannot come to us."[63] When, after the war, women threw themselves at the romantic figure Lowell Thomas created, they grasped empty air.

Lawrence's mother hoped he might marry Kathleen Scott, the attractive sculptress widow of Antarctic explorer Capt. Robert Scott. She was eminently eligible; knew what it was like to be hounded by the press; "had a weakness for wounded heroes"; and, sculpting Lawrence in 1920, "developed a crush" on him. After his death, his mother told her "that he had liked her." Nothing happened because nothing could happen between Lawrence and a woman. Lady Scott heard talk: that he had taken credit for a "great landing" that had not happened; that "he is the Royal Mistress" (Feisal's). She "received a 'foolish' letter from him which, 'coinciding with yesterday's talk causes antidote to acute attack of Lawrencitis.'"[64]

Ralph Isham characterized his "fear ... of a woman's love" as "a boy's fear." Lawrence himself said, "I'm frigid towards woman so that I can withstand her: so that I want to withstand her."[65] An example is his relation with Clare Sydney Smith, wife of the Mount Batten commander under whom he served from 1929–31. The Smiths treated Lawrence as a family member; he was often in their home and spent much time alone with Clare, exploring coastal waters in a motorboat. *The Golden Reign*, her glowing account of that time, does not mention that her marriage was shaky and she loved Lawrence, who did not respond. "Am I a beast?" he asked Lady Astor. "But she wants something which I want to keep, and she ought to understand it."[66]

Lawrence's conduct reflected not just his moral scruples but his abhorrence of sexual intercourse, his inability to view it as a loving act in which both parties gladly engage, as anything but an animal act leading to the yet more monstrously animal act of birth, the "disgust of reproduction." "Do you really like naked women? They express so little," he tells Eric Kennington.[67] A note for his contemplated book, *Leaves in the Wind,* says, "I take no pleasure in women. I have never thought twice or even once of the shape of a woman."[68] The thought of a man embracing a woman, even in dancing, offended, and the sexual embrace revolted, him.[69] It "must seem an unbearable humiliation to the woman…. I hate and detest this animal side." It "must leave a dirty feeling."[70]

At intervals, he envied the communion of bodies. "I … lamented myself most when I saw a soldier with a girl, or a man fondling a dog." But he could not become such a soldier; to judge from a photo, he could not even fondle a dog.[71] Women were to him prostitutes or "holy almost, despite the soilings they receive when men handle them."[72] The "soilings" had the infamous outcome of birth. "Honour thy father & thy mother—when we can see crawling out of her that bloody blinded thing (which was ourselves), the penalty of her fall to the sexual assault of the father."[73]

For someone so intelligent and widely read, who recorded the sexual conduct and talk of Bedouin and Britons in two books and discussed sexuality candidly with several friends, Lawrence was surprisingly naive, ill-informed, and contradictory about it. Probably the intense feelings stirred by his parents' sinfulness, Deraa, and his protracted juvenility overwhelmed his usually astute observation. Thus, he says, "I can't understand all the fuss about sex. It's as obvious as red hair: and as little fundamental." And, "I'm deeply puzzled and hurt by this Lady Chatterley…. Surely the sex business isn't worth all this damned fuss? I've met only a handful of people who really cared a biscuit for it."[74] Several years earlier, he declared, "Hut 12 shows me the truth behind Freud. Sex is an integer in all of us."[75] Quoting a preacher's remark that the period of sexual pleasure "lasts less than one and three-quarter minutes," *The Mint* adds, "the climax is … a razor-edge of time, which palls so on return that the temptation flickers out into the indifference of tired disgust." Disgust at an act he has not committed. It is a mistake to write about what you do not know. F. L. Lucas asked, "Is that genuine ignorance? …the reader cries 'Oh he *must* learn better, if only by hearsay."[76]

It is safe to conclude that Lawrence never had a relationship with anyone, man or woman, which was both loving and sexual. To that extent, I agree with Arnold Lawrence, John Mack, Jeremy Wilson, and many of Lawrence's friends who have made similar statements in rebutting assertions that he was a homosexual. "TE's virginity should be perceptible to any intelligent reader of his books, being one of the main causes or symptoms of his ill-adjustment," Arnold Lawrence protested.[77] But to stop at that point would misrepresent the facts.

The misrepresentation arises from the different usages of *homosexual*. Those who deny that Lawrence was a homosexual mean: he was not actively homosexual, shunned physical contact with men almost as much as with women, had no known male lover, and rejected overtures by homosexual friends. He rejected Vyvyan Richards's love; his love of Dahoum was not sexual; his affection for several servicemen stopped short of love or sex;[78] in 1934, he rejected Ernest Altounyan's love.[79] He expressed discomfort at the company of a writer who may have been too demonstrably homosexual[80] and told E. M. Forster, "I couldn't ever do it, I believe: the impulse strong enough to make me touch another creature has not yet been born in me...."[81]

Homosexuals are as varied as heterosexuals and bisexuals. Robert Stoller complains that "the word *homosexuality* has been used in so many ways that, unless one clearly says how it is employed, ... the surplus meanings stifle our understanding."[82] So let me say: by *homosexual,* I mean an erotic taste, preference, or disposition with or without overt sexual acts. Lawrence's astonishing hostility to and disgust at heterosexual congress, coldness to a woman's body, and warm depiction and approval of overt homosexual acts clearly reflect a homosexual disposition. He liked the company of men in Carchemish, Arabia, and the RAF. He said, "men's bodies, in repose or in movement ... appeal to me directly and very generally." Upon reading *The Mint,* Noel Coward recognized that he "despised his own body, and ... loved the better bodies of other younger men...."[83] Conceding that T.E. "was impressed often with the physical beauty and animal grace of the young, particularly the young male, in uncivilised countries," Arnold Lawrence added that homosexuality "repulsed him physically but not morally."[84] But that is untrue. He expressed both physical and moral repulsion for a man's sexual engagement only with a woman. One must scour his writing for any criticism of homosexual conduct, whereas praise of its "cleanliness" abounds.

Irving Howe suspected that his "sexual impulses were usually passive and suppressed."[85] The forced passivity of the Deraa whipping and sodomy was so "lascivious" he yearned to, and did, repeat it. The beatings he arranged apparently peaked in mid–1933 but continued thereafter with a planned session interrupted by his death. The sessions have been interpreted as a reprise of Deraa. But whipping alone was not the core of Deraa and would not repeat it. The core elements were whipping, sodomy, sexual pleasure, and resultant feelings of debasement and self-hatred.

Robin Maugham recounts an episode (others may be imagined but are undocumented) in which whipping was combined with the sodomy for which Lawrence most despised himself. In December 1939, Maugham was posted to Bovington for tank training.

> One of the sergeant-instructors, in a pub one night, took me to an upstairs room which ... he rented occasionally. He produced half a bottle of rum ... and we drank it. He drew his chair closer to mine and ... told me a story which at the time I disbelieved but which has since been partially confirmed. When Colonel T. E. Lawrence was at Bovington [1923–25]..., he had made friends with the instructor—who was then a lance-corporal. T. E. Lawrence had rented the very room in which we now sat. One evening he had invited the lance-corporal to drink with him. He had then persuaded the lance-corporal to whip him and then to penetrate him.[86]

Some persons dismiss this story because Maugham and the instructor were homosexual, because it may be invented, because there is no corroboration; Lawrence might have invited the sergeant to drink, but for him to drink is more questionable. Yet the story was told decades before his whippings were known; the timing coincides with the savage time at Bovington and the onset of Bruce's punishment. Like a key inserted in a lock, the story *fits*, it is a clue to several mysteries. It would explain why Lawrence hated and loathed himself and why these feelings were so entrenched.

Lawrence's implication in Britain's "betrayal" of the Arabs, once seen as a reason for his enlistment, now seems less relevant. The "betrayal" is arguable; he was not responsible for it; he himself said that the 1921 Cairo settlement fulfilled most of Britain's promises. His revulsion at Deraa—and at himself for enjoying it— took strangely long to develop. We do not know his thoughts and feelings when Bruce's whippings were initiated. Did he hope, by silently enduring the pain, to redeem his submission at Deraa; to repeat the pleasure it yielded; or, by some strange internal chemistry, to do both ?

"Unclean!" he cried to Charlotte Shaw years later, blaming himself, not the Turks, for what happened. His secret beatings seem to have made his position more unforgivable. A secret vice is hinted at repeatedly in Lawrence's later letters, but guardedly and not twice to the same person. To E. M. Forster, he says, "If you knew all about me ... you'd think very little of me." To Eric Kennington, "If mankind started confessing ... the filth of which they were the fathers & mothers.... Oh NO: it won't do. There is not one of us righteous, not one." To Bruce Rogers, "we are all such mixtures, that it would be a miracle of suppression to be good all through."[87] He made similar remarks to David Garnett and Lincoln Kirstein.

It seems clear that Lawrence despised himself because he had good reason to feel despicable.

III
CONCLUSION

22

Summing Up

Lawrence was an extraordinary boy and man with a powerful mind, independent outlook, great resourcefulness, determination, and courage. To these native talents, study, experience, and effort added wide knowledge, many skills, strength, and endurance.

The Boy is Father of the Man

Visible continuities between the boy and man make me question explanations that attribute his postwar conduct to his wartime experience. Thus, it is said the RAF attracted him because he liked the wartime comradery of men. The explanation is not so much wrong as insufficient. Before the war he evidently enlisted in the Army, joined the high school rifle club and university Officers Training Corps, practiced with rifle and gun, and carried a gun in Syria. We may infer that, later, the military represented not only a refuge from fame but the same refuge from bourgeois and family life it had offered as a boy and the same opportunity to practice the arts of war, macho arts the small man cultivated.

Lawrence's adult fondness for pseudonyms, name changes, and anonymity was manifest in high school articles and the anonymity he sought for his Sinai survey report. His deviousness was manifest by the youth who told his family that he did not remember what article he had written for a college magazine and that he was perfectly well when he was deathly ill. His intrepidity and stamina were plain in boyhood excursions.

Thus, many features of the adult Lawrence were present in young Ned: his boyishness, ready grin, self-assurance, and intensity. Important, less evident features were also present, such as the ability to penetrate his parents' imposture and to keep the secret for years. Plainly, Lawrence's sharp perception, self-control, self-containment, and talent for concealment were established early.

Ned showed an energy and purposefulness that Privates Ross and Shaw lacked. Unhappy at school, bearing silently the secret of his bastardy, he nonetheless pursued his own goals with ebullience, determination, thoroughness, and, when necessary—the word and trait recur throughout his life—ruthlessness. Youth is a solvent for many ills. The boy gave no sign of the depression and apathy that beset the man.

The period in Syria and Egypt between 1909 and 1916, before the desert war, merits special attention for Lawrence can then be observed free of the legend and the disputes that later becloud him. In those years, age 21 to 28, an Oxonian known to no one but his archeologist colleagues, he impressed many—prominent figures, peasants, and laborers. His solitary summer walk through unsafe, oven-hot lands was comparable, in courage and hardihood, to his July 1917 ride to Damascus and other wartime episodes so bold or foolhardy some writers have dismissed them as fabrications. Near East traveler Gertrude Bell, Captain Stewart Newcombe, poet James Elroy Flecker were impressed by the "amazing boy," as Flecker called him. Small, cultured, alternately shy and brazen, his friendship with Kurdish and Arab chiefs and men, his easy management of Carchemish workmen presaged his masterful handling of feuding Bedouin.

What would have happened if, in 1916, Lawrence had remained in Cairo instead of entering the desert war? Arabists had admired and Indianists resented his trenchant analyses. Very likely he would have gained influence in setting Near East policies, but it is hard to imagine his becoming a celebrity at all like Lawrence of Arabia. "Lawrence of Arabia" signifies a man of action whom desk-bound leaders with regular mealtimes can rely on to do what they themselves could not. Without a great war that licensed trickery, destruction, murder, and massacre, he is unimaginable. He would not have won Feisal's friendship, would not have tested himself against other men and his own more severe standards, would not have written anything like *Seven Pillars of Wisdom*.

When, after the 1915 Gallipoli disaster, Prime Minister Asquith demanded Winston Churchill's resignation, Lady Churchill wrote him: "Winston may ...

have faults but he has the supreme quality which I venture to say very few of your present.... Cabinet possess, the power, the imagination, the deadliness to fight Germany."[1] Change Germany to Turkey and that is true of Lawrence, which may be why he and Churchill got on so well.

The Desert Hero

Seven Pillars contains no battle like Gallipoli, Verdun, or Passchendaele, but raids, demolitions, attacks, advances, retreats, marches, camps, scouting, recruiting, proselytizing. It is not a novel, where characters enact their drama as convincingly as the novelist's genius dictates, but an intense, protracted memoir, where events and actors are viewed solely as Lawrence recollects them and he alone is present in every scene. This or that detail may be wrong: it is not documented history but relived, deeply incised experience or, more strictly, the selective presentation and concealment of remembered experience mixed with later emotions. "There are no mass-effects. All is intense, individual, sentient.... Through all, one mind, one soul, one willpower. An epic, a prodigy, a tale of torment, and in the heart of it—a Man."[2]

As the desert war was the defining time of Lawrence's life, the time he "entered history," biographers have devoted disproportionate space to those two years—Thomas, Graves, and Liddell Hart, writing while Lawrence lived, around three-fifths of their text; Wilson and James, more recently, half of that. I have given it less, as my central concern is psychological, not historical. Even so, Lawrence's recapitulation of his part in the revolt offers abundant insight into his mind and character. Lawrence without *Seven Pillars* is unimaginable. The book has imposed itself on disparagers and admirers alike. Elie

Kedourie, no admirer, acknowledges its "immense influence."[3]

A school of biographers swimming in Richard Aldington's wake—Stewart, Dold, James, Sugarman, Asher—see little honesty, truth (save the self-criticism), or heroism in *Seven Pillars,* only imposture and self-aggrandizement. They dismiss the revolt as militarily inconsequential, Bedouin as brigands, and Lawrence as the barker of a sordid sideshow. What Lowell Thomas inflates they deflate; he sees romance, they, contrivance. James grants Lawrence "a quick intellect, great courage, stamina, superhuman willpower," but not heroism.[4] Is the word too honorific for him? Must heroism be unadulterated by any vain, weak, or ignoble trait? Then sagas, myths, and boys' adventure stories are full of heroes but history holds few and only a bald outline of their deeds can stand; a fuller account dare not be given. Alexander, Caesar, Napoleon do not pass muster or, in our time, MacArthur, Eisenhower, Patton, de Gaulle, Churchill, Montgomery, Rommel, Pershing, Foch, Scott, Byrd, Lindbergh. Their failings have been detailed by historians and biographers as assiduously as those of Lawrence.

If the ability to formulate, foster, and reach a goal are necessary to leadership, Lawrence was a leader. If brave, brilliant action is necessary to heroism, he was a hero. A live, not mythological, hero cannot be superhuman. He need not even succeed. (Scott did not return from the South Pole; Byrd did not reach the North Pole; Mallory died on Everest.) He is entitled to his quota of failings and may, like Lawrence, have a good many.

Lawrence rose too high too fast on a shaky personal and familial foundation. His success was too great. Without his assurance, no one would rebuff the King's honors or talk to the War Cabinet as he did—"You people don't understand yet the hole you have put us all into." In Paris, his inexperience bred vain expectations and a sense of crushing defeat that an experienced diplomat would not share. Thereafter, the cleavage in his character grew more manifest. "Who knoweth the spirit of man that goeth upward, and the spirit of the beast that goeth downward to the earth?" His All Souls stay, his virulent attack on government policy, and his Colonial Office work were positive efforts to settle into civilian life and deal with his personal and political wartime commitments. Leaving All Souls for an unheated attic, the depression and apathy during the latter phase of his Colonial Office stint, and the self-lacerating period writing *Seven Pillars* marked a downward thrust. Both movements were enacted upon the fantasy stage that Lowell Thomas and the press erected for the public.

Initially, the RAF may have been an escape from that stage, a place to pause and decide what to do next. When, ousted, Lawrence imprudently made readmission his major goal in life, the RAF became his prison. How dependent he became on its institutional care is clear from the despondent, vacant weeks following his discharge. His last months of freedom contrasted with his first months in Syria. Then, he was excited and enthusiastic; at Clouds Hill, he found nothing to absorb him. He was alone with himself and, used to the coarse comforts and companionship of the military, did not like it.

Lawrence said that to write about the RAF, he had to look at it from the bottom. To write about him, I have looked at the small details of how he lived and the larger elements of his character and conduct. I have tried to circumnavigate him, examining his body, bearing, and living habits; his money management and possessions; his relations with family members and friends; his view of himself, so conflicted and contradictory he might have been two different persons; his odd, sad sexuality;

and the masochistic cord binding his inner life.

The Lifelong Boy

Disliking his small body, Lawrence worked on it like the puny boy who builds his biceps in exercise advertisements. Emotionally detached from friends, he seemed also detached from his body, fed it sparingly, and punished it often. The two did not have a healthy relationship.

Lawrence's feelings and force were expressed and concealed in his eyes and lips. Often, he was expressionless, shy, absent; he would sit or stand withdrawn, immobile, looking at the floor. Suddenly he could come to life, grin, his eyes would flash and his soft-spoken voice and commanding presence would rule the conversation. In many ways, he remained a lifelong boy. His charm and daring, his liking for pranks, leg-pulling, and medieval romances fit the boyish model. He had an adolescent's view of intercourse, never outgrew his adolescent love-hate relation with his mother, was deferential and entertaining to older persons. Friends felt protective toward the boy they saw in the man's uniform.

Lawrence's eating and living habits were those of a camper, customer, or guest. The camper ate basic food and drink requiring little preparation; the guest chose what he liked from what was offered; the customer ate in a cafe or asked his neighbor to prepare a meal. He did not usually cook or keep fresh food, but could heat a kettle and serve a proper English tea, a not insignificant meal.

Camp living arrangements—food, cot, laundry, hot water, the exclusion of curious persons and reporters—and the company and services of comrades suited him. His cottage was equipped with necessities, not luxuries, as he defined them.

A gramophone, records, books, fireplace, hot bath were necessities; a stove, toilet, phone, even a bed (or so he declared) were luxuries. Not sleeping on it, he was honest, if duplicitous, and having no "bed" was a convenient way to refuse unwanted guests.

At the Colonial Office, Lawrence wore a proper dark suit, white shirt, tie, at times even a hat. Upon enlisting, a uniform was his standard dress motorcycling and visiting high- or low-placed friends. Occasionally, he wore a tweed jacket that grew worn and shabby. Though he bought an expensive suit for a comrade, he owned none.

Clouds Hill was untidy. Dirty cups and dishes were washed—insofar as pouring boiling water on them washed them—only when clean ones were exhausted. Spider webs were, on principle, preserved. Visitors who liked rough living were pleased; others found the place distasteful. Lawrence shared the cottage readily and, when stationed at distant camps, invited friends to use it. He was not possessive about his possessions. His motorcycle was borrowed and badly damaged. Most of the art commissioned for *Seven Pillars* was given away or sold to the subject and the sum given to the artist. Valuable copies of *Seven Pillars* were given away; some were sold and the money given to needy friends. A few Arabian mementos were eventually installed at Clouds Hill.

Lawrence's books and records, freely loaned, often disappeared. The most valuable were stored with friends. His goods and papers were scattered in half a dozen locations in London, Oxford, Cambridge, Dorset, and, as retirement approached, gradually, but never fully, assembled at Clouds Hill. Once he left the family's Oxford home, Lawrence was a wanderer on three continents, with no permanent home.

His money management was puzzling. He gave and lent it so freely you might think it was polluted. When he had a good income and fair capital, this may be judged generous and kind. When his capital and income dwindled, it seems heedless. Some call him saintly, but saints do not live with foul-mouthed men to keep war machines in good running order. Some said he emulated his kind, gentlemanly father: he was kind and gentlemanly enough, but, unlike his father, deliberately depleted his resources. In some ways, he lived like his mother, a rigid fundamentalist who lived simply. When he had no money to give, Lawrence borrowed and went into debt to do so. Giving begot giving and kept him in a straitened state. Was needless generosity, producing needless poverty, another way to punish himself?

Lawrence's Family

The improper liaison of Lawrence's parents, one a shy, besotted landowner, the other an attractive, firm-willed working-class woman, can only have been based on love and passion. Moving often from fear of exposure, they multiplied the fruits of their sin in a procession of sons from whom they diligently hid their secret. Only in 1919, when his father died, did T.E.'s mother tell him (not his two brothers) what he had long known, that he was illegitimate. That he had kept this secret to himself for so long attests to his remarkable control of his feelings.

A young boy who detected his parents' closely guarded secret may also have detected their sexual passion. There is no direct evidence for this surmise, but I think it reasonable. Doubtless, the parents were very discreet, but, year after year, could their passion be hidden from the shrewd spy in their midst? An undocumented story has it that Ned once surprised his parents making love. Such gross evidence was not needed to bolster his

thoughts of and disgust at the act that had made him a bastard.

Lawrence's letters to his father are respectful; his adult recollections, appreciative but not warm or intimate. They depict a kind, relaxed, supportive gentleman—and a weak, sinful man seduced by a stronger woman who was, like Lawrence, illegitimate. The love for his mother expressed in early letters later grows cool and hostile. After Thomas's death, Sarah reaches for love and wants to turn him toward her great consoler, Jesus. T.E. harshly rejects her God, her love, her sex. One reason he enters the RAF is to escape his mother. "She has given me a terror of families.... Knowledge of her will prevent my ever making any woman a mother."[5]

The adult Lawrence was concerned about his mother's welfare, but hostile to her intrusion into his affairs. He could never resolve his feelings toward her, could neither forget, nor establish a satisfactory relation with, her. She was too demanding; he, too sensitive, defensive, aggravated, angry. She too readily punctured the shield which hid his feelings.

Of his brothers, only Will played a significant emotional part in his life and one, Arnold, in his posthumous reputation. T.E. and Will, sixteen months younger, were close friends. Taller, handsomer, less introspective, better balanced, Will was a fine athlete and horseman, whereas T.E. shunned athletic competitions and disliked horses. Will won the love of Janet Laurie, whom T.E. liked. T.E. must have admired and envied him; Will, in turn, had great regard for T.E., great confidence in his powers, and yet enough detachment to question his friendship with a murderous Kurdish chief.

Millions of young men were massacred in the disastrous European war. A student of Lawrence must particularly mourn the death of Will whose life held great promise, would have illuminated, and might even have moderated that of his brother.

Arnold, twelve years younger than T.E., was the only brother to marry and father a child. As guardian of T.E.'s writings and reputation, he is responsible for much that we know (and some things we will never know) about Lawrence, especially the private man recorded in letters and recollections. Arnold discerned and regretted his brother's failings, but obstructed and tried to censor writers who believed that he was homosexual.

Lawrence's intense dislike of Arnold's wife Barbara, mentioned by no previous writer, seems out of character for a protective older brother. Arnold's marriage seemed to displease T.E. as much as the thought of marriage revolted him.

Friends

Lawrence's idea of an ideal friendship was one in which each friend knows the other so well that thoughts and feelings need hardly be expressed; words are spoken without subterfuge or ulterior motive; their meaning and feeling is understood and shared. Ideal friendship may end in a comfortable silence. It is doubtful if Lawrence ever had such a friend. Charlotte Shaw and he had a mother-son relation; she grew too possessive and he retreated. If he was closer to Dahoum, it was not a relation of equals; their friendship dispensed with a large realm of intellect, culture, and, probably, intimate confession. That may have been welcomed by Lawrence (and be why he found poorly educated servicemen congenial) as a relief from thinking, that, in him, worked itself into an introspective, self-destructive coil.

Not thinking and not talking brought a peace more easily reached in camp than with intellectual friends. Yet Lawrence, a man of many moods, could tire of camp

and rush off for a bout of intellectual fencing with G. B. Shaw; literary discussion with the Garnetts, Hardy, Forster, or Hanley; or art talk with Kennington, John, Rothenstein, Ede. Few prominent friends could accept his life in the ranks, rejecting and implicitly condemning their cultured world. "If you will permit me to say so: you ought not to be '338171 A C Shaw' residing in Room 2 ERS. RAF. Depot at Karachi: but your proper place is at home amongst men & women of intellect and culture like yourself."[6] Writing thus to Lawrence, the King's Private Secretary expressed what many friends felt.

They opposed his enlistment, could not credit it, thought him mad. Then they thought (as did Lawrence) it might be a phase with a limited purpose, such as writing a book, after which he would return to their world. Few could think of Lawrence without thinking of the desert hero, an Arab headdress, a camel. Comrades at least saw him living and working among them, like other former officers who could not adjust to civilian life; his choice was odd, but it flattered and did not insult them.

From childhood to adulthood, from obscurity to renown, Lawrence seems an outsider[7] with no intimate, intellectually and emotionally detached. Something was missing in every friendship: full equality, equal give and take, equal interest in the full range of personal concerns. He remained reserved; he defined the depth and range of each friendship. Some friends (Richards, Altounyan, Clare Smith) fell in love; he did not. Some friends (Guy, Forster, Charlotte Shaw) thrust closer; he thrust them back or withdrew.

His most satisfactory relations may have been those which, because of a marked difference in age or social standing, were relatively stable, neither friend asking too much of the other. He was considerate, content, and engaging with decidedly older friends (Hogarth, the Shaws,

Doubleday, Hardy, Rogers) with whom he could behave as a respectful, slightly mischievous son. When the Shaws became too prescriptive, he braked firmly. With service friends, he was usually an avuncular elder and they, respectful and helpful acolytes. Lawrence set a limit to each relationship. He was generous and helpful to friends and acquaintances, even some who were hostile; they found it hard to help him because he would be obligated to no one. He gave and lent money but accepted none that was offered (except, under protest, from his mother).

His conduct with strangers was changeable. Fan mail he usually discarded, but sometimes he responded courteously, sometimes forthrightly (telling Lincoln Kirstein he was an ordinary man with human vices and inviting him to visit and see for himself). He could curtly dismiss a stranger's greeting or reply politely, corresponded with and visited an elderly woman who sought advice on her writing.

He made few appointments because his mood might change; he preferred to knock on the door and drop in or try another friend. Thereby, he visited far more people and accepted more hospitality than he extended. His living standard was low, his cottage amenities were spare, and, like Greta Garbo (with whom he sympathized), he liked to be alone.

He was a mixture of extremes. Vain and narcissistic, he liked to spend time with himself—who else knew and understood him so well? He also hated himself for his many failings: his smallness and illegitimacy; his inability to love, to overcome his secret vices, to write great literature, to enjoy life like anyone else.

His genius was an ability to see in an immediate scene—the landmass and peoples of the Middle East, a rail line and guard post, a crashed plane, or the conversation at a conference—what should be said and done to achieve a given end. He was a natural leader of men, leading not by command but by incisive analysis clearly pointing the direction to be taken.

Conscious of his powers, Lawrence could overrate them, be arrogant, offensive, disdainful, and not accept correction. Condemning himself and his writing severely, he nonetheless rebutted criticism. Forgetting political and military realities and his exhausted state upon entering Damascus, he later dreamed of "changing the face of Asia." These dreams are not the only signs of his periodic megalomania and madness. He was too exacting, lonely, unrelenting, set himself too demanding standards, could not resolve the conflict between his aspirations and feelings, his outer and inner world.

Fawning was the obverse of megalomania. Lawrence fawned upon Forster, a good, not great, writer, and Manning, a precious one, as well as Shaw and Yeats; he called Augustus John "master," Elgar, Bruce Rogers, and Emery Walker, "monuments." Perhaps such homage served to demean his own literary talent. His overvaluation of artists did not fit with his principle that all men are equal. His adulation of Trenchard betrayed the yearning to debase himself that he fulfilled in varied masochistic rituals.

Masochism

Freud considered it "impossible to understand anyone without knowing his sexual constitution."[8] I do not claim to understand Lawrence fully. The evidence on key points is too thin and he is too slippery, tells too many indistinguishable truths, half-truths, and lies. To derive pleasure from pain is to reverse normal expectations. As David Hogarth observed, Lawrence was not normal. His masochism is not disputed. The chief point in dispute may be the range of conduct that should be assigned to it and the weight it should bear in each instance. I assign it a wide range and varying weights.

To be savagely beaten, swim in frigid waters, undergo electric shocks are plainly masochistic. To refuse treatment for a broken bone, sleep uncovered in the cold on hard ground, ride a motorcycle at high speed without goggles are evidently masochistic, though the search for pain and for hardihood can merge. They can merge in a spare diet and fast, marathon journeys. If needless ordeals are masochistic, what about needless penury, military discipline, and humiliation? Much of Lawrence's life, including heroic feats in Arabia, can be seen as the acting out of a drive for physical and emotional punishment, suffering, abasement. However, we should beware of explaining too much too simply. Lawrence was not a simple man.

The primary meaning of masochism is securing sexual pleasure by pain. Lawrence obtained sexual pleasure from his beating and rape at Deraa and the beatings that he later arranged. Whether any other punishment, such as horseback riding, generated such pleasure is unknown but conceivable. Mind and body can work in wondrous ways their pleasures to perform.

Since his death, many writers have contended that Lawrence was a practicing homosexual. Objecting strongly,[9] others cling to Arnold Lawrence's impossible notion of his sexless virginity. Attempting to make sense of all the evidence, I conclude that his disposition was homosexual. Throughout his life he fled sexually eligible women, admired handsome men, worshipped large men, sought and enjoyed male companionship. However, his sexual expression was largely inhibited. His one known love, for the Arab boy Dahoum, probably found physical expression only in friendly wrestling—rough enough to break two ribs. His one known physical re-lationship, with a young Scotsman, was perverse. He enjoyed his whipping and rape at Deraa and was driven to repeat the whippings, perhaps also the sodomy. But whatever he did was done secretly and the gratification was accompanied by self-hatred. Altogether, his sexual life is pitiable.

A Broken Hero

For Claire Keith, a long-time student of Lawrence and others involved in his life and afterlife (Lowell Thomas, Andre Malraux), this book "closes a process of demystification and addresses squarely the darker struggles of Lawrence's life." Nonetheless, she asks, "How are we to qualify … the effect Lawrence had and still has on most people? A number of words have been used (mind-reading, magnetism, genius, eternal youth, kindness, saintliness, uncommon power), which keep forcing themselves on our consciousness, and we sense them to be true in a diffuse way." I don't know what effect Lawrence still has on "most people," but, for me and many members of the T. E. Lawrence Society, what she says is true. Her words present the kindly face of a man who had other faces. He was not just kind, generous, even saintly. He could and did assault and kill men. He could be ruthless: no saint, but a strong, resolute man led the Bedouin in raids and massacres. Near Damascus, Barrow met a fierce, harsh man. A tough, most unsaintly man lived with Bovington toughs, drove powerful machines at dangerous speeds, manhandled newsmen, kept a gun and oiled the engines of war, castigated his sister-in-law, abominated sexual intercourse and childbirth. This man could be devious, deceitful, and self-centered as well as courteous, excessively generous, and very kind. Unfortunately, he was kinder to others than to himself. His self-hatred, we may say self-destruction, was his tragedy.

Robert Graves characterized Lawrence as "a broken hero who tried to appear whole."[10] That is a fair assessment of his life from 1922 onward. His conduct in the weeks after he left the RAF offers little ground for believing him ready to resume serious work. His preparation to visit Arthur Russell in Coventry and John Bruce in Scotland show him more inclined to live as Aircraftman Shaw than Colonel Lawrence. John Mack thinks, "Once he permitted himself to be involved with Bruce he could no longer return to public life, even if he had chosen."[11] That neglects the tough side of Lawrence, who had less to fear from Bruce than Bruce had to fear from him. At 46, he had lost the will, not the ability, to act.

Four years after Lawrence's death, Britain and Germany were at war. In June 1940, 120 German bombers attacked England and the Battle of Britain began. Had he lived, I do not believe that Lawrence would have tinkered in his cottage while German planes bombed British cities, RAF pilot friends fought them overhead, and his friend Churchill strove to save the land they both loved. However, that is idle speculation about what might have been.

We are all such stuff as dreams are made of and Lawrence was made of astonishing stuff.

Notes

Introduction

1. Brown and Cave, 223.
2. From a 1956? letter to David Garnett cited in Louis Allen, "French Intellectuals and T.E. Lawrence," *Durham University Journal*, 69 (1976), 60.
3. Ocampo, 19.
4. Aug. 18, 1935 letter to Liddell Hart quoted by Brian Reid, "T. E. Lawrence and Liddell Hart," *History*, June 1985, 231.
5. Aldington, 349, 376.
6. Aldington refers to Lawrence as a "pansy hero" and "an impudent pederast": see A. Kershaw and F.-J. Temple, eds., *Richard Aldington* (Carbondale: Southern Illinois University Press, 1965) 34 and Ian MacNiven and Harry Moore, *Literary Lifelines* (New York: Viking, 1961), 11.
7. Aldington, 331.
8. The story, first told by journalists Colin Simpson and Phillip Knightley in four articles in the (London) *Sunday Times*, June 9 to 30, 1968, was amplified in Knightley and Simpson's 1969 book.
9. June 29, 1954 letter to Liddell Hart (O'Prey, 1990, 137).
10. Mack, 433–4.
11. Wilson, 751.
12. R. G. Sims provides a collection of such stories.
13. Aldington, 386–7.
14. After detailing Lawrence's deception of Charlotte Shaw and Edward Garnett, Wilson (821) concludes, "it seems curious that he should so casually have deceived" them. He dismisses the evidence of vanity in the many portraits for which Lawrence posed, stating that he never "actually asked anyone to paint his portrait or photograph him" (12). His antiseptic remarks about Lawrence's sexuality were made in lengthy postings on his internet listserv.
15. E.g., "Jewish Personality Traits," *Commentary*, Oct. 1946, 377–83; "Infant Care and Personality," *Psychological Bulletin*, Jan. 1949, 1–48; "Some Attitudes toward Death," *Diogenes*, Fall 1957, 73–91; and *Adjustment to Adult Hearing Loss* (San Diego: College-Hill, 1985), 179–94.

Prologue: A Rocket Flared and Fell

1. *Seven Pillars*, Chapt. CXIX.
2. Wilson, 573, 576–7.
3. *Friends*, 195.
4. See Phillip Knightley, "Desert Warriors, Why are we in Saudi Arabia? Blame it on Lawrence," *M inc.*, Nov. 1990.

1. Childhood and Youth, 1888–1907

1. Mack, 5; for the Chapmans, see Wilson, 941–4.
2. Orlans, 1996, 20.
3. Though living in Dinard at the time, Sarah went to Jersey for Frank's birth in 1893, to ensure his British citizenship and exemption from French conscription.
4. *Friends*, 25.
5. Davis, 9.
6. July 14, 1927 letter to Richard Knowles (Wilson, 41 and Bodleian); *The Mint*, 154.
7. Comments by Lawrence in 1927 (*B:RG*, 61, 113).
8. *Friends*, 36–7.
9. *Friends*, 31.
10. Cadeli, 47; Richardson, 142.
11. Wilson, 32, and Liddell Hart, notes on a May 12, 1929 conversation with Lawrence (Texas).

12. April 14, 1927 letter to Charlotte Shaw (Brown, 326).

13. In *The Mint* (132), he said three months; at other times, six or eight months (*B:LH*, 24, 51). Some writers question this boyhood enlistment; Arnold Lawrence could not make up his mind about it.

14. Lawrence, Dec. 7, 1927 letter to Dick Knowles (Garnett, 553); Wilson, 31–2.

2. College and the East, 1907–1914

1. July 14, 1927 letter to Dick Knowles (Wilson, 41).

2. Eventually, the thesis became a study of *The Influence of the Crusades on European Military Architecture—to the End of the XIIth Century* (1910). It has been published in several editions; the most recent: T. E. Lawrence, *Crusader Castles*, Denys Pringle, ed. (Oxford: Clarendon Press, 1988).

3. Wilson, 52–3.

4. Feb. 3, 1909 letter to Lawrence (*Letters*, 37).

5. Aug. 2, 1909 letter to his mother (*Home*, 92, 89).

6. Sept. 7 and Aug. 2, 1909 letters (*ibid.*, 106, 96).

7. Brown and Cave, 32.

8. D. G. Hogarth, *Accidents of an Antiquary's Life* (1910), quoted in Wilson, 73.

9. T. W. Chaundy (*Friends*, 41).

10. *Friends*, 591.

11. Aug. 6, 1908 letter to his mother (*Home*, 67).

12. Dec. 1910 and April 11, 1911 letters (*Home*, 115–16; Brown, 34).

13. It has been suggested, and denied, that the British Museum provided archeological cover for intelligence activities. More precisely, that a patron of the dig also funded the 1914 Sinai survey that was, indeed, a cover for intelligence mapping. Dismissing this tenuous reasoning, Jeremy Wilson (1,008, note 96) observes that, when World War I broke out, Hogarth's difficulties "in finding war service appropriate to his specialist knowledge must surely be proof that he had no pre-war connections with British Intelligence." St. John Armitage points out that there was no need to spy on the railroad. "Travellers moved along the route with little … hindrance." A *Times* of India correspondent "drew plans, took photographs and set out the problems … in siting the bridge at Jerablus." (Dec. 9, 1997, telstudies@lists.netlink.co.uk).

14. June 2 and 23, 1912 letters (*Home*, 211, 218).

15. April 1, 1914 letter (*ibid.*, 293).

16. Oct. 2, 1912 and Feb. 1, 1913 letters (*ibid.*, 235, 246).

17. Woolley in *Friends*, 87.

18. *Secret*, 202–3.

19. M. O. Williams, *National Geographic Magazine*, 1913 (cited in Robinson, 8).

20. Oct. 22, 1912 letter to his family (*Home*, 239).

21. June 28 and May 11, 1912 letters home (*ibid.*, 221, 208).

22. Woolley (*Friends*, 89).

23. Sept. 12, 1912 letter to his family (*Home*, 229).

24. June 24, 1911 and June 28, 1912 letters (*ibid.*, 174, 220–1).

25. Bell, May 18, 1911 letter (Mack, 76); Flecker, 59; Hubert Young (*Friends*, 123).

26. Leonard Woolley (*Friends*, 91); E. H. R. Altounyan (*Friends*, 115); and Somerset de Chair, *The Golden Carpet* (London: Faber & Faber, 1944), 5.

27. Asher, 34; see Lawrence's March 20 and Feb.18, 1912 letters home (*Home*, 198) and to Flecker (Brown, 45).

28. July 29, 1911 letter from Jerablus (*Home*, 176). Before setting out on this trip, Lawrence told his family, "People seldom or never get ill here." (June 24, 1911 letter, *Home*, 173).

29. Sept. 13, 1912 and April 23, 1914 letters (*Home*, 232, 295).

30. William Lawrence, Aug. 9, 1911, Oct. 14, 1913, March 1914 letters (*Home*, 407; Garnett, 159; *Home*, 517).

31. William Lawrence, Aug. 27, 1913 letter (*Home*, 446–7).

32. Aug. 29, 1909 letter (*ibid.*, 105).

33. Dec. 10, 1913 letter to Vyvyan Richards (Garnett, 160–1).

34. *Friends*, 587. In addition to his thesis, Lawrence and Woolley wrote *The Wilderness of Zin* (Palestine Exploration Fund, 1915), a report on their 1914 Sinai survey; Lawrence also contributed to Woolley's *Carchemish*, Vol. I (British Museum, 1921).

35. Jan. 4, 1914 letter (*Home*, 280).

36. Feb. 28, 1914 letter to E. T. Leeds (93–5).

37. Woolley, 1962, 91–2.

38. Woolley, Nov. 26, 1919 letter to British Museum Director Frederick Kenyon (Winstone, 100–3, 287).

3. War, 1914–1918

1. In the spring of 1913, Kitchener, then British Agent in Cairo, requested a military survey of the Sinai; decades earlier, he had worked on a survey of western Palestine (Wilson, 136).

2. Nov. 16, 1914 letter to E. T. Leeds (105).

3. Letters: Dec. 24, 1914 to E. T. Leeds (106), July 21, 1920 to F. N. Doubleday (Bodleian), Sept. 29,1915 to his family (*Home*, 309).

4. Dec 27, 1914 diary entry of S. P. Cockerel, George Lloyd's friend (Wilson, 1003).

5. Nov. 15, 1914 and Jan. 21, 1915 letters (*Home*, 300–1).

6. Feb. 2, 1915 letter to D. G. Hogarth (Garnett, 192).

7. March 18 and 22, 1915 letters to Hogarth (*ibid.*, 193–6).

8. March 31, 1929 letter to Liddell Hart (Garnett, 195).

9. Monroe, 26; Gilbert, 291; Wilson, 171.

10. Nov. 16, 1915 letter to Leeds (110).

11. McMahon, March 20, 1916 letter to Cox (Wilson, 259); Mousa, 1997, 178–9.

12. McMahon, March 20, 1916 letter to Cox; Cox, April 7, 1916 letter to W. H. Beach (Wilson, 259, 267); Wilson, 263.

13. Aubrey Herbert, diary (FitzHerbert, 180).

14. Young (*Friends*, 123); Stirling, 1933, 494–5.

15. Wilson, 949–59.

16. Liddell Hart, 71; James, 125; Lawrence, July 1, 1916 letter to his family (*Home*, 328).

17. See, for example, Antonius, Dawn, Fromkin, Kedourie, Monroe, Tauber, and Wilson.

18. July 1, 1916 letter to his mother (*Home*, 327).

19. *Seven Pillars*, 63. Wilson (302 and 1030, note 68) shows that Clayton told Lawrence to accompany Storrs and "bring back a good appreciation of the situation."

20. *Seven Pillars*, 63; Oct. 12 and 14, 1916 diary entries (Storrs, 186–7).

21. In a footnote, Storrs (193) praises "the fine prose of *Seven Pillars*" yet questions Lawrence's "late memory."

22. Storrs, 204.

23. Oct. 22, 1916 cable (James, 141).

24. *Seven Pillars*, 67–8. Of course, manipulability was also important to Storrs. Abdulla, he noted, "has intelligence, energy and charm, requiring only firm but not too heavy or respectful guidance to prove a valuable asset." (Oct. 18, 1916 diary entry, Storrs, 193).

25. *Seven Pillars*, 220; Liddell Hart, 41.

26. *Seven Pillars*, 92, 98–9.

27. *Ibid.*, 117.

28. *Seven Pillars*, 337–40. This portion and the succeeding discussion of six Syrian cities (341–4), possibly a remnant of the book on seven Eastern cities Lawrence once planned to write, appeared in *The Arab Bulletin*, March 12, 1917.

29. Aug. 2, 1908 letter to his mother; the poem is Shelley's Julian and Maddalo (Garnett, 56).

30. D. G. Hogarth, Jan. 23, 1917 letter to E. T. Leeds (Wilson, 350).

31. The message was erased but decipherable (Wilson, 410).

32. The news was of the May 1916 Sykes–Picot agreement. Kedourie, Monroe, and Wilson have shown that the gist of this agreement was long known to Hussein, Feisal, and Lawrence. In May 1917, Sykes and Picot met with Arab leaders in Cairo and with Hussein in Jidda to discuss the Allies' postwar plans. Their presence must have heightened the sheikhs' awareness of, and Lawrence's embarrassment over, these plans.

33. Oxford Text, 299–300.

34. *Seven Pillars*, 283; Wilson, 414; Oxford Text, 300.

35. Raswan, 7.

36. In *Seven Pillars* (325), Lawrence says he reached Suez July 8, 49 hours out of Akaba. Attempting to duplicate the camel trip, Asher (254–60) found it impossible, berates Lawrence for lying, and notes that Lawrence's diary and July 10 report recorded the facts correctly.

37. Storrs, 466. A Companion of the Order of Bath was awarded, because the Syrian ride was not witnessed by a British officer; Lawrence was also promoted from Captain to Major (Wilson, 424–5).

38. Brown and Cave, 88.

39. D. G. Hogarth, Oct. 17, 1917 letter to his wife (Mack, 156); Storrs, 286.

40. Suleiman Mousa (75) says, "this story [of the Syrian trip] was entirely fabricated by Lawrence." Stewart (166–7) agrees and Fromkin (310), crediting him, states that Lawrence's report of his Syrian trip was "almost certainly fictitious."

41. Antonius, 221; Wilson, 410–14, 1069–70 note 41.

42. Mack, 49; *Seven Pillars*, 294.

43. Howe, 349. Stewart (188) terms the entire episode "a myth"; Yardley (113) says it "did not take place as Lawrence described." James (214) writes, "It seems absolutely certain that Lawrence fabricated the incident ... he was making a coded statement about his own sexuality." Little about Lawrence's well-hidden inner nature is "absolutely certain." Accepting James's account, Angus Calder (xvi) states, "we now know" that the Deraa episode "simply cannot have happened." What we "know" is too often based on the last book we read.

44. *Seven Pillars*, 453. The letter to Major W. F. Stirling, Deputy Chief Political Officer in Cairo, written June 28, 1919, when Lawrence was in Cairo, is printed in Brown (165–7).

45. *Seven Pillars*, 454; March 26, 1924 letter to Charlotte Shaw (2000, 70).

46. Storrs, 471 note 11; Wilson, 5 and 1976, 4.

47. Wilson, 471–2; *Seven Pillars*, 400, 471, 476. In a detailed analysis, Asher (296–7) contends that there were never more than 17 men in the bodyguard, not 90 as Lawrence claimed, and that most were humble peasants. Wilson concedes an error: the bodyguard was formed before Deraa.

48. *Seven Pillars*, 31; Malraux, 521; Young, 217.

49. James, 121; Rolls, 258; Wavell, 282 note 1.

50. *Seven Pillars*, 105.

51. James, 160; Robert Graves, letter, *Sunday Times*, July 31, 1927.

52. *Seven Pillars*, 192, 40.

53. Hubert Young (1926, 422), whom Lawrence designated as his successor if he were incapacitated, wrote that, after some time in Arabia, "three general rules of conduct were impressed upon me. The first was never to believe that a detachment of Sherifian regulars would start on the appointed day; the second, never to believe that they had started on any day at all unless I had actually seen

them on the move; and the third, to place no reliance whatever upon the Bedouin."

54. Feb. 11, 1918 letter to General Clayton (Wilson, 480); *Seven Pillars,* 347; Macphail, 319.

55. *Seven Pillars,* 648, 167, 176, 169.

56. *Seven Pillars,* 249, 267, 314, 380.

57. *Seven Pillars,* 412, 433; Pearman, 15.

58. Wilson, 537; Winterton, 1992, 20, 23, 26.

59. *Seven Pillars,* 68, 95, 138.

60. Villars, 141–2; *Seven Pillars,* 333–4.

61. "The British Government had gone very far in this direction," Lawrence adds (*Seven Pillars,* 573). In an October 1929 letter to William Yale, he said that Feisal's negotiations were "quite serious.... All is fair in love, war, and alliances" (Garnett, 672).

62. Mousa, 1997, 78; Lockman, 97–8.

63. George Lloyd, Oct. 20, 1917 letter to General Clayton (Charmley, 65).

64. *Seven Pillars,* 618, 639.

65. Lloyd, Sept. 30, 1917 letter to General Clayton (Charmley, 64); Lawrence, Feb. 12, 1918 letter to Clayton (Brown, 142).

66. *Seven Pillars,* 514–15; *B:LH,* 106.

67. Lönnroth, 42; Villars, 169; Jarvis, 297.

68. March 28, 1918 letter from Akaba (*Home,* 349).

69. Kedourie, 120; Wilson, 561.

70. *Seven Pillars,* 684; Oct. 22, 1929 letter to William Yale (Garnett, 670).

71. *Seven Pillars,* 607, 618, 635, 656, 654. The estimate of children and women killed is from Lawrence's report in the *Arab Bulletin* (*Secret,* 192).

72. *B:LH,* 153; *Seven Pillars,* 658; Oxford Text, 796.

73. Barrow, 211.

74. Oct. 15, 1924 letter to Lt. Col. W. F. Stirling, driver of that Rolls (Brown, 275).

75. Liddell Hart, 291; Arabella Rivington, notes of an interview with Beaumont (1968? IWM).

76. Grosvenor, 66; *B:LH,* 153.

77. *Seven Pillars,* 24.

78. *Ibid.,* 344–5.

79. *Friends,* 125; Antonius, 248.

80. *Seven Pillars,* 572, 136; Oct. 22, 1929 letter to William Yale (Garnett, 671).

81. *Seven Pillars,* 136; Antonius, 433–4.

82. Wavell, 285.

83. *Seven Pillars,* 682. Alec Dixon quotes Lawrence as saying, "Lenin will probably take his place as the greatest man of our time" (*Friends,* 375).

84. Report to General Staff, G.H.Q. (Brown, 155); Oxford Text, 815.

85. *Seven Pillars,* 582.

86. Wavell, 286.

87. *Seven Pillars,* 683; Wavell, 286; Oct. 22, 1929 letter to Yale (Garnett, 670).

88. July 14, 1941 BBC broadcast.

89. Oct. 14, 1918 letter to Major R. H. Scott (Garnett, 258).

4. *Undiplomatic Battles,* 1918–22

1. Wilson, 570–2.

2. Winterton, 65–6.

3. Wilson, 573.

4. Lord Cecil, who was present at the meeting, denied that Curzon had "burst into tears" (*B:RG,* 141). Crawford (187) cites a similar episode involving King Hussein as further reason to doubt Lawrence's account.

5. Wilson, 578.

6. Nov. 27, 1918 cabinet minute (Brown and Cave, 143); Wilson, 585.

7. Wilson, 581, 586.

8. The Nov. 26, 27, and 28, 1918 *Times* articles are reprinted in *Secret,* 226–42.

9. Wilson, 589.

10. *Ibid.,* 595–7.

11. D. G. Hogarth (1923), reprinted in *JTELS,* Autumn 1994, 31–2, 39.

12. Jan. 30, 1919 letter to his mother (*Home,* 352).

13. Shotwell, 121, 191; a 1928 entry in Cyril Connolly's journal (137–8) following a conversation with Berenson.

14. Lincoln Steffens, *Outlook and Independent,* Oct. 14, 1931, 203 (the article was written in 1919).

15. *Friends,* 117; Nicolson, 116.

16. Lönnroth, 88; Lawrence, Oct. 18, 1927 letter to Charlotte Shaw (Brown, 350).

17. Keynes, undated communication (1937?) to David Garnett (261).

18. Garnett, 279.

19. June 19, 1919 memorandum to Foreign Secretary Curzon (Wilson, 614).

20. Clark-Kerr, for Lord Curzon, Aug. 21, 1919 memo to Vansittart and Aug. 25, 1919 reply (Wilson, 617).

21. Sept. 27, 1919 memo and letter to Curzon (Garnett, 289, 291–2).

22. Lönnroth, 88.

23. Thomas, 128, 131, 196–8; also 201–5 for the following account of Thomas's show and meetings with Lawrence.

24. Hodson, 40.

25. Buchan, 1939, 372. Lawrence's mother told David Garnett (294) that, at home, he "would sometimes sit the entire morning between breakfast and lunch in the same position, without moving."

26. Mack, 285–6; Robert Graves (*Friends,* 33).

27. *B:LH,* 145; Wilson, 627, 1116 note 17. Lawrence told Liddell Hart that he put the bag under the table in the refreshment room and left it. He apparently told Alan Dawnay that he left the bag on the train while he got a sandwich and, when he returned, it was gone (Douglas Brownrigg, *Unexpected,* London: Hutchinson, n.d., 58).

28. *B:LH,* 68; *Friends,* 249.

29. 1922 letters: Aug. 26 to Edward Garnett, Nov. 12 to Robert Graves (Garnett, 360, 379).

30. Wilson, 629.

31. *Seven Pillars,* 92; Oxford Text, 696.

32. *Seven Pillars,* 283.

33. Holograph preface to the proposed abridgment, Nov. 18, 1922 (Oxford Text, Harvard copy).

34. Letter in *The Times,* July 22, 1920 (Garnett, 306–8).

35. Col. T. E. Lawrence, "France, Britain, and the Arabs," *The Observer,* Aug. 8, 1920 (Garnett, 311–15).

36. Gertrude Bell, Sept. 5 and 19, 1920 diary entries (Mack, 292–3).

37. Sept. 25, 1920 letter to H. R. Hadley (Garnett, 320).

38. Churchill (*Friends,* 197); Lawrence, Dec. 1920 letter to Robert Graves (Garnett, 324).

39. Lawrence's 1927 comment on the manuscript of Graves's biography (*B:RG,* 110).

40. This account is given by Sachar (378).

41. March 2, 1921 letter to Wilfred Blunt (Brown, 184).

42. Oct. 13, 1927 letter to Charlotte Shaw (Mack, 301).

43. Mack, 301.

44. Knightley and Simpson, 141–2.

45. Comment on the typescript of Graves's biography, 1927 (*B:RG,* 112).

46. Knightley and Simpson, 138–9.

47. Lawrence in *B:LH,* 131.

48. Aug. 2, 4, Sept. 7, 1921 cables to Prodrome, London (Brown, 188–90).

49. Benoist-Méchin, 157–8; Mack, 305.

50. Oct. 24, 1921 report to the Colonial Office (Garnett, 335).

51. Philby, 210, 108.

52. March 20, 1921 letter (*Home,* 352).

53. Alec Dixon (*Friends,* 373–4); "Eric Kennington's Arab Portraits" in Orlans, 98–101.

54. Jarvis, 1942, 84; Antonius, 321, 324; *B:RG,* 114, 112.

55. Philby, 210; Lawrence, Jan. 1922 letter to Hugh Trenchard (Hyde, 45).

56. Aug. 26, 1922 letter to Edward Garnett (Garnett, 360).

57. *B:RG,* 15.

58. Churchill (*Friends,* 198–9); Feb. 15, 1922 letter (Brown, 355).

59. Jan. 26, 1922 letter to Hornby (Bodleian); Arnold Lawrence, note in *The Mint,* 12.

60. *The Mint,* 20.

61. Hyde, 43–4.

62. Letter to Kennington, around May 1922 (*Friends,* 273).

63. Aug. 22, 1931 letter to Bertram Thomas (Orlans, 274).

64. July 23, 1922 letter to Wilfred Blunt (Brown, 197).

65. Garnett, 342; Hyde, 47.

66. Aug. 16, 1922 memo (Hyde, 48).

67. Aug. 17, 22, 23, and 26, 1922 letters to Edward Garnett (Garnett, 355–61).

68. Aug. 17 and 27, 1922 letters to G. B. Shaw (2000, 4, 8).

5. In and Out of the RAF, 1922

1. *The Mint,* 19.

2. Leeds, 120.

3. *The Mint,* 20; Arnold Lawrence, Introduction, *ibid.,* 12.

4. Peter B. Ellis and Piers Williams, *By Jove, Biggles!* (London: W. H. Allen, 1981) 107.

5. W. E. Johns, "How Lawrence joined R.A.F.," *Sun Times,* April 8, 1951, 5.

6. Sept. 1, 1922 letter (Garnett, 363–5).

7. Swann, letter (1936 or '37?) to David Garnett (363). Neither Marson, Trenchard's private secretary, nor Marsh expressed annoyance; both were friendly.

8. May 20, 1928 letter to Lawrence (*Letters,* 84).

9. Sept. 1, 1922 letter to Oliver Swann (Garnett, 365).

10. Letters: Sept. 7, 1922 to Edward Garnett, Aug. 6, 1928 to E. M. Forster (Garnett, 366, 619).

11. *The Mint,* 24, 26; cf. "that Handley crash in Rome" (38).

12. Sept. 28, 1925 letter to Charlotte Shaw (Brown, 291).

13 *The Mint,* 64.

14. *Seven Pillars,* 315, 677; Rutherford, *The Literature of War* (London: Macmilan, 1978), 56; Allen, 172.

15. Frank Lawrence, May 1, 1915 letter to his mother (*Home,* 713).

16. Jan. 23, 1924 letter to Jonathan Cape (Wilson, 734); Meyers, 1976, 131.

17. *The Mint,* 72; Sept. 7, 1922 letter to Edward Garnett, his Sept. 9 reply, and Lawrence's response (Garnett, 366–7; *Letters,* 89).

18. Hyde, 65.

19. *The Mint,* 105, 91.

20. Nov. 6, 1922 letter (Garnett, 375).

21. Sept. 7, 1922 letter (Garnett, 366).

22. Wilson (683–4) gives a choice number; e.g., Navy Captain Boyle: "A good face (hot as mustard, red-haired, socialist, ... disciplinarian: thinks the world made for Naval Officers: very decent: full of laughter of a slightly sharp sort: restless, impatient); a real bad sitter: but a first-rate face. Sinew and fire and tight skin."

23. Oct. 27, 1922 letter to Eric Kennington and Oct. 29 to D. G. Hogarth (Garnett, 373–4).

24. Nov. 9 and 19, 1922 letters to Swann (Garnett, 378, 381–2); Hyde, 69–70.

25. Dec. 27, 1922 letter to G. B. Shaw (2000, 21–2).

26. BBC, 9.

27. Oct. 29, 1922 letter to D. G. Hogarth (Garnett, 374).

28. Shaw, 2000, 11–12, 17–18, 23–4.

29. Wilson, 699. Stanley Weintraub also disputes Wilson's unlikely charge that G. B. Shaw "altered the course of T.E.'s life" (letter, *Times Literary Supplement,* July 20–26, 1990, 775).

30. *The Mint*, 20; Sept. 1, 1922 letter to Swann; Dec. 21, 1922 letter to R. V. Buxton (Garnett, 365, 389).

31. Nov. 11 and 24, 1922 letters to Blumenfeld (Brown, 211–14). Blumenfeld may have kept Lawrence's secret, but his newspaper broke the story while he was ill in a nursing home.

32. Hyde, 71–5; January 1923 letters to T. B. Marson, Trenchard's assistant (*ibid.*, Hyde, 75, 77).

33. Garnett, 351.

34. Jan. 30, 1923 letter (Garnett, 396).

35. 1923 letters: Feb. 4 to B. E. Leeson (Garnett, 398), Feb. 5 to Rothenstein (9).

36. Hoare, 257–8.

6. *The Tank Corps, 1923–25*

1. March 1, 1924 letter to Trenchard (Hyde, 99).

2. Four 1923 letters: March 27 and 28 to Lionel Curtis and Trenchard, respectively; April 1 to Hogarth (Garnett, 405, 407, 413); May 11 to Chambers (Bodleian).

3. April 12 and 24, 1923 letters to Edward Garnett (Garnett, 409–10).

4. May 14, 1923 letter to Lionel Curtis (Garnett, 415).

5. Mack, 346 note. Cf. Lawrence's remark to Curtis: "Don't take seriously what I wrote about the other men [in Bovington].… It's only at first that certain sides of them strike a little crudely" (March 19, 1923 letter, Brown, 228).

6. June 13, 1923 letter to D. G. Hogarth (Garnett, 425).

7. Trenchard resigned as RAF commander at the end of 1929. "I shan't feel as I do about the R.A.F. after he has gone," Lawrence said (Aug. 23, 1929 letter to T. B. Marson in Brown, 426).

8. The quotations in this and the preceding paragraph are from Lawrence's letters to Curtis (Garnett, 409–14).

9. In a March 19, 1923 letter to Curtis (Garnett, 412). The expression, now fashionable, was then little used.

10. Dixon, 294–7.

11. 1923 letters: Feb. 5 to Lady Scott (Garnett, 399–400); Nov. to Siegfried Sassoon (66).

12. Letters: Nov. 12 and 20, 1922 to Edward Garnett (Garnett, 380, 383); early 1923 to Vyvyan Richards (Brown, 223).

13. Huxley in Grover Smith, ed., *Letters of Aldous Huxley* (New York: Harper & Row, 1969, 273); Aldington, 1975, 80; Hughes, *The Spectator*, Aug. 2, 1936, 193; Read, 23; Bergonzi is cited in O'Donnell, 138; Malraux, 523; Woodcock, *Queen's Quarterly*, 1974, 609–10.

14. In letters written, Dec. 1920 to Aug. 1927, to (in order) Graves, G. B. Shaw, Edward Garnett, Granville-Barker, Kennington, Granville-Barker, E. M. Dowson, Cockerell, Edward Garnett, Buxton, Charlotte Shaw, Forster, and Curtis.

15. Feb. 7, 1924 letter to Granville-Barker (Garnett, 454).

16. Oct. 22, 1923 letter to Cockerell (Garnett, 437); Sassoon, Nov. 26, 1923 letter to Lawrence (*Letters*, 154).

17. Charlotte Shaw, Dec. 31, 1922 letter to Lawrence and Jan. 8, 1923 reply (Shaw, 2000, 26, 33).

18. June 13, 1923 letter to Hogarth (Bodleian).

19. Kipling, July 20, 1922 letter (*Letters*, 123); Lawrence, Dec. 27, 1922 letter to Shaw and Jan. 4, 1923 reply (Shaw, 2000, 21, 31).

20. *Friends*, 200; Jan. 8, 1923 letter to Charlotte Shaw (Brown, 219).

21. Isherwood, 24; Forster, Feb. 1924 letter (*Letters*, 60).

22. July 18, 1927 letter (*Letters*, 94).

23. Mann, Introduction, *The Short Novels of Dostoevsky* (New York: Dial Press, 1945), xviii.

24. May 11, 1923 letter to Col. Wavell (Brown, 235).

25. July 23, 1923 letter to Hogarth (Garnett, 429).

26. V. Thompson, 88.

27. Dec. 19, 1923 draft "To Subscribers to 'Seven Pillars'" (Garnett, 445–6).

28. The 127 subscriptions netted £4,000; the cost of production (including the press, paper, reproductions, and the two printers' salaries, but not the paintings) was £13,000.

29. Wilson, 727.

30. Letters: Aug. 29, 1924 to Buxton (Garnett, 465); April 12, 1925 to Hagberg-Wright, Librarian of the London Library (Brown, 278).

31. In a prize example of Lawrencian guile, he said, "no *subscriber* was asked to accept any condition … with his copy: though I did diddle old Shorter into refusing one, by asking for a pledge that he shouldn't write any of *his* muck about it!" (April 7, 1927 letter to Hogarth, Garnett, 512).

32. Dec. 18, 1923 letter from Shaw and Dec. 20 reply (Shaw, 2000, 50–1, 53).

33. Feb. 6, 1925 letter to Trenchard (Hyde, 105).

34. Dixon, 294; and Mack, 346.

35. Forster, March 23, 1924 letter in Wilson, 737, and Furbank, 121.

36. Forster, 344–8, and March 25, 1924 letter to Sassoon (Furbank, 121); BBC.

37. 1924 letters: July 27 to Dawnay (Brown, 270–1); July 19 to Eric Kennington (Bodleian).

38. "I wish Trenchard was a worm, for then I could ease myself by cursing him.… However T. is one of the really great people.…" (Dec. 27, 1923 letter to Wavell, in Garnett, 449); Hyde, 81.

39. Letters: Nov. 14, 1923 to Hogarth (Garnett, 440); March 1, 1924 to Trenchard (Hyde, 100).

40. 1923 letters: June 27 to Hogarth; Dec. 20 to G. B. Shaw (Garnett, 426, 447).

41. Jan. 2, 1925 letter to Curtis (Wilson, 750). "He told me," Curtis recalled, "that he would have got into prison if he could have done so without committing a crime." (*Friends*, 261).

42. Feb. 6, 1925 letter (Hyde, 106).

43. May 16, 1925 letter to Buxton (IWM).

44. June 13, 1925 letter (Garnett, 477).

45. Hyde, 107; John Bruce said that in mid–1925 he took Lawrence's gun from him after a scuffle at Clouds Hill. "There is no doubt he planned to end it, because the next day we destroyed eighteen letters which he had written to various people." (Knightley and Simpson, 197).

46. Garnett, 477.

47. 1925 letters: early May to Curtis, May 19 to Buchan (Brown, 279–80).

48. Janet Smith, 242.

7. Back in the RAF, 1925–26

1. July 5, 1925 letter to John Buchan (Garnett, 478).

2. Aug. 18, 1925 letter (Brown, 287).

3. Aug. 4, 1925 letter to Blumenfeld (Brown, 287).

4. Dec. 29, 1925 letter to Dixon (Garnett, 489).

5. *The Mint,* 172, 194 (my italics), 196, 183.

6. *Ibid.,* 189, 192, 191, 198.

7. Sept. 7, 1925 letter to E. Palmer (Garnett, 485).

8. Sept. 28, 1925 letter to Charlotte Shaw (2000, 149–51).

9. Sergeant Pugh (in Graves, 434); Lawrence, Dec. 26, 1925 letter to Charlotte Shaw (2000, 157–8) and May 25, 1926 letter to H. H. Banbury (Wilson, 770).

10. Sergeant Pugh in Graves, 434; Clare Smith, 14.

11. June 21, 1925 letter (*Friends,* 461).

12. Dec. 26, 1925 letter to Charlotte Shaw (2000, 158); Ede, 7.

13. Nov. 30, 1926 letter to Trenchard (Brown, 306).

14. Nov. 25, 1926 letter to J. G. Wilson (Garnett, 497).

15. Dec. 3, 1926 letter to Dick Knowles (Brown, 308).

8. India, 1927–28

1. Jan. 11, 1927 letter to Charlotte Shaw (Brown, 313–14).

2. These notes, "Leaves in the Wind," were apparently made for an expanded version of *The Mint* or a sequel on man's conquest of the air (Garnett, 502–3).

3. 1927 letters: Jan. 28 Charlotte Shaw (Brown, 316), and Feb. 8 to Dick Knowles (Garnett, 505–6).

4. May 12, 1927 letter to Charlotte Shaw (Brown, 328).

5. B. V. Jones, a Drigh Road airman (*Friends,* 414).

6. 1927 letters: Feb. 8 to Dick Knowles (Garnett, 506), March 1 to Curtis (Wilson, 777–8).

7. March 15, 1927 letter to Charlotte Shaw (Wilson, 777).

8. W. M. M. Hurley, adjutant at Drigh Road (*Friends,* 401).

9. From "Leaves in the Wind" (Garnett, 571).

10. When Graves started work in June, he had until the end of July to finish; Cape extended the deadline to mid–August (*B:RG,* 44, 47).

11. June 16, 1927 letter to Edward Eliot (Brown, 333). On June 28, Lawrence informed Graves that "the change [to "Shaw"] is legal" (*B:RG,* 54). He was wrong; it was not legal until August 30.

12. Wrench, 130–31.

13. Oct. 13, 1927 letter to Yeats-Brown (Wrench, 136).

14. Yeats-Brown in *Friends,* 424.

15. July 8, Aug. 18 and Sept. 9, 1927 letters to Yeats-Brown (Wrench); March 3, 1933 letter to Hanley (Orlans, 74).

16. 1927 letters: Dec. 7 to Dick Knowles, Dec. 22 to Curtis, Dec. 8 to Rothenstein (Garnett, 553, 557).

17. December 1927 draft agreement; Mrs. Hogarth, March 14, 1928 letter to Lawrence (Orlans, 296, notes 7 and 11).

18. July 17, 1927 letter to Hogarth (Garnett, 528).

19. Dec. 21, 1927 letter to Charlotte Shaw (Mack 369 and BM).

20. Aug. 12, 1927 and Jan. 4, 1928 letters to his mother (*Home,* 368, 370–1).

21. Nov. 24, 1922 letter to Cockerell (Dunbar, 236).

22. This count is kindly provided by Clifford Irwin, who has prepared an index of all Lawrence's known letters.

23. Dunbar, xi.

24. May 4 and Oct. 20, 1927 letters to Charlotte Shaw (BM).

25. A week after suggesting she interrupt her regular gifts, he asked for an Elgar symphony; two months later, for Handel and Wagner records (Oct. 27, 1927 and Jan. 26, 1928 letters, BM).

26. April 14, 1927 letter to Charlotte Shaw (Brown, 324–5).

27. Aug. 18 and March 29, 1927 letters (Brown, 344, 321).

28. May 12, 1927 letter (Brown, 328–9). Lawrence returned a letter from Trenchard to T. B. Marson, his private secretary, "'cause I can't tear 'em up: and it would put me into the guard room to be found with it by the C. O." (Commanding Officer) (Jan. 20, 1928 letter, Hyde, 142). Richards and Curtis stored his valuable books and papers.

29. Aug. 18, 1927 letter to Charlotte Shaw (Brown, 345).

30. March 6, 1939 letter to Dorothy Walker (Dunbar, 270).

31. Aug. 1 and Sept. 22, 1927 letters to Edward Garnett (Garnett, 532, 541).

32. Letters: July 23, 1929 to Wavell (Bodleian), Aug. 6, 1934 to Kennington (Garnett, 813).

33. April 23, 1928 letter to Edward Garnett (Garnett, 596); Stewart, 268.

34. March 22, 1928 letter (Garnett, 581). On May 17, Lawrence told Garnett, "G.B.S. and Mrs. Shaw had your text of The Mint shown them before it was posted you" (Garnett, 609).

35. March 16, 1928 letter to Charlotte Shaw (Wilson, 820).

36. Wilson, 820–1.

37. At least fifteen persons read the manuscript by February 1929; more probably did, since it could be read quickly and what is "secret" arouses special interest.

38. G. B. Shaw, quoted in Weintraub, 278. The story is too similar to another Shaw told to be accepted without question: "on letting them read his Oxford [Text] version he made them vow to keep it sacredly secret, making them believe that they alone enjoyed that priceless privilege; and when they presently discovered that it had been read by everyone within his reach…, they set him down as insincere and untruthful" (Shaw, 39–40).

39. Hyde, 127; Trenchard, Nov. 22, 1926 letter to Lawrence (Letters, 198). Something is wrong either with this date or Lawrence's "Dec. 5, 1926" inscription in Trenchard's Seven Pillars.

40. April 10 and July 5, 1928 letters to Lawrence (Letters, 200, 204).

41. May 2, 1928 letter to Arnold Lawrence (Garnett, 600).

42. Edward Garnett, May 29, 1928 letter to Lawrence (Bodleian copy).

43. April 26 and Aug. 28, 1928 letters to Savage (Bodleian).

44. Marsh, 238.

45. The Mint, 185; G. B. Shaw, April 12, 1928 letter to Lawrence (Letters, 174–8).

46. Storrs, 473; Buchan, 1939, 372, and March 12, 1935 letter to Lawrence (Letters, 22).

47. May 20, 1928 letter to Lawrence (Letters, 83) and David Garnett, 1962, 110.

48. Charlotte Shaw, April 9, 1928 letter to Lawrence (BM); Sassoon, Nov. 13, 1930 letter to Lawrence (BM, RP 2207).

49. Read, Jan. 7, 1929 letter to David Garnett (copy in Bodleian).

50. 1928 letters to Lawrence: Forster, July 5; Edward Garnett, April 22 (Letters, 67, 96–7).

51. 1928 letters to Lawrence: Forster, Nov. 12; David Garnett, May 20; Tomlinson, Aug. 5 (Letters, 70, 83, 191–2).

52. March 16 and 20, 1928 letters to Charlotte Shaw (BM).

53. March 22 and April 23, 1928 letters to Edward Garnett (Garnett, 581, 598).

54. July 23, 1929 letter to Wavell (Bodleian).

55. 1927 letters: March 4 to Robin Buxton, March 29 to Charlotte Shaw (Brown, 319, 323).

56. July 19, 1928 letter to Shaw (Garnett, 616–18).

57. 1927 letters: March 25 to Kennington, June 20 to Buchan (Brown, 320, 326).

58. 1927 letters: May 12 to Charlotte Shaw (Brown, 328); July 7 to Hogarth (Garnett, 528).

59. Letters: Dec. 7, 1927 to Dick Knowles, May 2, 1928 to Arnold Lawrence (Garnett, 554, 600–1).

60. March 29, 1927 letter to Charlotte Shaw (Brown, 323), April 14, 1927 to Forster (Kings), April 16, 1928 to Ede (Garnett, 592).

61. B. V. Jones and W. M. M. Hurley (Friends, 415, 410).

62. Mack, 368; Wilson, 1142 note 76, and 826.

63. Wilson, 827.

64. Lawrence, Dec. 23, 1929 letter to Trenchard (Hyde, 143).

65. June 30, 1928 letter to Ede (Garnett, 614–15).

66. See Hayter, The Star (London), May 23, 1935, 1.

67. Aug. 18, 1928 letter to Charlotte Shaw (Wilson, 830).

68. June 15, 1928 letter to Charlotte Shaw (Wilson, 829).

69. April 16, 1928 letter to Rogers and his footnote (Rogers).

70. June 30, 1928 letter to Rogers (ibid.) and Rogers, Sept. 3, 1928 letter to Lawrence (Wilson, 832–3).

71. Oct. 2 and 10, 1928 and Jan. 4, 1929 letters to Rogers (Rogers).

72. Oct. 16, 1928 letter to Charlotte Shaw (BM).

73. 1928 letters: Dec. 27 to Trenchard (Hyde, 172), Dec. 12 to Forster (Garnett, 625).

74. July 17, 1928 letter to Herbert Baker (Brown, 380).

75. Oct. 16, 1928 letter to Charlotte Shaw (BM).

76. The foregoing account is drawn mainly from Wilson, 834–44.

9. Seas and Shores, 1929–35

1. Jan. 22, 1929 letter to George Lloyd (Brown, 398–9).

2. Ernest Thurtle in Friends, 353.

3. Hyde, 185–6; Feb. 8, 1929 letter to Trenchard (Brown, 401).

4. 1929 letters: Feb. 22 to Marson (Brown, 402), April 1 to Doubleday (Princeton), May 5 to Graves (Garnett, 659).

5. 1929 letters: Feb. 28 to Dawnay, Feb. 8 to Newcombe (Brown, 404–5); Wilson, 848.

6. March 12, 1929 letter to Charlotte Shaw (Brown, 405).

7. Clare Smith, 33; Mack, 379.

8. 1929 letters: May 1 to Rogers (Brown, 420); Rogers, undated May reply (Wilson, 853–4).

9. John O'London's Weekly, May 4, 1929; The Vancouver Sun, June 8, 1929; Howard, Jan. 29, 1931 letter to Lawrence (Reading).

10. April 18, 1929 letter to H. A. Ford (Brown, 416).

11. July 22, 1929 letter to Nancy Astor (Garnett, 665).

12. March 13, 1930 and April 1, 1927 letters to Thurtle (Garnett, 685; Brown, 411).

13. April 16 and June 20, 1929 letters to Trenchard (Brown, 416; Hyde, 193).

14. June 20 and July 12, 1929 letters to Trenchard (Hyde, 193–5).

15. Hyde, 199; Wilson, 863.

16. Peter Davies would have printed twelve copies for £120; Lawrence gave up (or postponed) the idea because, he said, *The Mint* was "scrappy and arty and incompetent" (Aug. 7, 1930 letter to Frederic Manning in Hergenham, 246).

17. April 27, 1929 letter to Chambers (Garnett, 655); Foden, 320.

18. Letters: June 11, 1930 to unidentified recipient (Harvard); Sept. 6, 1930 to Williamson (2000, 104–5).

19. Nov. 19, 1930 letter to David Garnett (Garnett, 706).

20. Clare Smith, 102–4; *The Naval and Military Record,* Feb. 11,1931.

21. Feb. 6, 1931 letter to Charlotte Shaw (Hyde, 206).

22. Clare Smith, 106; March 2, 1931 letter to Lady Astor (Garnett, 713–4).

23. April 13, 1931 letter to Liddell Hart (Garnett, 718).

24. Letters: April 21, 1931 to Graves (Brown, 453), June 14, 1932 to Charlotte Shaw (BM).

25. Lawrence and Scott-Paine "shared a totally … impracticable notion that even large ships could be hard-chine planing craft…. Scott-Paine's designer, George Selman, knew that such applications were totally unsound…. [Lawrence], however, was clearly impressed by Scott-Paine's vision but lacked the technical appreciation to criticise its soundness" (Adrian Rance, *JTELS,* Summer 1992, 65).

26. 1930 letters: Jan. 19 to Charlotte Shaw (Brown, 436), May 3 to Williamson (2000, 102), Dec. 5 to Charlotte Shaw (Brown, 447).

27. Letters: Dec. 29, 1930 to Buxton and Dec. 5, 1930 to Edward Garnett (Garnett, 708), June 8, 1931 to Rogers (unpaged).

28. Aug. 20, 1931 letter (Rogers). Robert Fagles sensed "a marked falling off in intensity" in the last two books (George Steiner and Robert Fagles, eds., *Homer,* Englewood Cliffs, N.J.: Prentice-Hall, 1962, 162).

29. Joseph Blumenthal, *Bruce Rogers* (Austin: W. Thomas Taylor, 1989); 134; April 13, 1935 letter to Robin White (Bodleian copy).

30. *Publishers Weekly,* Dec. 10, 1932, 2166; *New York Times Book Review,* Dec. 18, 1932.

31. Oct. 12, 1932 letter to Geoffrey Cumberlage (Brown, 467).

32. March 22, 1932 letter (Brown, 461); Aug. 28, 1932 story (Wilson, 894–5).

33. In May 1933, Lawrence called the current commander a "paper man" more concerned with organizational details than with flying; hence the station atmosphere had changed (*B:LH,* 74).

34. 1932 letters: Sept. 16 to Charlotte Shaw, Oct. 22 to Forster, (Brown, 464–5).

35. Lawrence wrote the blurb in October 1932; later that year, he edited Ian Tyre's *Garoot,* published by Cape in 1933.

36. Sept. 3, 1932 letter to Hudd (Garnett, 741–2).

37. *B:RG,* 165, 169.

38. Jan. 24, 1933 letter to Graves (*ibid.,*169–70).

39. Dec. 21, 1933 letter to Beaumont (copy, IWM).

40. Nov. 5, 1933 letter (*Home,* 383). The "broad-as-long" bed "covered…with soft undyed leather" was "for lounging, not for sleeping" (Armitage, 284). Presumably, Lawrence got no comfort from sleeping in comfort.

41. May 18 and 14, 1934 letters to Mrs. Shaw and Williamson (Brown, 489, 488).

42. 1933 letters: March 21 to Philip Sassoon, Under Secretary for Air (Garnett, 763), March 10 to Nancy Astor (Reading), March 23 to Ede (56).

43. 1933 letters: Salmond, March 17 to Lawrence (Wilson, 902); Lawrence, April 22 to Lady Astor (Reading).

44. Oct. 28, 1929 letter to Liddell Hart (*B:LH,* 38), who did not begin work on the biography for another three years.

45. In the war and the RAF, Lawrence flew a great deal as a passenger but, it seems, not as a pilot. Asked by Liddell Hart "Have you ever piloted aeroplanes yourself?" he replied, "Never formally" (*B:LH,* 167). Upon reading the biography typescript, Lawrence changed "I learned to fly" to "I flew" (*ibid.,* 183).

46. June 26, 1933 letter to Liddell Hart (*B:LH,* 75).

47. *Ibid.,* 199–200.

48. The proposed title had been *Lawrence.* "I must protest (and shall protest publicly, if you insist still) that Lawrence, for this generation, is D.H.L.," Lawrence wrote Wren Howard at Cape. "Inverted commas are not enough to avoid trespass on him…. Colonel 'Lawrence' if you want to use that long name." (Dec. 17, 1933 letter, Garnett, 783–4).

49. Lawrence, Dec. 17, 1933 letter to his mother (*Home,* 384); *B:LH,* 38–9.

50. Garnett, 1979, 197; Lawrence, Nov. 26, 1933 letter to R. de la Bère (Garnett, 780). Mack (396) says that the last three chapters of *The Mint* were printed, not "a précis." Garnett suspected "the criminal" was Charlotte or Bernard Shaw (Lawrence's "Irishman").

51. Liddell Hart, 406; Mack, 432, 437.

52. *B:LH,* 181–2; May 11, 1934 letter to Kirstein (Brown, 486).

53. May 24, 1934 letter to Clare Smith (175).

54. Clare Smith (177).

55. 1934 letters: Feb. 2 to his mother (*Home,* 385), Nov. 15 to Clare Smith (179).

56. April 12, 1934 letter to Lincoln Kirstein (Garnett, 796–7).

57. Garnett, 1962, 112; BBC.

58. Liddell Hart, 353; Lawrence, Feb. 2, 1934 letter to Charlotte Shaw (Hyde, 226); *Friends*, 439, 593.

59. *Friends*, 545; Nov. 23, 1934 letter to Marson (Bodleian).

60. 1934 letters: Feb. 2 to his mother (*Home*, 385–6), June 5 to Bruce Rogers (1936), Sept. 26 letter to George Lloyd (Brown, 497).

61. 1934 letters: Dec. 20 to Buchan (Garnett, 836–7), Dec. 31 to Liddell Hart (Brown, 509). The Flecker passage is from "The Golden Journey to Samarkand."

62. 1935 letters: Jan. 3 to Ede, Jan. 31 to Storrs (Brown, 511, 518).

63. In London, Lawrence often made the rounds of publishers he knew, such as Cape, Faber, Heinemann, Peter Davies, Boriswood. Early in 1934, he did so again, "sounding them for a job in twelve months' time" (March 20, 1934 letter to Marshall in Wilson, 913).

64. 1934 letters: June 26 to Eliot and Nov. 23 to Rodd (Brown, 492, 500–01).

65. Jan. 3, 1935 letter to Russell (Brown, 512).

66. Jan. 31, 1935 letter to Knowles (Garnett, 846).

67. *B:RG*, 182–3; *Friends*, 560–1.

68. Garnett, 958–9; Mack, 406.

69. *Friends*, 406. Hanley places this conversation in 1931 but, as he says Lawrence "had about eighteen more months of Service life still to go," I place it later.

70. Quoted in Hyde, 242.

10. The Last Twelve Weeks, 1935

1. Bère, 44–5. Manning died February 22. *The Times* printed nothing until February 28, when Lawrence, stopping in Bourne (Manning lived a few miles west in Edenham), probably picked up the paper and saw the notice.

2. 1935 letters: Feb. 28 to Davies (Garnett, 859–60), May 5 to Rothenstein (*Friends*, 293), who had phoned *The Times* the late notice of Manning's death and had repeatedly tried to contact Lawrence; Manning's mother was hurt by his silence. On May 5, Lawrence finally responded to a second letter, c/o Mrs. Thomas Hardy, who forwarded it to Clouds Hill.

3. Feb. 5, 1935 letter to Buchan (Garnett, 858); Buchan, March 5, 1935 letter to his son John (Lownie, 64).

4. Buchan, 216; time may have mellowed Buchan's memory. Two days after the visit, he was more pessimistic. "I don't know what can be done with him." (March 5, 1935 letter, in Lownie, 64).

5. Jan. 31, Feb. 25, 1935 letters to Beaumont (Brown, 517, Wilson, 924, 926).

6. Brown, 526, and private conversation.

7. Wilson, 928, and Knowles, 40.

8. March 19, 1935 letter to Patrick Knowles (Garnett, 862).

9. Lawrence, April 20, 1935 letter to Beauforte-Greenwood (Texas); Hill, 596.

10. April 1, 1935 letter to Buchan (Garnett, 862–3); Eric Kennington, *Drawing the R.A.F.* (London: Oxford, 1942) 26, and Wilson, 1988, 235.

11. *The Mint*, 90; May 20, 1935 diary entry in Jones, 129.

12. Buchan, March 5, 1935 letter to his son (Lownie, 64–5).

13. *B:LH*, 230; Arnold Lawrence in *Friends*, 595.

14. Wilson, 934; Lawrence, May 8, 1935 letter to Lady Astor (Garnett, 872).

15. Liddell Hart, June 14, 1935 letter to Robert Graves (O'Prey, 252–3); Baker in *Friends*, 254.

16. 1935 letters: April 6 to Marson (Texas), April 5 to Greenwood (Garnett, 865), April 13 to Buxton (Brown, 531).

17. Mack, 410; May 5, 1935 letters to Nancy Astor and Beauforte-Greenwood and Norrington (Brown, 535, 534).

18. May 6, 1935 letters to Rogers and Kennington (Brown, 536–7).

19. Feb. 1935? note from "Leaves in the Wind" (Garnett, 854). Lawrence did not have to serve twelve years; he could leave at any time.

20. Letters: June 29, 1927 to Marson (Hyde, 141), April 5, 1935 to "Walter" (Mack, 407); Oct. 29, 1928 to Herbert Baker (Jesus).

21. April 20, 1935 letter to H. Norrington; David Garnett note (868).

22. Lawrence, "Leaves in the Wind," Feb. 1935 (Garnett, 854).

23. This account of the motorcycle crash draws on Knowles, 44; Legg, 86–7, who quotes local sources and testimony at the May 21, 1935 inquest; Harry Broughton, *Lawrence of Arabia and Dorset* (Wareham, Dorset: Pictorial Museum, 1966); Hyde, 249–53; and Marriott and Argent, 102 ff..

24. Knightley and Simpson, 269. Mathew Eden's *The Murder of Lawrence of Arabia* (1979) is at least a novel. Legg (93) intimates that British agents in the black car caused the accident to remove a man they deemed unsuited to head British intelligence, but Lawrence was not slated to do so and a miss is less effective than a hit.

25. That was George Brough's view: "The boy…glanced backwards and inadvertently swerved." (Dave Tunbridge, *With Lawrence in The Royal Air Force*, Sevenoaks: Buckland, 2000, 84). But the boys' testimony at the inquest did not confirm it.

26. Henry Williamson, *Goodbye West Country* (Boston: Little, Brown, 1938) 357; Chambers (BBC); Sarah Lawrence, Feb. 18, 1936 letter to Ede (Kettle's).

27. Rowse, 256.

28. *Seven Pillars*, 311.

29 "Address by the Coroner to the Jury" and certificate (copy, Bodleian, IWM).

30. Storrs, 478.

31. May 12, 1927 letter to an unnamed person—Guy? (Harvard); Shaw, quoted in *The Star* (London), May 20, 1935, 1.

32. *Seven Pillars*, 358–60.

33. Halifax in *Friends*, 17, 22.

11. Body and Appearance

1. August 1922 RAF recruiting station examination record.

2. For example, an officer who served in Palestine recalled Lawrence as "a wee mon...about 5 feet or 5 feet 1 inch" (Leggs, 16); Lowell Thomas (1967, 2) said 5' 3".

3. "The average height for a middle-class boy at the time would have been nearer five foot nine." (James, 16).

4. April 29, 1911 letter to his family (*Home,* 152); *Seven Pillars,* 451.

5. Mack, 65; Graves (BBC).

6. Tabachnick and Matheson, 45; Ralph Isham in *Friends,* 295; *Seven Pillars,* 477.

7. Lawrence Durrell, Nov. 4, 1957 letter in Ian MacNiven and Harry Moore, eds., *Literary Lifelines* (New York: Viking, 1981), 32; Liddell Hart (90); Hynes, *The Auden Generation* (Princeton: Princeton University, 1976), 191.

8. *Seven Pillars,* 330, and April 14, 1927 letter to Alan Dawnay (Bodleian).

9. July 19, 1924 letter to Edward Garnett (Bodleian) and *The Mint,* 98–9.

10. Lord Beaverbrook, *Men and Power* (London: Hutchinson, 1956), xxv. In May 1918, Rothermere wrote Bonar Law, "In getting rid of Trenchard I flatter myself I did a great thing for the Air Force With his dull unimaginative mind and his attitude of 'Je suis tout' he would within twelve months have brought death and damnation to the Air Force" (*ibid.,* 236); *The Mint,* 98.

11. Meinertzhagen (42), Nov. 20, 1955 diary.

12. Buchan, 212; *Friends,* 264–5.

13. Robert Graves in *B:RG,* 8; C. M. Devers, "With Lawrence in the Tank Corps," *World's Work,* Aug. 1927, 384–8; Buchan, in Lownie, 64.

14. Rowse, 256–7; *Seven Pillars,* 581, 580.

15. Aug. 26, 1906 letter to his mother (*Home,* 35); June 10, 1927 letter to Marsh (Garnett, 521); Graves, 41.

16. Without luggage, he said in 1907, "I could do 180 miles in the day with ease" (Garnett, 50).

17. Pencil notes for "Leaves in the Wind" (Bodleian).

18. Altounyan in *Friends,* 118–19.

19. *The Mint,* 47; May 14, 1923 letter to Lionel Curtis (Garnett, 416); *The Mint,* 148.

20. Letters: Dec. 4, 1928 to Edward Garnett (Bodleian), Dec. 8, 1927 to Rothenstein (Orlans, 209).

21. Dec. 27, 1927 letter to Charlotte Shaw (BM).

22. Graves and Hall in *Friends,* 331, 46; Sept. 12, 1912 letter to his family (*Home,* 229).

23. April 1, 1929 letter to Ernest Thurtle (Brown, 412); *The Mint,* 141.

24. *The Mint,* 138; Sept. 29, 1927 letter to Charlotte Shaw (BM).

25. David Garnett, 1979, 195–6; the episode may have occurred in late 1926.

26. Foden, 323; Villars, 350.

27. Kennington in *Friends,* 264–5; Wheeler, 104–5.

28. *Friends,* 364—Lawrence was then in the Tank Corps (1923–25).

29. Woolley in *Friends,* 91; Wilson, 1042 note 77.

30. Rolls, 151; Toynbee, 188.

31. Dunn in *Friends,* 444; Webb (107) Nov. 8, 1926 diary.

32. *B:RG,* 70; Graves in *Friends,* 325; Richards, 248; Legg, 16.

33. Garnett in *Friends,* 431; *The Mint,* 108.

34. Meinertzhagen, 38; *The Mint,* 108.

35. Cited by Larès in Tabachnick, 234; Villars, 9.

36. Hall in *Friends,* 46; Liddell Hart, 13.

37. Meinertzhagen, 38; Malcolm Ellis, *Express to Hindustan* (London: John Lane The Bodley Head, 1929), 8.

38. Hall and Altounyan in *Friends,* 46, 115.

39. Sims and Thurtle in *Friends,* 549, 352; *B:RG,* 165.

40. May 5, 1927 letter (*Home,* 366); Dec. 31, 1933 to Mrs. Shaw (BM).

41. Feb. 2, 1921 diary entry in Kennet, 188; Isham, *Friends,* 295; Bruce, *The Scottish field,* August 1938, 20.

42. Mack, 21, 476, note 23; Woolley in *Friends,* 91.

43. James J. Abraham, *Surgeon's Journey* (London: Heinemann, 1957), 227; Col. Edward Brémond quoted in Mack, 259; Kennington in *Friends,* 262.

44. Feb. 11 and 22, 1921 diary, Kennet, 189–90.

45. *Seven Pillars,* 400, 472; April 16, 1928 letter to Forster (Garnett, 593). Claire Keith calls my attention to Paul Fussell's discussion of "lad" in the literature of World War I. In Housman's usage, lad signified 'a beautiful brave doomed boy.' In Great War diction there are three degrees of erotic heat attaching to three words: men is largely neutral; boys is a little warmer; lads is very warm" (*The Great War and Modern Memory,* New York: Oxford, 1975, 282). However, Lawrence's body temperature was low; for him, lad was merely warm.

46. April 1932 letter reprinted in *T. E. Notes,* 8:3&4, 1997, 19.

47. Williamson, 9; *B:RG,* 165.

48. Shaw in *Friends,* 247; Feb. 9, 1944 conversation with Shaw (Lees-Milne, 22).

49. Isham in *Friends,* 296, 303.

50. April 6, 1928 letter to Charlotte Shaw (BM).

51. Woolley in *Friends,* 89–90.

52. Pryce-Jones, 8; Tomlinson, Dec. 5, 1928 letter to Lawrence (*Letters,* 189).

53. *Seven Pillars,* 583.

12. Eating and Living Habits

1. March 16, 1927 letter to Charlotte Shaw (BM); April 1907 letter to his mother (*Home*, 52).

2. Prys-Jones, 8; June 15, 1913 letter (*Home*, 258); Woolley in *Friends*, 91.

3. Jan. 31, 1917 letter to his family (*Home*, 334); *Seven Pillars*, 476–7.

4. *The Mint*, 39, 91; *B:RG*, 72.

5. To writers like Forster, Eliot, and Wells, John Carey notes, tinned food represented lower-class vulgarity, a repellent "mechanical and soulless … homogenized mass product" (*The Intellectuals and the Masses*, New York: St. Martin's, 1992, 18, 21–2). To Lawrence, it was a convenience he foisted on his friends.

6. Devas, 90–1; May 27 and Oct. 13, 1927 letters to Charlotte Shaw (BM).

7. July 19, 1928 letter to Bernard Shaw (Garnett, 617); Hayter, *The Star* (London), May 23, 1935, 1; Sims, *Friends*, 553–4.

8. Note of a 1934 conversation in Liddell Hart, *Memoirs* (London: Cassell, 1965, I) 350.

9. Williamson, *Friends*, 454; Allen, 173–7.

10. Woolley, *Friends*, 91; Isham, *Friends*, 299; for the glass of port (in 1922), see *The Mint*, 93; Meinertzhagen (31), April 8, 1919 diary entry. Declining a glass of champagne in 1934, Lawrence said, "Thanks, but I daren't drink anything. One sip, and I go all dithery" (Williamson, 63): indicating that he has gone dithery.

11. *The Mint*, 19; Dec. 25, 1923 letter (Texas). Of course, Mrs. Russell knew nothing about Lawrence's abstemiousness and he was being polite: "the cigarettes were very successful," he says—perhaps to the soldiers he gave them to.

12. *Friends*, 580; see also 554.

13. *The Mint*, 91; A. E. Chambers in *Friends*, 340; *B:RG*, 72–3.

14. See the photo in Tabachnick and Matheson, 16.

15. Woolley, *Friends*, 91; June 1912 letter (*Home*, 213).

16. Yardley, 65; Storrs, 211.

17. See the photos of Lawrence in Cairo, Jerusalem, and Transjordan in 1921 (Tabachnick and Matheson, 97, 138, 128, 139).

18. *Friends*, 275; Bère, 41; photo, Tabachnick and Matheson, 60.

19. Weblin and Jones, *Friends*, 545, 347.

20. Dec. 20, 1923 letter to G. B. Shaw (2000, 54); Spencer (BBC); Bennett, 54.

21. Aug. 30, 1924 letter to Charlotte Shaw (2000, 95).

13. Possessions and Finances

1. Aug. 14, 1928 letter to Kennington (Texas). Cf. his remark, "Possessions possess us, in their time" (Jan. 18, 1935 letter to Kennington, Texas).

2. Vyvyan Richards, *Friends*, 384.

3. Robert Graves, *Friends*, 329.

4. Feb. 15, 1922 letter to his mother (*Home*, 354).

5. Sept. 15, 1933 letter to Edward Garnett (Garnett, 776–7).

6. The books and records are listed in *Friends*, 476–510 and 523–9.

7. Dec. 23, 1923 letter to Buxton (Leatherdale, 65). My account of Lawrence's motorcycles is drawn largely from Leatherdale's excellent paper.

8. Feb. 25, 1924, March 16, April 6, 1925 letters to Buxton (Leatherdale, 66–8).

9. The list price, Jeremy Wilson (848) says, was £185; Robin Buxton arranged a £40 discount, so Lawrence paid £144.

10. Sept. 12, 1933 and May 3, 1934 letters to George Brough (Leatherdale, 83, 85).

11. Obituary, "Professor A. W. Lawrence," *The Independent*, April 4, 1991.

12. Hurley, *Friends*, 407; Hunt, 76–7.

13. Curtis heard he was going to sell the dagger and asked to buy it.

14. Sept. 17, 1923 letter to Doubleday (Wilson, 1993, 46); much of the other information about the cottage not otherwise identified here comes from this Wilson paper.

15. June 27, 1925 receipt (Bodleian).

16. Forster, 346–7; Russell.

17. Undated letter to Kennington (end 1924?) (Texas). Lawrence began *The Wilderness of Zin* with the same verse. Stanley Brown, Curator of Rare Books at Dartmouth, identifies it as from the Poem of the Nutbrown Maid, an anonymous, 15th century? poem.

18. March 31, 1927 letter to W. A. Knowles (Bodleian).

19. Sept. 20, 1945 diary entry in Lees-Milne, 236; Knowles, 32—the conversation may have occurred in 1931.

20. "There were some really granddaddy cobwebs there…and they were not disturbed" (Russell).

21. "Lady Astor said she wanted the toilet. Call from Lawrence, 'Russell, would you show Lady Astor the toilet please'. So I took her outside into the rhododendrons. I said 'You sit on that bough…', and I walked away" (Russell).

22. Knowles, 30.

23. 1933 letters: Oct. 3 to Charlotte Shaw (BM), Sept. 25 to his mother (*Home*, 380).

24. Letters: Alec Guinness, March 13, 1960 to Patrick Knowles (70); Lawrence, July 10, 1933 and May 18, 1934 to Marshall (Wilson, 1993, 55, 61), Nov. 5, 1933 to his mother (*Home*, 383).

25. Wilson (1993, 59) says the pool held 70,000 gallons; Lawrence said 7,000, which is a close estimate. If perfectly level and filled to the brim, it would hold 8,670 imperial gallons.

26. May 18, 1934 letter to Marshall (Garnett, 803).

27. Nov. 16, 1934 letter to Manning (Brown, 499).

28. J. C. in *The Private Library,* Spring 1973, 21; Jan. 15, 1934 letter to Lady Astor (Brown and Cave, 189, and Reading; Liddell Hart, 358).

29. Letters: Nov. 16, 1934 to Manning (Brown, 499), Dec. 17, 1933 to Graves (*B:RG,* 176).

30. *B:LH,* 78 and Liddell Hart, 3; March 4, 1927 letter to Charlotte Shaw (Brown, 325).

31. Wilson, 943, 983–4 note 28, and Orlans, 1996, 22–3, 30 note 7; Arnold Lawrence, June 8, 1987 letter to Jeremy Wilson, 984.

32. Thomas Lawrence, March 8, 1916 letter to Lawrence (BM, RP 2207); Wilson, 252, 944; Lawrence, Sept. 24, 1917 letter (*Home,* 341).

33. Letters: Sept. 5, 1917 (*Home,* 340), Sept. 10, 1930, Jan. 4, 1934 to Buxton (Bodleian).

34. Letters: April 11, 1911 and Sept. 24, 1917 to his mother (*Home,* 147, 341).

35. Letters: Dec. 7, 1922 to G. B. Shaw (2000, 16); Feb. 4, 1923 to Leeson (Garnett, 398).

36. Birdwood, 103; Lawrence said he had no pay at the Peace Conference (Feb. 16, 1923 letter to Leeson, Bodleian).

37. Lawrence told Graves his salary was £1,000 plus a £300 "bonus" (*B:RG,* 54); he told Liddell Hart it was £1,600 (*B:LH,* 143); Churchill said £1,200 (*Friends,* 199).

38. July 17, 1915 letter to Will (Wilson, 227).

39. "His mother...would have been bitterly angry if she had known. Will had consulted Janet before deciding to return from India to fight on the Western Front, and Mrs. Lawrence had always held her responsible for his death" (Wilson, 638).

40. June 27, 1923 letter to D. G. Hogarth (Bodleian).

41. Lawrence may have cooled toward Richards, have been distracted by his efforts on behalf of Feisal, or focussed on writing *Seven Pillars.* Why he continued to buy Pole Hill land while doing nothing to establish a press there is puzzling.

42. March 16, 1927 letter to Charlotte Shaw (BM). Three years earlier, he told Florence Hardy he had given up the idea (Jan. 27, 1924 letter, Texas).

43. Letters: Feb. 25, 1924, March 26, 1925 to Buxton (Bodleian; Garnett, 472); May 1, 1929 to Charlotte Shaw (BM).

44. In October 1935, Lawrence's books and paintings were valued at £726.10: the Chaucer at £120, a John portrait at £100, a Doves *Bible* £35 (Bodleian).

45. K. W. Marshall, *Broadsheet,* Feb. 1941. This *Ulysses* is now in the Humanities Research Center, University of Texas.

46. 1929 letters: May 5 to Bain (Harvard), July 29 to Ede, 37.

47. May 19, 1927 letter to Hogarth (Bodleian).

48. Wilson, 675; V. Thompson, 87.

49. Wilson, 796, 637. In Oct. 27, 1923, Lawrence told Sydney Cockerell (359) he had paid artists nearly £3,000; he commissioned more art after that date.

50. April 21, 1927 letter to Buxton (IWM); e.g., Lawrence bought John's Feisal portrait in 1919 and eighteen Kennington pastels in 1921.

51. They were portraits of Newcombe, Wingate, McMahon, and Buxton. Lawrence asked Buxton (and, very likely, the others) if he would buy his.

52. Paul Nash, Sept. 12, 1922 letter (Mack, 335); Lawrence, March 15, 1927 letter to Edward Eliot (Bodleian).

53. Feb. 16, 1923 letter to Leeson (Bodleian). After Thomas Lawrence's death, Sarah, his sole beneficiary, evidently gave each of her three living sons about £4,000 (Hyde, 34).

54. July 8 and September 27, 1923 letters to Jonathan Cape (Texas).

55. Letters: Dec. 3, 1926 to "Walter," a fellow serviceman (Bodleian); Nov. 1, 1927 to Charlotte Shaw (BM), April 1, 1929 to Thurtle (Brown, 412).

56. March 1, 1927 letter to Edward Garnett (Garnett, 510); July 29, 1930 telegram to Hilton Young (Cambridge).

57. Letters: Dec. 11, 1933 to Lady Astor (Reading), Dec. 31, 1934 to Mrs. Shaw (Brown, 510).

58. Storrs, 474.

59. Aug. 16, 1927 letter, *Contemporary Review,* Dec. 1974, 312.

60. June 10, 1927 letter to Buxton (IWM).

61. "...don't let the interest [on investments of the Epping money] come over £70 a year, otherwise I shall be due for income tax," Lawrence instructed Buxton (Oct. 5, 1930 letter, Bodleian).

62. Jan. 13, 1935 letter to Graves (*B:RG,* 179).

63. 1935 letters: Apr. 13 to Buxton (IWM), May 6 to Rogers (1936).

64. The short will, signed Thomas Edward Shaw and witnessed by two airmen on Aug. 28, 1926, gave Vyvyan Richards the Pole Hill land and the rest to Arnold or, should he be dead, his children. Arnold was asked to consult David Hogarth before publishing any of his writing.

65. Michael Howard, *Jonathan Cape, Publisher* (London: Jonathan Cape, 1971), 155, 94, 82.

66. Trust income was used to preserve historic buildings, aid poor artists and authors, give art to museums, and award scholarships. Illustrative awards were: £4,000 to the Birmingham Art Gallery for an Epstein sculpture, £1,500 to the British School of Archaeology in Iraq, £1,010 to the Ashmolean for an Oman coin collection, £2,490 to the National Trust ("The Lawrence Trusts," typed document, Bodleian).

67. Morris and Raskin, 33, 148.

68. Graves, Dec. 7, 1959 letter to Derek Savage (O'Prey, 1990, 186); Richard Graves put Graves's receipts from the Lean film at $20,000.

69. Morris and Raskin, 26; Crawford, 149.

70. July 7, 1927 letter to Charlotte Shaw (Wilson, 791).

71. May 1, 1928 letter to Trenchard (Bodleian).

72. March 25 and June 1, 1927 letters to Hogarth (Bodleian; Wilson, 775).

73. March 25, 1927 and April 14, 1928 letters to Buxton (Bodleian).

74. Letters: May 1, 1928 to Trenchard (Bodleian); June 1, 1927 to Hogarth (Wilson, 775).

75. Letters: Sept. 27, 1927 and undated (late 1927?) to Buxton (Bodleian).

14. Parents

1. Colin Simpson and Phillip Knightley, *Sunday Times,* June 9, 1968, 49; Lord Stamfordham, March 15, 1927 letter to General Sir Reginald Wingate (IWM).

2. Celandine Kennington, "Re Chapmans of Killua," Oct. 17, 1954, an eight-page typed report of interviews she conducted in Ireland (Texas); Stamfordham, *op. cit.*

3. Wilson, 941.

4. Arnold Lawrence in Flavell, 9 and "Biographical Notes," May 12, 1985 (2 typed pages, Bodleian).

5. Armitage, 20; Mack, 13; Lawrence, Aug. 27, 1924 letter to Edward Garnett (Bodleian).

6. *B:LH,* 67; A. W. Lawrence, "Biographical Notes."

7. Aug. 15, 1909 letter (*Home,* 103–4).

8. Jan. 14, 1911 letter to his family (*Home,* 126).

9. Jan. 22, 1911 and Oct. 16, 1913 letters (*Home,* 129, 269).

10. Leeds, 114.

11. Orlans, 1996, 20–1; A. W. Lawrence, "Biographical Notes."

12. April 14, 1927 letter to Charlotte Shaw (Brown, 325).

13. Caroline Chapman, Thomas's sister, left him £20,000 intended for his sons if he died after her, but he did not. Nonetheless, Lawrence hoped for some recognition from the Chapmans: "if my father's family felt inclined, my dream of £300 assured [yearly income] might come off," he wrote Liddell Hart (May 17, 1929 letter, Texas).

14. Dec. 22, 1933 letter to Mr. Ireland (Texas).

15. May 18, 1924 letter (Wilson, 743). I follow the original spelling in the Bodleian. Judging from a letter "Cousin Teresa" Frampton wrote to "My dear Ned," she and Sarah Lawrence were on friendly terms and met when Sarah stayed at Clouds Hill (1933 or '34 letter, Bodleian).

16. May 1, 1928 letter (Knightley and Simpson, 230); May 11, 1921 conversation noted in Lady Scott's diary (James, 1995, 256).

17. Jeremy Wilson, Dec. 8, 1997, telstudies @lists.netlink.co.uk.

18. Pritchett, 968.

19. This account of Sarah Lawrence's childhood is drawn from Wilson, 942–3, and Mack, 9.

20. Celandine Kennington, "Re Chapmans of Killua," 8-page Oct. 1954 typescript (Texas); A. Rivington, memorandum, 1968 interview with Mrs. Calvert (IWM).

21. Mack, 16, 32.

22. Mack, 33, 32.

23. Aug. 4 and 6, 1906, July 23 and Aug. 28, 1908 letters (*Home,* 6–8, 81).

24. Aug. 5, 1909 letter (*Home,* 101).

25. Aug. 13 and 29, 1909 letters (*Home,* 102, 105).

26. Dec. 1910 and Jan. 31, 1911 letters (*Home,* 113, 131).

27. June 24, 1911, Sept. 12, 1912, April 26, 1913 letters (*Home,* 173, 231, 254).

28. "I haven't written since I got your wire as I was waiting for details," he wrote on June 4 (*Home,* 303). That seems to have been the same wire whose receipt a friend witnessed. "A telegram had been handed to him at dinner, but Lawrence glanced at it, crumpled it into his pocket, and went on with what he was saying. After dinner I ventured to hope that his news was good. 'It was only about my brother,' he said. 'I can't think why they bothered to wire me.'…Whatever his feelings were…, Lawrence kept them almost savagely to himself" (Hill, 593).

29. Letters: June 4, 1915 and undated (June 1915?) (*Home,* 304).

30. June 16, July 3, 27, 1915 letters (*Home,* 305–7).

31. Garnett, 294; May 21, 1921 letter to Graves (Harvard).

32. Aldington, 350; Lawrence, April 14, 1927 letter to Mrs. Shaw (Brown, 325).

33. Leeds, 120.

34. Nov. 22, Dec. 19, 1923 letters (*Home,* 356).

35. Dec. 28, 1925, Dec. 1, 1926, July 6, 1926 letters (*ibid.,* 298, 363, 362).

36. 1927 letters: April 14 to Charlotte Shaw, June 16 to his mother (Brown, 325, 334), April 21 to Charlotte Shaw (BM).

37. July 10, 1928, April 14, 1927 letters to Charlotte Shaw (BM; Brown, 325).

38. Letters: April 14, 1927 to Charlotte Shaw (Brown, 325), July 27, 1934 to Lady Astor (Reading).

39. Celandine Kennington, "Mrs. Lawrence," 15-page paper, and "T. E. And His Mother," 3-page paper, both undated (195?), Bodleian; Louisa Young, 254–5.

40. Ocampo, 29–33.

41. May 18, 1924 letter (*Home,* 358).

42. Jan. 11, 1927 letter (Brown, 315). Lawrence had not felt that way about American missionaries educating Syrians.

43. Feb. 24, 1927 letter (*Home,* 365).

44. May 11, 1934 letter to Lady Astor (Brown, 487).

45. Jan. 4, 1928, Nov. 5, 1933, Sept. 27, 1933 letters (*Home,* 370, 382, 381).

46. Nov. 4, 1927 letter (*Home,* 369).

47. Aug. 17, 1929? letter from Sarah Lawrence to Lawrence (BM, RP 2207); Sept. 27 and Dec. 17, 1933 letters to his mother (*Home,* 382–3); Sarah Lawrence, Feb. 26, 1935 letter to T.E. (Bodleian).

48. Undated letter to Charlotte Shaw, Sept. or

Oct. 1929 (Mack, 381); Oct. 24, 1930 letter to Florence Hardy (Wilson, 1993, 52).

49. Nov. 23, 1932 letter to Mrs. Knowles (Wilson, 1993, 53); C. Kennington, "T. E. And His Mother," *op. cit.*

50. 1931 letters: April 25 to his mother (*Home,* 378); Sarah Lawrence, May 25 to Guy (Harvard).

51. Aug. 17, 1929, Aug. 17, 1934 letters (BM, RP 2207; Bodleian).

52. July 27, 1934 letter to Lady Astor (Brown, 494).

53. Sarah Lawrence, Feb. 26, 1935 letter (Bodleian); April 22, 1935 letter to Mrs. Hardy (Garnett, 869).

54. Knowles, 42; Sarah Lawrence, Feb. 26, 1935 letter (Bodleian).

55. Mack, 33; Brown, 298 note; C. Kennington, "T. E. And His Mother."

56. April 14, 1927 and May 8, 1928 letters to Charlotte Shaw (Brown, 324; Mack, 31).

15. Brothers

1. *Friends,* 28, 30.

2. Letters: May 12, 1927 to Charlotte Shaw (BM), July 27, 1934 to Lady Astor (Reading).

3. Lawrence, April 11, 1911 letter (*Home,* 147); Arnold Lawrence, Oct. 10, 1961 letter to Anthony Nutting dismissing a story that the brothers had vowed not to marry (Bodleian).

4. *Home,* 601, 611.

5. Oct. 30, 1914 and Jan. 2, 1915 letters to Will (*Home,* 630, 645–6).

6. T.E., May 19, 1911 letter home; Frank, Jan. 2, 1915 letter to Will (*Home,* 159–60, 646).

7. Nov. 16, 1914 letter delivered after Frank's death (*Home,* 718–9).

8. July 17, 1915 letter (Bodleian).

9. E. F. Hall in Mack, 15; Ernest Barker in *Home,* 397. T.E.'s remark was noted in Lady Scott's May 11, 1921 diary (James, 1995, 256).

10. Aug. 16, 1906 and June 8, 1911 letters (*Home,* 45, 164–5).

11. Will Lawrence, Feb. 26, 1914 letter (*Home,* 507).

12. 1913 letters: Sept. 16 to his father, Nov. 13 to his mother (*Home,* 442–3, 467).

13. May 19 and 29, 1911 letters home (*Home,* 164).

14. *Delhi Mission News* story quoted by Will and various letters to his family (*Home,* 567, 473, 476, 480, 504).

15. Oct. 28 and Jan. 1, 1914, and Dec. 4, 1913 letters (*Home,* 580, 487, 477).

16. Feb. 7, 26, and June 18, 1914 letters (*Home,* 501, 505, 545).

17. Various letters (*Home,* 544, 493, 502, 595).

18. Aug. 15 and June 3, 1914 letters (*Home,* 568, 539).

19. Jan. 27, 1915, July 30, 1914 letters (*Home,* 587, 562–3).

20. Various letters to his family (*Home,* 474, 512, 537, 541).

21. 1914 letters: Aug. 5, Sept. 23, Oct. 15, Nov.19 (*Home,* 565–6, 572, 576, 583).

22. Oct. 30, 1914, Jan. 21, 1915 letters (*Home,* 628, 584–5).

23. Mack, 14; Ernest Cox, *Friends,* 37; passage in T.E.'s Aug. 14, 1906 letter deleted in *Home Letters* (Mack, 53).

24. Mack, 65; Robert Lawrence, Oct. 15, 1969 letter to Stanhope Landick (18).

25. Letters: May 3, 1930 to Lucas (Garnett, 691); May 20, 1931 to Arnold Lawrence (Bodleian).

26. Note on the typescript of Liddell Hart's biography (*B:LH,* 79); July 27, 1934 letter to Lady Astor (Brown, 494).

27. *Home,* x. "The omitted passages…express anything critical or insulting about other persons or places, negative or discordant comments, some complaints, boyish accounts of politics,…various small kindnesses" (Mack, 51).

28. Oct. 15, 1969 letter to Landick (18); C. Kennington, "T. E. And His Mother," 3-page typescript, 1955? (Bodleian).

29. Jan. 29, 1965, Feb. 1, 1966, Sept. 16 and Oct. 16, 1968 letters to Landick (4, 6, 14, 15).

30. Sarah Lawrence, *Friends,* 29.

31. Arnold, *Friends,* 585; T.E., Dec. 31, 1910 and April 11, 1911 letters (*Home,* 123, 147).

32. Oct. 19, 1917 letter (*Home,* 342).

33. "About 1922 or 1923 [actually, 1924], Lawrence told…Arnold of his parents' legal inability to marry. Arnold laughed and T.E. told him that his parents did not regard it at all as a laughing matter and…he was 'practically a pervert' for taking it lightly" (Mack, 477). Lawrence himself purported to make light of it to his mother in 1919.

34. Obituary, "Professor A. W. Lawence," *The Times,* April 6, 1991.

35. Aug. 18, 1924 letter to his mother (*Home,* 359).

36. Jan. 28, 1926, May 15, 1927 letters to Cape (Bodleian; Texas).

37. April 20, 1926 letter (Bodleian); obituary notice of Arnold Lawrence (*The Independent,* April 1, 1991).

38. According to Clifford Irwin (Nov. 20, 1990 conversation).

39. Jan. 11 and Nov. 4, 1927 letters to his mother (Bodleian).

40. Letters: May 12, 1927 to Charlotte Shaw (BM), Jan. 4, 1928 to his mother (Bodleian).

41. 1927 letters: May 12 to Mrs. Shaw (BM), May 19 to Hogarth (Bodleian).

42. Arnold Lawrence, June 15, 1927 letter to Graves (Bodleian).

43. Letters: June 10, 1931 to Cockerell (Texas), Sept. 27, 1933 to his mother (Brown, 477).

44. "Letters of T. E. Lawrence (T. E. Shaw)," undated (1935) one-page printed sheet distributed to those who might have a letter from Lawrence (BM Ad. Ms. 56499).

45. Jeremy Wilson, Feb. 25, 1998, telstudies @lists.netlink.co.uk.

46. Graves, Dec. 10, 1935 letter to Liddell Hart and comments by Paul O'Prey (260, 268–9).

47. March 20, 1944 diary, Lees-Milne, 39.

48. R. M. Cook, obituary (*The Independent*, April 1, 1991).

49. 1951 letter to Patrick Knowles (62).

50. Cook, *op. cit.*; Mack, 17.

51. Feb. 23, 1955 letter to Alan Bird (Aldington, 1975, 15).

52. Save for £57,000 left to his two grandchildren, the bulk of the estate went to the *Seven Pillars* Trust.

53. Seymour-Smith, 497; Morris and Raskin, 35–6.

54. Morris and Raskin, 158, 175, 35, 147–8; they report (175) Arnold Lawrence as saying that £12,500 of the £17,500 he received for the film rights would go to charities (presumably via the Lawrence trusts). The latter figure does not match the £30,000 he was initially to receive.

55. Weintraub, March 19, 1992 letter to Fred Crawford (141–2).

56. *Sunday Times*, June 9, 16, 23, 30, 1968.

57. *Friends*, 592.

58. Knightley, 156. In an Oct. 31, 1990 letter to me, Colin Simpson blames the sensational third installment on Associate Editor Leonard Russell and says nothing about his own role or Knightley's. Knightley (157) states, "Leonard Russell…took the blame, diverting…[Arnold Lawrence's] wrath from me, Simpson and the newspaper by saying, incorrectly, that the decision [on the Bruce story] had been his and his alone."

59. This summary is derived from Knightley, 158–9, and a copy of the contract (IWM). The two sources are largely, but not entirely, consistent.

60. In a Dec. 1975 letter to Stewart, Arnold's wife Barbara said that "neither he [Arnold] nor the Bodleian" wish to admit more persons" (Stewart, letter, *Sunday Times*, June 26, 1977).

61. Colin Simpson, *Sunday Times*, June 12, 1977, 2.

62. Jeremy Wilson, Feb. 28, 1993 letter to Fred Crawford, *T. E. Notes*, May 1993, 4–5.

63. Wilson, 17; Brown, xi.

64. Ocampo, 33, 15.

16. Friends

1. This section draws on Orlans, 1995, where sources not otherwise identified are given.

2. Graves, *B:RG*, 10, and March 25, 1923 letter to Mrs. Hardy (Orlans, 50–1).

3. *B:RG*, 4; Sept. 16, 1926 letter (*B:RG*, 37–8).

4. Graves, undated (Sept. 1933?) letter (Seymour-Smith, 257).

5. Aug. 14, 1927 letter to Lionel Curtis (Garnett, 530).

6. Graves, 55, 407–8; Lawrence, Aug. 3, 1927 letter to Graves (*B:RG*, 116); Graves, Dec. 21, 1935 letter to Liddell Hart (O'Prey, 262).

7. Sept. 1933? letter (Seymour-Smith, 258).

8. Letters: May 5, 1929, Nov. 12, 1933, Dec. 17, 1933, May 4, 1934 (*B:RG*, 158, 174–6).

9. Nov. 1933 letter (*Letters*, 112–3).

10. Dec. 21, 1935, June 9, 1954, Feb. 6, 1955 letters to Liddell Hart (O'Prey, 262; O'Prey, 1990, 137, 142; *B:RG*, 135).

11. Forster, *Friends*, 282; Feb. 20, 1924 letter to Forster (Garnett, 455, 457).

12. *Friends*, 282; Forster, 344; March 23, 1924 letter to Alice Forster (Lago, 50).

13. Lawrence, July 24, 1924 letter to Forster (Garnett, 462); Forster, Dec. 12, 1926 letter to Florence Barger (Lago, 75).

14. Letters: Forster, Nov. 17, 1927 to Lawrence (Lago, 81); Lawrence, Dec. 21, 1927, Feb. 16, 1928 to Forster (Kings).

15. Letters: Forster, Aug. 9, 1927 to Lawrence (Lago, 80); Lawrence, Sept. 8, 1927 to Forster (Brown, 347).

16. Dec. 21, 1927 letter (Brown, 360–1).

17. March 15, 1928 letter to Lawrence (Lago, 83); *Friends*, 284–5; May 31, 1935 letter to Charles Mauron (Lago, 131–2).

18. March 20, 1923 letter (Orlans, 181–2).

19. Letters: Graves, March 25, 1923 to Mrs. Hardy (Texas); Lawrence, March 30, 1923 to Kennington (Garnett, 406).

20. 1923 letters: May 21 to Mrs. Hardy, July 23 to Hogarth, Sept. 8 to Graves (Garnett, 424, 429–30).

21. Titterington quote (Knight, 66); undated (Sept. 1924?) letter from Mrs. Hardy to Louise Yearley (Knight, 45).

22. Florence Hardy, April 11, 1924 letter to Sydney Cockerell (Knight, 35).

23. 1927 letters: Jan. 11 to Florence Hardy (Garnett, 503); Florence, June 13 to Graves (Legg, 53).

24. 1928 letters: Jan. 15 to Mrs. Hardy (Garnett, 564–5), March 5 to Lawrence (Mack, 373; Brown, 365 note).

25. 1928 letters: Charlotte Shaw, Jan. 16 (Dunbar, 265); Lawrence, April 14 (Garnett, 582).

26. Feb. 2, 1928 letter to Cockerell (Garnett, 574).

27. Letter (Aug. 1935?) to Marguerite Roberts (Knight, 106).

28. Richards, 20, 43; Richards, 1939, 19, 18.

29. Knightley and Simpson, 29); Richards, 1939, 132.

30. Their sensitivity to their sons' homosexual friends is evident in a letter from Will urging his mother not to worry about Frank's friend: "he has got sense…enough not to compromise anyone's reputation … he avoided a fresher…at St. John's, so that nobody would suspect the man of being of like sort to himself" (Jan. 22, 1914 letter, *Home*, 494).

31. Jan. 31, 1911 letter (*Home*, 132).

32. Dec. 10, 1913 and March 1916 letters to Richards (Garnett, 161, 201–2).

33. July 15, 1918 letter (Brown, 150–1).

34. March 29, 1927 letter to Charlotte Shaw (Brown, 321); Wilson, 681.

35. Richards, 189, 201, 218, 240; 1939, 13, 14, 29, 120, 125.

36. Early 1923 letter to Richards (Brown, 223).

37. May 1, 1955 letter to Liddell Hart (Texas).

38. Graves, 18.

39. Mack, 58–9.

40. April 11, 1911 letter to his mother (Brown, 35).

41. Mack, 59 (quoting Hogarth's son William).

42. "Our cook can't grasp a word of English, which explains his continued presence…after Woolley…had expressed his desire (in front of the whole camp) to bugger him with a rough stick," Lawrence wrote Leeds (89). E. M. Forster, but to my knowledge no one else, noted that Lawrence could be surprisingly bawdy.

43. Wilson, 115.

44. Dec. 7, 1927 letter to Dick Knowles (Garnett, 553); Kedourie, 94.

45. *Seven Pillars*, 57.

46. Rothenstein, n.p.

47. Garnett, 352.

48. June 13 and 27, 1923 letters (Garnett, 424–6).

49. Oct. 29, 1922, July 23, 1923 letters to Hogarth (Garnett, 374, 428–9).

50. 1924 letters: March 26 to Charlotte Shaw (Brown, 261), May 9 to his mother (*Home*, 357).

51. May 9, 1924 letter to Hogarth (Garnett, 460); undated letter (1925?) from Hogarth to Storrs (467, note).

52. 1927 letters: June 1 to Hogarth (copy, IWM); Oct. 9, Hogarth to Lawrence (Bodleian).

53. Letters: Nov. 10, 1927 to Buxton (copy, IWM), April 14, 1928 to Rothenstein (Garnett, 583); 1933 remark to Liddell Hart (*B:LH*, 168).

54. Laura Hogarth, Dec. 18, 1927, March 14, 1928 letters to Lawrence (Bodleian; Orlans, 296 note 11).

55. Feb. 25, 1928 letter to Charlotte Shaw (Orlans, 51).

56. 1922 letters: Aug. 17 to Shaw, Aug. 25 reply (Shaw 2000, 5, 7).

57. 1922 letters: Nov. 30 to Shaw, Dec. 1 reply (Shaw 2000, 11, 12).

58. 1922 letters: Dec. 7 to Shaw, Dec. 17 reply (Shaw 2000, 15–16, 18–19).

59. Cited in Orlans, 218–23.

60. Weintraub, 279.

61. Letters: Jan. 21, 1924 to Hogarth, April 14, 1928 to Rothenstein, July 2, 1931 letter to Hanley (Garnett, 452, 583, 728).

62. Shaw, May 31, Nov. 12, 1923 letters to Baldwin (Shaw 2000, 43, 46).

63. Lawrence, Jan. 14, 1924 letter to Shaw; Shaw, April 20, 1925 letter to Lawrence (Shaw, 2000, 58, 128).

64. Subscribers' edition, Aug. 15, 1926 preface.

65. Undated (June 1925?) letter from Shaw to Edward Garnett (Garnett, 477).

66. Bernard Shaw, Preface, *Catalogue of an Exhibition of Paintings…* (London: Leicester Galleries, 1927) 9–10.

67. Feb. 15, 1927 letter to Kennington (Garnett, 509); "bubble and squeak" is "A dish of meat and cabbage fried up together," named for the sounds made in cooking (*Oxford English Dictionary*).

68. *Friends*, 243, 246; Shaw, 40–1.

69. Dunbar, 232; Holroyd, 102.

70. June 17, 1926, Jan. 28, 1927 letters to Charlotte Shaw (Brown, 302; BM).

71. *Friends*, 247; Shaw, 39–40.

72. Letters cited by Holroyd, 102; Robert Boothby, *Recollections of a Rebel* (London: Hutchinson, 1978) 79.

73. Shaw, 40; Weintraub, 280.

74. Holroyd, 102; Weintraub, 280.

75. Dunbar, 76.

76. Nov. 4, 1896 letter to Terry (Dunbar, 111).

77. Dec. 31, 1922 letter to Lawrence (Shaw, 2000, 26).

78. June 10, 1924, July 4, 1925, Sept. 28, 1925 letters (Shaw, 2000, 78, 141, 149).

79. June 16 and March 29, 1927 letters (Wilson, 788; Brown, 305, 321–2).

80. Jan. 8, 1923, April 14, 1927 letters (Brown, 219, 324–5).

81. Dunbar, 250; May 17, 1927 letter to Lawrence (Dunbar, 251–3).

82. Letters: Dec. 5, 1930 to Mrs. Shaw (Brown, 447), June 28, 1929 to Doubleday (Garnett, 662); Holroyd, 102.

83. Shaw, 40.

84. Dunbar, 269; June 24, 1936 letter to Dorothy Walker (Dunbar, 270).

85. Wilson, 1141 note 43; March 6, 1939 letter to Dorothy Walker (Dunbar, 270).

86. March 10, 1923, April 27, 1929 letters (Garnett, 402, 655).

87. Jan. 26, 1935 letter (Garnett, 841–2); Aug. 29, 1972 interview with Mack (442).

88. Aug. 25, Sept. 7, 1925 letters (Garnett, 480–1, 485).

89. May 10, 1935 letter to Palmer (Brown, 539).

90. Feb. 22, 1923 letter to Kennington (Wilson, 703). The "Greek God" remark was Chambers's (Mack, 323); "vile," his recollection of what Lawrence had said. Lawrence refers to the accent more affectionately in his March 21, 1923 letter to Guy (Brown, 231).

91. March 21, 1923 letter to Guy (Brown, 230–1); Stewart, 276 (Lawrence's check was dated March 31, 1923).

92. Sept. 17, 1923 letter (Brown, 244). Misleading or false statements in this letter indicate that Lawrence made light of a substantial gift.

93. Dec. 25, 1923 letter (Brown, 253).

94. July 29, 1929, July 29, 1930, Sept. 30, 1931, Nov. 16, 1934 letters to Guy (Harvard).

95. Stewart, 275–6; Wilson, 703–4.

17. Illegitimacy and Pseudonyms

1. Malcolm Brown, Obituary, *The Independent*, April 4, 1991.

2. Mack, 26–7; April 14, 1927 letter to Charlotte Shaw (Brown, 325).

3. Mack, 12–13; Arnold Lawrence, "Knowledge of Illegitimacy," one page, handwritten, Feb. 1963 (Bodleian).

4. Mack, 29. Lord Vansittart, Lawrence's second cousin, said, "My father told me that Lawrence's father was really Chapman, an Anglo-Irish baronet…. He told it without censure. I listened without attention" (Vansittart, *Daily Telegraph?* Jan. 31, 1955).

5. April 14, 1927 letter to Charlotte Shaw (Brown, 325). Evidently, when Sarah was alone with T.E., she showed him a letter his father had prepared to be read by his sons after his death. That only T.E. saw this confession is indicated by his remark to David Hogarth, "I don't think my elder brother knows anything of that story of our origins which I sent you. I told A. [Arnold] a little of it, three years ago" (Sept. 15, 1927 letter, Orlans, 1996, 24). That jibes with Arnold Lawrence's recollection that "T.E.L. told me in 1924 that the story was still talked of in London society" ("Knowledge of Illegitimacy," Bodleian, 1963).

6. Vansittart, *op. cit.*; Garnett, 1962, 104.

7. Rowse, 255; Wilson, 667; Stamfordham, March 15, 1927 letter to General Wingate (IWM copy).

8. The confession may have been designed to win Amery's approval for Lawrence's enlistment in the Navy under a pseudonym.

9. *B:LH*, 78; Liddell Hart, 3–4.

10. Orlans, 1996, 20–1.

11. Kenneth Young, ed., *The Diaries of Sir Bruce Lockhardt* (New York: St. Martin's, 1973) vol. I, 320; Jones, 129.

12. Aug. 29, Sept. 4, 1946 letters (IWM, copies).

13. Mack, 11.

14. Oct. 22, 1912 letter (*Home*, 239).

15. Sept. 12, 1919 memorandum (Wilson, 618–19).

16. 1920 letters: Feb. 16 to Newcombe (Garnett, 299), April to Pound (Brown, 178).

17. March 20, 1920 letter to Doubleday (Garnett, 301).

18. *The Mint*, 135.

19. Dec. 21, 1922 letter to Robin Buxton (Garnett, 388).

20. Garnett, 350, 352.

21. Feb. 16, 1923 letter (Garnett, 401).

22. "Thomas Edward Ross" rented Clouds Hill and, in 1929, became its freehold owner. "John Hume Ross" had checking accounts in the Bank of Liverpool and Martins Bank. "T. E. Ross" registered at a Newquay hotel in May 1929 and became a Youth Hostels member in March 1935.

23. Feb. 6, 1925 letter to Trenchard (Brown, 277).

24. Aug. 3 and Dec. 1924 letters to Chambers (Bodleian).

25. "Smith only in U.J.C. [the Union Jack Club in London] Shaw here [Southampton] & everywhere else," he instructed Guy on Feb. 28, 1934 (Harvard).

26. Feb. 1, 1927 letter to Cape (Texas). Lawrence did not ask his solicitor to change his name to "Shaw" until June 16, 1927.

27. Letters: June 18, 1927 to Allanson (Texas); June 28, 1933 to Rogers (1936).

28. March 13, 1930 letter to Thurtle (Garnett, 685).

29. Jan. 4, 1923 letter (Shaw, 2000, 30).

30. Letters: Doughty, undated (1921?) (BM, RP 2207); Nov. 12, 1923, Shaw to Baldwin (Shaw, 2000, 45–6).

31. "For dinner, Winston made Lawrence put on his Arab robes. It was Winston who had kept the robes" (Patrick Buchan-Hepburn in Martin Gilbert, *In Search of Churchill*, New York: John Wiley, 1994, 306).

32. *Naval and Military Record*, Feb. 25, 1931. I am indebted to Robert Archibald for a copy of this story; *B:LH*, 177.

33. Oxford Text, 698; a similar passage appears in *Seven Pillars*, 583.

34. The implication of several remarks, Malcolm Brown (xxvi) writes, "is surely that he hoped he might somehow be able in due time to graft the 'Lawrence' branch of the family back into the family tree…. There is … a hint of weariness with his various identities." "Ramping" (*Journal of the Royal Air Force College*, Spring 1931) was signed "J.C."

35. From at least 1930 onward, he used the name A/C Smith at the Union Jack Club, London; in March 1934, he became a member of the London Central YMCA as "Mr. E. Smith."

36. Letters: Aug. 25, 1927 to Doubleday (Princeton); June 10, 1931 to Savage (Garnett, 721).

37. Mack, 446.

18. Sociable and Solitary

1. April 5, 1935 letter to H. S. Ede (61).

2. Aug. 1910 letter to his mother (*Home*, 110).

3. Dec. 7, 1931 letter to Edward Eliot, who asked him to talk at a girls' school (Brown, 460).

4. Lionel Curtis (*Friends*, 159–60).

5. Liddell Hart, 390.

6. Nov. 29, 1924 letter to Charlotte Shaw (2000, 115). The forest was New Forest, where the Lawrences lived before moving to Oxford.

7. May 14, 1923 letter to Curtis (Garnett, 416).

8. 1929 letters: May 9 to Ede (35); Feb. 28 to Lady Scott (Cambridge); Dec. 5 to Dawnay (Bodleian).

9. Letters: May 16, 1925 to Charlotte Shaw (2000, 135), Nov. 26, 1934 to Lady Astor (Brown, 502).

10. Forster (*Friends,* 285).

11. Letters: May 30, 1929 to Forster (Kings), May 6, 1935 to Kennington (Brown, 537).

12. Aug. 24, 1926 letter to Charlotte Shaw (2000, 196).

13. April 6, 1934, Nov. 5, 1933 letters to his mother (*Home,* 388, 383).

14. Letters: Dec. 11, 1934 to Williamson (70); May 6, 1935 to Kennington (Brown, 537).

15. 1935 letters: April 1 to Wrench, May 6 to Rogers (Brown, 530, 536).

16. May 10, 1935 letter to Palmer (Brown, 540).

17. Wilson, 1988, 183; Sergeant Pugh in Graves, 434.

18. Lawrence James, July 29, 1998 letter to author.

19. G. B. Shaw in *Friends,* 244; Siegfried Sassoon (187) called Russell "the Patroclus" of Clouds Hill.

20. A pocket-case for needles, threads, scissors, etc.

21. Sept. 7, 1925 letter to E. Palmer (Garnett, 484).

22. Garnett, 1979, 199–200.

23. Airman J. T. Parson and A. E. Chambers in *Friends,* 573, 341.

24. "My chauffeur is becoming impertinent (Rolls-Royce). Can you tell me where to get another man? Forgive my asking, but you know everything" (March 1, 1932 letter, Bodleian); the other letters cited in this paragraph are also in the Bodleian.

25. Letters: March 15, 1927 to Richards, Sept. 11, 1931 to Buxton (Bodleian).

26. March 30, 1932 letter to Manning Pike (Texas copy).

27. Jan. 30, 1933 letter (Bodleian copy).

28. I am indebted to Lawrence James, who interviewed this sailor (then in his seventies) in 1992 or '93, for this information.

29. July 4, 1932 letter to Marshall (Bodleian copy).

30. 1933 letters: May 30 and July 16, 1933 to C. J. Greenwood (Bodleian copies); Dec. 3 to Marshall (Texas).

31. 1934 letters: Nov. 16 to unidentified man (Harvard), July 20 to Jeffrey (Bodleian copy).

32. *Friends,* 591.

33. 1933 letters: Dec. 28 to Altounyan (Bodleian), Dec. 31 to Mrs. Shaw (BM).

34. Rev. H. D. Littler (Brown and Cave, 18–19); July 21, 1920 letter to Graves (*B:RG,* 7); Dunn (*Friends,* 449).

35. May 20, 1923 entry (Gregory, 214); Lawrence, Dec. 25, 1927 letter to Edward Garnett (Mack, 369).

36. Aug. 20, 1933 conversation with Liddell Hart (*B:LH,* 163).

37. *Seven Pillars,* 580; note on typescript of Graves's 1927 biography (*B:RG,* 80).

38. *Friends,* 92, 84; Fontana, Jan. 13, 1921 letter to Lawrence (Bodleian).

39. Hill, 593; Robinson, 102, 147.

40. Kennington (*Friends,* 264); Garnett, 1979, 198.

41. Dec. 31, 1933 letter to Ede (58).

42. Graves, 56; Forster (*Friends,* 285).

43. March 1, 1927 letter to Edward Garnett (Garnett, 511). "[I]n company … I felt fear, disgust, boredom, but anger very seldom; and I was never passionate. Only once or twice, when I was alone and lost in the desert,…did I break down" (Oxford Text, 644).

44. July 14, 1927 letter to Dick Knowles (Bodleian).

45. Arnold Lawrence (*Friends,* 591); Liddell Hart, notes of a June 27, 1935 conversation with Trenchard (Patrick).

46. July 19, 1934, July 14, 1927, Aug. 3, 1930 letters to Charlotte Shaw (BM).

47. Oxford Text, 40; July 7, 1925 letter to Kennington (Wilson, 1988, 64).

48. Oct. 15, 1924 letter to Francis Sterling (Brown, 275); Storrs, 474–5. In a BBC talk on the biography, Storrs said, "Lawrence's defects were recognised by most of us and discounted as not ultimately significant. We knew that he could be reckless in speech, irresponsible, misleading, tiresome, exasperating, maddening, stating as facts things which he knew nobody could or would accept." (The newspaper clipping from which this extract is taken was unidentified.)

49. April 1, 1935 letter to Wilfred Merton (Harvard); Lawrence gave elaborate instructions about how the copy should appear to come from Merton, though he would pay for it.

50. G. B. Shaw, Oct. 7, 1924 letter to Lawrence (Shaw, 1985, 885–6).

51. Nov. 2, 1923 letter to Buxton (Bodleian).

52. Letters: May 11, 1923 to Buxton (Jesus); March 15, 1927 letter to P. C. Joyce (Bodleian).

53. Feb. 7, 1964 letter to Donaree Gillespie posted Nov. 20, 1999 on TELIVES@aol.com.

54. Robert Graves (BBC); Williamson (Brown and Cave, 196).

55. Stirling, 83; Liddell Hart, *Memoirs* (London: Cassell, 1965) I, 356.

56. Taqui Altounyan, *Chimes from a Wooden Bell* (London: I. B. Tauris, 1990) 122; *Friends,* 312.

57. Cf. John Buchan (216), "I am not…much of a hero-worshipper, but I could have followed Lawrence over the edge of the world"; Rupert Hart-Davis, "I felt, for the only time in my life, that I could have followed him anywhere" (*The Power of Chance,* London: Sinclair-Stevenson, 1991, 81).

58. 1927 letters: May 12 to Charlotte Shaw (BM); Sept. 1 to Graves (Harvard).

59. March 29, 1928 letter to Graves (*B:RG,* 149).

60. *The Mint,* 205–6; letters: Aug. 6, 1928 to Forster (Garnett, 620), Dec. 7, 1927 to Dick Knowles (Knowles, 93).

61. Letters: July 25, 1933 to Marshall (Texas), Sept. 15, 1927 to Kennington (Wilson, 705).

62. Nov. 16, 1934 letter to Charlotte Shaw (BM); *Seven Pillars,* 30, 674.

63. *Friends*, 119–20; Simpson and Knightley, *Sunday Times*, June 23, 1968.

64. Jock Chambers (BBC); Arnold Lawrence in Flavell, 11.

65. Lady Scott, undated handwritten note (Cambridge). Louise Young (201) gives a similar version.

19. Political Outlook

1. George Orwell, "England Your England" (1941), *A Collection of Essays* (New York: Harcourt Brace Jovanovich, 1953), 274, 270.

2. Samuel Hynes, *The Auden Generation* (Princeton: Princeton University Press, 1982), 18.

3. Sept. 12, 1912 letter to Mrs. Rieder (Garnett, 148); undated letter inserted in the *Seven Pillars* Lawrence gave the Bodleian.

4. *Seven Pillars*, 24.

5. Kedourie, 88, 105. Robert Graves used identical words: "Ultimately, he was not interested in ideas." (Frank Kersnowski, ed., *Conversations with Robert Graves*, Jackson, MS: University Press of Mississippi, 1989, 105).

6. *Seven Pillars*, 22, 41.

7. "Hussein's usefulness did not extend beyond 1916" (Nov. 24, 1927 letter to Charlotte Shaw, BM).

8. *Seven Pillars*, 23.

9. Undated (1928) letter to D. G. Pearman (Garnett, 578).

10. November 1918 exchange recounted in Lawrence's Oct. 18, 1927 letter to Charlotte Shaw (Brown, 350).

11. "A slow progress, utilising only the resources of Syria itself, seems to me more desirable than foreign borrowing and a forcing bed of public enterprises," Lawrence wrote General Clayton in September 1917 (James, 168).

12. Dixon in *Friends*, 371; June 24, 1926 letter to Charlotte Shaw (2000, 186–7).

13. Isham and Shaw (*Friends*, 301–3, 245–6).

14. Webb, 107–8 and March 20, 1927 diary entry (118).

15. April 5, 1935 letter to Ede (61); Thurtle in *Friends*, 354–5.

16. Unidentified letter cited in Ernest Thurtle, *Time's Winged Chariot* (London: Chaterson, 1945), 355.

17. May 17, 1934 letter to Capt. Lloyd-James, a Mosley supporter (Wilson, 917). I read "pandering" in the Bodleian copy, not Wilson's "parading."

18. Letters: Dec. 20, 1934 to Day Lewis, March 21, 1930 to Buchan (Garnett, 839, 686).

19. Dec. 7, 1934 letter (Brown, 506).

20. Letters: April 20 and 29, 1931 to Charlotte Shaw (BM), Dec. 20, 1934 to Day Lewis (Orlans, 287).

21. *B:LH*, 211, 209, 222; July 29, 1929 letter to Thurtle (Garnett, 669).

22. Dec. 17, 1933 letter to his mother (*Home*, 384).

23. Letters: June 10, 1927 to Marsh, March 19, 1934 to Curtis (Garnett, 521–2, 792–3).

24. Jan. 7, 1935 letter to A. S. Frere-Reeves (Texas).

25. Lönnroth, 93. Peter Metcalfe identifies Lönnroth's source as Lüdecke's *I Knew Hitler* (London: Jarrolds, 1938) 287: "For years I tried to get in touch with him. Finally, in 1932, he sent me word through a mutual friend that in England the time was not ripe for action."

26. Williamson, *Goodbye West Country* (Boston: Little, Brown, 1938) 228 and *Friends*, 455.

27. "[N]owhere in the correspondence between these two men, nor in HW's diaries, or private papers have we found any mention of fascism or Adolf Hitler in connection with T. E. Lawrence. If such material existed, it would be there for HW never destroyed anything" (*Henry Williamson Society Journal*, March 1993, 29–30).

28. In a Feb. 8, 1955 letter to David Garnett, Williamson said, "the letter about the TEL–Hitler meeting (actually it was a peace-meeting or broadcast in London ... was written: and I thought posted: although hundreds...of letters... have, during the years, been thrown aside in books, cupboards, etc." (*Henry Williamson Society Journal*, September 1993, 16).

29. May 12, 1934 letter to Lloyd-James (Wilson, 916–7).

30. Liddell Hart notes of a June 25, 1934 talk with Lawrence (*B:LH*, 222).

31. May 17, 1934 letter to Lloyd-James (Bodleian copy; see also Wilson, 917).

32. Liddell Hart notes of a June 25, 1934 talk (*B:LH*, 223); I have added a few words from the original notes (Texas).

33. May 31, 1935 letter to Charles Mauron (Lago and Furbank, 131); Robert Graves and Alan Hodge, *The Long Week End* (New York: Macmillan, 1941), 207.

34. May 26, 1927 letter to Charlotte Shaw (BM).

35. Churchill and Isham (*Friends*, 194, 300, 307).

36. Wilson, 578; July 19, 1934 letter to Charlotte Shaw (BM).

37. Letters: June 11, 1928 to Charlotte Shaw (BM), April 25, 1928 to Richards (Bodleian), Jan. 15, 1934 to Lady Astor (IWM copy).

38. Trenchard, July 6, 1928 letter (Hyde, 161); Lawrence, Aug. 5, 1928 reply (Bodleian).

39. Letters: Forster, May 24, 1936 to Leonard Woolf (Lago, 141); Tomlinson, Dec. 5, 1928 to Lawrence (*Letters*, 191).

40. Letters: June 26, 1930 to Liddell Hart (Garnett, 694–5), May 23, 1933 and March 6, 1935 to Thurtle (Mack, 395, Garnett, 860).

41. Various passages of *Seven Pillars* (mainly) and other writings.

20. *"My Name Is Legion"*

1. Shaw, 1985, 853; *B:LH,* 186.
2. *B:RG,* 185; *Friends,* 439.
3. *Friends,* 439.
4. Buchan, 1939, 373; *Seven Pillars,* 30; Buchan, 213.
5. Frederic Manning, Aug. 28, 1931 letter to Lawrence (*Letters,* 141).
6. May 1, 1928 letter to Trenchard (Garnett, 599).
7. *Seven Pillars,* 200; June 26, 1933 letter (Garnett, 769); *Seven Pillars,* 621, 352.
8. Brown and Cave, 112; *Secret,* 160;
9. *Seven Pillars,* 569, 334.
10. Oxford Text, 362; *Seven Pillars,* 24; *Friends,* 125.
11. *Seven Pillars,* 595, 598.
12. Stirling, 1933, 504–5; Lunt, 294.
13. Charmley, 65–6; *Seven Pillars,* 634.
14. *Seven Pillars,* 580; Aug. 28, 1928 letter to Charlotte Shaw (BM).
15. Feb. 25, 1930 letter to Charlotte Shaw (Brown, 439).
16. A. Rivington, "Notes on a talk with Jock Chambers," Dec. 13, 1968 (IWM).
17. Letters: March 19, 1923 to Curtis (Garnett, 412), April 27, 1927 to Edward Garnett (*T. E. Lawrence: Fifty Letters,* Austin: University of Texas, 1962, 19).
18. Wilson, 12.
19. Zionist agronomist Aaronsohn 1917 diary entry after Lawrence lectured him about Jewish settlements and Arab sentiments (Anthony Verrier, ed., *Agents of Empire,* London: Brassey's, 289).
20. *Seven Pillars,* 485; Aug. 15, 1922 letter to Clayton (Brown, 198).
21. Villars, 13; Garnett, 352. Sidney Cockerell observed that Lawrence's letters "exhibit his self-centred nature to an unpleasant degree,…and the desire for self-effacement which was so curiously contradicted by his vanity" (1940 diary entry, Blunt, 208).
22. "…ashamed of my awkwardness, of my physical envelope, and of my solitary unlikeness" (*Seven Pillars,* 579).
23. Letters: Jan. 5, 1920 to Doubleday (Bodleian), Aug. 17, 1920 to Blunt (FM), April 4, 1929 to Dow (Bodleian).
24. April 16, 1929 letter (Harvard). This passage strikes St. John Armitage as a case of Lawrence "teasing a man who was his friend by imitating—or, less likely, being insubodinate by—in British service parlance, … 'taking the piss' out of a superior" (Dec. 3, 1997, telstudies@lists. netlink.co.uk).
25. Namier (*Friends,* 225); Isherwood, 24.
26. Wavell (*Friends,* 148); A. T. P. Williams (Mack, 57).
27. Lawrence, Feb. 15, 1927 letter to Kennington (Garnett, 508); Kennington (*Friends,* 279).
28. Garnett and Liddell Hart (BBC).
29. *Friends,* 296, 297; May 15, 1930 letter to Manning (Garnett, 692).
30. *Friends,* 591, 589–90; Wilson, 670.
31. *Seven Pillars,* 582.
32. Oxford Text, 810; *Seven Pillars,* 682, 684; "in skilled hands it would have been, not Damascus, but Constantinople which was reached in 1918" (*ibid.,*149).
33. *Seven Pillars,* 24.
34. Letters: Oct. 4, 1923 to Edward Garnett (Garnett, 434); Sept. 29, 1925 to Charlotte Shaw (2000, 150).
35. June 10, 1927 letter (Garnett, 522).
36. *B:LH,* 112; Liddell Hart, "Talk with Lord Trenchard," June 27, 1935 (Texas).
37. Churchill in *Friends,* 200. These sentences reflect *Seven Pillars* passages already quoted. Both Lawrence, in writing them, and Churchill forgot his emaciated, overstrained state in Damascus, when "I hopped off like a scalded cat and swore that I'd never go back" (Feb. 4, 1923 letter in Brown, 223). This was not the condition of a modern Alexander poised to conquer the rest of the Middle East.
38. Nov. 3, 1933 letter to David Garnett (569 note); *Seven Pillars,* 582.
39. Nov. 11, 1922 letter to R. D. Blumenfeld (Brown, 212).
40. *Seven Pillars,* 582–3; Mark Cocker, *Richard Meinertzhagen* (London: Secker & Warburg, 1989) 99.
41. Letters: Dec. 27, 1923 to Wavell (Garnett, 449), July 19, 1924 to Edward Garnett (Bodleian).
42. Edward Garnett, May 3, 1928 letter (*Letters,* 99).
43. Oct. 29, 1928 letter to Herbert Baker (Brown, 385).
44. Dec. 21 and May 1, 1928 letters to Trenchard (Brown, 391; Bodleian).
45. Spencer (BBC); Devas, 90.
46. Oct. 12, 1932 letters to Elgar and Yeats (Garnett, 743–5).
47. Letters: March 26, 1924 to Charlotte Shaw (2000, 71); July 24, 1924, Sept. 8, 1927 to Forster (Orlans, 156–8).
48. Feb. 25, 1930 and Sept. 1, 1931 letters to Manning (Orlans, 204–6); Marwil, 276.
49. *Seven Pillars,* 582; Arnold Lawrence in *Friends,* 589.
50. Oxford Text, 796.
51. *Seven Pillars,* 581; Howe, 356.
52. Scattered passages of *Seven Pillars* (400, 404–5, 471, 473, 475–6). In a careful analysis, Michael Asher (296–7) contends that, except for Abdulla, most members of the bodyguard were infirm, incompetent, or old Syrian peasants. He dismisses Lawrence's claim that sixty died in his service: at most, "one or two."
53. Oct. 1, 1921 letter to Kennington (Garnett, 334).
54. Jan. 18, 1923 letter to Graves (*B:RG,* 24).
55. Sept. 28, 1925 and Jan. 2, 1928 letters to Mrs. Shaw (2000, 151; Wilson, 1988, 203); in the 1928

letter, "this dirt" refers to the barrack-room language in *The Mint*.

56. *Seven Pillars*, 315, 677; *Mint*, 69–70.

57. Buchan, 215; Jan 2, 1928 letter to Charlotte Shaw (Wilson, 1988, 203).

58. July 11, 1924 letter to Dawnay (Bodleian).

59. Buchan, 215; March 22, 1928 letter to Edward Garnett (Garnett, 580).

60. Sydney Catt in *T. E. Lawrence Society Newsletter*, Spring 1998, 2.

61. Feb. 6, 1955 letter to Charles Curran in Bonnie Scott, ed., *Selected Letters of Rebecca West* (New Haven: Yale University Press, 2000) 287. West met Lawrence several times in the summer of 1923, when he visited H. G. Wells, with whom she was living in Swanage. Though her memory may have been affected by Aldington's biography, which she had just read, West was highly critical of Aldington. Right or wrong, her strong, independent intellect was evident throughout her writing career.

62. *B:RG*, 126, 80; Sept. 10, 1930, Oct. 26, 1929 letters to Charlotte Shaw (BM; Brown, 430).

63. Forster, 1964, 142 and *Friends*, 283, 285; Villars, 347.

64. Wendy Hughes, (1967?) interview with Pat Knowles (IWM).

65. Richards, 187, and 1923 reply (Brown, 225).

66. Dunn (*Friends*, 447); Lawrence, April 1, 1929 letter to Doubleday (Princeton).

67. Letters: Feb. 4, 1935 to Graves (*B:RG*, 182), July 17, 1928 to Charlotte Shaw (BM); *The Mint*, 107.

68. Richards, 29. Graves calls the poem "exquisitally masochistic."

69. Letters: Sept. 25, 1933 to Ede (57); Oct. 15, 1924 to Stirling (Brown, 275)—I have restored the original ampersands.

70. Howe, 357; Coward, 265.

71. March 26, 1924 letter to Charlotte Shaw (2000, 71); Cherry-Garrard (*Friends*, 189).

72. Churchill in *Friends*, 198; Aldous Huxley, Dec. 12, 1946 letter in Grover Smith, ed., *Letters of Aldous Huxley* (New York: Harper & Row, 1969), 559; Kedourie, 88.

73. *Seven Pillars*, 581, 477.

74. *Seven Pillars*, 477, 579, 684.

75. Sept. 1, 1927 letter to Graves (Harvard).

76. *Seven Pillars*, 582.

77. Lewinsky, "On Some Aspects of Masochism," cited in Margaret Hanly, 198.

78. *Seven Pillars*, 30; Lönnroth, xiv.

79. Written on the draft of Liddell Hart's biography (*B:LH*, 106); Graves, June 29, 1954 letter to Liddell Hart (O'Prey, 1990, 137); *Seven Pillars*, 682.

80. Mack, 286, 310.

81. May 14, 1923 letter to Curtis (Garnett, 416).

82. Lady Gregory's May 19, 1923 entry while staying at Ayot St. Lawrence (Gregory, 212); 1924 letters: July 11 to Dawnay (Bodleian), Nov. 25 to Buxton (Garnett, 471).

83. 1928 letters: Aug. 6 to Forster, July 19 to G. B. Shaw (Garnett, 620, 618).

84. *Cats*, 39; Jan 3, 1935 letter to Ede, who deleted this sentence in Ede, 59; Brown, 511, reinstates it.

85. *Seven Pillars*, 477.

86. Kennington (*Friends*, 277); *B:RG*,63.

87. Mack, 368; Lawrence, Dec. 20, 1934 letter to Day Lewis (Garnett, 839).

88. *Seven Pillars*, 30, 477.

89. Namier in *Friends*, 227; Garnett, 1962, 110.

90. *Seven Pillars*, 356; Oct. 6, 1924 letter to H. C. Armstrong (Texas).

91. *B:RG*, 74; July 29, 1929 letter to Thurtle (Garnett, 669); Altounyan in *Friends*, 121.

92. *Seven Pillars*, 38, 421–2.

93. May 15, 1930 letter to Frederic Manning (Garnett, 692–3); Bennett, 52.

94. Letters: Aug. 28, 1908 to his mother (*Home*, 81); Dec. 22, 1927 to Curtis (Garnett, 559).

95. Letters: Feb. 4, 1935 to Lord Carlow, Dec. 20, 1934 to Day Lewis (Garnett, 850, 839).

96. Oxford Text, 697; Dec. 22, 1927 letter to Curtis (Garnett, 559).

97. February 1934 conversation with Williamson (62).

98. Graves, 49; Colin Wilson, *The Outsider* (London: Gallancz, 1956) 153; Pritchett, 386.

99. Letters: March 21, 1923 to Guy; Nov. 28, 1925 to Mrs. Shaw (Brown, 231, 289).

100. March 19, 1923 letter to Curtis (Garnett, 411); *Seven Pillars*, 582; Liddell Hart, 434.

101. Letters: April 9, 1931 to Marshall (Orlans, 286); Dec. 7, 1934 to Pound (Brown, 507).

102. February 1934 conversation with Henry Williamson (61).

103. Feb. 24, 1927 letter to Charlotte Shaw (Brown, 317); Kennington in *Friends*, 278–9.

104. "Hungry time has taken from me year by year more of the Creed's clauses till now only the first four words ["I believe in God"] remain. Them I say defiantly" (*The Mint*, 149).

21. Masochism and Sexuality

1. Villars, 45; Sept. 12, 1912 letter (*Home*, 231).

2. *Seven Pillars*, 387, 450, 459, 254, 461.

3. *Ibid.*, 40, 476; Pritchett, 385–6; cf.Vyvyan Richards (236–7), "He hated to be touched, he says; though I think that turned most upon your impulse in touching him."

4. Durrell (36), 1935 letter; Garnett in *Friends*, 433.

5. Lawrence, April 16, 1928 letter to Forster (Garnett, 594); Read, 2 (the review first appeared in 1938).

6. *Seven Pillars*, 454–5; Nov. 12, 1922 letter to Edward Garnett (Garnett, 380).

7. Letters: March 26, 1924 to Mrs. Shaw, May 14, 1923 to Curtis (Brown, 261, 236).

8. Mrs. Shaw, June 24, 1936 letter to Dorothy Walker (Dunbar, 269); Curtis in *Friends*, 260.

9. David Garnett (351).

10. Rodd, 383. The wrist incident occurred in mid–1926 (Graves, 430–1).

11. Garnett, 351. Fred Crawford (165) speculates that Lawrence may have refused hospitalization to conceal scars from a recent whipping.

12. Ede (49) places this episode in August 1931.

13. Hyde (33) suggests that T.E. was beaten with a tawse, a Scottish instrument "consisting of a leather strap or thong, divided into narrow strips." However, it was a cane. In a school paper on cricket, written at age 15, Lawrence says, "one player who has had a most extensive and varied acquaintance with canes, both at home and abroad [in France], declares that no cane *ever* stung like this [cricket] bat" (*JTELS*, Summer 1993, 8).

14. "As Mlle. Lambercier had a mother's affection...[she] sometimes carried it so far as to inflict...the punishment of infants.... I felt in my pain...a mixture of sensuality which left more desire than fear to experience it again from the same hand.... Who would believe it, that this childish chastisement, received at eight years old from the hand of a girl of thirty, should decide my tastes, my desires, my passions, for the rest of my days...?" (Rousseau, *Confessions,* Glover, tr., Book I).

15. *Seven Pillars,* Chapter LXXX.

16. June 28, 1919 memo to Stirling (Brown, 165–6).

17. March 26, 1924 letter to Charlotte Shaw (2000, 70).

18. Arthur Russell is said to be the source of this report.

19. Dec. 21, 1927 letter to E. M. Forster (Brown, 360).

20. A. Rivington?, memo on interview with T. W. Beaumont, 1967? (IWM).

21. Oxford Text, 513. The bracketed words were given by Jeremy Wilson, Jan. 3, 1998, telstudies@lists.netlink.co.uk.

22. The whippings were first revealed in four June 1968 *Sunday Times* articles by Colin Simpson and Phillip Knightley, especially the third (June 23), and, corrected and augmented, in Knightley and Simpson's *The Secret Lives of Lawrence of Arabia* (1969) and John Mack's *A Prince of Our Disorder* (1976). Arnold Lawrence learned of them in 1935 but kept the knowledge to himself. Robert Graves, Liddell Hart, Eric Kennington, and Charlotte Shaw seem to have known something about them, but published nothing (Mack, 523–4 note 51).

23. John Bruce, untitled 85-page manuscript (photocopy, IWM). This is the only instance I know where Lawrence so condemned his father; usually, he blamed his mother for "capturing" him.

24. Knightley and Simpson, 173–7.

25. *Seven Pillars,* 580.

26. Mack, 434.

27. May 11, 1923 and Dec. 27, 1922 letters from Lawrence to Wavell and G. B. Shaw, respectively (Brown, 235; Garnett, 390).

28. Mack, 434–5.

29. Mack, 433, evidently quoting the service companion he interviewed.

30. *Friends*, 591–2. Theodor Reik (284) notes that "The flagellation which originally served the purpose of self-castigation with early Christian monks and ascetics later became a means of sexual excitement.... Ultimately the Church was forced to forbid too severe expiatory practices because they frequently led to sexual gratification."

31. Mack, 438–9, 437.

32. *Ibid.,* 438, 433. Interviewed by Mack in 1968, an RAF witness to whippings said that he "had to look at [Lawrence's penis] ... to see if it liquidated, and it did" (Lockman, 132, note 7).

33. Oct. 31, 1990 letter to the author.

34. Mack, 437.

35. *Hampshire Chronicle* story, March 15, 1985, reprinted in *T. E. Notes,* 3&4, 1997, 18–29; and June 30, 2000 posting on www.auctions-on-line.com/phillips/auct/index.html by Phillips, London auctioneers.

36. Knightley and Simpson, 199–200.

37. Buchan, 216; Aug. 18, 1930 letter to F. N. Doubleday (Garnett, 698–72).

38. Oct. 31, 1990 letter from Colin Simpson to the author.

39. For example, Wilhelm Reich (232) asserts that "the masochistic character cannot be a leader" and tends "to feel stupid or ... appear stupid"; Karen Horney (277), that the masochist "is incapable ... of putting all his energies into the service of a cause."

40. Reik, 287; Marcus, 260.

41. Reich, 232; Freud, "The Economic Problem of Masochism," in Hanley, 276.

42. Reik, 323–4.

43. Horney, 274–5; Reich, 227.

44. Stoller, 19; Mack, 431, 436.

45. Stoller, 24–5; 1975, 122.

46. Marcus, 127; *Sweet Retribution,* a flagellist work cited in Edward Anthony, *Thy Rod and Staff* (London: Little, Brown, 1995) 276–7.

47. Sept. 8, 1927 letter (Brown, 347).

48. Quoted in Knightley and Simpson, 29.

49. The poem may also contain an echo of Deraa in "the inviolate house ... shattered."

50. *Friends,* 89.

51. Col. Brémond noted that Lawrence "was always strictly shaven in a country where the lack of a beard gives rise to suspicions which he was not spared" (Villars, 313).

52. Kirkbride, 7; Rolls, 151; Dec. 10, 1917 diary entry—though many entries in this diary were revised years later (Meinertzhagen, 28).

53. *Seven Pillars,* 28. His views about the "sexless" purity of Arab homosexuality, Desmond Stewart (118, 237) writes, are his, not theirs: "an unwritten law ... condemned the passive partner in sexual activities between males"; "some bedouin

may conceivably have slept with others; they will have done so furtively."

54. Oxford Text, 542; *Seven Pillars,* 356.

55. *Seven Pillars,* 244, 521. Note Lawrence's use of "slaked," here and earlier in this paragraph, for both physical and emotional release.

56. Jeffrey Meyers's words (Tabachnick, 128).

57. *The Mint,* 106, 186.

58. Aside from an unauthenticated story of boyhood masturbation, which, as most boys can attest, hardly needs authentication.

59. Knightley and Simpson, 29; Graves, Feb. 19, 1954 letter to Liddell Hart (O'Prey, 123); Williamson, Dec. 16, 1957 letter to Storrs (IWM copy).

60. In an Aug. 20, 1933 conversation (*B:LH,* 163); see also Liddell Hart, 13.

61. Mack, 64–6.

62. Dec. 17, 1963 letter to Miss Early (Brown, xxvii).

63. Jan. 9, 1932 letter to C. Shaw (BM).

64. Louise Young, 185, 200–1; the words within single quotes are from Scott's diary; "yesterday's talk" refers to a Feb. 25, 1921 talk with Col. Charles Vickery, who served in Arabia, disliked Lawrence, and regarded him as a homosexual. Scott's May 11, 1921 diary entry says Lawrence "Admitted his proclivities"—presumably, his homosexual disposition (James, 1995 edition, 256).

65. *Friends,* 295–6; Lawrence, March 19, 1924 letter to Cockerell (Garnett, 458).

66. Nov. 26, 1934 letter to Lady Astor (Brown, 502; the name "Mrs. Smith," was deleted) written after the Smiths left Mount Batten for Manston, on the coast east of London, which Mrs. Smith implored Lawrence to visit. It does not pertain to the earlier period when, often alone with Lawrence, she had more opportunity to express her love. Perhaps it had not ripened or Lawrence's strict propriety restrained its expression.

67. Letters: Dec. 5, 1924 to Granville-Barker (Salmon, 400); June 16, 1927 to Kennington (Garnett, 524).

68. Mack, 425.

69. "Few post-war innovations more dismayed Lawrence than the custom of a man and woman arising from the dinner … table to dance together." (Arnold, 105). Lawrence's mother also disapproved of dancing (Mack, 10).

70. Letters: June 10, 1924 to Charlotte Shaw, Nov. 6, 1928 to Graves (Brown, 268, 389).

71. *Seven Pillars,* 581. A photo in Clare Smith (33) shows him touching the head of Smith's dog with a forefinger, not his hand. Nonetheless, Lawrence had a special knack with dogs, notably Thomas Hardy's ferocious Wessex, who terrified most visitors but was meek with him.

72. Jan. 2, 1928 letter to Charlotte Shaw (Wilson, 1988, 202).

73. Lawrence, three undated, almost illegible pages of handwritten notes (Bodleian, copy).

74. 1929 letters: April 1 to Thurtle (Brown, 412), April 18 to Marsh, who had given him a copy of *Lady Chatterley's Lover* (Garnett, 652)

75. March 27, 1923 letter to Curtis (Garnett, 414). Cf. also Lawrence's Feb. 7, 1924 letter to Granville-Barker, "Here in camp it's the lesson stamped into me with nailed feet hour after hour: that at bottom we are carnal" (Garnett, 453).

76. *The Mint,* 109; Lucas, March 9, 1929 letter to Lawrence (Mack, 422).

77. March 24, 1954 letter to Liddell Hart (Texas).

78. I agree with Jeremy Wilson (702–5), who dismisses suspicions of homosexual relations between Lawrence and Guy or other service friends. But he is wrong to dismiss the erotic aspect of Lawrence's pleasure in the company of handsome young men and to imagine that he was a normal, virginal Englishman whose sexual maturation was halted by the Deraa rape. This view can be sustained only by ignoring almost everything Lawrence said, did, and did not do about women, men, and sex.

79. Altounyan, then under a psychiatrist's care, wrote Lawrence passionate love letters.

80. "Queer; he makes me feel restless & on guard while I am with him. Some sort of sex warning, I fancy," Lawrence said of Yeats-Brown (Aug. 9, 1930 letter to Charlotte Shaw, BM). The remark is puzzling, for Lawrence expressed pleasure at the company of Farraj and Daud and other homosexual Arabs, and showed no discomfort with such homosexual Britons as Richards, Altounyan, Sassoon, and Forster, including the first two, who wanted a physical relation. Perhaps he was comfortable only with men he could control.

81. Dec. 21, 1927 letter to Forster (Brown, 360).

82. Stoller, 1985, 93.

83. Lawrence, "Confession of Faith" (Mack, 425); Aug. 11, 1963 diary entry (Coward, 540).

84. Oct. 4, 1965 letter to Maurice Larès (Bodleian, copy).

85. Howe, 349.

86. Maugham, 116.

87. Letters: Sept. 8, 1927 to Forster (Garett, 537); Sept. 15, 1927 to Kennington (Texas); April 16, 1928 to Rogers (Garnett, 580).

22. Summing Up

1. Martin Gilbert, *In Search of Churchill* (John Wiley: New York, 1994) 65.

2. Winston Churchill in *Friends,* 200.

3. Kedourie, "The Real T. E. Lawrence," *Commentary,* July 1977, 54.

4. Asked, "Is Lawrence rightly singled out above others for his role in Arabia? Was he a real hero in the desert war?" James replied, "Lawrence's part in the affair was vital," but would not call him a hero. "Real heroes were everywhere in the Middle East: I would plump for those civilians in arms, Turkish, British, Australian, and

Indian who did their duty steadfastly" (in Orlans, 1993, 232).

5. May 14, 1927 letter to Charlotte Shaw (Brown, 325).

6. Lord Stamfordham, Jan. 1, 1928 letter (*Letters*, 185).

7. See Colin Wilson's discussion of Lawence in *The Outsider* (London: Gollancz, 1956), 70–84.

8. July 15, 1934 letter in Ernest Freud, ed., *The Letters of Sigmund Freud and Arnold Zweig,* New York: Harcourt Brace Jovanovich, 1970, 85.

9. "'I do not believe there is a shred of proven evidence that he was gay,' one outaged academic wrote…. 'I find it rather disheartening that a series such as this [*Gay Men and Lesbians*] would include him without proof documented.' If by 'proof docu-mented' one means a picture of Lawence in the bedroom … there of course will be none…. Some will say that what Lawrence did with Bruce wasn't homosexuality, or even sexuality…. But why not? Can anyone believe that to Lawrence either the sex of the person beating him or the fact of his orgasm was unimportant? Or is sex only defined when genital meets genital, or as a process that involves pleasure but no pain…? A better question to ask seems to be why it is so important for heterosexuals to wrench Lawrence from the homosexual category" (Wolfe, 144–5). The answer to the last question is: it violates their image of Lawrence.

10. June 29, 1954 letter to Liddell Hart (O'Prey, 1990, 137).

11. Mack, 441.

Bibliography

Key words used for citations in the notes are included below; the specific edition cited is given. Where several works by an author are listed, the first entry (usually the one cited most often) is identified in the notes solely by the author's name; other entries, by the name and year.

Aldington, Richard, *Lawrence of Arabia, A Biographical Enquiry,* London: Collins, 1955.

Aldington, 1975: Miriam Benkovitz, ed., *A Passionate Prodigality, Letters to Alan Bird from Richard Aldington 1949–1962,* New York: New York Public Library, 1975.

Allen, M. D., *The Medievalism of Lawrence of Arabia,* University Park, PA: Pennsylvania State University, 1991.

Antonius, George, *The Arab Awakening,* Philadelphia: J. B. Lippincott, 1939.

Armitage, Flora, *The Desert and the Stars,* New York: Henry Holt, 1955.

Arnold, Julian B., *Giants in Dressing Gowns,* London: Macdonald, 1945.

Asher, Michael, *Lawrence, The Uncrowned King of Arabia,* London: Viking, 1998.

Barrow, General Sir George, *The Fire of Life,* London: Hutchinson, 1942.

BBC: Maurice Brown, producer, "Lawrence of Clouds Hill" script, BBC Third program, Dec. 3, 1958.

Bennett, Alan R., *Horsewoman, The Extraordinary Mrs. D,* Milborne Port, Dorset: Dorset Publishing, 1979.

Benoist-Méchin, Jacques, *Arabian Destiny,* Denis Weaver, tr., London: Elek, 1957.

Bère, Rupert de la, "Aircraftman T. E. Shaw, A Last Conversation" (1935), *JTELS,* Summer 1992, 40–8.

Birdwood, Lord, *Nuri As-Said,* London: Cassell, 1959.

B:LH: *T. E. Lawrence to his Biographer Liddell Hart* (1938), Garden City, NY: Doubleday, 1963.

Blunt, Wilfrid, *Cockerell,* New York: Knopf, 1965.

BM: British Museum, Department of Manuscripts, British Library, London.

Bodleian: Letters by and to Lawrence and related papers in the Bodleian Library, Oxford, reserved until the year 2000.

B:RG: *T. E. Lawrence to his Biographer Robert Graves* (1938), Garden City, NY: Doubleday, 1963.

Brown, Malcolm, ed., *The Letters of T. E. Lawrence,* London: Dent, 1988.

Brown, Malcolm, and Julia Cave, *A Touch of Genius,* London: Dent, 1988.

Buchan, John, *Pilgrim's Way* (1940), New York: Carroll & Graf, 1984.

Buchan, 1939: "T. E. Lawrence," *Canadian Defense Quarterly,* July 1939, 371–8.

Cadell, James, *The Young Lawrence of Arabia,* London: Max Parrish, 1962.

Calder, Angus, Introduction, *Seven Pillars of Wisdom,* Ware, Herts: Wordsworth, 1997.

Cambridge: Cambridge University Library.

Cats: *Cats and Landladies' Husbands, T. E. Lawrence in Bridlington,* Denby Dale, W. Yorks: Fleece, 1995.

Charmley, John, *Lord Lloyd and the Decline of the British Empire,* New York: St. Martin's, 1987.

Cockerell: Viola Meynell, ed., *The Best of Friends, Further Letters to Sydney Carlyle Cockerell,* London: Rupert Hart-Davis, 1956.

Connolly: David Pryce-Jones, ed., *Cyril Connolly, Journal and Memoir,* London: Collins, 1983.

Coward: Graham Payn and Sheridan Morley, eds., *The Noel Coward Diaries,* Boston: Little, Brown, 1982.

Crawford, Fred D., *Richard Aldington and Lawrence of Arabia,* Carbondale: Southern Illinois University, 1998.

Crawford, Fred, and Joseph Burton, "How Well Did Lowell Thomas Know Lawrence of Arabia?"

English Literature in Transition, 39:3, 1996, 299–318.

Dawn, C. Ernest, *From Ottomanism to Arabism,* Urbana, IL: University of Illinois, 1973.

Devas, Nicolette, *Two Flamboyant Fathers,* London: Collins, 1966.

Dixon, Alex, *Tinned Soldier,* London: Jonathan Cape, 1941.

Dold, Bernard, *T. E. Lawrence: Writer and Wrecker,* Rome: Herder, 1988.

Dunbar, Janet, *Mrs. G.B.S.: A Portrait,* New York: Harper & Row, 1963.

Durrell: Alan Thomas, ed., *Spirit of Place, Letters and Essays on Travel, Lawrence Durrell,* London: Faber & Faber, 1969.

Ede: *Shaw-Ede, T. E. Lawrence's Letters to H. S. Ede 1927–1935,* London: Golden Cockerel, 1942.

FitzHerbert, Margaret, *The Man Who Was Greenmantle,* Oxford: Oxford University (1983), 1985.

Flavell, A. J., *T. E. Lawrence, The Legend and the Man,* Oxford: Bodleian Library, 1988.

Flecker, James E., *Some Letters from Abroad,* London: Heinemann, 1930.

FM: Fitzwilliam Museum, Cambridge.

Foden, George, "Strange Encounter," *Aeroplane Monthly,* June 1982, 320–3.

Forster, E. M., *Two Cheers for Democracy,* New York: Harcourt, Brace, 1951.

Forster, 1964: *Abinger Harvest* (1936), New York: Harcourt Brace Jovanovich, 1964.

Friends: A. W. Lawrence, ed., *T. E. Lawrence by His Friends,* London: Jonathan Cape, 1938.

Fromkin, David, *A Peace to End All Peace,* New York: Avon, 1985.

Furbank, P. N., ed., *E. M. Forster, A Life,* Vol. II, New York: Harcourt Brace Jovanovich, 1978.

Garnett: David Garnett, ed., *The Letters of T. E. Lawrence,* New York: Doubleday, Doran, 1939.

Garnett, 1962: *The Familiar Faces,* London: Chatto & Windus, 1962.

Garnett, 1968: ed., *The White/Garnett Letters,* London: Jonathan Cape, 1968.

Garnett, 1979: *Great Friends,* London: Macmillan, 1979.

Gilbert, Martin, *Churchill, A Life,* New York: Henry Holt, 1991.

Graves, Robert, *Lawrence and the Arabs,* London: Jonathan Cape, 1927.

Gregory: Lennox Robinson, ed., *Lady Gregory's Journals 1916–1930,* London: Putnam, 1946.

Grosvenor, Charles, *The Portraits of T.E. Lawrence,* Hillsdale, NJ: Otterbein, 1975.

Hanley, Margaret, ed., *Essential Papers on Masochism,* New York: New York University, 1995.

Harvard: Houghton Library, Harvard University.

Hergenham, L. T., "Some Unpublished Letters from T. E. Lawrence to Frederic Manning,"*Southerly,* 23: 1963, 242–52.

Hill, Margot, "T. E. Lawrence: Some Trivial Memories," *Virginia Quarterly Review,* Oct. 1945, 587–96.

Hoare, Samuel (Viscount Templewood), *Empire of the Air,* London: Collins, 1957.

Hodson, Joel C., *Lawrence of Arabia and American Culture,* Westport, CT: Greenwood, 1995.

Hogarth, D. G., "Great Britain, France, and Syria following The Armistice of the 30th October 1918" (1923), *JTELS,* Autumn 1994, 29–63.

Holroyd, Michael, *Bernard Shaw,* Vol. III, *1918–1950, The Lure of Fantasy,* New York: Random House, 1991.

Home: M. R. Lawrence, ed., *The Home Letters of T. E. Lawrence and His Brothers,* Oxford: Basil Blackwell, 1954.

Horney, Karen, *The Neurotic Personality of Our Time,* New York: Norton, 1937.

Howe, Irving, "T. E. Lawrence: The Problem of Heroism," *Hudson Review,* Autumn 1962, 333–64.

Hunt, Bob, *The Life and Times of Joyce E. Knowles,* Weymouth: E.V.G. Hunt, 1994.

Hyde, H. Montgomery, *Solitary in the Ranks,* London: Constable, 1977.

Isherwood, Christopher, *Exhumations,* London: Methuen, 1984.

IWM: Knightley-Simpson Papers, Imperial War Museum, London.

James, Lawrence, *The Golden Warrior,* London: Weidenfeld & Nicholson, 1990 (1995, revised edition).

Jarvis, C. S., *Three Deserts,* New York: Dutton, 1937.

Jarvis, 1942: *Arab Command: The Biography of Lieutenant-Colonel F. G. Peake Pasha,* London: Hutchinson, 1942.

Jesus: Jesus College, Oxford.

Jones, Thomas, *A Diary with Letters, 1931–1950,* London: Oxford University, 1954.

JTELS: The Journal of the T. E. Lawrence Society.

Kedourie, Elie, *England and the Middle East,* London: Bowes & Bowes, 1956.

Kennet, Lady (Kathleen Scott), *Self-Portrait of an Artist,* London: John Murray, 1949.

Kettle's: papers and letters to and by H. S. Ede, Kettle's Yard, Cambridge.

Kings: Kings College, Cambridge.

Kirkbride, Sir Alec Seath, *A Crackle of Thorns,* London: John Murray, 1956.

Knight, Ronald, *Colonel T. E. Lawrence Visits Mr and Mrs Thomas Hardy,* Weymouth: R. D. Knight, 1985.

Knightley, Phillip, "T. E. Lawrence," in Jeffrey Meyers, ed., *The Craft of Literary Biography,* New York: Schocken, 1985, 154–72.

Knightley, Phillip and Colin Simpson, *The Secret Lives of Lawrence of Arabia,* London: Thomas Nelson, 1969.

Knowles, Patrick, *"An Handful With Quietness,"* Weymouth: E.V.G. Hunt, 1992.

Lago, Mary and P. N. Furbank, eds., *Selected Letters of E.M. Forster,* Vol. Two, *1921–1970,* Cambridge, MA: Belknap, 1985.

Landick, Stanhope, ed., *Letters from Dr. M. R. Lawrence … to Stanhope Landick,* Millbrook, Jersey: privately printed, 1981.

Leatherdale, Mike, "Lawrence and his Brough Superiors," *JTELS*, Winter 1991–92, 63–96.

Leeds: J. M. Wilson, ed., *T. E. Lawrence: Letters to E. T. Leeds*, Andoversford, Gloucestershire: Whittington, 1988.

Lees-Milne, James, *Prophesying Peace*, New York: Scribner's, 1977.

Legg, Rodney, *Lawrence of Arabia in Dorset*, Sherborne, Dorset: Dorset Publishing, 1988.

Letters: A. W. Lawrence, ed., *Letters to T. E. Lawrence*, London: Jonathan Cape, 1962.

Liddell Hart, B. H., *Colonel Lawrence, The Man Behind the Legend*, New York: Dodd, Mead, 1935.

Liddell Hart, 1936: "Lawrence. The Artist in War and Letters," in B. H. Liddell Hart and Ronald Storrs, *Lawrence of Arabia*, Corvinus, 1936, unpaged.

Lockman, J. N., *Scattered Tracks on the Lawrence Trail*, Witmore Lake, MI: Falcon, 1996.

Lönnroth, Erik, *Lawrence of Arabia, An Historical Appreciation* (1943), Ruth Lewis, tr., London: Vallentine, Mitchell, 1956.

Lownie, Andrew, "The Friendship of Lawrence and Buchan," *JTELS*, Autumn 1995, 56–67.

Lunt, J. D., "An Unsolicited Tribute," *Blackwood's*, April 1966, 289–96.

Mack, John E., *A Prince of Our Disorder*, Boston: Little, Brown, 1976.

Macphail, Sir Andrew, *Three Persons*, London: John Murray, 1929.

Malraux, André, "Lawrence and the Demon of the Absolute," *Hudson Review*, Winter 1956, 519–32.

Marcus, Steven, *The Other Victorians*, New York: Basic Books, 1966.

Marriott, Paul, *The Young Lawrence of Arabia, 1888–1910*, Oxford: Paul Marriott, 1977.

Marriott, Paul and Yvonne Argent, *The Last Days of T. E. Lawrence*, Alpha: Brighton, 1996.

Marsh, Edward, *A Number of People*, London: Heinemann, 1939.

Marwil, Jonathan, *Frederic Manning, An Unfinished Life*, Durham, NC: Duke University, 1988.

Meinertzhagen, Col. Richard, *Middle East Diary 1917–1956*, London: Cresset, 1959.

Meyers, Jeffrey, *The Wounded Spirit*, London: Martin Brian & O'Keefe, 1973.

Meyers, 1976: *A Fever at the Core*, New York: Barnes & Noble, 1976.

Minorities: J. M. Wilson, ed., T. E. Lawrence (ed.), *Minorities* (1927), London: Jonathan Cape, 1971.

The Mint: T. E. Lawrence, *The Mint* (1927, 1955); unexpurgated text, London: Jonathan Cape, 1973.

Monroe, Elizabeth, *Britain's Moment in the Middle East, 1914–1971*, Baltimore: Johns Hopkins, 1981.

Morris, L. Robert, and Lawrence Raskin, *Lawrence of Arabia*, New York: Doubleday, 1992.

Mousa, Suleiman, *T. E. Lawrence, An Arab View*, London: Oxford University, 1966.

Mousa, 1997: *Cameos*, Amman: Ministry of Culture, 1997.

Nicolson, Harold, *Peacemaking 1919*, London: Constable, 1933.

O'Brien, Philip, *T. E. Lawrence: A Bibliography*, Winchester: St. Paul's Bibliographies, 1988.

Ocampo, Victoria, *338171 T.E. (Lawrence of Arabia)* (1942), David Garnett, tr., New York: Dutton, 1963.

O'Donnell, Thomas J., *The Confessions of T. E. Lawrence*, Athens, OH: Ohio University, 1979.

O'Donnell, 1977: "The Confessions of T. E. Lawrence," *American Imago*, Summer 1977, 115–32.

O'Prey, Paul, ed., *In Broken Images: Selected Letters of Robert Graves 1914–1946* (1982), Mt.Kisco, NY: Moyer Bell, 1988.

O'Prey, 1990: ed., *Robert Graves, Between Moon and Moon, Selected Correspondence* (1984), Mt. Kisco, NY: Moyer Bell, 1990.

Oriental: A. W. Lawrence, ed., T. E. Lawrence, *Oriental Assembly*, New York: Dutton, 1940.

Orlans, Harold, ed., *Lawrence of Arabia, Strange Man of Letters*, Cranbury, NJ: Fairleigh Dickinson, 1993.

Orlans, 1993, ed., "The Many Lives of T. E. Lawrence: A Symposium," *Biography*, 1993, 224–48.

Orlans, 1995: "The Friendship of Lawrence and Graves," *JTELS*, Spring 1995, 50–60.

Orlans, 1996: "The Ways of Transgressors," *JTELS*, Autumn 1996, 20–33.

Oxford Text: T. E. Lawrence, *Seven Pillars of Wisdom* (1922), Fordingbridge, Hants.: Castle Hill, 1997.

Patch, Blanche, *Thirty Years with G.B.S.*, London: Gollancz, 1951.

Patrick, David, "The T. E. Lawrence Collection," *The Library Chronicle of the University of Texas at Austin*, 20:3, 1990, 16–47.

Pearman, Capt. D. G., *The Imperial Camel Corps with Colonel Lawrence and Lawrence and the Arab Revolt*, lecture notes, London: Newton, 1928.

Philby, H. St. John B., *Arabian Days*, London: Robert Hale, 1948.

Princeton: Firestone Library, Princeton University.

Pritchett, V. S., *Complete Collected Essays*, New York: Random House, 1991.

Pryce-Jones, A. G., "Recollections of T. E. Lawrence," *Jesus College Record*, 1986, 7–11.

Raswan, Carl, "An Episode in the Life of Lawrence of Arabia," *Breeders' Service Bulletin*, 1978, 7:1&2.

Read, Herbert, *A Coat of Many Colours*, London: Routledge, 1945.

Reading: University of Reading Library.

Reich, Wilhelm, *Character-Analysis*, Theodore Wolfe, tr., New York: Orgone Institute, 1949.

Reik, Theodor, *Of Love and Lust*, New York: Jason Aronson, 1974.

Richards, Vyvyan, *Portrait of T. E. Lawrence*, London: Jonathan Cape, 1936.

Richards, 1939: *T. E. Lawrence* (1939), London: Duckworth, 1954.

Richardson, Frank M., *Mars without Venus, A Study of Some Homosexual Generals*, Edinburgh: William Blackwood, 1981.

Robinson, Edward, *Lawrence the Rebel*, London: Lincolns-Prager, 1946.

Rodd, Sir James Rennell, *Social and Diplomatic Memories (Third Series) 1902–1919,* London: Edward Arnold, 1925.

Rogers, Bruce, ed., *Letters from T. E. Shaw to Bruce Rogers,* privately printed by William E. Rudge, 1933, unpaged.

Rogers, 1936: ed., *More Letters from T. E. Shaw to Bruce Rogers,* privately printed, 1936, unpaged.

Rolls, Sam C., *Steel Chariots in the Desert,* London: Jonathan Cape, 1937.

Rothenstein, William, *Since Fifty, Men and Memories, 1922–1939,* London: Faber & Faber, 1939.

Rothenstein, 1920: *Twenty-Four Portraits,* London: Allen & Unwin, 1920.

Rowse, A. L., *Homosexuals in History* (1977), New York: Dorset, 1983.

Russell, Arthur, "September 23, 1990 talk to the T. E. Lawrence Society," *T.E. Notes,* 1997, 8:1&2.

Rutherford, Andrew, *The Literature of War,* New York: Barnes & Noble, 1978.

Sachar, Howard M., *The Emergence of the Middle East: 1914–1924,* New York: Knopf, 1969.

Salmon, Eric, ed., *Granville-Barker and His Correspondents,* Detroit: Wayne State, 1980.

Sassoon: Rupert Hart-Davis, ed., *Siegfried Sassoon Diaries, 1923–1925,* London: Faber & Faber, 1985.

Scotland: National Library of Scotland, Edinburgh.

Secret: Malcolm Brown, ed., T. E. Lawrence, *Secret Despatches from Arabia* (1939), London: Bellew, 1991.

Seven Pillars: T. E. Lawrence, *Seven Pillars of Wisdom* (1926, 1935), London: Jonathan Cape, 1952.

Seymour-Smith, Martin, *Robert Graves,* New York: Holt, Rinehart & Winston, 1982.

Shaw, George Bernard, *Flyleaves,* Austin, TX: W. Thomas Tylor, 1977.

Shaw, 1985: Dan H. Laurence, ed., *Bernard Shaw, Collected Letters, 1911–1925,* New York: Viking, 1985.

Shaw, 2000: Jeremy and Nicole Wilson, eds., *T. E. Lawrence, Correspondence with Bernard and Charlotte Shaw 1922–1926,* Woodgreen Common, Hants.: Castle Hill, 2000.

Shotwell, James T., *At the Paris Peace Conference,* New York: Macmillan, 1937.

Sims, R. G., *The Sayings & Doings of T. E. Lawrence,* Wakefield, W. Yorkshire: Fleece, 1994.

Smith, Clare Sydney, *The Golden Reign,* London: Cassell, 1949.

Smith, Janet Adam, *John Buchan* (1965), Oxford: Oxford University, 1985.

Sperber, Manès, *The Achilles Heel,* Constantine FitzGibbon, tr., Port Washington, NY: Kennikat, 1959.

Stewart, Desmond, *T. E. Lawrence,* London: Hamish Hamilton, 1977.

Stirling, Walter F., *Safety Last,* London: Hollis & Carter, 1953.

Stirling, 1933: "Tales of Lawrence of Arabia," *Cornhill Magazine,* April 1933, 494–510.

Stoller, Robert J., *Pain and Passion,* New York: Plenum, 1991.

Stoller, 1975: *Perversion, The Erotic Form of Hatred,* New York: Pantheon, 1975.

Stoller, 1985: *Observing the Erotic Imagination,* New Haven: Yale University, 1985.

Storrs, Ronald, *The Memoirs of Sir Ronald Storrs,* New York: Putnam's, 1937.

subscribers' edition: T. E. Lawrence, *Seven Pillars of Wisdom,* privately printed, 1926.

Sugarman, Sidney, *A Garland of Legends,* Hanley Swan, Worcs.: privately printed, 1992.

Tabachnick, Stephen E., ed., *The T. E. Lawrence Puzzle,* Athens: University of Georgia, 1984.

Tabachnick, Stephen E., and Christopher Matheson, *Images of Lawrence,* London: Jonathan Cape, 1988.

Tauber, Eliezer, *The Arab Movements in World War I,* London: Frank Cass, 1993.

Texas: Harry Ransom Humanities Research Center, University of Texas, Austin.

Thomas, Lowell, *Good Evening Everybody,* New York: William Morrow, 1976.

Thomas, 1967: *With Lawrence in Arabia* (1924), Garden City, NY: Doubleday, 1967.

Thompson, V.M., *'Not a Suitable Hobby for an Airman'—T. E. Lawrence as Publisher,* Oxford: Orchard, 1986.

Thompson, Walter H., *Assignment: Churchill,* New York: Farrar, Straus & Young, 1955.

Toynbee, Arnold J., *Acquaintances,* London: Oxford University, 1967.

Vansittart, Robert G., *The Mist Procession,* London: Hutchinson, 1958.

Villars, Jean Beraud, *T. E. Lawrence or the Search for the Absolute* (1955), Peter Dawnay, tr., New York: Duell, Sloan & Pearce, 1959.

Wavell, General Sir Archibald, *Allenby, A Study in Greatness,* London: George Harrap, 1940.

Webb, Beatrice, Norman and Jeanne MacKenzie, eds., *The Diary of Beatrice Webb,* Vol. Four, *1924–1943,* Cambridge, MA: Belknap, 1985.

Weintraub, Stanley, *Private Shaw and Public Shaw,* New York: George Braziller, 1963.

Westrate, Bruce, *The Arab Bureau,* University Park, PA: Pennsylvania State University, 1992.

Wheeler, Charles, *High Relief,* Feltham: Hamlyn, 1968.

Williamson, Henry, *Genius of Friendship, 'T. E. Lawrence',* London: Faber & Faber, 1941.

Williamson, 1994: *Threnos for T. E. Lawrence and Other Writings,* Longstanton, Cambs.: The Henry Williamson Society, 1994.

Williamson, 2000: *T. E. Lawrence, Correspondence with Henry Williamson,* Woodgreen Common, Hants.: Castle Hill, 2000.

Wilson, Jeremy, *Lawrence of Arabia, The Authorised Biography of T. E. Lawrence,* London: Heinemann, 1989.

Wilson, 1976: "Sense and Nonsense in the Biography of T. E. Lawrence," *T. E. Lawrence Studies,* Spring 1976, 3–10.

Wilson, 1988, *T. E. Lawrence, Lawrence of Arabia,* London: National Portrait Gallery, 1988.

Wilson, 1993: "T. E. Lawrence at Clouds Hill," *JTELS*, Summer 1993, 45–65.

Winstone, H. V. F., *Woolley of Ur*, London: Secker & Warburg, 1990.

Winterton, Edward T., *Fifty Tumultuous Years*, London: Hutchinson, 1955.

Winterton, 1992: "Arabian Nights and Days" (1920), *JTELS*, Summer 1992, 7–32.

Wolfe, Daniel, *T. E. Lawrence*, New York: Chelsea House, 1995.

Woolley, C. Leonard, *Dead Towns and Living Men*, New York: Oxford University, 1929.

Woolley, 1962: *As I Seem to Remember*, London: Allen & Unwin, 1962.

Wrench, John Evelyn, *Francis Yeats-Brown, 1886–1944*, London: Eyre & Spottiswoode, 1948.

Yardley, Michael, *Backing Into the Limelight*, London: Harrap, 1985.

Young, Hubert, *The Independent Arab*, London: John Murrray, 1933.

Young, 1926: "Makik, A Soldier in the Desert," *Cornhill*, Oct. 1926, 409–28; Nov. 1926, 537–56.

Young, Louisa, *A Great Task of Happiness, The Life of Kathleen Scott*, London: Papermac, 1996.

Index

Dostoevsky 65

Doubleday, Frank N. (1862–1934, publisher) 43, 44, 83, 130, 173, 179, 182, 185

Doubleday, Doran (publisher) 134

Doughty, Charles M. (1843–1926, writer, poet) 16, 52, 57, 76–7, 129, 167, 169, 181, 184; see also *Travels in Arabia Deserta*

Dunbar, Janet 171

Dunn, G.W. 103

Durrell, Lawrence 111, 218

Ede, H.S. (b1895, Tate Gallery curator) 72, 101, 103, 132, 219

Egypt 25–8

Elgar, Edward 209

Elles, Col. Hugh 61

Ellington, Edward 98

Ellis, Havelock 223

enlistment: boyhood 14, *244n13*; in RAF 8, 54–5; in Tank Corps 61

Evans, Harold 157

Farnborrough, RAF Photography School, Hampshire 58–60, 111, 174, 175, 194

Feisal ibn Hussein (1885–1933, Prince, son of Sherif Hussein, king of Iraq 1921–1933) 8, 23, 30, 34–7p, 39–45p, 47–9p, 71, 112, 131, 204, 208

filth: interest in 34, 56, 74, 121, 209–11

finances 75, 78, 83, 128–35, 161, 190, *225n44, 255n61*

Flecker, James Elroy (1884–1915, poet, British consul at Beirut) 21, 97, 234

Fletcher, Frank 104

Fontana, Winifred 101, 191

The Forest Giant (*Le Gigantesque*) 65, 131–2p, 175

Forster, Edward Morgan (1879–1970, writer) 65, 67, 81, 111, 125–6p, 132, 162–3, 175, 187–8p, 191, 199–200p, 209, 211

Fortescue, John 72

Frampton, Henry R.F. 138

Frampton, Teresa *256n15*

France: L opposes 31, 37, 39–45p, 49–51p; L's home 12; Mid-East policy 26, 40, 42; trips in 15, 140, 146; see also Sykes-Picot Treaty; Syria

Freud, Sigmund 62, 213, 227

friendships 1, 96–7, 160–76, 187, 238–9

Garnett, David (1892–1981, writer, son of Edward) 1, 55, 60, 81, 90, 96–7p, 103, 114, 157, 178, 182, 189, 191, 195, 206, 215, 218

Garnett, Edward (1868–1937, publisher's reader) 53, 57, 65, 68, 72, 79–81p, 116, 131, 161, 169, 170, 174, 179, 183, 205, 208

generosity 52, 71, 129–32p, 161, 174–5p, 186, 189–90p

George V (1865–1936, king 1910–1936) 7, 42, 45, 57, 72, 171, 196, 199

Germany: aids Turks 36; building railway over Euphrates 18, 20; declares war 23; troops in Arabia 7

The Golden Reign 227

Granville-Barker, Harley 179

Graves, Philip 106

Graves, Robert (1895–1985, writer, poet, L biography 1927) 2, 46, 51,60, 67, 76–7p, 94, 98, 111–6p, 129, 132, 134, 155–7p, 160–2, 163, 169, 181, 193, 199, 202, 211, 241

Gregory, Augusta, Lady 191

guerrilla fighting 7, 35, 196, 204

Guido, Peggy 159

Guilfoyle, W.J.Y. (Farnborough commander) 59, 82

Guinness, Alec 126, 156, 157

guns 14, 19–20, 122, 124, 148, 233

Guy, Rob A.M. (Farnborough comrade) 175–6, 183, *259n90*

Haig, Douglas 57

Hajim Bey (Deraa governor) 33

Halifax, Edward, Viscount 107

Hallsmith, Laurie 154, 226; *see also* Laurie, Janet

Hamish Hamilton (publisher) 158

Hanley, James (1901–1985, writer) 76, 98, 170

Hardy, Florence (1879–1937, Mrs. Hardy, m1914) 106, 123, 141, 160, 161, 163–5

Hardy, Thomas (1840–1928, writer, poet) 63–4p, 160–1p, 163–5, 179, 184, 192, *266n71*

Hargreaves, Albert 104

Harmsworth, Esmond 101

Headlam, Cuthbert 66

Heartbreak House 170

Heidenstam, Verner von 93

Hejaz 26, 28–32, 43, 51

Her Privates We 90, 184, 209

Herbert, Aubrey (1880–1923, military intelligence, M.P.) 25, 27

hero: L as 1–4, 8, 36–7, 45–6, 96, 235, *266n4*

Hirtzel, Arthur 42, 44

Hitler, Adolf 198

Hoare, Samuel (1880–1959, air minister 1922–1929) 59, 60, 67, 68, 86

Hodgson, Herbert 132

Hogarth, David G. (1862–1927, Mid-East scholar, Ashmolean Museum head) 16–9p, 25–6p, 31–2p, 36, 42–3p, 46–8p, 65, 76, 77, 80, 82, 117, 123, 129, 132, 134, 167–9, 179, 181, 187, 192, 194

Hogarth, Laura (Mrs. David Hogarth) 77, 137, 169

Hogarth, William (son) 77, 137, 169

Holroyd, Michael 173

Hornby, S. John 51

Horney, Karen *265n39*

Houghton Library, Harvard 57

House, Edward M. (colonel, adviser to President Wilson) 43

Howard, Gwen 88, 190

Howe, Irving (literary critic) 33, 209, 212, 228

Hudd, Walter 94

Hughes, Richard 63

Hussein ibn Ali el-Aun, Sherif (1854–1931, emir of Mecca, king of Hejaz) 28–9, 31, 34, 37, 40, 42–3p, 49–50, 51, 57, 196, 204

Hussein, Sheik (Druse chief) 32

Huxley, Aldous 63, 212

Hyde, H. Montgomery (writer, L biography 1977) 158, 187

Hythe 91–3, 144

I, Claudius 162

Ibn Saud (1888–1953, founder of Saudi Arabia) 49–51p, 196

illegitimacy 13, 18, 76, 142, 177–80, *257n33, 260n5*

illness 13–6, 22, 37, 52, 77, 82, 93, 140, 163

Imperial Camel Corps 35, 42, 192